I0575348

Joseph Hatton

Henry Irving's Impressions of North America

Narrated in a Series of Sketches, Chronicles, and Conversations

Joseph Hatton

Henry Irving's Impressions of North America
Narrated in a Series of Sketches, Chronicles, and Conversations

ISBN/EAN: 9783337010669

Printed in Europe, USA, Canada, Australia, Japan

Cover: Foto ©Thomas Meinert / pixelio.de

More available books at **www.hansebooks.com**

HENRY IRVING'S
IMPRESSIONS OF AMERICA,

NARRATED IN A

SERIES OF SKETCHES, CHRONICLES, AND
CONVERSATIONS.

BY

JOSEPH HATTON

AUTHOR OF "CLYTIE," "CRUEL LONDON," "THREE RECRUITS,"
"JOURNALISTIC LONDON," "TO-DAY IN AMERICA," ETC.

NEW AND CHEAPER EDITION.

London:
SAMPSON LOW, MARSTON, SEARLE, & RIVINGTON,
CROWN BUILDINGS, 188, FLEET STREET.
1884.

LONDON :
PRINTED BY GILBERT AND RIVINGTON, LIMITED,
ST. JOHN'S SQUARE.

TO THE ENGLISH PUBLIC.

THE interest taken by you in our American experiences has been made manifest to us in many ways on this side of the Atlantic. We have received the "God speed" of friends and associates, and a record of our trip will, I believe, be interesting to many.

My own share in this book is but small ; and to my friend, Joseph Hatton, belongs whatever credit there may be in it. It will, I hope, be accepted only for what it professes to be,—a series of sketches, chronicles, and conversations regarding a tour which the American people made for us, by their welcome and by their bounteous hospitality, a delightful progress.

In our intercourse with our friends, old and new, throughout the United States, nothing has impressed us more than their fondness for the old country. The greetings which we have everywhere received we take to be as much a token of the love of Americans for the English people, as an expression of personal good-feeling toward ourselves.

HENRY IRVING.

NEW YORK, April 30, 1884.

TO THE AMERICAN PUBLIC.

THIS book is the outcome of a desire to chronicle, in a lasting form, some of the events of a tour which your kindness has made a delight to Ellen Terry and myself. Before leaving London I ventured upon a prophecy that in journeying to America we were going amongst friends. That prophecy has been fulfilled.

In the history of the stage the Lyceum Company is the first complete organization which has crossed the Atlantic with the entire equipment of a theatre.

As the tour is, I believe, unique, so also is this record of it; and I particularly desire to emphasize a fact concerning its authorship. I am, myself, only responsible for my share in the conversations and dialogues that are set down, everything else being the work of my friend, Joseph Hatton, well known to you as the author of "To-day in America."

I can but trust that I have not erred in expressing, for publication, some passing thoughts about a country which has excited my profound admiration, and which has the highest claims upon my gratitude.

HENRY IRVING.

NEW YORK, April 30, 1884.

CONTENTS.

〜〜〜〜

I.

AT HOME.

II.

NEW YORK.

III.

FIRST IMPRESSIONS.

IV.

AT THE LOTOS CLUB.

V.

THE NIGHT BEFORE THE PLAY.

X.

BOSTON AND SHYLOCK.

XI.

A CITY OF SLEIGHS.

XII.

LOOKING FORWARD TO CHRISTMAS.

XXII.

"THE LONGEST JOURNEY COMES TO AN END."

IMPRESSIONS OF AMERICA.

I.

AT HOME.

Talking of America — Warned against the Interviewer—
"Travellers' Tales"—International Gossip—A mythical
Palace on the Thames—Reports from "A little English
Friend"—The Grange—A Grafton Street Interior—Sou-
venirs and Portraits—An Actor on his Audiences—Hamlet
at the Lyceum—Critics and Public Opinion—The final
Verdict—First Nights — Anonymous Letters — Notable
Gifts—The Character of Louis XI.—" A poor Mother who
had lost her Son "—Scene Calls—Stories of a " Dresser "
—Behind the Scenes—" Waking up "—The original Beef-
steak Club Room—Host and Guests.

I.

" AND I don't think he believes a word I have said,"
was Mr. John T. Raymond's own commentary upon a
series of romances of " the wild West " which he had
related to Mr. Henry Irving [1] with an intensity that
was worthy of Col. Sellers himself.

[1] John Henry Brodripp Irving was born at Keinton, near
Glastonbury (the scene of the tradition of the sacred thorn),
February 6, 1838. In 1849 his father sent him to the private
school of Dr. Pinches, in George Yard, Lombard Street, London.
During his school days he evinced a taste for dramatic poetry.
He was placed in the office of an East India house, and
might, had he liked his occupation, have become a prosperous
merchant ; but his ambition gravitated towards the stage. He
made personal sacrifices in many ways to educate himself in the
direction of his taste for dramatic work. He read plays, studied

B

The comedian's reminiscences were graphic narratives of theatrical and frontier life, with six-shooters and bowie-knives in them, and narrow escapes enough to have made the fortunes of what the Americans call a ten-cent novel.

" Oh, yes, I believe it is the duty of the door-keeper at a Western theatre to collect the weapons of the audience before admitting the people to the house; that what we call the cloak-room in London, you might call the armoury out West; and that the bowie-knife of a Texan critic never weighs less than fourteen pounds. But I am not going as far as Texas, though one might do worse if one were merely crossing the Atlantic in search of adventures."

America was at this time a far-off country, about which travellers told Irving strange stories. I recall many a pleasant evening in the Beefsteak Club Room of the Lyceum Theatre, when famous citizens of the

the theatre and dramatic literature, became an expert fencer, practised elocution with a famous actor, and in 1855 left London and obtained an engagement in a provincial theatre. An earnest student always, he fought his way through a world of troubles, and made his first success at the St. James's Theatre, London, October 6, 1866, as Doricourt in "The Belle's Stratagem." He afterwards played in eccentric comedy with Toole; made a hit in melodrama at the now defunct Queen's Theatre; then went to Paris with Sothern, and played Abel Murcot in "Our American Cousin." Returning to London, he filled important engagements at the Gaiety and Vaudeville Theatres. His appearance at the Lyceum Theatre, London, followed. Here, after his friend, Manager Bateman, had staked and lost everything on "Fanchette," Mr. Irving advised the production of "The Bells," which restored the fortunes of the house, and was the beginning of a series of artistic and financial successes, both for the management and the leading actor. On the death of Mr. Bateman, and the withdrawal of his widow from the lesseeship of the theatre, Mr. Irving entered upon management. One day I hope to tell the story of his life and adventures. Placidly as the river of his fortunes may seem to have flowed since he became lessee of the Lyceum, in October, 1878, the incidents of his early struggles are not more interesting than his managerial battles and victories in these latter days of London.

United States, actors more particularly, have sat at his round table, and smoked the Havannah of peace and pleasant memories : Booth, Barrett, Boucicault, McCullough, Raymond, Florence, and others of their craft : Generals Horace Porter, Fairchild, Merritt, Mr. Sam. Ward, Mr. Rufus Hatch, Mr. James R. Osgood, Mr. Hurlbert, Mr. Crawford, Col. Buck, Mr. Dan Dougherty, and many others. They all promised him a kindly reception and a great success.

"I question, however," said an English guest, taking the other side, as Englishmen love to do, if only for the sake of argument, "if America will quite care for the naturalness of your effects, the neutral tones of some of your stage pictures, the peaceful character, if I may so style it, of your representations. They like breadth and colour and show ; they are accustomed to the marvellous and the gigantic in nature ; they expect on the stage some sort of interpretation of these things,— great rivers, lofty mountains, and the startling colours of their fall tints. Your gentle meads of Hampton, the poetic grace of ' Charles the First,' the simplicity of your loveliest sets, and the quiet dignity of your Shylock, will, I fear, seem tame to them."

"Human nature, I fancy," Irving responded, "is the same all the world over, and I have played to many Americans in this very theatre. You will say, perhaps, that they will accept here in London what they would not care for on the other side of the Atlantic. You would say we are an old country, with fairly settled tastes in art, a calm atmosphere, a cultivated knowledge ; and that possibly what we, in our narrower ways, regard as a subtilty of art, they may not see. That may be so, though some of their humour is subtle enough, and the best of it leaves a great deal to the imagination. I know many persons, American and English, have talked to me in your strain ; yet I never saw quieter or more delicate acting than in Jefferson's Rip Van Winkle. As I said before, human nature is ever the same : it loves and hates, it quarrels and murders, it honours valour, sympathizes with the unfortunate, and delights in seeing human passions delineated on the stage. Moreover, are not the Americans, after all, our own flesh and blood? I never think of them in the sense of foreigners, as one does of the French and Germans, and the other European nations who do not speak our language; and I have yet to learn that there is any difference between us so marked that the jangle of ' The Bells ' shall not stir their imagination as much as the sorrows of Charles shall move their hearts, and the story of Louis heighten their pulses. We shall see. I cannot exactly say that my soul's in arms and eager for the fray, but I have no doubt about the result. That love of breadth, of largeness, of colour, you talk of, should go hand in hand with a catholic taste, devoid of littleness and combined with a liberal criticism that is not always looking for spots on the sun."

" You are not nervous, then, as to your reception ? "

" No, I am sure it will be kindly; and, for their criticism, I think it will be just. There is the same honesty of purpose and intention in American as in English criticism, and, above all, there is the great play-going public, which is very much the same frank, generous, candid audience all over the world."

" But there is the American interviewer! You have not yet encountered that interesting individual."

" Oh, yes, I have."

" Has he been here, then ? "

" Yes; not in his war-paint, nor with his six-shooter and bowie-knife, as he goes about in Raymond's Texan country, yet an interviewer still."

" And you found him not disagreeable ? " asked the travelled guest.

" I found him well informed and quite a pleasant fellow."

" Ah, but he was here under your own control, probably smoking a cigar in your own room. Wait until he boards the steamer off New York. Then you will see the sort of fellow he is, with his string of questions more personal than the fire of an Old Bailey lawyer at a hostile witness under cross-examination. The Inquisition of old is not in the race with these gentlemen, except that the law, even in America, does not allow them to put you to physical torture, though they make up for that check upon their liberty by the mental pain they can inflict upon you. Apart from the interviewers proper, I have known reporters to disguise themselves as waiters, that they may pry into your secrets and report upon your most trivial actions."

" You have evidently suffered," said Irving.

" No, not I; but I have known those who have. Nothing is sacred from the prying eyes and unscrupulous pens of these men. ' You smile, old friend,' to quote your ' Louis the Eleventh,' but I am not exaggerating nor setting down aught in malice. You will see! The interviewers will turn you inside out."

" You don't say so ! Well, that will be a new sensation, at all events," answered Irving ; and, when our friend had left, he remarked, " I wonder if Americans, when they visit this country, go home and exaggerate our peculiarities as much as some of our own countrymen, after a first trip across the Atlantic, evidently exaggerate theirs ?"

" There are many travellers who, in relating their experiences, think it necessary to accentuate them with exaggerated colour ; and then we have to make allowances for each man's individuality."

" How much certain of our critical friends make of that same 'individuality,' by the way, when they choose to call it ' mannerism ! ' The interviewers, I suppose, will have a good deal to say on that subject."

" English papers and American correspondents have given them plenty of points for personal criticism."

" That is true. They will be clever if they can find anything new to say in that direction. Well, I don't think it is courage, and I know it is not vanity; yet I feel quite happy about this American tour."

II.

No man was ever more written of or talked about in America than Henry Irving; probably no man was ever more misrepresented as to his art and his life. A monster, according to his enemies; an angel, if you took the verdict of his friends; he was a mystery to untravelled American journalists, and an enigma to the great play-going public of the American cities. They were told that people either loved or hated him at first sight. American tourists carried home contradictory reports of his appearance, though the majority were enthusiastic in praise of him as an actor and as a man. The American newspaper correspondent is naturally a trifle more sensational in the style of his work than his English colleague, because his editor favours graphic writing, entertaining chronicles, picturesque descriptions. Then the sub-editor or compiler of news from the foreign exchanges looks out for " English personals," gossip about the Queen, notes on the Prince of Wales, out-of-the-way criticisms of actors and public persons of all classes; and so every *outré* thing that has been published concerning Irving in England has found its way into the ubiquitous press of America. Added to this publicity, private correspondence has also dealt largely with him, his work, his manners, his habits; for every American, who travels, writes letters home to his family and often to his local paper, and many English people who have visited America keep up a pleasant epistolary communication with their good friends in the New World.

III.

BEING in New York ahead of Mr. Irving's arrival, I found much of the curious fiction of which gossip had made him the hero, crystallized into definite assertions that were accepted as undisputed facts. A day's sail from the Empire city, in a pretty Eastern villa, I discovered the London gossip-monger's influence rampant. But if a prominent critic in London could publicly credit Mr. Irving's success as an actor to his hospitable dispensation of "chicken and champagne," one need not be surprised that social gossips should draw as liberally on their imagination for illustrations of his social popularity. A leading figure in the world of art, and a person of distinction in Vanity Fair, it is not to be wondered at that Jealousy and Mrs. Grundy, standing outside his orbit, should invent many startling stories about him. I have not exaggerated the following conversation, and I am glad to use it here, not only as illustrative of the singular misrepresentations of Irving's life and habits, but to bind up in this volume a sketch of the actor and the man which has the merit of being eminently true, and at the same time not inappropriate to these pages.

"Lives in chambers!" exclaimed an American lady, during an after-dinner conversation in a pleasant Eastern home. "I thought he owned a lovely palace."

"Indeed; where, madam?" I asked, "in Utopia?"

"No, sir; on the banks of your Thames river. A little English friend of mine told me so, and described the furnishing of it. I understand that it is as splendid as Claude Melnotte's by the Lake of Como."

"And as real?"

"I don't know what you mean; but, if what she says is true, it is wickeder, any way. You do not say that it is all false about his banquets to the aristocracy, his royal receptions? What about the Prince of Wales, then, and Lord Beaconsfield and Mr. Gladstone and the Poet Laureate visiting him? And his garden parties and the illuminations at night, parterres of flowers mixed up with coloured lamps; his collections of rhododendrons and his military bands?"

"Were you ever at a botanical *fête* in Regent's Park?" I asked.

"I have never crossed the Atlantic."

"Your little English friend evidently knows the Botanical well."

"She is acquainted with everything and everybody in London. I wish she were here now. Perhaps she knows a little more than some of Mr. Irving's friends care to admit."

"Does she know Mr. Irving?"

"She knows his house."

"By the Lake of Como?"

"No, sir; by the Thames."

"One comes from home to hear news. Will you not tell us all about it, then?"

"No, I will not. I think you are positively rude; but that is like you English. There, I beg your pardon; you made me say it. But, seriously now, is not Mr. Irving as rich as—"

"Claude Melnotte?"

"No; Crœsus, or Vanderbilt, or Mackay? And does he not live in that palace, and have crowds of servants, and visit with the court and the aristocracy? Why, I read in the papers myself, quite lately, of an estate he had bought near, let me see—is there such a place as Hammersmith?"

"Yes."

"Is that on the Thames?"

"Yes, more or less."

"Well, then, is that true? More or less, I suppose. You are thinking how inquisitive I am. But you started the subject."

"Did I?"

"You said he lives in chambers."

"I answered your own question."

"Ah!" she said, laughing merrily, "now I know my little English friend spoke the truth, because I remember she said there was a mystery about Mr. Irving's lovely house; that he only receives a certain princely and lordly set there. How could she have described it if she had not seen it? A baronial castle, a park, lovely gardens, great dogs lying about on the lawns, wainscoted chambers, a library full of scarce books and costly *bric-à-brac*, Oriental rugs, baths, stained-glass windows, suits of armour, and a powerful bell in a turret to call the servants in to meals."

" Beautiful! But if there is a mystery about it, what of those gorgeous receptions ? "

" Oh, don't ask me questions. It is I who am seeking for information. There is no public person in the world just at this moment in whom I take a deeper interest. If he were not coming to America, I should have been obliged to go to London, if only to see what you call a first night at the Lyceum. We read all about these things. We are kept well informed by our newspaper correspondents—"

" And your little English friend."

" Yes, she writes to me quite often."

" Well, now I will tell you the truth about that palace on the Thames," I said.

" Ah! he confesses," exclaimed the bright little lady, whose friends suspect her of writing more than one of the famous American novels.

An interested and interesting group of ladies and gentlemen brought their chairs closer to the conversational centre of the company.

" A few years ago, Irving and a friend, strolling through the purlieus of Brook Green (a decayed village that has been swallowed up by the progress of West End London) towards Hammersmith, saw a house to be sold. It was low and dilapidated, but it had an old-fashioned garden, and the lease was offered at a small sum. Irving knew the house, and he had a mind to examine its half-ruined rooms. He did so, and concluded his investigation by buying the lease. It cost him about half the money you would pay for an ordinary house off Fifth Avenue in New York; less than you would pay for a house in Remsen Street, Brooklyn ; in Michigan Avenue, Chicago ; or in Commonwealth Avenue, Boston. Since then it has been one of his

few sources of amusement to lay out its garden, to
restore the old house and make it habitable. It is a
typical English home, with low red roofs, ancient
trees, oaken stairs, and a garden with old-fashioned
flowers and fruit in it; but it is the home of a yeo-
man rather than a prince, the home of a Cincinnatus
rather than the palace of an Alcibiades. The staff of
servants consists of a gardener and his wife, and I have
been present at several of the owner's receptions. The
invitation was given in this wise : ' I am going to drive
to the Grange on Sunday afternoon,—will you bring
your wife, and have a cup of tea ? ' And that described
the feast; but Irving, looking at his gilliflowers and
tulips, watching the gambols of his dogs, and discussing
between whiles the relative cost of carpets and India
matting, illustrated the truth of the philosophy, that
there is real recreation and rest in a mere change of
occupation. Those persons who tell you that Irving's
tastes are not simple, his private life an honour to him,
and his success the result of earnestness of purpose,
clearness of aim, deep study and hard work, neither
know him nor understand how great a battle men
fight in England, who cut their way upwards from
the ranks, to stand with the highest at head-
quarters."

Quite a round of applause greeted this plain story.

" Why, my dear sir," exclaimed my original inter-
locutor, " I am right glad to hear the truth. Well,
well, and that is Mr. Irving's real home, is it ? But I
thought you said he lives in chambers."

" One day he hopes to furnish and enjoy the simplicity and quiet of that cottage in a garden, four miles
from his theatre; but he still lives, where he has lived
for a dozen years or more, in very unpretentious rooms
in the heart of London."

And now, courteous reader, come straightway into
this little company of the friendly and the curious, and
I will show you where Henry Irving lived until he set
sail for America, a week ago, and you shall hear him

talk about his art and his work; for my good friend, the editor of *Harper's Magazine*, commissioned me to describe the famous English actor at home, and here is the result :—

IV.

AT the corner of Grafton Street, where ˙the traffic of a famous West End artery ebbs and flows among picture exhibitions and jewellery stores, lives the most popular actor of his time. It is a mysterious-looking house. The basement is occupied by a trunk store. From the first floor to the top are Mr. Henry Irving's chambers. They present from the outside a series of dingy, half-blind windows that suggest no prospect of warmth or cheer. "Fitting abode of the spirit of tragic gloom!" you might well exclaim, standing on the threshold. You shall enter with me, if you will, to correct your first impressions, and bear testimony to the fact that appearances are often deceptive. This sombre door, the first on the left as we enter Grafton Street from Bond Street, leads to his chambers. Two flights of stairs—not bright, as a Paris staircase, not with the sunlight upon the carpet, as in New York, but darkened with the shadows of a London atmosphere —and we enter his general room. With the hum of the West End buzzing at the windows, the coloured glass of which shuts out what little sunlight falls there, the apartment is characteristic of a great artist and a great city. The mantelpiece recalls the ancient fashion of old English mansions. It is practically an oak cabinet, with a silver shield as the centre-piece. On the opposite side of the room is a well-stocked book-case, surmounted by a raven that carries one's thoughts to, Poe and his sombre story. On tables here and there are materials for letter-writing, and evidence of much correspondence, though one of the actor's social sins is said to be the tardiness with which he answers letters. The truth is, the many pressing claims on his time

do not enable him to act always upon the late Duke
of Wellington's well-known principle of immediately
replying to every letter that is addressed to him.
A greater philosopher than his Grace said many
letters answer themselves if you let them alone, and
I should not wonder if Irving finds much truth in the
axiom. *Bric-à-brac,* historic relics, theatrical properties, articles of *virtù,* lie about in admired disorder.
Here is Edmund Kean's sword, the one which was presented to Irving on the first night of his Richard III.
by that excellent and much-respected artist Mr.
Chippendale, who had acted with Edmund Kean, and
was his personal friend. In a glass case near this
precious treasure is a ring that belonged to David
Garrick. It is an exquisite setting of a miniature of
Shakespeare. This was given to Irving by the Baroness
Burdett-Coutts. In a cabinet near one of the windows, the order of the George which Edmund Kean
wore in "Richard III.," and his prompt-book of
"Othello." Close by are three marble busts,—one
of Young, with a faded wreath upon its brow; another
of Mrs. Harriet Brown, "a most dear and valued
friend" (to use his own words); and the third, of
Ellen Terry, sculptured by Irving's friend, Brodie,—
a portrait of Rossi (presented by the actor) as Nero;
a photograph of Charles Dickens (presented by Miss
Mary Dickens),—the one by Gurney, of New York,
which the great author himself thought an excellent
portrait; medallions of Émile Devrient and John
Herschell (the latter a gift from Herschell's daughter);
and a sketch of a favourite Scotch terrier (very well
known to his friends as "Charlie"), which during
the last year or two has become his most constant
companion at home and at the theatre. The adjoining
room continues the collection of the actor's art
treasures,—not the mere connoisseur's museum of
articles of *virtù,* but things which have a personal
value and a special history associated with the art
their owner loves.

It is a frank smile that greets us as the actor enters and extends his long, thin hand. I know no one whose hand is so suggestive of nervous energy and artistic capacity as Irving's. It is in perfect harmony with the long, expressive face, the notably æsthetic figure !

"You want to talk shop," he says, striding about the room, with his hands in the pockets of his loose gray coat. "Well, with all my heart, if you think it useful and interesting."

"I do."

"May I select the subject?"

"Yes."

"Then I would like to go back to one we touched upon at your own suggestion some months ago."

"An actor on his audiences?"

"Yes. The subject is a good one; it interests me, and in that brief anonymous newspaper sketch of a year ago you did little more than indicate the points we discussed. Let us see if we cannot revive and complete it."

"Agreed. I will 'interview' you, then, as they say in America."

"By all means," replied my host, handing me a cigar, and settling himself down in an easy-chair by the fire. "I am ready."

"Well, then, as I think I have said before when on this subject, there has always appeared to me something phenomenal in the mutual understanding that exists between you and your audiences; it argues an active sympathy and confidence on both sides."

"That is exactly what I think exists. In presence of my audience I feel as safe and contented as when sitting down with an old friend."

"I have seen Lord Beaconsfield, when he was Mr. Disraeli, rise in the House of Commons, and begin a speech in a vein and manner evidently considered beforehand, which, proving at the moment out of harmony with the feelings of the House, he has entirely altered from his original idea to suit the immediate

mood and temper of his audience. Now, sympathetic
as you are with *your* audience, have you, under their
influence in the development of a new character, ever
altered your first idea during the course of the representation ? "

"You open up an interesting train of thought," he
answered. "Except once, I have never altered my
original idea under the circumstances you suggest;
that was in 'Vanderdecken,' and I changed the last
scene. I can always tell when the audience is with
me. It was not with me in 'Vanderdecken;' neither
was it entirely on the first night of 'Hamlet,' which is,
perhaps, curious, considering my subsequent success.
On the first night I felt that the audience did not go
with me until the first meeting with Ophelia, when
they changed toward me entirely. But as night
succeeded night, my Hamlet grew in their estimation;
I could feel it all the time, and now I *know* that they
like it—that they are with me heart and soul. I will
tell you a curious thing about my 'Hamlet' audience.
It is the most interesting audience I play to. For any
other piece there is a difficulty in getting the people
seated by half-past eight. For 'Hamlet' the house
is full and quiet, and waiting for the curtain to go up,
by half-past seven. On the first night the curtain
dropped at a quarter to one."

"In what part do you feel most at home with your
audience, and most certain of them ? "

"Well, in Hamlet," he replied thoughtfully.

"Has that been your greatest pecuniary success ? "

"Yes."

"What were two unprecedented runs of 'Hamlet?'"

"The first was two hundred nights; the second, one
hundred and seven; and in the country I have often
played it ten times out of a twelve nights' engagement.
But, as we have got into this line of thought about
audiences, it should be remembered that, with the
exception of two or three performances, I had never
played Hamlet before that first night at the Lyceum.

Indeed, so far as regards what is called the classic and legitimate drama, my successes, such as they were, had been made outside it, really in eccentric comedy. As a rule, actors who have appeared for the first time in London in such parts as Richard III., Macbeth, Hamlet, and Othello, have played them previously for years in the country ; and here comes a point about my audiences. They knew this, and I am sure they estimated the performance accordingly, giving me their special sympathy and good wishes. I believe in the justice of audiences. They are sincere and hearty in their approval of what they like, and have the greatest hand in making an actor's reputation. Journalistic power cannot be over-valued ; it is enormous ; but, in regard to actors, it is a remarkable fact that their permanent reputations, the final and lasting verdict of their merits, are made chiefly by their audiences. Sometimes the true record comes after the players are dead, and it is sometimes written by men who possibly never saw them. Edmund Kean's may be called a posthumous reputation. If you read the newspapers of the time, you will find that during his acting days he was terribly mauled. Garrick's impersonations were not much written about in his day. As to Burbage, Betterton, and other famous actors of their time, whose names are familiar to us, when they lived there were practically no newspapers to chronicle their work."

" You believe, then, that merit eventually makes its mark in spite of professional criticism, and that, like Masonic rituals, the story of success, its form and pressure, may go down orally to posterity ? "

" I believe that what audiences really like they stand by. I believe they hand down the actor's name to future generations. They are the judge and jury who find the verdict and pronounce sentence. I will give you an example in keeping with the rapid age in which we live. I am quite certain that within twelve hours of the production of a new play of any import-

ance all London knows whether the piece is a success
or a failure, no matter whether the journals have
criticized it or not. Each person in the audience is
the centre of a little community, and the word is
passed on from one to the other."

"What is your feeling in regard to first-night
audiences, apart from the regular play-going public ?
I should imagine that the sensitive nature of a true
artist must be considerably jarred by the knowledge
that a first-night audience is peculiarly fastidious and
sophisticated."

"I confess I am happier in presence of what you
call the regular play-going public. I am apt to become depressed on a first night. Some of my friends
and fellow-artists are stimulated and excited by a
sense of opposition. I fear it lowers me. I know
that while there is a good, hearty crowd who have
come to be pleased, there are some who have *not* come
to be pleased. God help us if we were in the hands of
the few who, from personal or other motives, come
to the theatre in the hope of seeing a failure, and
who pour out their malice and spite in anonymous
letters ! "

"Detraction and malicious opposition are among
the penalties of success. To be on a higher platform
than your fellows is to be a mark for envy and slander,"
I answered, dropping, I fear, into platitude, which my
host cut short with a shrug of the shoulders and a
rapid stride across the room.

He handed to me a book, handsomely bound and
with broad margins, through which ran a ripple of old-
faced type, evidently the work of an author and a
handicraftsman who love the memories both of Caxton
and his immediate successors. It was entitled "Notes
on Louis XI. ; with some short extracts from Com-
mines' Memoirs," and was dated "London, 1878—
printed for the author."

"That book," said my host, "was sent to me by a
person I had then never seen or heard of. It came to

me anonymously I wished to have a second copy of it, and sent to the printer with the purpose of obtaining it. He replied by telling me the work was not for sale, and referring me to the author, whose address he sent to me. I made the application as requested; another copy was forwarded, and with it a kind intimation that if ever I should be near the house of the writer, 'we should be glad to see you.' I called in due course, and found the author one of a most agreeable family. 'You will wonder,' they said at parting, 'why we wrote and compiled this book. It was simply for this reason : a public critic in a leading journal had said, as nothing was really known of the character, manners, and habits of Louis XI., an actor might take whatever liberties he pleased with the subject. We prepared this little volume to put on record a refutation of the statement, a protest against it, and a tribute to your impersonation of the character.' Here is another present that I received soon afterwards,—one of the most beautiful works of its kind I ever remember to have seen."

It was an artistic casket, in which was enshrined what looked like a missal bound in carved ivory and gold. It proved, however, to be a beautifully bound book of poetic and other memorials of Charles the First, printed and illustrated by hand, with exquisite head and tail pieces in water-colours, portraits, coats-of-arms, and vignettes, by Buckman, Castaing, Terrel, Slie, and Phillips. The work was "imprinted for the author at London, 30th January, 1879," and the title ran: "To the Honour of Henry Irving: to cherish the Memory of Charles the First: these Thoughts, Gold of the Dead, are here devoted." As a work of art, the book is a treasure. The portraits of the Charleses and several of their generals are in the highest style of water-colour painting with gold borders; and the initial letters and other embellishments are studies of the most finished and delicate character.

C

"Now these," said their owner, returning the volumes to the book-shelves over which the raven
stretched its wings, "are only two out of scores of
proofs that audiences are intellectually active, and that
they find many ways of fixing their opinions. These
incidents of personal action are evidences of the spirit
of the whole. One night, in ' Hamlet,' something was
thrown upon the stage. It struck a lamp, and fell
into the orchestra. It could not be found for some
time. An inquiry was made about it by some person in
the front,—an aged woman, who was much concerned
that I had not received it,—so I was informed at
the box-office. A sad-looking woman, evidently very
poor, called the next day; and, being informed that
the trinket was found, expressed herself greatly
pleased. 'I often come to the gallery of the theatre,'
she said, 'and I wanted Mr. Irving to have this family
heirloom. I wanted him alone in this world to possess
it.' This is the trinket, which I wear on my watch-
chain. The theatre was evidently a solace to that poor
soul. She had probably some sorrow in her life; and
she may have felt a kind of comfort in Hamlet, or
myself, perhaps, possessing this little cross."

As he spoke, the actor's lithe fingers were busy at his
watch-chain, and he seemed to be questioning the secret
romance of the trinket thrown to him from the gallery.

"I don't know why else she let it fall upon the
stage ; but strange impulses sometimes take hold of
people sitting at a play, especially in tragedy."

The trinket about which he speculated so much is an
old-fashioned gold cross. On two sides is engraved,
"Faith, Hope, and Charity;" on the front, "I believe
in the forgiveness of sins;" and on the reverse, "I
scorn to fear or change."

"They said at the box-office," went on the actor,
musingly, "that she was a poor mother who had lost
her son;" and then rousing himself, he returned
brightly to the subject of our conversation. "One
example," he said, "of the generous sympathy of

audiences serves to point the moral of what I mean;
and in every case the motive is the same, to show an
earnest appreciation, and to encourage and give pleasure to the actor. At Sheffield one night, during the
grouse season, a man in the gallery threw a brace of
birds upon the stage, with a rough note of thanks and
compliments; and one of the pit audience sent me
round a knife which he had made himself. You see,
the people who do these things have nothing to gain;
they are under no extraneous influence; they judge for
themselves; and they are representative of that great
Public Opinion which makes or mars, and which in the
end is always right. When they are against you, it is
hard at the time to be convinced that you are wrong;
but you are. Take my case. I made my first success at the St. James's. We were to have opened
with 'Hunted Down.' We did not. I was cast for
Doricourt in 'The Belle's Stratagem'—a part which
I had never played before, and which I thought did
not suit me. I felt that this was the opinion of the
audience soon after the play began. The house appeared to be indifferent, and I believed that failure was
conclusively stamped upon my work, when suddenly,
on my exit after the mad scene, I was startled by a
burst of applause, and so great was the enthusiasm of
the audience that I was compelled to reappear on the
scene,—a somewhat unusual thing, as you know,
except on the operatic stage."

"And in America," I said, "where scene-calls are
quite usual, and quite destructive of the illusion of the
play, I think."

"You are right; and, by the way, if there must be
calls, I like our modern method of taking a call after
an act on the scene itself. But to proceed. I next
played 'Hunted Down,' and they liked me in that; and
when they do like, audiences are no niggards of their
confessions of pleasure. My next engagement was at
the Queen's Theatre, where I was successful. Then I
went to the Gaiety, where I played Chevenex. I fol-

lowed at Drury Lane in 'Formosa,' and nobody noticed me at all."

"Do you think you always understand the silence of an audience? I mean in this way : on a first night, for example, I have sometimes gone round to speak to an actor, and have been met with the remark, 'How cold the audience is!' as if excessive quietness were indicative of displeasure, the idea being that when an audience is really pleased, it always stamps its feet and claps its hands. I have seen an artist making his or her greatest success with an audience that manifested its delight by suppressing every attempt at applause."

"I know exactly what you mean," he answered. "I recall a case in point. There was such an absence of applause on the first night of 'The Two Roses,' while I was on the stage, that I could not believe my friends when they congratulated me on my success. But with experience one gets to understand the idiosyncrasies and habits of audiences. You spoke of the silence of some audiences. The most wonderful quiet and silence I have ever experienced as an actor, a stillness that is profound, has been in those two great theatres, the one that was burned down at Glasgow, and the Standard, in London, during the court scene of 'The Bells.'"

V.

GENIUS is rarely without a sense of humour. Mr. Irving has a broad appreciation of fun, though his own humour is subtle and deep down. This is never better shown than in his Richard and Louis. It now and then appears in his conversations; and when he has an anecdote to tell, he seems to develop the finer and more delicate motives of the action of the narrative, as if he were dramatizing it as he went along.

We dropped our main subject of audiences presently to talk of other things. He related to me a couple of stories of a "dresser" who was his servant in days gone by. The poor man is dead now, and these incidents of his life will not hurt his memory.

"One night," said Irving, "when I had been playing a new part, the old man said, while dressing me, 'This is your master-piece, sir!' How do you think he had arrived at this opinion? He had seen nothing of the piece, but he noticed that I perspired more than usual. The poor fellow was given over to drink at last; so I told him we must part if he did not mend his ways. 'I wonder,' I said to him, 'that, for the sake of your wife and children, you do not reform; besides, you look so ridiculous.' Indeed, I never saw a sillier man when he was tipsy; and his very name would set children laughing—it was Doody. Well, in response to my appeal, with maudlin vanity and with tears in his eyes, he answered, 'They make so much of me!' It reminded me of Dean Ramsay's story of his drunken parishioner. The parson, you remember, admonished the whisky-drinking Scot, concluding his lecture by offering his own conduct as an example. 'I can go into the village and come home again without getting drunk.' 'Ah, minister, but I'm sae popular!' was the fuddling parishioner's apologetic reply."

A notable person in appearance, I said just now. Let me sketch the famous actor as we leave his rooms together. A tall, spare figure in a dark overcoat and grayish trousers, black neckerchief carelessly tied, a tall hat, rather broad at the brim. His hair is black and bushy, with a wave in it on the verge of a curl, and suggestions of gray at the temples and over the ears. It is a pale, somewhat ascetic face, with bushy eyebrows, dark dreamy eyes, a nose that indicates gentleness rather than strength, a thin upper lip, a mouth opposed to all ideas of sensuousness, but nervous and sensitive, a strong jaw and chin, and a head inclined to droop a little, as is often the case with men of a studious habit. There is great individuality in the whole figure, and in the face a rare mobility which photography fails to catch in all the efforts I have yet seen of English artists. Though the popular idea is rather to associate tragedy with the face and manner of Irving, there is nothing sunnier than his smile. It lights up all his countenance, and reveals his soul in his eyes; but it is like the sunshine that bursts for a moment from a cloud, and disappears to leave the land-scape again in shadows, flecked here and there with fleeting reminiscences of the sun.

The management of the Lyceum Theatre has a moral and classic atmosphere of its own. A change came over the house with the success of " The Bells." " Charles I." consummated it. You enter the theatre with feelings entirely different from those which take possession of you at any other house. It is as if the management inspired you with a special sense of its responsibility to Art, and your own obligations to sup-port its earnest endeavours. Mr. Irving has intensified all this by a careful personal attention to every detail belonging to the conduct of his theatre. He has stamped his own individuality upon it. His influence is seen and felt on all hands. He has given the colour of his ambition to his officers and servants. His object is to perfect the art of dramatic representation, and elevate the profession to which he belongs. There is no commercial consideration at work when he is mounting a play, though his experience is that neither expense nor pains are lost on the public.

VI.

WHEN Mr. Irving's art is examined, when his Hamlet or his Mathias, his Shylock or his Dei Franchi, are discussed, he should be regarded from a broader stand-point than that of the mere actor. He is entitled to be looked at as not only the central figure of the play, but as the motive power of the whole entertainment—the master who has set the story and grouped it, the controlling genius of the moving picture, the source of the inspiration of the painter, the musician, the costumer, and the machinist, whose combined efforts go to the realization of the actor-manager's conception and plans. It is acknowledged on all hands that Mr. Irving has done more for dramatic art all round than any actor of our time, and it is open to serious question whether any artist of any time has done as much. Not alone on the stage, but in front of it, at the very entrance of his theatre, the dignified influence of his management is felt. Every department has for its head a man of experience and tact, and every person about the place, from the humblest messenger to the highest officer and actor, seems to carry about with him a certain pride of association with the management.

Mr. Irving's dressing-room at the theatre is a thorough business-like apartment, with at the same time evidences of the taste which obtains at his chambers. It is as unpretentious, and yet, in its way, as remarkable as the man. See him sitting there at the dressing-table, where he is model to himself, where he converts himself into the character he is sustaining. His own face is his canvas, his own person, for the time being, the lay figure which he adorns. It is a large square table in the corner of the room. In the centre is a small, old-fashioned mirror, which is practically the easel upon which he works; for therein is reflected the face which has to depict the passion and fear of Mathias, the cupidity of Richard, the martyrdom of Charles, the grim viciousness of Dubosc, the implacable justice of the avenging Dei Franchi, and the touching melancholy of Hamlet.

As a mere matter of "make-up," his realizations of the historical pictures of Charles the First and Philip of Spain are the highest kind of art. They belong to Vandyck and Velasquez, not only in their imitation of the great masters, but in the sort of inspiration for character and colour which moved those

famous painters. See him sitting, I say, the actor-
artist at his easel. A tray on the right-hand side
of his mirror may be called his palette; it contains
an assortment of colours, paint-pots, powders, and
brushes; but in his hand, instead of the maul-stick, is
the familiar hare's-foot—the actor's "best friend"
rom the earliest days of rouge and burnt cork. To
the left of the mirror lie letters opened and unopened,
missives just brought by the post, a jewel-box, and
various "properties" in the way of chains, lockets, or
buckles that belong to the part he is playing He is
talking to his stage-manager, or to some intimate
friend, as he continues his work. You can hear the
action of the drama that is going on—a distant cheer,
the clash of swords, a merry laugh, or a passing
chorus.

The "call-boy" of the theatre looks in at intervals to report the progress of the piece up to the
point where it is necessary the leading artist should
appear upon the stage. Then, as if he is simply going
to see a friend who is waiting for him, Irving leaves
his dressing-room, and you are alone. There is no
"pulling himself together," or "bracing up," or
putting on "tragic airs" as he goes. It is a pleasant
"Good-night," or "I shall see you again," that takes
him out of his dressing-room, and you can tell when
he is before the audience by the loud cheers that come
rushing up the staircases from the stage. While he
is away, you look around the room. You find that the
few pictures which decorate the walls are theatrical
portraits. Here is an etching of Garrick's head.; there
a water-colour of Ellen Terry; here a study of
Macready in Virginius; there a study in oil of Edmund
Kean, by Clint, side by side with a portrait of George
Frederic Cooke, by Liversiege. Interspersed among
these things are framed play-bills of a past age and
interesting autograph letters. Near the dressing-table
is a tall looking-glass, in front of it an easy-chair,
over which are lying a collection of new draperies and

costumes recently submitted for the actor-manager's approval. The room is warm with the gas that illuminates it, the atmosphere delightful to the fancy that finds a special fascination behind the foot-lights.

VII.

A REFLECTIVE writer, with the power to vividly recall a past age and contrast it with the present, might find ample inspiration in the rooms to which Mr. Irving presently invites us. It is Saturday night. On this last day in every acting week it is his habit to sup at the theatre, and in spite of his two perform-ances he finds strength enough to entertain a few guests, sometimes a snug party of three, sometimes a lively company of eight or ten. We descend a car-peted staircase, cross the stage upon the remains of the snow scene of the " Corsican Brothers," ascend a wind-ing stair, pass through an armoury packed with such a variety of weapons as to suggest the Tower of Lon-don, and are then ushered into a spacious wainscoted apartment, with a full set of polished ancient armour in each corner of it, an antique fireplace with the example of an old master over the mantle, a high-backed settee in an alcove opposite the blind windows (the sills of which are decorated with ancient bottles and jugs), and in the centre of the room an old oak dining-table, fur-nished for supper with white cloth, cut glass, and silver, among which shine the familiar beet-root and tomato.

" This was the old Beefsteak Club Room," says our host ; " beyond there is the kitchen ; the members dined here. The apartments were lumber-rooms until lately."

Classic lumber-rooms truly ! In the history of the clubs no association is more famous than the Sublime Society of Beefsteaks. The late William Jerdan was the first to attempt anything like a concise sketch of the club, and he wrote his reminiscences thereof for me and *The Gentleman's Magazine* a dozen years ago, in the popular modern days of that periodical. Jerdan gave me an account of the club in the days when he visited it.

"The President," he said,—"an absolute despot during his reign,—sat at the head of the table, adorned with ribbon and badge, and with the insignia of a silver gridiron on his breast ; his head, when he was oracular, was crowned with a feathery hat, said to have been worn by Garrick in some gay part on the stage. He looked every inch a king. At the table on this occasion were seated the Bishop, Samuel Arnold, the patriotic originator of English opera and strenuous encourager of native musical talent. He wore a mitre, said to have belonged to Cardinal Gregorio ; but, be that as it might, it became him well, as he set it on his head to pronounce the grace before meat, which he intoned as reverently as if he had been in presence of the Archbishop of Canterbury instead of a bevy of Steakers. Near him was John Richards, the Recorder, whose office in passing sentence on culprits was discharged with piquancy and effect. Captain Morris, the Laureate, occupied a distinguished seat ; so also did Dick Wilson, the Secretary, a bit of a butt to the jokers, who were wont to extort from him some account of a Continental trip, where he prided himself on having ordered a 'boulevard' for his dinner, and *un paysan* (for *faisan*) to be roasted ; and last of all I can recall to mind, at the bottom of the plenteous board sat the all-important 'Boots,' the youngest member of the august assembly. These associated as a sort of staff with a score of other gentlemen, all men of the world, men of intellect and intelligence, well educated, and of celebrity in various lines of life— noblemen, lawyers, physicians and surgeons, authors, artists, newspaper editors, actors,—it is hardly possible to conceive any combination of various talent to be more efficient for the object sought than the Beefsteaks.

"The accommodation for their meetings was built, expressly for that end, behind the scenes of the Lyceum Theatre, by Mr. Arnold ; and, among other features, was a room with no daylight to intrude, and this was the dining-room, with the old gridiron on the ceiling, over the centre of the table. The cookery on which the good cheer of the company depended was carried on in what may be called the kitchen, in full view of the chairman, and served through the opposite wall, namely, a huge gridiron with bars as wide apart as the 'chess' of small windows, handed hot and hot to the expectant hungerers. There were choice salads (mostly of beet-root), porter, and port.

"The plates were never overloaded, but small cuts sufficed till almost satiated appetite perhaps called for one more from the third cut in the rump itself, which his Grace of Norfolk, after many slices, prized as the grand essence of bullock ! "

Other times, other manners. The rooms are still there. The gridiron is gone from the ceiling, but the one through which sliced bullock used to be handed " hot and hot " to the nobility of blood and intellect remains. It and the kitchen (now furnished with a fine modern cooking-range) are shut off from the dining-room, and neither porter nor port ever weighs down the spirits of Mr. Irving's guests. He sometimes regales a few friends here after the play. The *menu* on these occasions would contrast as strangely with that of the old days as the guests and the subjects of their conversation and mirth. It is classic ground on which we tread, and the ghosts that rise before us are those of Sheridan, Perry, Lord Erskine, Cam Hobhouse, and their boon companions. Should the notabilities among Irving's friends be mentioned, the list would be a fair challenge to the old Beefsteaks. I do not propose to deal with these giants of yesterday and to-day, but to contrast with Jerdan's picture a recent supper of guests gathered together on an invitation of only a few hours previously. On the left side of Irving sat one of his most intimate friends, a famous London comedian; on the right, a well-known American tragedian, who had not yet played in London; opposite, at the other side of the circular-ended table, sat a theatrical manager from Dublin, and another of the same profession from the English midlands; the other chairs were occupied by a famous traveller, an American gentleman connected with literature and life insurance, a young gentleman belonging to English political and fashionable society, the editor of a Liverpool journal, a provincial playwright, and a north-country philanthropist.

The repast began with oysters, and ran through a few *entrées* and a steak, finishing with a rare old Stilton cheese. There were various salads, very dry sherry and champagne, a rich Burgundy, and, after all, sodas and brandies and cigars. The talk was "shop" from first to last—discussions of the artistic treatment of certain characters by actors of the day and of a previous age, anecdotes of the stage, the position of the drama, its purpose and mission. Every guest contributed his quota to the general talk, the host himself giving way to the humour of the hour, and chatting of his career, his position, his hopes, his prospects, his ambition, in the frankest way. Neither the space at my disposal nor the custom of the place will permit of a revelation of this social dialogue; for the founder of the feast has revived, with the restored Beefsteak rooms, the motto from Horace's "Epistles" (paraphrased by the old club Bishop), which is still inscribed on the dining-room wall :—

> Let no one bear beyond this threshold hence
> Words utter'd here in friendly confidence.

II.

NEW YORK.

Going to meet the *Britannic*—The *Blackbird*—Skirmishers of the American Press—The London *Standard's* Message to New York, Boston, and Chicago—"Working" America—"Reportorial" Experiences—Daylight off Staten Island—At Quarantine under the Stars and Stripes—"God Save the Queen!" and "Hail to the Chief!"—"Received and Interviewed"—"Portia on a Trip from the Venetian Seas"—What the Reporters think, and what Irving says—The Necessity of Applause—An Anecdote of Forrest—Mr. Vanderbilt and the Mirror—Miss Terry and the Reporters—"Tell them I never loved home so well as now"—Landed and Welcomed—Scenes on the Quay—At the Brevoort.

I.

FOUR o'clock in the morning, October 21, 1883. A cheerful gleam of light falls upon a group of Lotos guests, as they separate at the hospitable door-way of that famous New York club. Otherwise Fifth Avenue is solitary and cold. The voices of the clubmen strike the ear pleasantly. "Going to meet Irving," you hear some of them say, and "Good-night," the others. Presently the group breaks up, and moves off in different directions. "I ordered a carriage at the Brevoort House," says one of the men who pursue their way down Fifth Avenue. They are the only persons stirring in the street. The electric arcs give them accompanying shadows as black as the night-clouds above them. The Edison lamps exhibit the tall buildings, sharp and clear, against the darkness. Two guardians of a carpet-store, on the corner of

Fourteenth Street, sleep calmly among the show bales
that decorate the side-walk. An empty car goes
jingling along into Union Square. A pair of flickering
lights are seen in the distance. They belong to "the
carriage at the Brevoort House." It will only hold
half our number. The civilities that belong to such a
situation being duly exchanged, there are some who
prefer to walk; and an advance is made on foot and
on wheels towards the North River.

For my own part I would, as a rule, rather walk
than ride in a private carriage in New York. The
street cars and the elevated railroad are comfortable
enough; but a corduroy road in a forest-track is not
more emphatic in its demands upon the nerves of a
timid driver than are the pitfalls of a down-town
street in the Empire city. I nevertheless elect to ride.
We are four; we might be any number to one who
should attempt to count us, so numerous does the
jolting of our otherwise comfortable brougham appear
to make us. We are tossed and pitched about as persistently as we might be in a dinghy during a gale off
some stormy headland. Presently the fresh breeze of
the river blows upon us, as if to justify the simile;
then we are thrown at each other more violently than
ever; a flash of gaslight greets us; the next moment
it is dark again, and we stop with alarming sudden-
ness. "Twenty-second Street Pier," says our driver,
opening the door. We are received by a mysterious
officer, who addresses us from beneath a world of com-
forters and overcoats. "Want the *Blackbird?*" he
asks. We do. "This way," he says. We follow
him, to be ushered straightway into the presence of
those active scouts and skirmishers of the American
press—the interviewers. Here they are, a veritable
army of them, on board Mr. Starin's well-known river
steamer, the *Blackbird,* their wits and their pencils
duly sharpened for their prey. Youth and age both
dedicate themselves to this lively branch of American
journalism. I tell a London friend who is here to

"mind his eye," or they may practise upon him, and that if he refuses to satisfy their inquiries they may sacrifice him to their spleen; for some of them are shivering with cold, and complaining that they have had no rest. Finding an English artist here from the *Illustrated London News,* I conduct him secretly to the "ladies' cabin." It is occupied by a number of mysterious forms, lying about in every conceivable posture; some on the floor, some on the sofas; their faces partially disguised under slouch hats, their figures enveloped in cloaks and coats. They are asleep. The cabin is dimly lighted, and there is an odour of tobacco in the oily atmosphere. "Who are they?" asks my friend in a whisper. "Inter-viewers!" I reply, as we slip back to the stove in the saloon. "What a picture Doré would have made of the ladies' cabin!" says the English artist.

II.

WE encounter more new-comers in the saloon. Two of them bring copies of the morning papers. I recognize several of the interesting crowd, and cannot help telling them something of the conversation of the Beefsteak Club Room guest, who drew their pictures in London, as a warning to the traveller whom they were going to meet. I find them almost as ill-informed, and quite as entertaining, concerning Irving's mannerisms, as was the traveller in question touching their own occupation. They talk very much in the spirit of what has recently appeared here in some of the newspapers about Irving and his art-methods. New York, they say, will not be dictated to by London; New York judges for itself. At the same time they do not think it a generous thing on the part of the London *Standard* to send a hostile editorial *avant-courier* to New York, to prejudice the English actor's audiences and his critics.[1] Nor do they think this "British malevo-

[1] The following cablegram appeared in the *Herald* on October

lence" will have any effect either way, though the *Standard* practically proclaims Mr. Irving and Miss Terry, as impostors. This article has been printed by the press, from New York to San Francisco, while the Lyceum company and its chief are on the Atlantic. I have often heard it said in England that Irving had been wonderfully "worked" in America. Men who are worthy to have great and devoted friends unconsciously make bitter enemies. Irving is honoured with a few of these attendants upon fame. If the people who regard his reputation as a thing that has been "worked" could have visited New York a week before his arrival, they could not have failed to be delighted to see how much was being done against him and how little for him. An ingenious and hostile

the 18th, and it was alluded to in the editorial columns as "a hint" which "will not be lost upon the theatrical critics :"—
                                    "*London*, Oct. 17, 1883.
"The *Standard*, in an editorial this morning, thus appeals to America for a dispassionate judgment of Henry Irving:—
"American audiences have a favourable opportunity of showing that they can think for themselves, and do not slavishly echo the criticisms of the English press. We confess that, though one has read many eulogistic notices of Mr. Irving, and listened in private to opinions of different complexions, it is difficult to find anything written respecting him that deserves to be dignified with the description of serious criticisms. Cannot New York, Boston, and Chicago supply us with a little of this material? Are we indulging vain imaginings if we hope that our cousins across the water will forget all that has been said or written about Irving and the Lyceum company this side of the ocean, and will go to see him in his chief performances with unprejudiced eyes and ears, and send us, at any rate, a true, independent, unconventional account of his gifts and graces, or the reverse?"
"Most Englishmen naturally will be gratified if the people of the United States find Irving as tragic, and Miss Terry as charming, as so many people in this country consider them. But the gratification will be increased, should it be made apparent that a similar conclusion has been arrived at by the exercise of independent judgment, and if in pronouncing it fresh light is thrown upon the disputed points of theatrical controversy."

pamphleteer was in evidence in every bookseller's window. Villainous cheap photographs of "actor and manager" were hawked in the streets. Copies of an untruthful sketch of his career, printed by a London weekly, were circulated through the mails. The *Standard's* strange appeal to New York, Boston, and Chicago was cabled to the *Herald,* and republished in the evening papers. Ticket speculators had bought up all the best seats at the Star Theatre, where the English actor was to appear, and refused to sell them to the public except at exorbitant and, for many play-goers, prohibitive rates. So far as "working" went, the London enemies of the Lyceum manager were so actively represented in New York that his friends in the Empire city must have felt a trifle chilled at the outlook. The operations of the ticket speculators, it must, however, be admitted, seemed to project in Irving's path the most formidable of all the other obstacles.

III.

BUT Irving's ship is sailing on through the darkness while I have been making this "aside," and the *Blackbird* is in motion; for I hear the swish of the river, and the lights on shore are dancing by the port-holes. Mr. Abbey's fine military band, from the Metropolitan Opera House, has come on board; so also has a band of waiters from the Brunswick. Breakfast is being spread in the saloon. The brigands from the ladies' cabin have laid aside their slouch hats and cloaks. They look as harmless and as amiable as any company of English journalists. Night, and dark-lanterns might convert the mildest-mannered crowd into the appearance of a pirate crew.

I wish the Irving guest of my first chapter could see and talk to these interviewers. I learn that they represent journals at Boston, Philadelphia, Chicago, St. Louis, and other cities besides New York. One of them has interviewed Lord Coleridge; another was

D

with Grant during the war; a third was with Lee.
They have all had interesting experiences. One is an
Englishman; another hails from "bonnie Scotland."
There is no suggestion of rowdyism among them. I
owe them an apology on the "excuse accuse"
principle, for saying these things; but the "interviewer" is not understood in England; he is often
abused in America, and I should like to do him
justice. These gentlemen of the press, who are going
out to meet Irving, are reporters. Socially they occupy
the lowest station of journalism, though their work is
of primary importance. Intellectually they are capable
men, and the best of them write graphically and with
an artistic sense of the picturesque. They should, and
no doubt do, develop into accomplished and powerful
journalists; for theirs is the best of education. They
study mankind; they come in contact with the most
prominent of American statesmen; they talk with all
great foreigners who visit the United States; they are
admitted into close intercourse with the leading spirits
of the age; they have chatted on familiar terms with
Lincoln, Sheridan, Grant, Garfield, Huxley, Coleridge,
Arnold, Patti, Bernhardt, Nilsson, and they will
presently have added to the long list of their personal
acquaintances Irving and Miss Terry. They are
travellers, and, of necessity, observers. Their press-
card is a talisman that opens to them all doors of
current knowledge; and I am bound to say that these
men on board the *Blackbird* are, in conversation
and manners, quite worthy of the trust reposed in
them by the several great journals which they
represent.

IV.

"BRITANNIC ahead!" shouts a voice from the gangway. We clamber on deck. It is daylight. The air
is still keen. The wooded shores of Staten Island are
brown with the last tints of autumn. Up the wide
reaches of the river, an arm of the great sea, come all

kinds of craft : some beating along under sail; others, floating palaces, propelled by steam. These latter are ferry-boats and passenger steamers. You have seen them in many a marine picture and panorama of American travel. The *Blackbird* is typical of the rest,—double decks, broad saloons, tiers of berths, ladies' cabins, and every ceiling packed with life-buoys in case of accident. We push along through the choppy water, our steam-whistle screaming hoarse announcements of our course. The *Britannic* lies calmly at quarantine, the stars and stripes at her topmast, the British flag at her stern. She is an impressive picture,—her masts reaching up into the gray sky, every rope taut, her outlines sharp and firm. In the distance other ocean steamers glide towards us, attended by busy tugs and handsome launches. One tries to compare the scene with the Mersey and the Thames, and the only likeness is in the ocean steamers, which have come thence across the seas. For the rest, the scene is essentially American,—the broad river, the gay wooden villas ashore, the brown hills, the bright steam-craft on the river, the fast rig of the trading schooners, and above all the stars and stripes of the many flags that flutter in the breeze, and the triumphant eagles that extend their golden wings over the lofty steerage turrets of tug and floating palace.

Now we are alongside the *Britannic.* As our engines stop, the band of thirty Italians on our deck strikes up " God save the Queen." One or two British hands instinctively raise one or two British hats, and many a heart, I am sure, on board the *Britannic* beats the quicker under the influence of the familiar strains. A few emigrants, with unkempt hair, on the after-deck, gaze open-mouthed at the *Blackbird.* Several early risers appear forward and greet with waving hands the welcoming crowd from New York. One has time to note the weather-beaten colour of the *Britannic's* funnels.

" What sort of a passage ? " cries a voice, shouting
in competition with the wind, that is blowing hard
through the rigging.

" Pretty rough," is the answer.

" Where is Mr. Irving ? " cries out another *Blackbird*
passenger.

" In bed," is the response.

" Oh ! " says the interrogator, amidst a general laugh.

" Beg pardon, no," presently shouts the man on the
Britannic,—" he's shaving."

Another laugh, drowned by a salute of some neighbouring guns. At this moment a boat is lowered
from the splendid yacht *Yosemite,* which has been
steaming round about the *Britannic* for some time.
It is Mr. Tilden's vessel. He has lent it to Mr.
Lawrence Barrett. He has come out, with Mr. William Florence, to meet Irving and Miss Terry, intending to carry them free from worry or pressure to
their several hotels. The two well-known actors are
in the yacht's pinnace, and some of us wonder if they
are good sailors. The waves, which do not stir the
Britannic, and only gently move the *Blackbird,* fairly
toss the *Yosemite's* boat ; but the occupants appear to
be quite at home in her. She disappears around the
Britannic's bows to make the port side for boarding,
and as she does so Mr. Irving suddenly appears between the gangway and the ship's boats, on a level with
the deck of the *Blackbird,* about midships. " There
he is ! " shout a score of voices. He looks pale in the
cold, raw light ; but he smiles pleasantly, and takes
off a felt bowler hat as the *Blackbird* gives him a cheer
of welcome.

" Won't you come here ? The quarantine authorities
object to our visiting the ship until the doctor has
left her."

A plank is thrust from our paddle-box, Irving climbs
the *Britannic's* bulwark, and grasps a hand held out
to steady him as he clambers aboard the *Blackbird,*
right in the midst of the interviewers. Shaking hands

with his manager, Mr. Abbey, and others, he is introduced to some of the press-men, who scan his face
and figure with undisguised interest. By this time
Messrs. Barrett and Florence appear on the *Britannic*.
They have got safely out of their boat, and have a
breezy and contented expression in their eyes. Irving
now recrosses the temporary gangway, and is fairly
embraced by his two American friends. The band
strikes up, " Hail to the Chief! " Then the gentlemen
of the press are invited to join Mr. Irving on board
the *Yosemite*. They are arrested by what one of them
promptly designates " a vision of pre-Raphaelitish
beauty." It is Miss Ellen Terry.[2] Every hat goes off
as she comes gaily through the throng. " Portia, on
a trip from the Venetian seas! " exclaims an enthusiastic young journalist, endeavouring to cap the
æsthetic compliment of his neighbour. Escorted by
Mr. Barrett, and introduced by Mr. Irving, she is
deeply moved, as well she may be, by the novel scene.
Britannic passengers crowd about her to say good-bye ;
the band is playing " Rule, Britannia ;" many a gay
river boat and steamer is navigating the dancing
waters ; the sun is shining, flags fluttering, and a score
of hands are held out to help Portia down the gangway
on board the *Yosemite*, which is as trim and bright
and sturdy in its way as a British gun-boat. While

[2] The *Tribune's* reporter drew Miss Terry's picture with
studied elaboration :—
" As she stepped with a pretty little shudder over the sway-
ing plank upon the yacht she showed herself possessed of a
marked individuality. Her dress consisted of a dark greenish-
brown cloth wrap, lined inside with a peculiar shade of red ; the
inner dress, girt at the waist with a red, loosely-folded sash,
seemed a reminiscence of some eighteenth-century portrait, while
the delicate complexion caught a rosy reflection from the loose
flame-coloured red scarf tied in a bow at the neck. The face
itself is a peculiar one. Though not by ordinary canons beautiful, it is nevertheless one to be remembered, and seems to have
been modelled on that of some pre-Raphaelitish saint,—an effect
heightened by the aureole of soft golden hair escaping from
under the plain brown straw and brown velvet hat."

the heroine of the trip is taking her seat on deck, and kissing her hand to the *Britannic,* the *Yosemite* drives ahead of the ocean steamer. Mr. Irving goes down into the spacious cabin, which is crowded with the gentlemen against whose sharp and inquisitive interrogations he has been so persistently warned.

V.

"WELL, gentlemen, you want to talk to me ?" he says, lighting a cigar, and offering his case to his nearest neighbours.

The reporters look at him and smile. They have had a brief consultation as to which of them shall open the business, but without coming to any definite arrangement. Irving, scanning the kindly faces, is no doubt smiling inwardly at the picture which his London friend had drawn of the interviewers. He is the least embarrassed of the company. Nobody seems inclined to talk; yet every movement of Irving invites interrogatory attack.

"A little . champagne, gentlemen," suggests Mr Florence, pushing his way before the ship's steward and waiters.

" And chicken," says Irving, smiling ; " that is how we do it in London, they say."

This point is lost, however, upon the reporters, a few of whom sip their champagne, but not with anything like fervour. They have been waiting many hours to interview Irving, and they want to do it. I fancy they are afraid of each other.

"Now, gentlemen," says Irving, "time flies, and I have a dread of you. I have looked forward to this meeting, not without pleasure, but with much apprehension. Don't ask me how I like America at present. I shall, I am sure; and I think the bay superb. There, I place myself at your mercy. Don't spare me."

Everybody laughs. Barrett and Florence look on curiously. Bram Stoker, Mr. Irving's acting manager, cannot disguise his anxiety. Loveday, his stage-manager and old friend, is amused. He has heard many curious things about America from his brother George, who accompanied the famous English comedian, Mr. J. L. Toole (one of Irving's oldest, and perhaps his most intimate, friend), on his American tour. Neither Loveday nor Stoker has ever crossed the Atlantic before. They have talked of it, and pictured themselves steaming up the North River into New York many a time; but they find their forecast utterly unlike the original.

" What about his mannerisms ? " says one reporter to another. " I notice nothing strange, nothing *outré* either in his speech or walk."

" He seems perfectly natural to me," the other replies; and it is this first " revelation " that has evidently tongue-tied the " reportorial " company. They have read so much about the so-called eccentricities of the English visitor's personality that they cannot overcome their surprise at finding themselves addressed by a gentleman whose grace of manner reminds them rather of the polished ease of Lord Coleridge than of the *bizarre* figure with which caricature, pictorially and otherwise, has familiarized them.

" We are all very glad to see you, sir, and to welcome you to New York," says one of the interviewers, presently.

" Thank you, with all my heart," says Irving.

" And we would like to ask you a few questions, and to have you talk about your plans in this country. You open in ' The Bells,'—that was one of your first great successes ? "

" Yes."

" You will produce your plays here just in the same way as in London ? " chimes in a second interviewer.

" With the same effects, and, as far as possible, with the same cast ? "

" Yes."

" And what are your particular effects, for instance, in ' The Bells' and ' Louis XI.,' say, as regards mounting and lighting ? "

" Well, gentlemen," answers Irving, laying aside his cigar and folding his arms, " I will explain. In the first place, in visiting America, I determined I would endeavour to do justice to myself, to the theatre, and to you. I was told I might come alone as a star, or I might come with a few members of my company, and that I would be sure to make money. That did not represent any part of my desire in visiting America. The pleasure of seeing the New World, the ambition to win its favour and its friendship, and to show it some of the work we do at the Lyceum,—these are my reasons for being here. I have, therefore, brought my company and my scenery. Miss Ellen Terry, one of the most perfect and charming actresses that ever graced the English stage, consented to share our fortunes in this great enterprise ; so I bring you almost literally the Lyceum Theatre."

" How many artists, sir ? "

" Oh, counting the entire company and staff, somewhere between sixty and seventy, I suppose. Fifty of them have already arrived here in the *City of Rome.*"

" In what order do you produce your pieces here ? "

" ' The Bells,' ' Charles,' ' The Lyons Mail,' ' The Merchant of Venice,' we do first."

" Have you any particular reason for the sequence of them ? "

" My idea is to produce my Lyceum successes in their order, as they were done in London ; I thought it would be interesting to show the series one after the other in that way."

" When do you play ' Hamlet ' ? "

" On my return to New York in the spring."

" Any special reason for that ? "

" A managerial one. We propose to keep one or
two novelties for our second visit. Probably we shall
reserve ' Much Ado ' as well as ' Hamlet.' Moreover,
a month is too short a time for us to get through our
répertoire."

" In which part do you think you most excel ? "

" Which do you like most of all your range of
characters ? "

" What is your opinion of Mr. Booth as an
actor ? "

These questions come from different parts of the
crowd. It reminds me of the scene between an English
parliamentary candidate and a caucus constituency,
with the exception that the American questioners are
quite friendly and respectful, their chief desire evidently
being to give Mr. Irving texts upon which he can
speak with interest to their readers.

" Mr. Booth and I are warm friends. It is not
necessary to tell you that he is a great actor. I acted
with him many subordinate parts when he first came
to England, about twenty years ago."

" What do you think is his finest impersonation ? "

" I would say ' Lear,' though I believe the American
verdict would be ' Richelieu.' Singularly enough
' Richelieu ' is not a popular play in England. Mr.
Booth's mad scene in ' Lear,' I am told, is superb. I
did not see it ; but I can speak of Othello and Iago :
both are fine performances."

" You played in ' Othello ' with Mr. Booth in London,
you say ? "

" I produced ' Othello ' especially for Mr. Booth, and
played Iago for the first time on that occasion. We
afterwards alternated the parts."

" Shakespeare is popular in England,—more so now
than for some years past, I believe ? "

" Yes."

" What has been the motive-power in this revival ? "

" England has to-day many Shakespearian societies,
and our countrymen read the poet much more than

they did five-and-twenty years ago. As a rule our
fathers obtained their knowledge of him from the
theatre, and were often, of course, greatly misled as to
the meaning and intention of the poet, under the
manipulation of Colley Cibber and others."

" Which of Shakespeare's plays is most popular in
England ? "

" ' Hamlet.' And, singularly, the next one is not
' Julius Cæsar,' which is the most popular after
' Hamlet,' I believe, in your country. ' Othello '
might possibly rank second with us, if it were not
difficult to get two equally good actors for the two
leading parts. Salvini's Othello, for instance, suffered
because the Iago was weak."

" You don't play ' Julius Cæsar,' then, in England?"

" No. There is a difficulty in filling worthily the
three leading parts."

By this time Mr. Irving is on the most comfortable
and familiar terms with the gentlemen of the press.
He has laid aside his cigar, and smiles often with a
curious and amused expression of face.

" You must find this kind of work, this interviewing,
very difficult," he says, presently, in a tone of friendly
banter.

" Sometimes," answers one of them; and they all
laugh, entering into the spirit of the obvious fun of a
victim who is not suffering half as much as he expected
to do, and who indeed is, on the whole, very well
satisfied with himself.

" Don't you think we might go on deck now and see
the harbour ? " he asks.

" Oh, yes," they all say; and in a few minutes the
Yosemite's pretty saloon is vacated.

Irving and his friends go forward; Miss Terry is
aft, in charge of Mr. Barrett. She is looking intently
down the river at the far-off *Britannic*, which is
now beginning to move forward in our wake, the
Yosemite leaving behind her a long, white track of
foam.

The interviewers are again busily engaged with Mr. Irving. He is once more the centre of an interested group of men. Not one of them takes a note. They seem to be putting all he says down in their minds. They are accustomed to tax their memories. One catches, in the expression of their faces, evidence of something like an inter-vision. They seem to be ticking off, in their minds, the points as the speaker makes them; for Irving now appears to be talking as much for his own amusement as for the public instruction. He finds that he has a quick, intelligent, and attentive audience, and the absence of note-books and anything like a show of machinery for recording his words puts him thoroughly at his ease. Then he likes to talk " shop," as who does not ? And what is more delightful to hear than experts on their own work ?

"Do your American audiences applaud much ? " he asks.

"Yes," they said; " oh, yes."

"Because, you know, your Edwin Forrest once stopped in the middle of a scene and addressed his audience on the subject of their silence. ' You must applaud,' he said, ' or I cannot act.' I quite sympathize with that feeling. An actor needs applause. It is his life and soul when he is on the stage. The enthusiasm of the audience reacts upon him. He gives them back heat for heat. If they are cordial, he is encouraged; if they are excited, so is he; as they respond to his efforts he tightens his grip upon their imagination and emotions. You have no pit in your American theatres, as we have ; that is, your stalls, or parquet, cover the entire floor. It is to the quick feelings and heartiness of the pit and gallery that an actor looks for encouragement during his great scenes in England. Our stalls are appreciative, but not demonstrative. Our pit and gallery are both."

Irving, when particularly moved, likes to tramp about. Whenever the situation allows it, he does so upon the stage. Probably recalling the way in which pit and gallery rose at him—and stalls and dress circle, too, for that matter—on his farewell night at the Lyceum, he paces about the deck, all the interviewers making rapid mental note of his gait, and watching for some startling peculiarity that does not manifest itself.

"He has not got it; why, the man is as natural and as straight and capable as a man can be," says one to another.

"And a real good fellow," is the response. "Ask him about Vanderbilt and the mirror."

"Oh, Mr. Irving!—just one more question."

"As many as you like, my friend," is the ready reply.

"Is it true that you are to be the guest of Mr. Vanderbilt?"

"And be surrounded with ingeniously-constructed mirrors, where I can see myself always, and all at once. I have heard strange stories about Mr. Vanderbilt having had a wonderful mirror of this kind constructed for my use, so that I may pose before it in all my loveliest attitudes. Something of the kind has been said, eh?" he asks, laughing.

"Oh, yes, that is so," is the mirthful response.

"Then you may contradict it, if you will. You may say that I am here for work; that I shall have no time to be any one's guest, though I hope the day may come when I shall have leisure to visit my friends. You may add, if you will" (here he lowered his voice with a little air of mystery), "that I always carry a mirror of my own about with me wherever I go, because I love to pose and contemplate my lovely figure whenever the opportunity offers."

"That will do, I guess," says a gentleman of the interviewing staff; "thank you, Mr. Irving, for your courtesy and information."

"I am obliged to you very much," he says, and then, having his attention directed to the first view of New York, expresses his wonder and delight at the scene, as well he may.

Ahead the towers and spires of New York stand out in a picturesque outline against the sky. On either hand the water-line is fringed with the spars of ships and steamers. On the left stretches far away the low-lying shores of New Jersey; on the right, Brooklyn can be seen, rising upwards, a broken line of roofs and steeples. Further away, joining "the city of churches " to Manhattan, hangs in mid-air that marvel of science, the triple carriage, foot, and rail road known as the Brooklyn Bridge. Around the *Yosemite*, as she ploughs along towards her quay, throng many busy steamers, outstripping, in the race for port, fleets of sailing vessels that are beating up the broad reaches of the river before the autumn wind.

VI.

" SHE is not quite pretty," says a New York reporter, turning to me during his contemplation of Miss Terry, who is very picturesque, as she sits by the taffrail at the stern; " but she is handsome, and she is distin-guished. I think we would like to ask her a few questions; will you introduce us ? "

I do the honours of this presentation. Miss Terry is too much under the influence of the wonderful scene that meets her gaze to receive the reporters with calmness.

"And this is New York ! " she exclaims. "What a surprising place ! And, oh, what a river ! So different to the Thames ! And to think that I am in New York ! It does not seem possible. I cannot realize it."

" If you had a message to send home to your friends, Miss Terry, what would it be ? " asks Reporter No. 1, a more than usually bashful young man.

The question is a trifle unfortunate.

" Tell them I never loved home so well as now," she answers in her frank, impulsive way.

She turns her head away to hide her tears, and Reporter No. 2 remonstrates with his companion.

" I wouldn't have said it for anything," says No. 1.

" I was thinking how I would add a few words for
her to my London cable,—that's a fact."

" It is very foolish of me, pray excuse me," says
the lady ; " it is all so new and strange. I know my
eyes are red, and this is not the sort of face to go into
New York with, is it ? "

" I think New York will be quite satisfied, Miss
Terry," says a third reporter; "but don't let us
distress you."

" Oh, no, I am quite myself now. You want to ask
me some questions ? "

" Not if you object."

" I don't object ; only you see one has been looking
forward to this day a long time, and seeing land again
and houses, and so many ships, and New York itself,
may well excite a stranger."

" Yes, indeed, that is so," remarks No. 1, upon
whom she turns quickly, the " Liberty " scarf at
her neck flying in the wind, and her earnest eyes
flashing.

" Have you ever felt what it is to be a stranger just
entering a strange land ?   If not, you can hardly
realize my sensations.   Not that I have any fears
about my reception. No, it is not that; the Americans on the ship were so kind to me, and you are so
very considerate, that I am sure everybody ashore
will be friendly."

" Do you know Miss Anderson ? "

" Yes.   She is a beautiful woman. I have not seen
her upon the stage; but I have met her."

" Do you consider ' Charles I.' will present you to a
New York audience in one of your best characters ? "

" No ; and I am not very fond of the part of
Henrietta Maria either."

" What are your favourite characters ? "

" Oh, I hardly know," she says, now fairly interested
in the conversation, and turning easily towards her
questioners for the first time. " I love nearly all I
play ; but I don't like to cry, and I cannot help it in

' Charles I.' I like comedy best,—Portia, Beatrice, and Letitia Hardy."

" Do you intend to star on your own account ?·"

" No, no."

" You prefer to cast your fortunes with the Lyceum company ? "

" Yes, certainly. Sufficient for the day is the Lyceum thereof. There is no chance of my ever desiring to change. I am devoted to the Lyceum, and to Mr. Irving. No one admires him more than I do ; no one knows better, I think, how much he has done for our art; no one dreams of how much more he will yet do if he is spared. I used to think, when I was with Charles Kean,—I served my apprenticeship, you know, with Mr. and Mrs. Charles Kean,—that his performances and mounting of plays were perfect in their way. But look at Mr. Irving's work; look at what he has done and what he does. I am sure you will be delighted with him. Excuse me, is that the *Britannic* yonder, following in our wake ? "

" Yes."

She kisses her hand to the vessel, and then turns to wonder at the city, which seems to be coming towards us, so steadily does the *Yosemite* glide along, hardly suggesting motion.

Then suddenly the word is passed that the *Yosemite* is about to land her passengers. A few minutes later she slips alongside the wharf at the foot of Canal Street. The reporters take their leave, raising their hats to Miss Terry, many of them shaking hands with Mr. Irving. Carriages are in waiting for Mr. Barrett and his party. A small crowd, learning who the new-comers were, give them a cheer of welcome, and Henry Irving and Ellen Terry stand upon American soil.

" I am told," says Mr. Irving, as we drive away, " that when Jumbo arrived in New York he put out his foot and felt if the ground was solid enough to bear his weight. The New Yorkers, I believe, were very much amused at that. They have a keen sense of fun. Where are we going now?"

"To the Customs, at the White Star Wharf, to sign your declaration papers," says Mr. Florence.

"How many packages have you in your state-room, madame?" asks a sturdy official, addressing Miss Terry.

"Well, really I don't know; three or four, I think."

"Not more than that?" suggests Mr. Barrett.

"Perhaps five or six."

"Not any more?" asked the official. "Shall I say five or six?"

"Well, really, I cannot say. Where's my maid? Is it important,—the exact number?"

There is a touch of bewilderment in her manner which amuses the officials, and everybody laughs—she herself very heartily—when her maid says there are fourteen packages of various kinds in the state-room of the *Britannic*, which is now discharging her passengers. A scene of bustle and excitement is developing just as we are permitted to depart. A famous politician is on board. There is a procession, with a band of music, to meet him. Crowds of poor people are pushing forward for the *Britannic* gangway, to meet a crowd of still poorer emigrant friends. Imposing equipages are here to carry off the rich and prosperous travellers. Tons of portmanteaus, trunks, boxes, baggage of every kind, are sliding from the vessel's side upon the quay. Friends are greeting friends. Children are being hugged by fathers and mothers. Ships' stewards are hurrying to and fro. The express man, jingling his brass checks, is looking for business; his carts are fighting their way among the attendant carriages and more ponderous waggons. A line of Custom-house men form in line, a living cord of blue and silver, across the roadway exit of the wharf. There is a smell of tar and coffee and baked peanuts in the atmosphere, together with the sound of many voices; and the bustle repeats itself outside in the rattle of arriving and departing carts and carriages. Above all one hears the pleasant music of distant car-bells. We dash along, over level crossings, past very continental-looking river-side *cabarets* and rum-shops, under elevated railroads, and up streets that recall Holland, France, Brighton, and Liverpool, until we reach Washington Square. The dead leaves of autumn are beginning to hide the fading grass; but the sun is shining gloriously away up in a blue sky. Irving is impressed with the beauty of the city as we enter Fifth Avenue, its many spires marking the long line of street as far as the eye can see. The Brevoort House has proved a welcome, if expensive, haven of rest to many a weary traveller. To-day its bright windows and green sun-blinds, its white marble steps, and its wholesome aspect of home-like comfort suggest the pleasantest possibilities.

Let us leave the latest of its guests to his first experiences of the most hotel-keeping nation in the world.

III.

FIRST IMPRESSIONS.

I.

"It is not like my original idea of it, so far," said Irving the next morning,—" this city of New York. The hotel, the Fifth Avenue, the people,—everything is a little different from one's anticipations; and yet it seems to me that I have seen it all before. It is London and Paris combined. I have been round to call on Miss Terry. She is at what she calls ' The Hotel—ahem ! '—the Hotel Dam, in Union Square. Dam is the proprietor. It is a handsome house. A fine square. The buildings are very tall. The cars, running along the streets, their many bells, the curious, wire-drawn look of the wheels of private carriages,—all a little odd. Fifth Avenue is splendid ! And what a glorious sky ! "

He rattled on, amused and interested, as he stood in the back room of his suite of three on the ground floor at the Brevoort.

" Several interviewers in there," he said, pointing to the folding-doors that shut us out from the other

apartment. " One reporter wanted to attend regularly
and chronicle all I did,—where I went to, and how;
what I ate, and when; he wished to have a record of
everybody who called, what they said, and what I said
to them."

"An enterprising chronicler; probably a ' liner,' as
we should call him on the other side,—a liner un-
attached."

" He was very civil. I thanked him, and made him
understand that I am modest, and do not like so much
attention as he suggests. But these other gentlemen,
let us see them together."

It was very interesting to hear Irving talk to his
visitors, one after the other, about his art and his
work. I had never seen him in such good conversational form before. So far from resisting his in-
terrogators, he enjoyed their questions, and, at the
same time, often puzzled them with his answers. Some
of his visitors came with minds free and unprejudiced
to receive his impressions, with pens ready to record
them. Others had evidently read up for the interview;
they had turned over the pages of Hazlitt, Lamb, and
Shakespeare with a purpose. Others had clearly
studied the ingenious pamphlet of Mr. Archer; these
had odd questions to ask, and were amazed at the
quickness of Irving's repartee. As a rule they reported
the new-comer correctly. The mistakes they made
were trivial, though some of them might have seemed
important in prejudiced eyes. I propose, presently,
to give an example of this journalistic work.

After dinner Irving went to a quiet little reception at the house of a friend, and at night he visited
the Lambs Club. The members are principally actors,
and Sunday night is their only holiday. Once a month
they dine together. On this night they held their first
meeting of the season. The rooms were crowded.
Irving was welcomed with three cheers. Mr. William
Florence, Mr. Raymond, Mr. Henry Edwards, Mr.
Howson, and other well-known actors introduced him

to their brother members, and a committee was at once formed to arrange a date when the club could honour itself and its guest with a special dinner.

"It is very delightful to be so cordially received," said Irving, "by my brother actors. I shall be proud to accept your hospitality on any evening that is convenient to you. It must be on a Sunday, of course. I am told New York is strict in its observance of Sunday. Well, I am glad of it—it is the actor's only day of rest."

II.

On Monday morning the newspapers, from one end of the United States to the other, chronicled the arrival of Mr. Irving and Miss Terry. The New York journals rivalled each other in columns of bright, descriptive matter, with headings in more than customary detail. The *Herald* commenced its announcement in this way :—

IRVING—TERRY.

Arrival of the Famous English Actor and the Leading Lady of the Lyceum.

A Hearty Welcome Down the Bay by Old Friends.

AN INTERVIEW WITH MR. IRVING.

His Views on the Drama and Stage of To-day.

PLANS FOR THE FUTURE.

The *Sun* greeted its readers with,—

UP EARLY TO MEET IRVING!

A BUSINESS-LIKE HAMLET AND A JOLLY OPHELIA ARRIVE.

What the Famous English Actor Looks Like and How He
Talks—A Stentorian Greeting Down at
Quarantine before Breakfast.

The morning *Journal* (the latest success in cheap
newspaper enterprise) proclaimed :—

ENGLAND'S GREAT ACTOR.

Henry Irving Cordially Welcomed in the Lower Bay.

He Tells of His Hopes and Fears, and Expresses Delight
over Dreaded Newspaper Interviewers—
Miss Terry Joyful.

A leading Western journal pays a large salary to a
clever member of its staff, whose duty is confined to
the work of giving to the varied news of the day
attractive titles. The New York press is less exuberant
in this direction than formerly.

The sketches of the arrival of the *Britannic's*
passengers are bright and personal. They describe
the appearance of Mr. Irving and Miss Terry. The
vivacity of Miss Terry charmed the reporters. The
quiet dignity of Irving surprised and impressed them.
The " interviews " generally referred to Mr. Irving's
trip across the Atlantic, his programme for New York,
his hopes of a successful tour, his ideas of the differences between American and English theatres, what
he thought of Booth, and other points which I have
myself set forth, perhaps more in detail than was
·possible for the journals, and, what is more important,
from the platform of an interested English spectator.
The following conversation is, in the main, a revised
edition of an interview that appeared in the *Herald.*

" And now to speak to you of yourself as an actor,
and also of your theatre,—let me ask you, to what
mainly do you attribute your success ? "

" The success I have made, such as it is, has been

made by acting—by acting alone, whether good or bad." [1]

" There is a notion in America, Mr. Irving, that your extraordinary success is due to your *mise en scène* and the research you have given to the proper mounting of your pieces."

" Indeed, is that so ? And yet ' The Cup ' and ' Romeo and Juliet ' were the only two pieces I have done in which the *mise en scène* has been really remarkable. During my early association with the Lyceum nothing of that kind was attempted. For instance, the churchyard scene in ' Hamlet ' was a scene painted for ' Eugene Aram,' as the then manager of the Lyceum (my old friend, Mr. Bateman) did not believe in the success of ' Hamlet.' The run of

---

[1] These simple facts prove that, aside from his acting, with which it is not our duty to deal at present, Mr. Irving is one of the most remarkable men of this or any other age. But he is unquestionably right when he asserts that he owes his success to his acting alone. It has been said that the splendid manner in which he puts his plays upon the stage is the secret of his popularity ; but he first became popular in plays which were not splendidly mounted, and his greatest financial and artistic successes have been made in pieces upon which he expended no unusual decorations. It has been said that Manager Bateman made Irving ; but, as we shall presently prove, Irving made Manager Bateman in London, and has been doubly successful since Manager Bateman's death. It has been said that his leading lady, Ellen Terry, is the Mascot of Irving's career ; but his fame was established before Miss Terry joined his company, and he has won his proudest laurels in the plays in which Miss Terry has not appeared. It has been said that the financial backing of the Baroness Burdett-Coutts gave Irving his opportunity ; but he had been overcrowding the London Lyceum for years before he made the acquaintance of the Baroness. No ; the unprecedented and unrivalled success of Mr. Irving has been made by himself alone. He became popular as an actor in a stock company ; his popularity transformed him into a star and a manager ; and, as a star and a manager, he has widened, deepened, and improved his popularity. He has won his position fairly, by his own talents and exertions, against overwhelming odds, and he has nobody to thank for it but himself, in spite of the theories which we have exploded.—*Spirit of the Times, New York*, Oct. 27, 1883.

the play was two hundred nights. I have been associated with the Lyceum since 1871, eleven years, and, until the production of 'The Corsican Brothers' and 'The Cup,' in 1880-81, no play in which I acted had ever been elaborately mounted. Before the time of these plays I had acted in 'The Bells,' 'Charles I.,' 'Eugene Aram,' 'Philip,' 'Richelieu,' 'Hamlet,' 'Macbeth,' 'Louis XI.,' 'Othello,' 'Richard III.,' 'The Merchant of Venice,' 'The Iron Chest,' and others; and this, I think, is sufficient answer to the statement that my success has, in any way, depended upon the mounting of plays. When I played 'Hamlet,' under my own management, which commenced in December, 1878, I produced it with great care; and many things, in the way of costume and decoration, which had been before neglected, I endeavoured to amend. But take, for instance, 'The Merchant of Venice,'—it was put upon the stage in twenty-three days."

"It will be impossible for managers to go back to the bad system of mounting formerly in vogue, will it not?"

"I think so. Indeed, it is impossible for the stage to go back to what it was in any sense. Art must advance with the times, and with the advance of other arts there must necessarily be an advance of art as applied to the stage. In arranging the scenery for 'Romeo and Juliet' I had in view not only the producing of a beautiful picture, but the illustration of the text. Every scene I have done adds to the poetry of the play. It is not done for the sake of effect merely, but to add to the glamour of the love story. That was my intention, and I think that result was attained. I believe everything in a play that heightens and assists the imagination, and in no way hampers or restrains it, is good, and ought to be made use of. I think you should, in every respect, give the best you can. For instance, Edwin Booth and I acted together in 'Othello.' He alone would have drawn a great public; yet I took as much pains with it as any play I ever put upon the stage. I took comparatively as much pains with the ' Two Roses ' and the ' Captain of the Watch ' as with ' Romeo and Juliet.' But there is no other play in Shakespeare that seems to me to so much require a pictorial setting as ' Romeo and Juliet.' You could not present plays nowadays as they formerly did, any more than you could treat them generally as they were treated."

" How did you come to identify yourself so much with the revival of Shakespearian acting ? "

" I will try to tell you briefly what I have done since I have been before the London public.   Much against the wish of my friends, I took an engagement at the Lyceum, then under the management of Mr. Bateman. I had successfully acted in many plays besides the 'Two Roses,' which ran three hundred nights.   It was thought by everybody interested in such matters that I ought to identify myself with what they called ' character parts ; ' though what that phrase means, by the way, I never could exactly understand, for I have a prejudice in the belief that every part should be a character.   I always wanted to play in the higher drama.   Even in my boyhood my desire had been in that direction.   When at the Vaudeville Theatre I recited the drama of ' Eugene Aram,' simply to get an idea as to whether I could impress an audience with a tragic theme.   I hoped I could, and at once made up my mind to prepare myself to play characters of another type.   When Mr. Bateman engaged me, he told me he would give me an opportunity, if he could, to play various parts, as it was to his interest as much as to mine to discover what he thought would be successful—though, of course, never dreaming of ' Hamlet ' or ' Richard III.'   Well, the Lyceum opened, but did not succeed. Mr. Bateman had lost a lot of money, and he intended giving it up. He proposed to me to go to America with him.   By my advice, and against his wish, ' The Bells ' was rehearsed, but he did not believe in it much.   He thought there was a prejudice against the management, and that there would probably be a prejudice against that sort of romantic play. It produced a very poor house, although a most enthusiastic one. From that time the theatre prospered. The next piece was a great difficulty. It was thought that whatever part I played it must be a villain, associated with crime in some way or other; because I had been identified with such sort of characters, it was thought my *forte* lay in that direction. I should tell you that I had associated histrionically with all sorts of bad characters, housebreakers, blacklegs, assassins. When ' Charles I.' was announced, it was said that the bad side of the king's character should be the one portrayed, not the good, because it would be ridiculous to expect me to exhibit any pathos, or to give the domestic and loving side of its character. After the first night the audience thought differently. Following ' Charles I.' ' Eugene Aram ' was, by Mr. Bateman's desire, produced. In this we have a character much like that of Mathias, but with a pathetic side to it. Then Mr. Bateman wished me to play ' Richelieu.' I had no desire to do that, but he continued to persuade, and to please him I did it. It ran for a long time with great success. What I did play, by my own desire, and against his belief in its success, was ' Hamlet;' for you must know that at that time there was a motto among managers,— ' Shakespeare spells bankruptcy.' "

" What is your method in preparing to put a play on the stage ?—say one of Shakespeare's,—would you be guided by the tradition of Shakespearian acting ? "

" There is no tradition of Shakespearian acting ; nor is there anything written down as to the proper way of acting Shakespeare. We have the memoirs and the biographies of great actors, and we know something of their methods ; but it does not amount to a tradition or to a school of Shakespearian acting. For instance, what is known on the stage of Shakespeare's tradition of Richard ?　Nothing.　The stage tradition is Colley Cibber.　' Off with his head—so much for Buckingham!' is, perhaps, the most familiar line of his text. We have had some men who have taken this or that great actor as their exemplar; they have copied him as nearly as they could.　Actors, to be true, should, I think, act for themselves."

" You would advise an actor, then, to go to the book and study the play out for himself, and not take this or that character by rote ? "

" Certainly; take the book, and work the play out to the best of your intelligence.　I believe my great safeguard has been that I have always tried to work out a character myself.　As a boy I never would see a play until I had studied it first."

" That would be an answer to the strictures which have been made on you, that you have not kept to the old acting versions, but have made versions for yourself? "

" True; and why should I not, if I keep, as I do, to Shakespeare ?　For many actors Shakespeare was not good enough.　A picture which hangs in my rooms affords an instance in point.　It represents Mr. Holman and Miss Brunton in the characters of Romeo and Juliet, and gives a quotation from the last scene of Act V.　Juliet says,—' You fright me.　Speak; oh, let me hear some voice beside my own in this drear vault of death; or I shall faint.　Support me.'　Romeo replies,—' Oh !　I cannot.　I have no strength, but want thy feeble aid.　Cruel poison ! '　Not one word of which, as you know, is Shakespeare's."

" You referred just now to the necessity of an actor acting ' from himself;' in other words, not sinking his own individuality in the part he is trying to represent,—would it not be an answer to those who charge you with mannerisms on the stage?　Is it not true, in short, that the more strongly individual a man is, the more pronounced his so-called mannerisms will be ? "

" Have we not all mannerisms ? I never yet saw a human being worth considering without them."

" I believe you object to spectators being present at your rehearsals. What are your reasons for that course ? "

" There are several, each of which would be a valid objection."

" For instance ? "

" Well, first of all, it is not fair to author, manager, or actor, as the impression given at an incomplete performance cannot be a correct one."

" But surely by a trained intellect due allowance can be made for shortcomings ? "

" For shortcomings, yes ; but a trained intellect cannot see the full value of an effort, perhaps jarred or spoiled through some mechanical defect ; or if the trained intellect knows all about it, why needs it to be present at all ? Now, it seems to me that one must have a reason for being present, either business or curiosity ; and business cannot be properly done, while curiosity can wait."

" Another reason ? "

" It is unjust to the artists. A play to be complete must, in all its details, finally pass through one imagination. There must be some one intellect to organize and control ; and in order that this may be effected, it is necessary to experimentalize. Many a thing may be shown at rehearsal which is omitted in representation. If this be seen, and not explained, a false impression is created. A loyal company and staff help much to realize in detail and effect the purpose of the manager ; but still, all are but individual men and women, and no one likes to be corrected or advised before strangers."

" As to the alleged dearth of good modern English plays, what do you think is the cause of their non-production ? "

" I deny the dearth, except so far as there is always a dearth of the good things of the world. I hold that

there are good English plays. I could name you
many."

" What are your opinions of the stage as an educational medium ? I ask the question, because there is a
large class of people, both intelligent and cultured,
who still look upon the stage and stage plays, even if
not downright immoral, as not conducive to any
intellectual or moral good."

" My dear sir, I must refer you to history for an
answer to that problem. It cannot be solved on the
narrow basis of one craft or calling. Such ideas are
due to ignorance. Why, in England, three hundred
years ago,—in Shakespeare's time,—in the years when
he, more than any other human being in all that great
age of venture and development, of search and research,
was doing much to make the era famous, actors were
but servants, and the stage was only tolerated by court
licence. A century later, in London city, actors were
pilloried and the calling deemed vagrancy ; while in
France a Christian burial was denied to Molière's
corpse. The study of social history and development
teaches a lesson in which you may read your answer.
When bigotry and superstition fade and toleration
triumphs, then the work of which the stage is capable
will be fairly judged, and there will be no bar to
encounter. The lesson of toleration is not for the
player alone ; the preacher must learn it."

III.

THE first week in New York was, in a great measure,
spent between the theatre and the hotel. Invitations
to dinner and receptions were, as a rule, declined.
The exceptions were breakfasts given by Mr. Vanderbilt
and Judge Shea. Many distinguished persons called.
All kinds of polite attentions were offered, some of
which, it is to be feared, Irving had not time or
opportunity to acknowledge as he could have wished.
One gentleman placed his carriage at Mr. Irving's
disposal ; another offered to lend him his house ; another

his steam launch. These courtesies were tendered gracefully and without ostentation. Flowers were sent regularly from unknown hands to the Hotel Dam. Miss Terry went driving with friends in the park, and found the trotting-track a fascinating scene. Within forty-eight hours Irving was a familiar figure in the lower part of Fifth Avenue and Union Square, as he walked to and from the theatre. He and Miss Terry made their first acquaintance at Delmonico's in company with myself and wife. An elegant little dinner, of which the ice creams were its most successful feature. Artistic in construction, they were triumphs of delicate colour. I think they were the *chef's* tributes to Miss Terry's supposed æsthetic taste. No wonder the Delmonicos made millions of dollars, when it is possible that the chief reminiscence of a dinner may be associated with the ice creams and sweets. On Tuesday, after a rehearsal and a drive down town on a pouring wet day, I piloted the new-comer to Sieghortner's, in Lafayette Place. This well-known *café* occupies the house in which the Astors lived. It is a building characteristic of the early days of New York's first millionaires,—marble steps, heavy mahogany doors, rich Moorish decorations, spacious hall-ways. Close by is the Astor Library, a valuable institution, and the street itself has quite an Old-World look. It was once the most fashionable quarter of New York; but wealth has moved towards the park, and left Lafayette Place to restaurants, boarding-houses, public-baths, and stores. Sieghortner himself is a typical Dutchman, a veritable Knickerbocker of hotel-keepers, and a *gourmet*. He is almost the only "landlord" (as we should call him at home) in New York who will condescend to wait upon his guests. It is a pleasure to look upon his beaming face when you order a dinner and leave *menu* and wines to his judgment. As he stands by your chair, directing his attendants, he is radiant with satisfaction if you are pleased, and would no doubt be plunged into despair if you were dissatisfied. Shrewsbury oysters, gumbo soup, cutlets, canvas-back ducks, a *soufflé*, Stilton cheese, an ice, a *liqueur*, a dish of fruit, and a bottle of hock that filled the room with its delicious perfume.

" It was perfection, Mr. Sieghortner," said Irving, as he sipped his coffee, and addressed the old man,—" the canvas-back superb.   You are so interested in the art of dining that you will appreciate a little experience of mine in connection with the great American bird,—I don't mean the eagle, but the duck."

Sieghortner rubbed his hands, and said, " Oh, yes,— why, of course ! "

" An old American friend of mine,—dead now, alas !—when he was in his prime, as they say, frequently had numbers of canvas-back ducks sent to London from New York.   On the first great occasion of this kind he invited thirty guests to eat thirty ducks. He spent a day or two instructing the *chef* of a well-known club how to cook them.   The kitchen was to be well heated, you know, and the ducks carried gently through."

" Oh, yes, that's the way," said Sieghortner, rubbing his hands.

" Well, the night came.   His guests were in full force.   The ducks were served.   They had a whity-brown and flabby appearance.   Bateman cut one and put it aside.   He tried another, and in his rage flung it under the table.   The dinner was an utter failure."

" Dear ! dear ! " exclaimed Sieghortner.

"My friend did not forget it for months.   He was continually saying, ' I wonder how that fool spoiled our ducks; I have tried to find out, but it is a mystery.' Nearly a year afterwards I heard of the *chef's* sudden death.   Meeting my friend, I said, ' Have you heard of poor So-and-so, the *chef* at the club ?—he is dead ! '— ' I am very glad of it ! ' he exclaimed.   ' Do you know, he cooked those ducks over the gas ! ' "

" Dear ! dear ! " exclaimed Sieghortner, a quick

expression of anger on his face, " why, he ought to have been hanged ! "

IV.

It is customary in American theatres for the orchestra to play the audience out as well as in.

" We will dispense with that," said Irving to his conductor, Mr. Ball.

" It is a general habit here," remarked the Star manager.

" Yes, I understand so," Irving replied ; " but it seems to me a difficult .matter to select the music appropriately to the piece. What sort of music do you usually play ? "

" A march."

" Ah, well, you see our plays are so different, that a march which would do one night would be entirely out of place the next. Have you the score of ' The Dead March in Saul ? ' "

" No," was the conductor's reply.

" Well, then, I think we will finish as we do in London,—with the fall of the curtain. If we make a failure on Monday night, the most appropriate thing you could play would be ' The Dead March.' As you have no score of it, we will do without the exit music."

" And who knows," said Irving, as we walked back to the hotel, " whether we shall have a success or not ? The wild manner in which the speculators in tickets are going on is enough to ruin anything.' They have

---

² Speculation in theatre tickets seems now to have reached its height. Folks thought it had come to a lively pass when Sarah Bernhardt was here, and some $23,000 worth of seats were disposed of for her engagement on the opening day of the sale. But, bless you, that was a mere drop in the bucket. A man named McBride, who has from keeping a small news-stand gradually come forward until he is now one of the richest of the ticket speculators, "got left," as he picturesquely observed, on the Bernhardt affair. In other words, rival speculators got all the best seats. So McBride put twelve men on duty in front

bought up every good seat in the house, I am told, and will only part with them at almost prohibitive prices. The play-goers may resent their operations and keep away; if they pay ten and twenty dollars for a seat, instead of two and a half or three, they cannot be expected to come to the house in a con-

of the Star Theatre box-office three days before the Irving sales were to open, and there they stayed on duty day and night until the window was finally thrown open. Each one of these men got ten season tickets for the Irving engagement, which is to last four weeks. In other words, every one of these men bought 280 tickets of admission to the Star Theatre, so that McBride now holds for the Irving season a neat little pile of 3360 tickets. They were bought at season ticket prices of $60 per set of twenty-eight, and therefore cost the speculator the sum of $7200. Now you will see how the speculator happens to have the bulge on the Irving management. The box-office price of a ticket for a single performance is $3, and even if the demand should not happen to be as immense as to warrant a long advance on the box-office tariff, McBride can sell his tickets at the regular price of $3 apiece, and get the sum of $10,080 for them, which will leave him a profit of nearly $3000 upon his short investment. There is, however, little or no likelihood that he will be obliged to resort to this manner of doing business. For the first night he has already sold seats for $10 and $15 each, and it is quite reasonable to suppose that as the time approaches, and tickets become scarce, he can advance to a still higher price. These ticket speculators have regular customers, who willingly pay them the ordinary price they ask rather than bother about going to the box-office. When Anna Dickinson wants to visit a theatre in New York, she invariably buys her tickets of Tyson, who charges her $2 for a $1.50 seat. So it is with a good many other people, particularly the rich and reckless down-town brokers, who purchase their tickets during the day, and who, rather than take the trouble to send a messenger away up to the theatre they intend to visit, go to the speculator's branch office and pay the advance demanded for whatever they want. There are only a few regular ticket speculators in New York. Old Fred Rullman, a Dutchman, was for a long time the chief operator in theatre tickets, but he seldom appears nowadays in any of the big deals. He works mostly in opera tickets, and is contented not to take heavy risks. McBride is the longest chance-taker of the lot. Tyson is not a risky buyer, but confines his purchases pretty closely to the demands of his regular customers.—*New York Correspondent of St. Louis Spectator.*

tented frame of mind. The more money they have
been plundered of, the more exacting they will be in
regard to the actors; it is only natural they should.
Then we have no pit proper, and the lowest admission
price to the gallery is a dollar. I would have preferred to play to Lyceum prices; but in that case they
say I should only have been putting so much more
into the pockets of the speculators. These operators
in tickets are protected by the law; managers are
obliged to sell to them, and the dealers have a right to
hawk them on the pavement at the entrance of the
theatres."

"This is a State or city law, only applying to New
York. I don't think it exists anywhere else in the
Union. It certainly does not at Philadelphia and
Boston."

"It is an outrage on the public," he replied. "Legitimate agencies for the convenience of the public, with
a profit of ten or twenty per cent. to the vendor, is
one thing; but exacting from the public five and ten
dollars for a two and a half dollar seat is another.
After all, a community, however rich, have only a
certain amount of money to spend on amusements.
Therefore the special attractions and the speculators
get the lion's share, and the general or regular amusements of the place have to be content with short
commons."

"If the *Sun* reporter could hear you, he would congratulate himself on having called you 'a business-like
Hamlet.'"

IV.

AT THE LOTOS CLUB.

The Savage Club of America—Thackeray and Lord Houghton
—A great Banquet—Mr. Whitelaw Reid on Irving and
the Actor's Calling—" Welcome to a country where he
may find not unworthy brethren "—An Answer to the
Warnings of the English Traveller of Chapter I.—" Shakespeare's Charles the First "—A Night of Wit and Humour
—The Knighting of Sullivan—The Delineator of Romance
visiting the Home of America's Creator of Romance—
After-dinner Stories—Conspiring against the Peace of a
harmless Scotchman—A pleasant Jest.

I.

THE Lotos Club is the Savage of America, as the
Century is its Garrick; each, however, with a difference. The Lotos admits to membership gentlemen
who are not necessarily journalists, authors, actors,
and painters, earning their subsistence out of the
arts. They must be clubable and good fellows in the
estimation of the committee, and herein lies their best
qualification. This combination of the arts proper
with trade and finance has made the club a success in
the broadest sense of the term. Their home is a
palace, compared with that of the Savage in London.
The general atmosphere of the Century is more akin
to that of the Garrick, and it is a far closer corporation
than the Lotos. Mr. Thackeray spent a good deal of
his time there when he was in New York; while Lord
Houghton, it is said, preferred the more jovial fireside
of the Lotos. In those days the younger club was in
humbler, but not less comfortable, quarters than those

it now occupies; while the Century, conservative and conscious of its more aristocratic record, is well content with the house which is associated with many years of pleasant memories.

The Lotos honoured Irving with a banquet; the Century welcomed him at one of its famous monthly reunions. The Lotos dinner was the first public recognition, outside the press, of Irving in America. He had accepted its invitation before sailing for New York, and sat down with the Lotos-eaters on the Saturday (October 27) prior to his Monday night's appearance at the Star Theatre. The club-rooms had never been so crowded as on this occasion. Dishes were laid for a hundred and forty members and guests in the dining-room and *salon* of the club, and fifty others consented to eat together in the restaurant and reading-room upstairs, and fifty or sixty others had to be content to come in after dinner. Mr. Irving sat on the right hand of the President of the club, Mr. Whitelaw Reid, editor of the *Tribune.* At the same table were Chauncey M. Depew, Dr. A. E. Macdonald, General Horace Porter, E. Randolph Robinson, Algernon S. Sullivan, R. B. Roosevelt, Thomas W. Knox, H. H. Gorringe, W. H. Smith, Rev. Robert Laird Collier, and F. R. Lawrence. Among others present were Lawrence Barrett, Joseph Jefferson, William J. Florence, R. W. Gilder, Dr. Fordyce Barker, D. G. Croly, General Winslow, and A. Oakey Hall. In a window alcove behind the President's chair stood an easel, holding a large portrait of Irving as Shylock.

Coffee being served, Mr. Irving was conducted upstairs to be introduced to the diners in his honour who were crowded out of the lower rooms. They received him with a loud cheer, and then accompanied him to join the other guests. The company broke up into groups, stood about the door-ways, and thronged around the President, who thereupon arose and addressed them as follows :—

" You must excuse the difficulty in procuring seats. You know the venerable story which Oscar Wilde appropriated about the sign over the piano in a far-western concert-hall: ' Don't shoot the performer ; he's doing the best he can.' (Laughter.) The committee beg me to repeat in their behalf that touching old appeal. They've done the best they could. There are five hundred members of this club, and only one hundred and forty seats in this dining-room ; they have done their utmost to put the five hundred men into the one hundred and forty seats. Don't shoot. They'll come down, apologize, retreat, resign—do anything to please you. They've thoroughly tried this thing of putting two men in one seat and per-suading the other three that standing-room is just as good ; and to-night, as the perspiration rolls from their troubled brows, their fervent hope and prayer is that the manager for your distinguished guest may be haunted by that self-same trouble all through his American tour ! (Applause and laughter.)

" London appropriated our national anniversary, to do honour to its favourite actor as he was about to visit us. On that occasion, on the Fourth of July last, at a banquet without a parallel in the history of the British stage, and to which there are actually none to be compared, save the far less significant, but still famous, entertainments to Kean and Macready,—at that banquet your guest said, ' This God-speed would alone insure me a hearty welcome in any land. But I am not going among strangers. I am going among friends.' (Applause.)

" Let us take him at his word. Once we were apt to get our opinions from the other side. If that grows less and less a habit now, with the spread among us, since we attained our national majority, of a way of doing our own thinking, we are still all the more glad to welcome friendships from the other side.

" We know our friendly guest as the man whom a great, kindred nation has agreed to accept as its foremost living dramatic representative. We know that his success has tended to elevate and purify the stage, to dignify the actor's calling, to widen and better its influence. We know the scholarship he has brought to the representation of the great dramatists, the minute and comprehensive attention he has given to every detail, alike of his own acting and of the general management. His countrymen do not say that if he were not the foremost actor in England he would be the first manager; they declare that he is already both. (Applause.)

" We bid him the heartiest of welcomes to a country where he may find not unworthy brethren. Our greeting indeed takes a tone of special cordiality not so much from what we know of his foreign repute, or from our remembering the great assemblage of representative countrymen gathered to give him their farewell and God-speed. It comes even more from our knowing him as the friend of Edwin Booth (applause), and Joseph Jefferson (applause), and Lawrence Barrett (applause), and John McCullough (applause), and William Florence (applause). And if anything else were needed to make the grasp of every man's hand in this club yet warmer, it is furnished when we remember that his conspicuous friend among English actors is our friend, John Toole. (Applause.)

" It would not be fair to our distinguished but unsuspicious guest, adventuring into these foreign parts, if, before sitting down, I did not warn him that all this, and much more which he is likely to hear, is said around the dinner-table. Let him not think that he wholly knows us, and is fairly naturalized, until he has read the papers the morning after his first performance. What they may contain no living man knoweth (laughter); but others have sometimes groaned that we treat our guests with too much attention; that we accord them, in fact, the same distinguished honour we give our national bird—the turkey,—which we first feed and afterwards carve up. (Great laughter.) ·

"But the prologue is an antiquated device, now pretty well banished from the stage, because it merely detains you from what you came to hear. I will detain you no longer. I give you, gentlemen, Our Guest,—

'O trumpet set for Shakespeare's lips to blow.'

"Health to Henry Irving, and a hearty welcome!" (Great applause.)

II.

THE toast was drunk with ringing cheers, and in its report of the reply the *Tribune* says, "Mr. Irving spoke in measured tones, and with a singularly clear and effective enunciation, his frequent ironical sallies being received with bursts of laughter and applause." He said :—

"Mr. Chairman and Gentlemen,—It is not in my power to thank you, with eloquence, for the reception that you have given me to-night. In spite of the comforting words and suggestions of our friend, the chairman, that on Tuesday morning my feelings may undergo a change, I am quite determined that to-night and to-morrow night, if all be well, I shall have a good night's rest. I *do* feel naturalized; and, whatever may be said to the contrary, I shall always bear away with me the impression that I am among my own flesh and blood. (Applause.) The simile of the turkey did not affect me very much; for if the ill-omened bird (I do not know whether he is as familiar in your country as he is in mine), the *goose,* is not served up, I shall be very content. (Applause.)

"You have received me, not as a stranger, but as a welcome friend (applause), and that welcome I appreciate with all my heart and soul. In coming here amongst you I really had—I may as well confess it— but one terror. The Atlantic I would brave; the wind and weather I would scorn; even sea-sickness I would enjoy; but there was one terror,—the interviewer. (Laughter.) But I am very glad to tell you that that is passed; and I have said so much to the interviewer that I have very little left to say to you. I must, however, also tell you that I find the interviewer a very much misrepresented person. He seemed to me to be a most courteous gentleman, who had but an amiable curiosity to know a little about myself that he did not know before; and I was very well satisfied to gratify him as much as I could. I was told that he would turn me inside out; that he would cross-examine me, and then appear against me the following morning. (Laughter.) But I found nothing of the sort; and if I had any complaint to make against him, the comments with which he tempered his suggestions were so flattering and so gratifying to myself that I forgave him the suggestions that he made. The only thing that I would quarrel with him for was for saying that I reminded him of Oscar Wilde. (Laughter.) Oscar Wilde is a very clever fellow, and I am not going to descant upon him. You know more about him than I do; and I hope that when Oscar Wilde reads what I have said—as I suppose he will—he will take no offence. I am extremely indebted to the interviewer, also, for telling me that I was classed with Edwin Booth. With that I have no fault to find.

" To the courtesy and kindness of American gentlemen I have long been accustomed; for if you have not in London, as you have in Paris, an American quarter, it is really because Americans are found everywhere in London; and I think that everywhere in London they are welcome. (Applause.) Our interests are mutual; and in our art we are getting day by day more closely allied. London is now talking with raptures of your Mary Anderson (applause); of your great tragedian, Booth (applause); of your great comedian, Jefferson (applause)—I dislike the words 'tragedian' and 'comedian;' actor is so much better, and it is a household word. McCullough and Clarke, and my friends Florence and Raymond, have had amongst us the

heartiest of welcomes. And I am quite sure that your
famous actress, Clara Morris, need only come amongst
us—as my friend, Lawrence Barrett, is coming—to
have another welcome.

" Mr. Whitelaw Reid has spoken of my work in my
art in the kindest and most appreciative way. If I
have done anything to gain that commendation, it is
because I have striven to do my duty; and but for the
appreciation of many of my countrymen, who have
thought so, and· but for the appreciation that I receive
now at this table, I am quite sure that my work would
have been in vain.

" I do not intend to bore you with any ideas of mine
about my art, either histrionically or pictorially. My
method, histrionically, is a very simple one. I merely
endeavour to go to the fountain-head to get my inspiration; and by what my work is I know that you will
judge it, and judge it fairly. I am quite sure of this :
that no people will go to a theatre with a greater desire
to do justice to an actor than you will go to the theatre
to see me on Monday night. (Applause.) If you like
me, you will express it; and, if you do not like me,
still you will treat me kindly.

" Our art is cosmopolitan. Every actor has his own
methods, as every painter has his methods, and every
writer has his style. The best actor amongst us has a
great deal to learn. It is only at the end of his career
that he finds how short is his life, and how long is
his art. Concerning the mounting of plays, I give
to a play of Shakespeare the same advantage that I
would give to any modern author ; and, until a greater
man than Shakespeare arrives, I think I shall continue
to do so. (Applause.)

" In my own dear land I am glad to tell you that
the love for Shakespearian drama is very greatly increasing. Shakespearian societies throughout our land
have done much to encourage that. You know very
well that there was a time when Shakespeare was said
by a London manager to spell ' bankruptcy,' and Lord

Byron 'ruin.' I remember that at one of the revivals of Shakespearian plays at the Lyceum, a gentleman leaving the theatre was heard to express the opinion that the play was not a bad one; that he thought it might have a tolerable run, but that it would be very much improved if it had not contained so many quotations. (Laughter.) The play was 'Macbeth.' (Laughter.) I have been told that that gentleman is sometimes to be found in the British Museum, in the old reading-room devoted to Shakespearian manuscripts, and that he is very frequently found turning them over; but with what success I do not know. I also remember that once, when a play was produced, a friend of mine asked me what the subject of it was. I said to him that the subject was Charles I., at which he hemmed and hawed and said, 'Very good; *very* good; oh, capital! Charles I. Yes, I should think that would do very well. Let me see. Charles I. Do you mean Shakespeare's Charles I.?' (Laughter.) However, these things are improving, and even the old play-goer,—I do not know whether such a character exists amongst you,—who is amongst us a very dreadful creature; even he is beginning to tolerate the student who goes to the book, instead of to traditional characters, for his inspiration.

"We are very hypocritical, however, some of us, in England. We go to the Crystal Palace to see the play of 'Hamlet,' and go to the Crystal Palace because it is not a theatre; and when we would not go to a theatre to see the play of 'Hamlet,' we will go to the Crystal Palace, or some other such place, to see the 'Pink Dominoes.' (Laughter.) We will crowd sometimes to the French theatre, without understanding the nationality, the gesture of the actors, or a word of their language, when we will desert our own theatres where these pieces are being played. But fortunately no such difference as that can exist between us; and I cherish the hope that it will be my good fortune, and more especially the good fortune of my fellow-workers, and especially of my gifted companion and friend, Ellen Terry (Great applause),—I say that I cherish the hope that we shall be able to win your favour. (Applause.) I dare say that you will find many of us very strange and very odd, with peculiarities of speech, and with peculiarities of manner and of gesture; but it would, perhaps, not be so pleasurable if we were all just alike. (Laughter.) It is not our fault, you know, if we are Englishmen.

" Gentlemen, I thank you with all my heart for the greeting you have given me. I thank you for the brotherly hand that you have extended to me. And if anything could make one feel at home, and comfortable, and sure of having a real good time amongst you, it is the cordiality with which I have been received to-night. The very accents of your hearty greeting, and the very kindness of your genial faces, tell me that there are in your hearts good and kind overflowing wishes. Gentlemen, I thank you with all my heart; and I feel that there is a bond between us which dates before to-night."

The speaker sat down amidst great applause. His manner and matter had evidently given great satisfaction. How he had been misrepresented as to his mannerisms is unconsciously admitted by the note of the *Tribune* reporter, that he spoke clearly. He did; and in that quiet, self-possessed, conversational style which was remarked as so effective at the London banquet.

III.

It was late before the Lotos eaters parted, although London clubmen take more out of the night than is the habit with New-Yorkers. The raciness of the evening's speeches was repeated in the stories that were told by the genial few, who sat and talked and smoked with their guest, until Fifth Avenue was as quiet and deserted as it was when a crowd of admiring friends went out to meet the *Britannic* a week previously.

Apropos of an amusing anecdote, with a practical joke in it, which was related, I think, by Colonel Knox, the courteous honorary secretary of the club, Irving said, "I am not much of a hand at that kind of fun, but I remember an incident in which my old friend Toole, a Glasgow doctor, and myself were engaged, that may amuse you. Some years ago we found ourselves with a holiday forced upon us by the Church of Scotland. We utilized it by going out a short distance into the country and dining together at a famous roadside inn. The house was quite empty of guests, and we claimed the privilege of travellers, on our way to the next town, to sit over our dinner a trifle later than it was the custom to keep the bar open. The landlord was very civil, and we had an excellent dinner. The waiter who attended to our wants was a quaint old fellow—one of those rugged sort of serving-men with whom Sir Walter Scott has made us all so well acquainted. While he was respectful, he was, nevertheless, very talkative. He told us there had been of late many robberies in the neighbourhood. The constabulary, he said, were quite out of their reckoning in regard to tracing the thieves. He wondered if the country was going back again to the coaching days when cracksmen and highwaymen had it all their own way in those parts. The old fellow was a little superstitious too, and a lover of the marvellous, as many of the country people who live outside great cities are apt to be.

"'You seem a trifle hipped,' I said; 'take a glass of wine.'

"'I am just a wee bit low,' he said; 'what wi' the bad weather, the dull times—'

"'And the robberies you've lately had about here,' I suggested.

"'Ah, weel, they're nae calculated to raise one's sperrits. Good health to you, gentlemen!'

"We thanked him, and I filled his glass again.

"'This house,' said Toole, 'is rather a lonely place; you don't have many guests staying here?'

"'Not at this time o' the year,' he replied; 'only just chance customers.'

"I filled his glass again before he went for the cheese. When he came back I took up a fork, and expressed some surprise that the master should, in these thieving days, entrust his guests with real silver plate.

"'I dinna bring it oot for everybody,' he replied; 'but for a pairty o' gentlemen like yoursels, it's a defferent thing.'

"'Is the salver there,' asked Toole, taking up the running and pointing to the sideboard, 'real silver?'

"'Indeed it is, and all the plate aboot is silver, and I ken they dinna mak' sich silver nowadays.'

"'Bring us a little whisky!— a pint in a decanter; a drop of the best,' I said.

"Having planted the right kind of seed in his mind for the working of a little jest I had in my own, my companions and myself entered into a conspiracy against the peace of this harmless Scotchman. Invited to take a nip of whisky, he readily complied, and just as readily took a seat. We drew him out about all the robberies and murders he could remember, and then deftly got from him the statement that his master had gone to bed, leaving up only himself, the bar-maid, and his wife. Presently the doctor looked at his watch, and said it would soon be time for us to go. 'I think you had better get our bill, Sandy,' I said, for by this time I was quite on familiar terms with him, and he with me. 'You need not be in a hurry; let us have it in about a quarter of an hour,' added Toole, somewhat mysteriously. 'We are not quite ready to go yet.'

"'Vary weel, and thank ye,' he said, at the same time making us a bow which was quite a study of manner, combining independence and servility. He was a fine old fellow, straight as a poplar, but with a face full of wrinkles, and a characteristic gait that some people would call a mannerism.

" The moment he left the room each of us seized a piece of plate until we had cleared up every bit of silver in the room. We noted the exact places from which we took every piece ; then we opened the window. It was a very dark night, but we had noticed that close by the window there were some thick shrubs. We put out the gas, but left alight two candles on the table, so that we could see from our hiding-place what Sandy's face would look like when it should dawn upon him that we were a pack of thieves—perhaps part of the gang of swell-mobsmen who had become the terror of the district.

" I shall never forget the bewildered expression of the poor fellow's face as he stared at the empty room. Amazement gave place to fear, and fear to indignation, when he discovered that the silver had been carried off.

" ' Great heevens ! ' he exclaimed. ' Thieves ! berglers ! robbers ! An' if the rogues hae nae carried off the plate and gan awa' wi'out payin' their score into the bargain, my name is nae Sandy Blake ! '

" He rushed to the open window and peered wildly out into the darkness.

" ' The scoundrels were just fooling me, like any softy.'

" Then he began to shout ' Thieves ! ' and ' Murder ! ' and ran off, as we hoped and expected he would, to alarm the house. We all crept back to the room, closed the window, drew down the blind, relighted the gas and our cigars, put each piece of silver back into its proper place, and sat down to wait for our bill. We could hear Sandy, at the top of his voice, telling the story of the robbery ; and in a few minutes we heard evidently the entire household coming pell-mell to the dining-room. Then our door was flung open ; but the crowd, instead of rushing in upon us, suddenly paused *en masse*, and Sandy exclaimed, ' Great God ! Weel, weel ! Hae I just gane clean daft ? '

" ' Come awa', drunken foo', come awa' !' exclaimed

the landlord, pulling Sandy and the rest back into the passage and shutting the door; but we could hear how both master and wife abused poor Sandy, who did nothing but call upon his Maker and declare, if he had to die that minute, when he went into the room it was empty of both guests and silver. He was told to go to bed and sleep off his drunk, and thank his stars that his long service saved him from instant dismissal.

" We rang the bell. The landlord himself answered it. We asked for an explanation of the hubbub. It was nothing, he said, only that his man had got drunk and made a fool of himself. Was that all? we asked. Well, yes, except that he was very sorry to have so disturbed us. To have all the house burst in upon us, we said, was such a strange proceeding, that we begged he would explain it. He said he did not like to do so. It was the first time Sandy had ever been known to get so drunk as to lose his senses, and all he could do was to express his regret that his servant had made a fool of himself; but he would not insult his guests by telling them how great an ass the fellow was. We coaxed him, however, to explain the entire business; and at last, with many apologies, he told us how the drunken fool had mistaken us for a pack of thieves, and swore we had run off without paying our bill and taken the plate with us. We humoured the landlord for a time, and when he was at last in a genial temper we told him the true story, and he enjoyed the joke as well as any of us. Then we had him send for Sandy, who was so glad to discover that he had not lost his wits that a couple of sovereigns left him, at our departure, just as happy and contented a man as he was before making the acquaintance of 'a parcel of actors,' who are still regarded in some remote corners of Great Britain as the 'rogues and vagabonds' they are proclaimed in our ancient statute books."

V.

THE NIGHT BEFORE THE PLAY.

The Vividness of first Impressions—New York Hotels—On the
Elevated Road with "Charlie" — Trotting-horses —
Audiences on both sides of the Atlantic—"A man knows
best what he can do"—"Americanisms," so called—A
satirical Sketch, entitled "Bitten by a Dog"—Louis
and the Duke of Stratford-on-Avon—Macready and the
Forrest Riots.

I.

" A JOURNALIST from Chicago is anxious to know your
opinion of New York, and to have some suggestions
about the state of your feelings concerning your first
appearance in America," I said; "and if you will talk
to him, I have undertaken to collaborate with him in
writing the interview, so that I may revise and adopt
it for our book of impressions."

" Is he here ? "

" Yes, he has come over a thousand miles to see you,
and his chief is an old friend of mine, the proprietor of
the *Daily News.*"

" I am quite willing," he said, "if you think my impressions are of sufficient importance to record, after
only a week of New York."

" First impressions of a new country are always the
most vivid. I believe in first impressions, at all
events, in your case. · It is another matter when one
comes to treat them as a basis for philosophical argument. Your friend, Mr. Matthew Arnold, was not
backward in discussing the American people, their

cities, their institutions, their manners and customs, before he had crossed the Atlantic at all."

" Well, let us talk to Chicago then, if you wish it."

" So far, are you satisfied with your reception in this country ? "

" More than satisfied; I am delighted, I might say amazed. It is not only the press and the public who have shown me so much attention, but I have received many courtesies privately, — some from American friends whom I have met in London, some from gentlemen whom I have never seen."

" What is your general impression of New York, its theatres, hotels, streets, and its social life ? "

" I think Wallack's, or the Star, as it is called, one of the most admirable theatres I have ever seen, so far as the auditorium is concerned, and, in some respects, as to the stage. The appointments behind the footlights are rather primitive; but, as a whole, it is a fine house."

" Is it as good as your own in London ? "

"'Better, in many respects. As for the hotels, they are on a far larger scale, and seem more complete in their arrangements than ours. The Brevoort is, I am told, more like an English house than any other in the city. The genial proprietor evidently desires to make his guests think so. Portraits of Queen Victoria, the late Prince Consort, and pictorial reminiscences of the old country meet you at every turn. As for social life in New York, what I have seen of it is very much like social life in London—a little different in its forms and ceremonies, or, I might say, in the absence of ceremony—and with this exception, that there does not appear to be what you would call an idle class here, —a class of gentlemen who have little else to do but to be amused and have what you call ' a good time.' Everybody seems to be engaged in business of some kind or another."

" Is this your first visit to America ? "

" Yes ; though I seem to have known it for a long
time. American friends in London have for years been
telling me interesting things about your country. I
had heard of the elevated road, Brooklyn Bridge,
and the splendid harbour of New York. But they
are all quite different to what I had imagined
them. The elevated railway is a marvellous piece of
work. I rode down-town upon the Sixth Avenue
line yesterday. They compelled me to carry my
dog Charlie ; and I notice, by the way, a remarkable absence of dogs in the streets. You see them
everywhere, you know, in London. Charlie, an old
friend of mine, attracted great attention on the
cars."

" More than you did ? "

" Oh, yes; much more. He's a well-bred little
fellow, and one gentleman, who took a great interest
in him, tried to open negotiations to buy him from me.
Poor Charlie !—he is getting old and blind, though he
looks sprightly enough. He has travelled with me in
Europe and Africa, and now in America—some day we
hope to see Asia together."

" Does he go with you to the theatre ? "

" Always ; and he knows the pieces I play. I suppose he knows them by the colour of the clothes I
wear. During some plays he sniffs about all night
—during the long ones he settles quietly down. When
' Hamlet' is played he is particularly sedate. He
hates the ' Lyons Mail,' because there is shooting in it.
When the murder-scene comes he hides away in the
furthermost corner he can find."

" You are fond of animals ? "

" Yes, very ; and the most characteristic thing I
believe I have yet seen in America is your trotting-
horse. I have been twice upon the track beyond the
park ; it is a wonderful sight."

" Have you no trotting-horses in England ? "

" Nothing like yours, and no light vehicles such as
yours. I could only think of the old chariot races as I

G

watched the teams of magnificent trotters that rushed by me like the wind. I hear you have a fine race-course at Chicago. Our friend Hatton told me long ago about seeing the famous Maud S. make her great time there."

"Oh, yes. I remember how astonished he was. Maud S. and our fire-engine service captured his fancy. He described the racing in ' To-day in America.' You are coming to Chicago ? "

"Yes. I am informed that I shall strike quite a different civilization in your city to that of New York, that public life with you is even more ardent than it is in the Empire city, and that the spirit of your commerce is more energetic. I can hardly understand that; but I long to see your wonderful new streets and your city boundaries that daily push their way into the prairie. John McCullough, I remember, once gave me a startling description of Chicago."

" I see that Mr. Sala, in the *Illustrated London News,* warns you to expect our press to attack you. Is Mr. Sala a friend of yours ? "

" Yes; and a dear friend, and a very remarkable man. But we are wandering a little from the subject you came to talk about."

•   " Not much. May I ask if you have any nervous-ness as to your first appearance ? "

" Yes, the natural nervousness that is part of an actor's first appearances everywhere. I cannot think that the taste for the drama is any different in New York and Chicago from Dublin, Edinburgh, Glasgow, Liverpool, Birmingham, or London, in my own country."

" Very much is expected of you. It would be hardly possible for you to realize the exaggerated ideas of some people. If you were a god you could not satisfy their expectations."

" Nor, if I were a demon, could I achieve the attitudes and poses of my caricaturists. Between the two there is hope."

" You feel that it is a great ordeal anyway ? "

" Yes."

" Some of your methods are new, more particularly as to Shakespearian productions ? "

" I believe so. In my early days I had little opportunity to see other actors play Shakespeare, except on the stage where I acted with them, and then I was so occupied with my own work that I had little time to observe theirs. I had consequently to think for myself. It does not follow, of course, that I have always done the right thing, but my principle has been to go straight to the author. I have not taken up the methods of other actors, nor modelled my work on this or that tradition. A man knows best what he can do, and it seems to me just as absurd for one actor to imitate another—to recite this speech, or impersonate that action, as he has seen some other actor recite or impersonate—as it would be for a writer to print a historical incident just as some other had done, or for a modern novelist to write his stories on the lines of Fielding, Richardson, or Thackeray, without giving play to his own talents, or reins to his own imagination and conception of character."

" I will not weary you by going over the old ground concerning your alleged mannerisms ; but I see that a New York paper has already taken you to task for jesting about the Pilgrim fathers. Did you notice that ? "

" Oh, yes ; you mean as to the Pilgrim mothers. I had no intention to jest about Plymouth rock. I only repeated a story told me by an American friend, the point of which was that the austerity of the Pilgrim fathers must have made them trying persons for the Pilgrim mothers. A very harmless bit of fun. One of my interviewers makes me speak of ' Americanisms ' too. The word should have been ' mannerisms.' In regard to the so-called Americanisms of American actors, all I have heard in that way have fallen from the lips of Raymond and Florence, just as you would

G 2

hear Cockneyisms from our humorous comedians,
Toole and Brough. The accent of your great actors
does not strike me as different to our own; though a
reporter on board the *Britannic*, last Sunday, told me
he had understood I had a very strange accent, and
was surprised to find that I spoke English as well as
he did."

II.

THE night before Irving's first appearance at the Star
Theatre was spent at a quiet little supper given to a
few private friends, at the Manhattan Club. The
conversation turned chiefly upon English actors.

"I was once at a dinner of a Theatrical Fund, over
which a famous old actor presided," said Irving.
"His proposal of the first toast of the evening was a
pathetic incident. His mind was wandering back to
his early days. After alluding to the loyalty of all
classes of Englishmen, and of actors in particular, he
raised his glass and said, 'Gentlemen, I beg to give
you the health of his Majesty King George the
Third!'"

Somebody suggested that the ocean trip had done
Irving a great deal of good.

"It was the most perfect rest I ever remember to
have had," he said; "nothing to do, nothing to think
of, no letters to answer—none to receive, for that
matter; nothing to do but to rest. I took plenty of
exercise, also, on deck. I must have walked many
miles a day."

Later in the evening, over a last cigar, he said to me,
"But I did a little writing on board the *Britannic*. I
think it will amuse you. Watson asked me to send
him something for the Christmas number of his newspaper,—an anecdote, or sketch of some kind. Shortly
before I left Liverpool there appeared in the journals a
paragraph to the effect that I had been bitten by a dog
at some very aristocratic house. It occurred to me
on the *Britannic* that this would make a good little

story. You were telling me last night about my estate and palace on the Thames, and yet I don't suppose any man leads a quieter life than I do. I call my story ' Bitten by a Dog.' "

He read as follows, and, like most humourists, was tickled with his own fun, laughing now and then with real enjoyment at the suggestiveness of his satirical references to newspaper gossips, who, not knowing him personally, or being in any way acquainted with his habits, undertake to describe his inner life :—

" We regret to hear that Mr. Henry Irving, while on a visit near ——, was severely bitten by a favourite dog, belonging to his host. He bled profusely, but we sincerely hope that he will not seriously suffer from this occurrence.—*Newspaper Paragraph.*

" The circumstance thus recorded was somewhat novel to me, and having received several telegrams and letters of condolence upon my sad misfortune, I thought I would attempt, during my leisure upon the good ship *Britannic,* to tell this little story of ' The Bite of a Dog,' with a veracity equalling that of the inventor of the above-quoted paragraph.

" Seated in one of the suite of rooms which I invariably occupy in the hotels of the United Kingdom during my provincial tours—which have become alike the wonder and amazement of the entire dramatic profession—I was gazing into one of the many mirrors before which it is my regular habit to study grace of pose and poetry of expression. I was surrounded by the secretaries without whom I never travel; some telegraphing to the four corners of the globe the astounding success and enormous profit which accompany all my undertakings; others translating some of those essays on dramatic art which have done so much to regenerate the British drama; others copying in manifold certain not uncomplimentary criticisms of my own composition upon the most subtle and sublime of my impersonations; for, with Garrick, I agree that the actor should ever embrace the opportunity of becoming the critic of his own performances.

" In the midst of this multitudinous work a messenger was announced from the Duke of Stratford-upon-Avon. With a thrill of pleasure I sprang to my feet, and, greeting the messenger with a fascinating smile, begged him to be seated. Then throwing myself with a careless ease upon the velvet-pile sofa which adorned my room (a present from one of my admirers, and which I always carry with me, as I do my many mirrors), I crossed my graceful right over my still more graceful left leg, broke the duke's seal, and perused his letter.

" It was an invitation to sojourn from Saturday to Monday at the duke's feudal home, some fifteen miles from the town I was then appearing in. Throughout my life it has been my practice to solicit the favour and patronage of the great; for it is my firm belief that, to elevate one's art, one should mix as much as possible with the nobility and gentry.

'To grovel to the great is no disgrace,
For nothing humble can be out of place.'

" This social opportunity was not to be lost; hesitation there was none; the invitation was accepted.

" On the night of my visit to his Grace, the theatre was crammed from floor to ceiling with an audience attracted by that cold curiosity which characterizes the public with regard to my performances. The play was ' Louis XI.,' and the difficult feat which I had to accomplish was to catch a train after the performance, in order to present myself at the mansion of my noble host in time to participate in the ducal supper.

" Throughout the play I laboured with all heart and earnestness to cut short the performance by every means in my power. I was determined to sleep under the roof of the Stratford-upon-Avons that night, come what would.

" The curtain fell only five minutes before the time of the train starting; so, throwing on my overcoat of sable furs (a handsome adjunct to my American expedition), and, still attired as King Louis,—for I had no time to change my costume,—I rushed into the brougham, ready at the stage door, and, followed by my valet, drove frantically to the station.

" I was thrust immediately through the open door of the nearest compartment—the door was locked—the whistle shrieked—away sped the train—and, panting and breathless, I was left to my meditations.

" ' Ah ! horror ! most dreadful thought ; too dreadful to relate ! I have left the theatre without my teeth, —my beautiful teeth ! '

" In order to heighten the realism of my impersonation when I first acted Louis, I had several teeth extracted by one of our most eminent dentists, who has offered, as an advertisement, to take out any others in the like liberal manner.[1] In my insane hurry to catch the train I had left my teeth in a glass on my dressing-room table.

" But regrets are useless ; the train has stopped, and I enter the duke's chariot, in waiting at the station, and, through the broad woodlands, soon reach the duke's home.

" I alight from the ancestral coach and enter the ancestral hall, in which a cheerful fire is blazing upon the ancestral hearth.

" Suddenly I find myself in the presence of my host, surrounded by many scions of the nobility of ' England, Home, and Beauty.' The oddness of my position (dressed as I was, and minus my teeth), and the natural inferiority which I always feel when in the presence of

---

[1] This story was reprinted in several American papers. A dentist of some note in a leading city, not appreciating its satire, wrote a long letter to Mr. Irving, offering to make him a new set of teeth, on a patented system of his own, which had given great pleasure to a number of eminent American ladies and gentlemen. He enclosed a list of his clients, and the price of their teeth. As an inducement for Irving to accept his proposals, he quoted " very moderate terms," on condition that " if satisfactory " he should " have the use of his name " in public, thus " acting up to the liberal principles of the English practitioner."

the real aristocrat, robbed me for the moment of my
self-possession, and I unconsciously permitted two of
the gentlemen in powder to divest me of my overcoat,
and there I stood revealed as that wicked monarch
Louis XI.

"Now, this character I have long had an idea of
abandoning, for in art the eye must be pleased ; and,
though it is commendable to follow nature and truth,
yet if this can only be accomplished at the cost of one's
personal appearance, nature and truth should certainly
give way.   But to resume.

" Surprise at my aspect was in every face.   There
was a painful pause, and then a burst of laughter.

"' What is it ? ' whispered one.

"' Who is it ? ' whispered another.

"' Irving,' said a third.

"' Who's Irving ? ' asked a fourth.

"' What ! don't you know ?—the actor—Irving,
the actor—I've seen him at the Gaiety ! '

" I was profoundly relieved by the duke coming to
my rescue and graciously suggesting that I might,
before supper, wish to see my room.   I thanked his
Grace with the dignity with which nature has endowed
me, and strode like Marshal Stalk across the marble
vestibule, when a fierce sanguinary Blenheim spaniel
flew from the lap of a dowager duchess, and, with a
terrific howl, buried its fangs in the calf of my
beautiful left leg.

" Consternation and pallor were in every countenance ;
the dowager ran to seize her pet ; but, to the dismay of
all, the dog's hold would not relax.   They pulled and
pulled again, and ' Fido ' howled at every pull.   His
teeth, unlike mine, would not be extracted.

" There was a pause of painful silence.   Mingled
fear and compassion sat on every brow.   The dowager
was on the point of swooning in the arms of the duke,
when the dignity and distinction which sometimes support me in emergencies came to my aid.   Turning to
the gentle assembly, with a seraphic smile upon my

noble features, I said, as well as my articulation would
permit,—

"'Be not alarmed, fair ladies ; be not alarmed ! The
dog has not torn my leg; he has only torn my padding.'"

III.

"GOOD-NIGHT," I said, "and good luck ! When next
we say good-night, New York will have pronounced
its verdict."

"I don't believe in luck," he answered. "It will be
all right nevertheless. But it seems strange, after all
our talks of America, that to-morrow night I am to act
here in New York. How everything comes to an end !
Next year at this time, all being well, we shall be looking back upon the whole tour, recalling incidents of
New York, Boston, Philadelphia, Chicago, Baltimore,
Washington ; and I dare say it will appear very much
like a dream. It was not far from this hotel where
Macready found refuge from the mob, in a friend's
house. During this week several persons who were
present have mentioned the riots to me, and they all
blame Forrest. I told them Forrest had some reason
to believe that Macready had set Forster against him,
which, no doubt, helped to embitter Forrest's mind.
They say, however, that Forrest's hatred of English
actors amounted to something like a mania. He must
have been a remarkable and great actor in many
parts."

Irving little thought that in the reminiscences of a
past, which had yet to come, would be an incident that
should inseparably link his own name with the Forrest-
Macready riots.

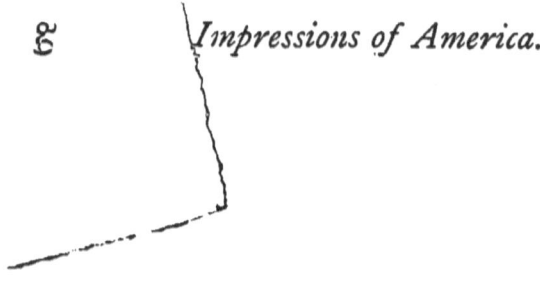

VI.

THE BELLS.

A stormy Night in New York—Ticket Speculators at work—
A first-night Audience—Mathias received with Enthu-
siasm—Behind the Scenes—Lighting the Stage—Return-
ing Thanks—Criticism of the Crowd—John Gilbert's
Opinion—Actor and Audience—English Play-goers and
Londoners — Laughter and Applause — An artistic
Triumph.

I.

Torrents of rain without, and a great fashionable
crowd within the Star Theatre, inaugurated Irving's
first appearance on the American stage.

The electric lights, away up among the wet clouds
that emptied themselves over Union Square, flashed
coldly on untended roadways, which vehicles of all
kinds churned into rivers of mud. The architectural
surroundings of the place, and the well-appointed carriages that dashed along to the Star Theatre and the
opera, were singularly out of keeping with the broken
streets and the everlasting telegraph poles of the
American continent.

It was a night on which London would have hesi-
tated to turn out of its comfortable homes to greet
even the most illustrious stranger; for the rain was
tropical in its density. It splashed on the pavements
in great drops, or, taken hold of by the wind, came
at you in sheets of water. Carriage-horses were protected with "rubber-cloths," and the people who
stepped out of the cars at the top of Broadway, or

were driven to the door of the theatre in the public stages, were enveloped in " water-proofs." Nevertheless, the moment they alighted they were mobbed by a band of ticket speculators, who followed or preceded them into the broad vestibule of the theatre, hawking seats even under the box-office windows. In appearance these energetic dealers were the counterpart of the betting men you may see on any English racecourse,—the same in manner, and almost in voice. They were warmly and well clad, had satchels strapped to their shoulders; but, instead of shouting, " Two to one, bar one!" " I'll bet on the field!" and other similar invitations to do business, they announced, in hoarse tones, " I have seats in the front row!" " Orchestra seats, third row!" " I have the best seats in the orchestra!" These New York speculators held in one hand a thick bundle of notes, and a packet of tickets in the other. They had change ready for any note you might offer them, and their tickets were frequently what they represented them to be, " for the choicest locations."

For some time a notable crowd of persons, distinguished in New York society, pushed their way to seats which they had already secured, many of them at a premium of one hundred per cent. beyond the box-office rates.[1] A large number of persons waited

[1] Among the audience (says the *Tribune*) were Miss Ellen Terry herself, accompanied by an elderly gentleman, with gray hair, who to some was known to be Felix Moscheles, Mendelssohn's godson, with his wife, and a young man of boyish appearance, known to many as the son of Lord Coleridge. In the other boxes were W. H. Vanderbilt, Chauncey M. Depew, Judge Brady, Augustus Schell, Algernon S. Sullivan, John H. Starin and Mrs. Starin, Howard Carroll and Mrs. Carroll, Madame Nilsson, Dr. Doremus and Mrs. Doremus, Mrs. Lester Wallack and Mrs. Arthur Wallack, Mr. and Mrs. William Bond, Mr. and Mrs. John Foord, Mrs. Charles Leland, Henry Rosener and Mrs. Rosener, and Mr. and Mrs. Theodore Moss. Among other well-known faces in the audience were noticed those of ex-Judge Horace Russell, General Horace Porter, Colonel and Mrs. Tobias, of Philadelphia; General Winslow, Dr. Fordyce

in the vestibule until the curtain should go up, in the hope that the speculators would, for a moderate consideration, relax their grip on "choice seats." Many tickets were sold, however, in the street and in the vestibule of the theatre for sums varying from five to ten dollars. Later in the evening, during the first and second acts of the play, the speculators parted with the balance of their property at box-office rates, which they readily obtained.

The entire floor of an American theatre is devoted to stall seats. Ladies and gentlemen who occupied the back seats had to submit to constant arrivals all through the first and second acts. The doors at the Star Theatre open right upon the audience. They were swinging backwards and forwards during the first half-hour of the piece. It is a universal habit in America for audiences not to be seated at the time announced for the curtain to go up. Add to this the obstruction of the ticket speculators and the premium they offer to late comers. Supplement these disturbing elements with a wet night; the natural annoyance of individuals who have paid large premiums for their seats; the prejudice against Irving which had been persistently promoted by his few but active enemies; and you will understand the severity of the ordeal of Irving's first appearance in the United States.

II.

A ROUND of applause greeted the rise of the curtain upon the first scene of "The Bells." The audience thus testified their desire to be kindly; but, as the first part of the story was told, there was a certain

Barker, George J. Gould, John Gilbert, Rafael Joseffy, Dr. Robert Laird Collier, of Chicago; Oscar Meyer and Mrs. Meyer, Mrs. John T. Raymond, Harry Edwards, Daniel Bixby, Charles Dudley Warner, John H. Bird, Mrs. John Nesbitt, Miss Jeffrey Lewis, Laurence Hutton, Mr. E. A. Buck, Mr. Whitelaw Reid, Colonel Knox, ex-Governor Dorsheimer, William Winter, and Dr. Macdonald.

impatience even in their recognition of the artistic simplicity of the scene. "The Bells" opens more like a novel than a play, and yet the suggestiveness of the narrative at the table, as the topers chat and drink, is singularly dramatic. On this first night the play seemed to drag, and the audience were on the tiptoe of expectation. Those who were comfortably seated were anxious for the appearance of Irving; those who poured in to fill vacant seats at the back, and the hundreds who pushed in to stand behind them, created an uncomfortable sensation of disquiet. Had the Star been a London theatre, the patience of the people who were seated would have been so seriously taxed that they would hardly have permitted the play to proceed until order had been secured in all parts of the house.

At last the door of the burgomaster's home-like inn is flung open, and Irving stands there in his snow-sprinkled furs, his right hand raised above his head in the action of greeting his family, his left hand grasping his whip. His entrance was never more natural, never more picturesque. The audience hardly heard his opening words,—" It's I ! " They greeted him with thunders of applause, and shouts of welcome. He presently stepped forward from the door. Those who knew him would not fail to detect an effort to control his emotions, when he bowed his acknowledgments of a greeting as spontaneous as it was hearty. I had seen him in his dressing-room only a short time before. He was anxious, but firm as a rock; not in doubt of his own powers, but impressed, as any man might be, under similar circumstances, with the knowledge of how high the expectations of the people had been raised; how great the task of even approaching the standard of their excited hopes.

And now that the audience, touched by the artistic novelty of his appearance, and moved by their sentiments of hospitality, had given vent to their feelings, they settled down to allow the actor, of whose methods they had heard so much, to conquer their favourable opinion if he could. Despite the prejudices of some, and the annoyance of those who had been victimized by the speculators, auditors were willing to be captured,—nay, were desirous, if they could honestly do so, to endorse the verdict of their cousins of England, as to the place which Henry Irving holds in dramatic art.

"The Bells" is a weird play. Its lines are simple; it never halts. Mathias is an inn-keeper. He murders his guest, a Polish Jew, murders him on the highway for his gold, and is for ever haunted by his crime. The jangle of the sleigh-bells, as the Jew's horse gallops away after its master's death, is continually in the assassin's ears. Their sad music trickles through the story like the ripple of a rising stream through stubble-fields in autumn. It sweeps over the dramatic narrative like the sighing of the wind in "chill October." Remorse takes possession of the criminal; he dreams he is being tried for his life.

This scene affords special opportunities for illustrating Irving's dramatic magnetism. The judicial court of his dreamland forces him to submit to the operations of a mesmerist. Under this influence he makes confession of his crime by re-enacting it. Nothing more weirdly suggestive can be imagined. Before an audience as breathless as the court, the actor went through the pantomime of stopping the Jew's horse, cutting down the Jew with an axe, plundering the body and thrusting it into a limekiln. Then, convicted and condemned, the murderer dies under the violent shock to his nerves of this retributive force of imagination,—dies while the church-bells are ringing for his daughter's marriage,—his last agonizing words, "Take the rope from my throat!"

Only a daring artist would undertake such a part; only a great one could succeed in it. Most of the second and last acts is a monologue; and, in a country like America, which is accustomed to rapidity of thought and action, Irving was courageous in risking the result of so serious a strain upon the mind of a highly strung audience. The experiment, however, was entirely a triumph, notwithstanding the previously-mentioned discomforts attending an over-crowded house, and the rain that stormed without.

III.

THE curtain having fallen on the first act, Irving received the honour of a triple call, after which I went to his room, and found him reading some of the numerous cables and telegrams from home and from several distant American and Canadian cities, wishing him success.

"How kind everybody is!" he exclaimed, as he handed me a bundle of despatches. "You should have seen the hundreds of telegrams and letters that were sent to me on board the steamer as I was leaving Liverpool!"

"You are pleased?"

"More than pleased," he said "What an audience! I never played to a more sympathetic lot of people in my life. They respond to every movement and point of the scene with a marvellous promptitude."

"You still feel that you are among friends?"

"I do, indeed."

"I believe you played that first act to-night better than ever you played it in London."

"Do you think so? 'Art is long and life is fleeting.'"

There was in the atmosphere behind the footlights something of the electricity of a first night at the Lyceum,—no fuss, but a suppression of feeling, a kind of setting of the teeth and a girding up of the loins. The fine " property " horse of the vision scene, covered with snow that would not melt, had been dragged to the rear, and the stage was being set for the trial scene. Mr. Frank Tyars had donned his ermine as the judge, the mesmerist was ready at the wing, the last nail was being driven into the judicial bench. The local stage-hands and supers were at last evidently impressed with the importance of attention to some little matter of detail which they had daily tried to shirk at rehearsal. There had even been difficulties, on the stage and off, in regard to the regulation of the lights. Prominent gas-brackets had been removed from the auditorium, but the lowering of the lights down nearly to darkness for the last act of " The Bells " had been resisted. Later, however, Mr. Loveday found his New York collaborators in this respect willing allies ; and within the first week the man who had charge of the calcium lights said, " I have seen them all ; every one of the great actors and stage-managers ; and they don't begin to know as much about lighting the stage as this Mr. Henry Irving has forgotten ! "

A breathless silence testified to the impressiveness of the last act. You might almost have fancied you heard, in the car-bells of the streets, faint echoes of the sleigh-bells that jangled in the ears of Mathias. I remember the first night of " The Bells " at the Lyceum. The stillness in this New York house, as Mathias died of imaginary strangulation, reminded me of the London theatre on that occasion. The sensation in the two houses was the same. Nobody moved until the thud of the drop-curtain roller emphatically announced the end. Then the Star audience, as the Lyceum audience had done before them, gave vent to their enthusiasm.

Called and recalled, Irving appeared before the curtain. Then there was a cry of " Speech ! " " Speech ! " whereupon he said,—

" Ladies and Gentlemen,—I believe it is a custom with you to allow an actor to thank you for the pleasure you have given to him; and I will avail myself of that custom now, to say that I thank you with all my heart and soul. It seems to me that the greatness of your welcome typifies the greatness of your nation. I thank you, and ' beggar that I am, I am even poor in thanks.' Let me say that my comrades are also deeply sensible of your kindness, and let me add that I hope you will give a warmer welcome, if such were possible, than I have received to my associate and friend, Miss Ellen Terry, who will have the honour of appearing before you to-morrow night. And, finally, if it be not a liberty, will you allow me to express the hope ' that our loves may increase even as our days do grow ' ? "

As the audience left the theatre, the opinions expressed accentuated the reality of the actor's success. " The things that have been said about his mannerisms are shameful;" " Why, he has no more mannerisms than Booth ! " " I never was more agreeably surprised ;" " He speaks like an educated American ;" " And in the street looks like a Yale or Harvard professor ;" " Never saw anything finer ;" " Most awfully impressive scene, that last act ;" " Stage magnetism in the highest degree ;" " Guess he is safe for the biggest run of popularity of any actor or any man who has ever come to this country ;" " Oh, he is immense ! " " Did you hear Tony Pastor say it's the intensest acting he's ever seen,—that's a compliment, from what you may call a low comedian ;" " Madame Nilsson,— wasn't she delighted ? " " Yes, she wouldn't sing to-night; would have a box to come and see Irving." These were some of the remarks one caught as the audience left the theatre ; and the most practical criticism is often heard as one leaves a theatre among the crowd.

Coming upon a group of critics and others, I learn that the critic of *The Telegram* says, " Irving is, indeed, a revelation ! " while Mr. Oakey Hall, of *Truth*, thanks God he has lived to see such an actor. Several members of the Press Club join in the chorus of praise. Buck and Fiske, of *The Spirit of the Times*, smile quietly, as much as to say, " We told you so." The famous critic of the *Tribune* goes out, saying, "Yes, it is great; there is no denying it." Mr. Wallack, who, too ill to walk, had been carried to his box, expresses his hearty admiration of the actor whom for so many years he had longed to see; and Mr. Gilbert,[2] the

---

[2] "Twelve Americans," a graphic series of biographical sketches, by Howard Carroll, devotes some interesting pages to the story of John Gilbert's life and work. For upwards of fifty years an actor, this veteran of the American stage was born on the 27th of February, 1810, at Boston, in a house "adjoining that in which Miss Cushman, the greatest of American actresses first saw the light." His parents were in a good position, and, while they were not bigots, they did not altogether hold the theatrical profession as a highly reputable one. Young Gilbert was head of his class in declamation at the Boston High School. When he left school he was sent into a commercial house with a view to his becoming a dry-goods merchant. He disliked business, and after reciting Jaffer, in "Venice Preserved," to the manager of the Tremont Theatre, he was granted an appearance. After opening the store where he was engaged he read with delight in the newspaper, that in the evening "a young gentleman of Boston" would make his *début* in the play of "Venice Preserved." He appeared and "did well," in spite of his uncle (who was his master) scowling at him in front. "O John! what have you done?" was the broken-hearted exclamation of his mother the next day. John had not dared to go to the store, and felt himself quite an outcast. He was forgiven, however, in due course, and made a second appearance as Sir Edward Mortimer, in "The Iron Chest." He was successful beyond his expectations, and as "a boy actor" was praised as a phenomenon. Later he joined the stock company, and was reduced to "speaking utility" parts. Though disliking the drudgery of his place, he grew up with his work, and with the physical capacity for leading business he showed that he had also the mental strength for it. He played with Macready and Charlotte Cushman at the Princess's Theatre, London. At the close of his engagement there he attended the leading English theatres to study actors and their methods. Thence he went to Paris to complete his studies. On his return to America he filled important engagements for some years at the old Park Theatre; then he went for a time to Boston, where he was a great favourite; and finally he joined the Wallacks, in New York, where he has familiarized the Empire city with the best interpretations of Sir Peter Teazle, old Dornton, old Hardy, Sir Anthony Absolute, Major Oakley, Master Walter, Hardcastle,

veteran comedian and stage-manager at Wallack's, is "impressed beyond expression, especially with the business of counting the dowry."

There is a rush of critics, reporters, correspondents, " down-town" to chronicle the night's success. One or two writers, whose eccentricities give a commercial value to their work, go away to maintain their lively reputations; but, on the whole, it is evident that everybody, press men and public, is greatly pleased. Many American journals in distant States were represented at the theatre by their own critics and by correspondents. Long telegraphic despatches were wired to the leading cities of the Union; the Associated Press sent out special messages; the London journals were in evidence, and a new Anglo-French paper in Paris had commissioned its New York correspondent to cable some thousand or more words of Irving's opening night. Since the Forrest-Macready riot no theatrical event had created so general an interest as the first appearance of Irving in America.

IV.

GOING behind the scenes after the play, I found a representative of the *Herald* already ensconced in Mr. Irving's dressing-room. He was pressing the actor for his views of the audience, and for some contrasts of his sensations under the influence of this audience and others before whom he had played in England. At first Irving seemed inclined to say no more than to express satisfaction at his success. But the *Herald* representative was a quiet, cultivated, and experienced journalist. Evidently a gentleman of education, a travelled man, and discreet, he led the actor into the conversational direction he desired him to go, and the result was a pleasant and instructive interview :—

Sir Harcourt Courtley, Adams, and other high-class comedy characters of the century. He is still to New York what the elder Farren was to London.

H 2

" When I first stepped into view of the audience, and saw and heard the great reception it gave me, I was filled with emotion. I felt that it was a great epoch in my life. The moment I faced the people·I felt that we were friends. I knew that they wished to like me, and would go away, if I disappointed them, saying, 'Well, we wanted to like him ; but we couldn't.' Who could stand before such an audience, on such an occasion, and not be deeply moved? All I can say is, that it was a glorious reception, and typical of your great people."

" But as to the merits of the audience—theatre-goers will judge your acting—what is your opinion of them ?"

" The audience was a fine one. Apart from the marks of intelligence, which could be read with the naked eye, it was a fine assembly. I never played before a more responsive or sympathetic audience. It did not miss a point. I could tell all through the play that every motion I made was being closely watched; that every look, gesture, and tone was carefully observed. It is stimulating to an actor to feel that he has won his audience."

" You felt confident that you had made an impression upon the audience, and that there was no flattery in the applause ?"

" After the first burst of welcome was over, yes. I had not been on the stage five minutes before I knew that I had control of my hearers, and that I could make every point in the play tell. Then the silence of the people—the greatest compliment that could be paid to one in such a play—was always succeeded by genuine applause at the end of the act !"

" Did you get such a reception when you appeared as Mathias first before a London audience ?"

" Oh, no. Don't you see, I was comparatively little known then."

" Mr. Irving, an English newspaper a few days ago

expressed a hope that you would be judged by your merits, independent of anything that had previously been said or written about you, and that Americans in this case would not slavishly echo English opinion.[3] Was there any trace of independence in the manner of the audience?"

"Yes, yes,—there was, certainly," said the actor, rising and pacing the room. "It is not presumption in me to say that I am sure I was judged solely on my merits, and that the audience went away pleased with me. There were times to-night when I could feel the sympathy of my hearers—actually feel it."

"The audience was quiet in the first act. The interest is worked up to the climax so smoothly and gradually that there was no opportunity for applause until the end?"

"There, now, you have found one of the differences between the judgment of my audience to-night and those I have played to in London. In the first part of the play the English audiences laughed a great deal; quite boisterously, in fact, at some of the comedy scenes. But the absence of this to-night, I think, was due to the fact that the people were straining to get the exact run of the play, and were labouring under anxiety—it is not presumption if I say so—to see me."

"Was there any other feature of this kind that you noticed?"

"Yes; when Christian yields to my demand for a promise that he will never leave the village while I am alive, I say, 'It was necessary!' This point has generally provoked laughter in England. To-night it evoked earnest applause. On the other hand, for the first time I heard the audience laugh at 'Now the dowry to be given to our dear son-in-law, in order that our dear son-in-law may love us.'"

---

[3] This statement and question were founded upon the *Standard's* message, previously referred to; but which Mr. Irving himself neither saw nor heard of until within a few days of the close of his New York engagement.

"Are you willing to be judged as an actor by to-night's performance, Mr. Irving?"

"For that character, yes."

"Is Mathias not your greatest *rôle*?"

"My best? Well, now, that's hard to say. There is no ground for comparison,—Charles the First is so different; he is full of qualities that are foreign to Mathias. I cannot name a character in which I feel I am best. They afford opportunities for the display of different powers. I am fond of the part of Mathias, it is true."

"Did your company play up to the standard of their work in the Lyceum?"

"Well, you have not seen them all; you have not seen Miss Terry or Mr. Howe."

"But did those of the company who were in the cast to-night do as well as usual?"

"They were rather slower, but quite good. Of course every one was excited, more or less. There is only one strong part in the play, and that is mine. Mr. Terriss was excellent. Don't you think he is a fine fellow?"

Suiting the action to the word, Irving unconsciously dropped into a military attitude, stretched his hand out and threw back his head,—a perfect fac-simile of Mr. Terriss' impersonation of Christian.

"Is the scenery the same that was used in the Lyceum?"

"Exactly the same. You prompt me to mention a particular point, now. Did you notice how little the scenery had to do with the play? I have it so on purpose. Why, there is practically no scenery. I try to get as near truth as possible, as Caleb Plummer says. I have sometimes heard that I rely on scenery. So far I do: if it were the hovel of King Lear I would have a hovel, and if it were the palace of Cleopatra I would make it as gorgeous as the possibilities of art would allow."

"Do you look upon your reception to-night as a success?"

"In every way. One of your greatest actors told me that American audiences are proverbially cold on first nights. He was trying to save me from a possible disappointment. In addition to this, 'The Bells' is not a play for applause, but for earnest, sympathetic silence. Need I say that the demonstrations which burst forth on every occasion that good taste would allow, are the best evidences that to-night I have won an artistic triumph."

VII.

"RED LETTER DAYS."

Miss Ellen Terry's first appearance in New York—The Press on
Charles and the Queen—A Professional *Matinée*—An
audience of Actors to see Louis XI.—How they impressed
the Actor, and what they thought of him—A visit to
Henry Ward Beecher—At Church and at Home—Mrs.
Beecher and Miss Terry—Reminiscences—Studies of Death,
Physiological and Idealistic—Louis's Death and Hamlet's
—A strange Story.

I.

NEW YORK received Miss Terry, on her first appearance before an American audience, as cordially as it had
welcomed Irving. It was as Henrietta Maria that she
spoke her first words on the stage of the New World.[1]

[1] In " Charles the First " Irving confirmed the good impression he had made. Miss Terry received a most cordial reception,
and made so excellent an impression upon the audience, both by
her charming personality and admirable acting, that long before
the evening was over she had firmly established herself in the
good graces of her new public, who more than once, at the fall of
the curtain, invited her, with every enthusiastic mark of appro-
bation, to come before the ·house to receive in person its
acknowledgments and congratulations. Her success was un-
questionable. In the second act the curtain fell on the conclusion of one of the grandest results that any actor has achieved
in New York for years. A continued succession of plaudits
came from all parts of the house. The performance was profoundly conceived, acted out with infinite care, elaborated with
rare skill, and invested with naturalness that deserved all praise.
Irving, in his finale, merited fully every word that has been
written of his power, intensity, and dramatic excellence; and
he was enthusiastically called before the curtain, in order that
the audience might assure him of that verdict. Miss Terry

There is no more tenderly poetic play in the *répertoire* of the modern drama than " Charles the First." The story in Irving's hands is told with a truthful simplicity that belongs to the hightest form of theatrical art. All the leading critics recognized this. The effect of the well-known Hampton Court cloth was so perfect in its way, and so new to some of them, that it was regarded as a cut cloth, with " raking " and water-pieces. The *Tribune* interpreted the general opinion of the audience, when it said, "what most impressed them was Irving's extraordinary physical fitness to the accepted ideal of Charles Stuart, combined with the passionate earnestness and personal magnetism that enable him to create and sustain a perfect illusion ;" while it may be said to have just as happily expressed the views of another class in the words : " To the student Mr. Irving's Charles is especially significant, as indicative of the actor's method in applying what is termed ' natural ' treatment to the poetic drama."

"Louis XI.," " The Merchant of Venice," " The Lyons Mail," and " The Belle's Stratagem," were the other pieces produced during the four weeks in New York. The theatre was crowded nightly, and on the Saturday *matinées*. The speculators found it easier to dispose of their tickets, as the weeks wore on, than even during the first five or six days of the engagement. Nothing damped the public ardour. The opera war between Mapleson and Abbey, as representatives of two great parties of wealthy art patrons, had no apparent influence on the receipts at the Star Theatre. One of the greatest nights of the month marked the first

made the impression of a charming actress. There was something very captivating in the sweetness of her manner, the grace of her movements, and the musical quality of her tones. In acting, her points were made with remarkable ease and naturalness. There was an entire absence of theatrical effect, there was a symplicity of style in everything she did, a directness of method and sincerity of feeling that, as we have said, was the simplicity of true art, and yet not the exaggeration of the simplicity of nature.—*New York Herald.*

appearance of Patti at the Academy of Music. Inclement weather, abnormal charges for seats, strong counter-attractions at the other houses, including the two grand Italian Opera Companies, might have been expected to discount the financial success of any rival entertainment. They made no difference to Irving. He was the talk, not of New York, but of America; and after her appearance as Portia, Miss Ellen Terry was almost as much written about as he himself. Unrivalled in the higher walks of comedy, Miss Terry is to the American public as new as Irving in the naturalness of her methods.

Shylock excited controversy, Louis inspired admiration, Dubosc and his virtuous double commanded respect, and the method of presenting the plays was a theme of praise and delight in and out of the press. Of Louis the *Sun* said, " Mr. Irving won his audience. to him almost at once. It was impossible to withstand the intensity, the vivid picturesqueness, and imposing reality of his portrayal, and after each great scene of the play he was called again and again before the curtain by hearty and most demonstrative applause. It was a wonderful performance, and the impression that it left is one that can never be laid aside." The *Times* was struck with his appearance. " His make-up is as perfect in its kind as that of Charles the First, and nobody would imagine the actor to be the same as the actor in either of the other parts which he has presented. But the verisimilitude here goes much deeper than the make-up. There is the senile garrulity and the senile impatience of garrulity, the senile chuckle over successful strokes of business. And this character is deepened as the play advances. The occasional expressions of energy are spasmodic ; and after each the patient relapses into a still more listless apathy, and this decay is progressive until the death-scene which is the strongest and most impressive piece of realism that Mr. Irving has yet given us." The *Herald* commended Shylock to the Shakespearian student, " as the best exposition of the character that can be seen on the stage ;" while the *Tribune* said of Miss Terry, " Her simple manner, always large and adequate, with nothing puny or mincing about it, is one of the greatest beauties of the art which it so deftly conceals. Her embodiment of a woman's loveliness, such as in Portia should be at once stately and fascinating, and inspire at once respect and passion, was felicitous beyond the reach of descriptive phrases. Her delivery of the Mercy speech was one of the few perfectly modulated and entirely beautiful pieces of eloquence that will dwell for ever in memory. Her sweet and sparkling by-play in the ' business ' about the ring and in her exit can only be called exquisite. Better comedy has not in our time been seen." [2]

[2] Miss Terry was born at Coventry, Feb. 27, 1848. Her parents were members of the theatrical profession. Her first appearances on the stage were in " The Winter's Tale " and " King John " (Mamillius and Arthur), during the Shakespearian revivals of Charles Kean, in 1858. As Prince Arthur she had repeated the success of her eldest sister Kate, who had made her first appearance in the part six years previously. Mr. Irving, during his conversations and speeches in this book of "Impressions," has referred to the stock companies which, at one time, were the provincial schools which supplied London with its principal actors. When Ellen Terry was a girl, the late Mr. Chute presided over the fortunes of two of the best stock companies in the country. He was the lessee of the Bristol and Bath theatres, and he played his Bristol company at Bath once or twice a week. Some twenty years ago I remember a stock company at the Bristol theatre, which included Marie Wilton, Miss Cleveland (Mrs. Arthur Stirling), Miss Mandelbert, Madge Robertson (Mrs. Kendall) and her mother, Arthur Stirling, George Rignold, William Rignold, Arthur Wood, Fosbroke, and the fathers, respectively, of Marie Wilton and Madge Robertson. At that time Kate Terry and Ellen Terry had left for London, Ellen having joined the Bristol company at the close of Charles Kean's management of the Princess's. She played Cupid to her sister Kate's Diana in Brough's extravaganza of "Endymion" at Bristol, in 1862. She made her *début* in London, March, 1863, as Gertrude, in the "Little Treasure." The critics of the time recognized in her art " an absence of conventionality and affectation," and they

II.

At the written request of the leading actors and
theatrical companies of New York, Irving gave a

look back now to trace in her interpretations of "the buoyant
spirits, kindly heart, and impulsive emotions" of Gertrude for
the undoubted forecast of her present success, more particularly
in those characters which give full play to the natural sympathetic and womanly spirit of her art. From March, 1863,
till January, 1864, she played Hero, in "Much Ado About
Nothing," Mary Meredith, in "The American Cousin," and
other secondary parts. She married and left the stage while
still a mere child, and was not yet twenty when she made her
reappearance at the end of October, 1867, in "The Double
Marriage," adapted from the French by Charles Reade for the
New Queen's Theatre, London. She also played Mrs. Mildmay,
in "Still Waters," and Katharine in the ordinary stage version
of the "Taming of the Shrew," known as "Katharine and
Petruchio." It was in this comedy, on the 26th of December,
1867, that she and Mr. Irving first acted together. She left the
theatre in January, 1868, and did not reappear on the London
stage until 1874, when she succeeded Mrs. John Wood in the
part of Phillippa Chester, in Charles Reade's "Wandering
Heir," which was produced under the author's management at
the Queen's Theatre. She afterwards joined Mr. and Mrs.
Bancroft's company at the Prince of Wales's, and was the Portia
to Mr. Coughlan's Shylock, in the ambitious production of
"The Merchant of Venice," which was to be a new departure in
the history of the famous little house near Tottenham Court
Road. Shakespeare did not prosper, however, at the Prince of
Wales's, though his great comedy was daintily mounted, and
Miss Terry's Portia was as sweet and gracious as the art of the
actress could make that sweet and gracious heroine. From the
Bancrofts, Miss Terry went to their rivals (Mr. Hare and the
Kendalls), at the Court Theatre. The sterling natural qualities
which some critics noted in her method when a child were
abundantly apparent in her Ophelia, a fresh, graceful, touching
performance, of which *Punch* said, January 11, 1879, "If anything more intellectually conceived or more exquisitely wrought
out than Miss Terry's Ophelia has been seen on the English
stage in this generation, it has not been within *Punch's*
memory." She closed her engagement at the Court Theatre on
the offer of Mr. Irving to take the position of leading lady at
the Lyceum Theatre, where she made her first appearance, December 30, 1878, and since which time she has shared with him
the honours of a series of such successes as are unparalleled in

"professional *matinée*" at the Star Theatre. The play was "Louis XI." It was the first time Irving had appeared before an audience of actors in any country. The house was packed from floor to ceiling. It was a singularly interesting and interested audience. No actor, proud of his profession, could have looked at it without a thrill of pleasure. Well-dressed, beaming with intelligence and intellectuality, it was on good terms with itself, and it settled down in stalls, boxes, and dress circle with an air of pleasant expectation that was refreshing to contemplate.[3]

the history of the stage. They include the longest runs ever known of "Hamlet," "The Merchant of Venice," "Romeo and Juliet," and "Much Ado About Nothing." This is not the place to do more than give these brief biographic notes of a brilliant career. But one is tempted to quote a singularly happy sketch of Miss Ellen Terry, which appeared, on the eve of her departure for America, in the *St. Stephen's Review*, July, 1883 : "It is well for the stage that it possesses such a gift as Ellen Terry. The age is, on the whole, terribly unromantic and commonplace ; it deals in realism of a very uncompromising form ; it calls a spade a spade, and considers sentiment an unpardonable affectation. But Ellen Terry is the one anachronism that the age forgives ; she is the one living instance of an ideal being that the purists pardon. As she stands before these cold critics in her classical robes as Camma ; as she drags at their heart-strings as the forlorn and abandoned Olivia ; as she trips upon the stage as Beatrice ; as she appears in a wondrous robe of shot-red and gold, or clothed "in white samite, mystic, wonderful," as Ophelia, or, as she falls a-weeping as the heart-broken queen on the breast of Charles the First, even these well-balanced natures pronounce her inexplicable but charming. She is the one actress who cannot be criticized ; for is she not Ellen Terry ? "

[3] "All that has been said in recognition of Mr. Irving's intellectual leadership, and of his puissant genius and beautiful and thorough method of dramatic art, was more than justified by his impersonation of Louis XI., given yesterday afternoon, before an audience mainly composed of actors, at the Star Theatre. He has not, since the remarkable occasion of his first advent in America, acted with such a noble affluence of power as he displayed in this splendid and wonderful effort. It was not only an expression, most vivid and profound, of the intricate, grisly, and terrible nature of King Louis ; it was a disclosure of the manifold artistic resources, the fine intuition, the repose, and the

Nothing could be more satisfactory to Mr. Irving and to his friends, after the demonstrative applause of this very remarkable audience, than the "Interviews" of many of the best-known actors and actresses which appeared in the *Herald* on the following morning. Irving had no idea that such a tribute was to be paid to him when, in talking with some gentlemen of the press, at the close of the play, he said,—

"I never played before such an audience, so spontaneous in its appreciation and applause, and it will remain with me as one of the most interesting and most memorable events in my dramatic career. It is very commonly said that actors are the worst judges of acting. But I would ask why should actors be worse judges of their art than painters of paintings, or musicians of music?"

"Your audience was very enthusiastic, was it not?"

"It could not well have been more so. You see actors know well from experience that an actor, to be stimulated, needs applause, and plenty of it. Applause is as necessary to an actor as to an orator. The greater the applause the more enthusiasm the actor

commanding intellectual energy of the actor himself. An intellectual audience—eager, alert, responsive, quick to see the intention almost before it was suggested, and to recognize each and every point, however subtle and delicate, of the actor's art —seemed to awaken all his latent fire, and nerve him to a free and bounteous utterance of his own spirit; and every sensitive mind in that numerous and brilliant throng most assuredly felt the presence of a royal nature, and a great artist in acting. Upon Mr. Irving's first entrance the applause of welcome was prodigious, and it was long before it died away. More than one scene was interrupted by the uncontrollable enthusiasm of the house, and eight times in the course of the performance Mr. Irving was called back upon the scene. A kindred enthusiasm was communicated to the other actors, and an unusual spirit of emulation pervaded the entire company and representation. . . . . At the close there was a tumult of applause, and the expectation seemed eager and general that Mr. Irving would personally address the assembly. He retired, however, with a bow of farewell. 'Louis XI.' will be repeated to-night."—*The Tribune, November* 21.

puts into his work. Therefore those who applaud most get most, and consequently my audience of this afternoon—"

" Got the most out of your performance ? "

" Well, they certainly excited me so that I felt the effect of their appreciation on my own work. I felt an elation for them, and an elation such as I have rarely experienced. I happened to walk into Mr. Millais' studio before leaving England. He had just finished a painting in which I was interested—in fact, it was a portrait of myself. I found him in an extraordinarily cheerful mood. He clapped his hands with delight, as he said, pointing to the portrait, ' Watts has just been here, and says it is the best thing I have ever done.' Millais was especially pleased, for this compli-ment came from a brother artist. I dare say you will see the parallel in this my especial pleasure in re-ceiving the plaudits of my brother artists."

"And how did the audience differ from the audiences you have been playing to here ? "

" This is the distinction, I think,—actors applaud all the touches as you put them on ; a general audience applaud the whole effect when made. And so it was that all the little asides and touches of by-play this afternoon were taken with as keen an appreciation of them as of the whole effect of any scene or situation. I felt that my audience thoroughly knew what they were applauding for. I felt that they applauded my-self and our company because they were really pleased, and I will say again that my first professional *matinée* has proved to be one of the pleasantest events of my life."

" It was a great performance," said Mr. Edward Gilmore, one of the managers of Niblo's Garden. " I have seen a good deal of acting," said Mrs. Agnes Booth ; " but I can honestly say I have never seen anything that pleased me more: it was simply perfect."

" I have seen most of the performances in Europe of

recent times," said Mdme. Cottrelly, who had been a
leading German actress and manager before appearing
on the Casino stage; " but I have never seen anything
that equalled Mr. Irving's performance this afternoon.
I have never seen anything in the theatrical line that
has been mounted more correctly. It has not been
surpassed in the finest German Court theatres that I
have attended."

" I think it is altogether one of the greatest performances the American public and profession have
ever seen," said Mr. Dan Harkins. " The wonderful
perfection of detail and subtlety of by-play is, I think,
greater than I have seen in any other performance,
excepting, perhaps, Mr. Forrest's ' King Lear.' Mr.
Irving also is in a constant state of activity; when he
is not talking he is acting. He is making some clever
point all the time. The whole performance is great.
It is great in the leading character, great in all that
is subordinate to it, which, by an excellent stage
management and a fine company, are brought into
unusual prominence."

Mr. McCaull remarked : " It's a long way the finest
piece of character-acting I have ever seen. Of
course, I'm a young man, and haven't seen much; but
I've seen Mr. Irving twice in this part, and when I go
to see a performance—out of my own theatre—
twice, I can tell you that, in my opinion, it must be a
very fine one."

" I am very familiar with ' Louis XI.,' " said Mr.
Harry Edwards, " as I have played in it myself a
great deal. I appeared as Nemours with Mr. Gusta-
vus V. Brooke, and his performance of Louis XI.
was a very fine one. I then travelled for a year
with Charles Kean, and played Courtier, the Physician, in ' Louis XI.,' and once appeared with Kean as
Courtier. I also played Nemours with Charles Coul-
dock. Well, I say all this to show you that I am
pretty familiar with the play, and with great actors
who have played ' Louis XI.' Mr. Irving's Louis is one

of the greatest performances I have ever seen as a whole, and far superior to that of any of his predecessors. He brings depth, more intensity, and more variety to the character than any of them. His facial action is something wonderful. His performance stands on the highest plane of dramatic excellence, and on the same plane as Macready's famous Werner. I may say that I am not an admirer of Mr. Irving in all parts, but his Louis is unapproachable. I never enjoyed a performance so much in my life, and I felt that I could sit it out for a week if I were given the opportunity."

"He is the greatest actor who speaks the English language," said Mr. Lewis Morrison. "I claim to know what good acting is. I have supported Salvini, whom I regard as the greatest artist on the foreign stage, and my preceptor was Edwin Booth. But even in Mr. Booth's presence I must say that I have been moved to-day as I never was before. I am not given to gushing over an actor; but I never before saw a man's soul as I did in King Louis this afternoon. It was simply perfection. It was not the actor; it was Louis XI. that I saw. I must admit that I went to the theatre with a little prejudice against Mr. Irving. I had never seen him, and, from certain things which other actors had told me, I was prepared to find an over-rated man. But what a performance it was! It was wonderful!—wonderful!"

"As a manager," said Mr. Palmer, of the Union Square Theatre, "it was a revelation to me to see such conscientious attention to detail. Every little thing in which good stage management could have been exhibited was shown by Mr. Irving's company. They worked as one man. I have heard but one opinion among members of our company,—everybody was delighted."

"What can I say that is strong enough?" exclaimed Miss Cary, of the Union Square Theatre company. "I was delighted beyond measure. What

I

a wonderful teacher Irving must be, and what a master of his art in every way! What impressed me particularly was the perfect harmony of the entire performance. How carefully and patiently everybody must have been drilled, and every detail which would add to the effect looked after!"

"I have only one word to say on this subject," said Mr. John Gilbert, "and that is, that it is wonderful; perhaps I, however, may supplement that by saying that it is 'extraordinary.' I have seen Mr. Irving play 'Louis XI.' before to-day, and, in fact, I have attended nearly all his performances at the Star Theatre; but this afternoon he exceeded anything that he has done here before. He was clearly moved, in no slight degree, by the almost incessant applause of his professional brethren. I don't know that I remember having seen a greater performance by any actor, not even excepting Macready's Werner. I am not astonished at Mr. Irving's great popularity in England. I am sure he deserves it."

Mrs. G. H. Gilbert, of Daly's theatre, thought that it was the finest performance within her experience. "In the confession scene," she said, "I thought him especially remarkable. I had seen him in 'The Lyons Mail' in London, and, now that I have seen his Louis XI., I want to see him in all his characters. The great applause that was given him by the vast gathering of his profession was, I assure you, not complimentary applause, but it was given in pure admiration of his great achievements.

"Mr. Irving's Louis," said Mr. Dan Frohman, "is a vivid and powerful transcript from history. Once or twice, at the end of an act, he lapsed into his natural voice; but this may be excused from the great draught that such a character must make upon his strength. As a picture of the subtle, crafty, and avaricious old monarch, his representation was absolutely perfect. I think Mr. Irving's Louis XI., in a word, is a sort of dramatic liberal education. Every actor can learn something from him. I wish our actors could keep the integrity of their characters as perfectly as Mr. Irving does."

" Mr. Irving is the greatest actor I have ever seen," said Mr. Tony Pastor. "I have been to see him several times, and this is my opinion. It ain't buncombe. It comes from the heart. I've seen all the greatest actors, and have been a great deal to the theatres since I have been in this business; but I have never seen any one as good as Mr. Irving. This is a compliment I am paying to a man I am not personally acquainted with, and perhaps we shall never meet."

" Mr. Irving's Louis," Mr. Colville said, " is superior beyond criticism. It is the most perfect performance I have ever witnessed. I was acting manager of the old Broadway Theatre when Charles Kean played there, and, of course, saw him in the part."

III.

" IF one had arranged events in America to one's own liking one could not have had them go along more pleasantly," said Irving, one Sunday afternoon, when he was giving me an account of his visit to Mr. Henry Ward Beecher and Mrs. Beecher, at Brooklyn; " indeed one would have had to lay in a stock of vanity to even dream of such a reception as we have had. It needs a little hostility here and there in the press at home and on this side to give a wholesome flavour to the sweets. It is a great reward, all this, for one's labour. I was struck the other day with some passages of Emerson, in his essay on Fate, where he says, ' Concentration is the secret of strength in politics, in war, in trade; in short, in all management of human affairs. One of the high anecdotes of the world is the reply of Newton to the inquiry, how he had " been able to achieve his discoveries :" " By always intending my mind." *Diligence passe sens,* Henry VIII. was wont to say, or, ' Great is drill.'

I 2

John Kemble said that the worst provincial company
of actors would go through a play better than the best
amateur company. No genius can recite a ballad at
first reading so well as mediocrity can at the fifteenth
or twentieth reading. A humorous friend of mine
thinks the reason Nature is so perfect in her art, and
gets up such inconceivably fine sunsets, is, that 'she
has learned at last by dint of doing the same thing
so very often.' A wonderful writer, Emerson! He
gives the right cue to all stage managers,—rehearsal!
rehearsal! Mr. Beecher has evidently been a hard
worker all his life, a persistent man; and nothing is
done without it. First lay down your lines; settle
what you mean to do, what you find you can do, and
do it; the greater the opposition the more courageous
and persevering you must be; and if you are right, and
strength and life hold out, you must win. But I want
to tell you about the visit to Brooklyn. Miss Terry
and I were invited to visit Mr. Henry Ward Beecher.
We went on Sunday to his church. He preached a
good, stirring sermon, full of strong common-sense.
It was what might, in some respects, be called an
old-fashioned sermon, though it was also exceedingly
liberal. The spirit of its teaching was the doctrine of
brotherly love. The preacher told his congregation
that a man was not simply a follower of Christ, because
he went to church on Sundays. A man could, he said,
be a follower of the Saviour without going to church
at all. He could also be a follower of Christ if he
wished, and belong to any church he liked,—Baptist,
Wesleyan, Lutheran. A Pagan could be a follower of
Christ if he lived up to His doctrine of charity. To
do good is the chief end and aim of a good life. It
was an extemporaneous sermon so far as the absence
of manuscript or notes went, and was delivered with
masterful point and vigour, and with some touches of
pure comedy — Mr. Beecher is a great comedian.
After the service he came to us, and offered his
arm to Miss Terry. She took one arm, his wife the
other. I followed with his son and several other rela-

tions.   A few members of the congregation joined the
little procession.   Following Mr. Beecher and the
ladies, we walked down the aisle and into the street,
to his house.   There was something very simple and
dignified about the whole business, something that to
me smacked of the primitive churches, without their
austerity.   Mrs. Beecher is seventy-one years of age;
a perfect gentlewoman, Quaker-like in her dress and
manners, gentle of speech, but with a certain suggestion of firmness of purpose.   Beecher struck me as a
strong, robust, genial, human man, a broad, big
fellow.   We had dinner,—the early dinner that was
in vogue when I was a boy.   It was, I should say, a
regular solid New England meal,—rich soup, plenty
of fish, a joint of beef; and some generous port was on
the table.   The host was most pleasant and simple,
the hostess most unsophisticated and kindly.   She took
greatly to Miss Terry, who also took greatly to her."

" Mr. Beecher had been at the theatre the night
before ? "

" Yes, to see ' Louis XI.' "

" Did he talk much ? "

" Oh, yes, and his conversation was most interesting.   He related, and very graphically, an incident of
the troubled times before the abolition of slavery.
' One day in the pulpit,' he said, ' I asked my people,
suppose you had a sister, and she came to you and
said, ' I would like to stay in your city of Brooklyn ;
I think I would be very happy here; but I must go
away, I cannot stay ; I must depart, probably to live
with a reprobate, some hard, cruel man, who will lay
claim to me, body and soul.'   You say, ' Why, why
must you go ? '   She answers, ' Because my body
is worth so much, and I am to be sold; and my little
child—it, too, is of value in the same way—my child
will be sold, and we shall be separated.'   There was
a dead silence in the church.   ' My friends,' I said,
' you have a sister in that position; and I want you to
buy that woman ! '   ' Come up here, Dinah Cullum '
(or whatever her name was), I said, and out of the

congregation stepped a beautiful woman, a mulatto, and I said, 'Here she is; here is my sister, your sister!' The collecting basket was sent around. More than enough was realized to buy the woman. And I said to her, 'Dinah Cullum, you are free.' Then addressing my people again, I said, 'Now you can buy the child;' and they did, and we gave the child to its mother!"

"It used to be said of Lord Beaconsfield," Irving continued, "that his Oriental blood and his race instincts gave him his fondness for jewels; but Beecher seems to have the same kind of taste. He brought out from a cabinet a handful of rings, and asked me which I thought Miss Terry would like best. Then he took them to her, and she selected an *aqua marina*, which he placed upon her finger, and begged her to accept as a souvenir of her visit to Brooklyn. 'May I?' said Miss Terry to Mrs. Beecher. 'Yes, my dear, take it,' said Mrs. Beecher, and she did. It was quite touching to see the two women together, so different in their stations, their years, their occupations. Miss Terry was the first actress Mrs. Beecher had ever known. To begin with, she was very courteous; her greeting was hospitable, but not cordial. The suggestion of coldness in her demeanour gradually thawed, and at the close of the visit she took Miss Terry into her arms, and the two women cried. 'One touch of nature makes the whole world kin.' Human sympathy,—what a fine thing it is! It is easy to understand how a woman of the training and surroundings that belong to the class in which Mrs. Beecher has lived might regard an actress, and especially one who has made a name, and is therefore the object of gossip. All the more delightful is the bit of womanly sympathy that can bind together two natures which the austerity of professed religionists would keep asunder."

"It is a greater triumph for the stage than you, perhaps, quite appreciate,—this visit to the home of a popular preacher; for, however liberal Mr. Beecher's sentiments may be in regard to plays and players, there are members of his congregation who will not approve of his going to the theatre, and who will probably be horrified at his entertaining you at his own home."

"No doubt," Irving replied. "Beecher said to me, 'I wish you could come and spend a week with me at my little country-house. You might leave all the talking to me, if you liked. I would give you a bit of a sermon now and then, and you in return should give me a bit of acting. Oh, we should have a pleasant time! You could lie on your back and smoke and rest. I suppose some day you will allow yourself a little rest.'"

"What was the Beecher home like? New or old,—characteristic of the host or not?"

"Quite characteristic, I should say. It impressed me as a home that had been gradually furnished over a period of many years. That was particularly the case with regard to the library. Around the walls were a series of cabinets, with old china and glass in them. The room nad an old English, or what I suppose would be called an old New England, appearance. Books, pictures, china, and a wholesome perfume of tobacco-smoke. Mr. Beecher does not smoke, but his sons do. 'I cannot pretend to put down these small vices,' he said. 'I once tried to, I believe.' 'Oh, yes,' said one of his sons, a fine fellow, 'the only thrashing he ever gave me was for smoking a cigar; and when the war broke out, and I went to the front, the first present I received from home was a box of cigars, sent to me by my father.' Altogether I was deeply impressed with Beecher. A robust, fearless man, I can quite understand how great he might be in face of opposition. Indeed, I was witness of this on the occasion of his famous platform fight at Manchester, during the war. I was acting in a stock company there at the time, and either in the first or last piece, I forget which, I was able to go and hear him speak. The inci-

dent, as you know, is historical on this side of the
Atlantic, and it created quite a sensation in Manchester.
The lecture-room was packed with secessionists.
Beecher was attacking the South, and upholding the
Federal cause. The great, surging crowd hooted and
yelled at him. I fear I did not know much about the
rights or wrongs of the matter. I had my work to
do, and, though I watched the course of the American
trouble, I had no very definite views about it. But I
admired the American preacher. He faced his opponents with a calm, resolute face,—stood there like a
rock. Whenever there was a lull in this commotion
he would speak, and his words were defiant. There
was the sound of the trumpet in them. We English
admire courage, worship pluck, and after a time the
men who had tried their hardest to shout Beecher
down evidently felt ashamed. There presently arose
cries of ' Hear him ! ' and ' Fair play ! ' Beecher stood
there firm and defiant, and I felt my heart go out to
him. Once more he got a few words in. They bore
upon the rights of free speech, and in a little while
he had the floor, as they say in America, and kept it.
It seemed as if he were inspired. He spoke with a
fervid eloquence I don't think I have ever heard
equalled. In the end he carried the entire meeting
with him. The crowd evidently knew no more
about the real merits of the quarrel between North
and South than I did. They entered the hall Confederates, and left it out-and-out Federals, if one
should judge by the thundering cheers that broke out
every now and then during the remainder of Beecher's
oration, and the unanimous applause that marked the
finish of it."

IV.

AMONG the little suppers which Irving accepted
after the play was a cosy entertainment given by
Major Frank Bond, at which a dozen gentlemen of
distinction in politics, science, and the army, were

present. Dr. Fordyce Barker, who was intimate with Dickens, during that illustrious author's visits to America, was one of the guests. He started, among other subjects, a very interesting conversation.

"Have you ever made studies of deaths for stage purposes ?" asked Dr. Barker.

" No."

" And yet your last moments of Mathias and of Louis XI. are perfectly consistent and correct psychologically."

" My idea is to make death in these cases a characteristic Nemesis; for example, Mathias dies of the fear of discovery; he is fatally haunted by the dread of being found out, and dies of it in a dream. Louis pulls himself together by a great effort of will in his weakest physical moment, to fall dead—struck as if by a thunderbolt—while giving an arrogant command that is to control heaven itself; and it seems to me that he should collapse ignominiously, as I try to illustrate."

" You succeed perfectly," the doctor replied, " and from a physiological point of view, too."

" Hamlet's death, on the other hand, I would try to make sweet and gentle as the character, as if the 'flights of angels winged him to his rest.'"

" You seem to have a genius for fathoming the conceptions of your authors, Mr. Irving," said the doctor; "and it is, of course, very important to the illusion of a scene that the reality of it should be consistently maintained. Last night I went to see a play called 'Moths,' at Wallack's. There is a young man in it who acts very well ; but he, probably by the fault of the author more than his own, commits a grave error in the manner of his death. We are told that he is shot through the lungs. This means almost immediate unconsciousness, and a quick, painless death ; yet the actor in question came upon the stage after receiving this fatal wound, made a coherent speech, and died in a peaceful attitude."

"Talking of interesting psychological investigations," said Irving, "I came upon a curious story, the other day, of the execution of Dr. de la Pommerais, in 1864. He was a poisoner, somewhat after the Palmer type. I was present, then a boy, during the trial of the English murderer, and was, therefore, all the more interested in the last hours of the Frenchman. He was a skilled physician, it seems, and a surgeon named Velpeau visited him in his prison, the night before his execution, in the pure interest of physiological science. 'I need not tell you,' he said to De la Pommerais, 'that one of the most interesting questions in this connection is, whether any ray of memory or sensibility survives in the brain of a man after his head is severed from his body.' The condemned man turned a startled and anxious face to the surgeon. 'You are to die; nothing, it seems, can save you. Will you not, therefore, utilize your death in the interest of science?' Professional instinct mastered physical fear, and De la Pommerais said, 'I will, my friend; I will.' Velpeau then sat down, and the two discussed and arranged the proposed experiment. 'When the knife falls,' said Velpeau, 'I shall be standing at your side, and your head will at once pass from the executioner's hands into mine. I will then cry distinctly into your ear: 'Count de la Pommerais, can you at this moment thrice lower the lid of your right eye while the left remains open?' The next day, when the great surgeon reached the condemned cell, he found the doomed man practising the sign agreed upon. A few minutes later the guillotine had done its work,—the head was in Velpeau's hands, and the question put. Familiar as he was with the most shocking scenes, it is said that Velpeau was almost frozen with terror as he saw the right lid fall, while the other eye looked fixedly at him. 'Again!' he cried frantically. The lids moved, but they did not part. It was all over. A ghastly story. One hopes it may not be true."

VIII.

A QUIET EVENING.

A first Visit behind the Scenes — Cooper and Kean—The University Club—A very notable Dinner—Chief Justice Davis and Lord Chief Justice Coleridge—A *Menu* worth discussing—Terrapin and canvas-back Duck—"A little Family Party"—Florence's Romance—Among the Lambs —The Fate of a Manuscript Speech—A Story of John Kemble—Words of Welcome—Last Night of the New York Engagement—*Au revoir !*

I.

"TURN the gas down a little."

"Yes, sir," said the attentive Irish-American waiter at the Brevoort House.

"And don't let us be disturbed."

"Very well, sir."

"The fire-light glows on the walls as if the so-called volcanic sunset had taken possession of the place," said Irving, stretching his legs upon the hearth; "what a rest it is to sit and talk to a friend and look into the fire ! "

"It is, indeed. Let us have a chat in that spirit and call the chapter 'A quiet evening.' "

"You mean a talk for the book ? "

"Yes ; one gets so few opportunities of this kind that it is worth while to avail ourselves of the present one. I think you had better tell me what you have done in New York, and I will chronicle it from your own lips."

"Do you mean generally, or in detail ? There

are some things that fix themselves in one's memory, not to be forgotten. Of course, the first night at the Star Theatre—one is not likely to forget that ! "

" No, I shall always remember you standing in the door-way of the burgomaster's inn. It had seemed as if hours were passing between the rise of the curtain and your appearance ! "

" Ah, I dare say; we were all more or less anxious."

" But let us get away from the theatre. What do you look back upon so far, to remember with special pleasure, in the way of social entertainment and American hospitalities ? "

" It is difficult to select, is it not? It is bewildering to try to select the incidents. The Lotos dinner,—that was glorious, eh! How well Whitelaw Reid spoke!—and Mr. Depew, Dr. Macdonald, General Porter, Mr. Oakey Hall,—everybody, in fact. A great gift to be able to express your thoughts well, standing up in the presence of others ! Then the Lambs Club. I felt their reception as a very pleasant thing, because there were so many actors present. I think I got well out of the speech-making there by adopting Florence's written oration. That amused me greatly, and I think Florence enjoyed it as much as the others. Well, those are two of the New York events. I am endeavouring to think of them in their order, categorically. The breakfast which Mr. Joseph Harper gave me at the University Club,—what a rare lot of men! Mr. George William Curtis [1] struck me as one who might be very eloquent as a speaker."

[1] On a later occasion Mr. Curtis (whose eloquence on the platform and in the press, and whose independent career in politics, are familiar to all Americans and to many English) and Mr. Joseph Harper had a box to see " The Merchant of Venice." Irving invited them to go behind the scenes, and afterwards to join him at supper in his room at the Brevoort. Mr. Curtis said it was the first time he had been on that side of the footlights. " I am not sure whether I regret it or not;

"He is."

"So I should have thought, and he talks of the stage with the unsophistication of one who knows nothing about it mechanically, but is full of the romantic and poetic spirit of it. Let me see, it was at Franklin Square where we saw that modern Dutch interior."

"The private room at Harpers and Brothers?"

"Yes, and where we again met Mr. Curtis, Mr. Alden, the editor of the magazine, and Mr. Conant of *The Weekly*, I remember. Don't you think that when America once takes up the work of a complete representation of legitimate and established plays, she will

I think I am sorry to have the illusion of that last lovely scene at Belmont set aside even for a moment." While he was talking to Miss Terry in her dress as the Lady of Belmont, Loveday's men were bringing on some of the scenery of "The Lyons Mail." Said Harper, "Behind the scenes is always to me a good deal like the 'tween decks of a ship; the discipline is just as strict, too." During the evening, after supper, Mr. Curtis discussed with his host the question of how much an actor may lose himself in a part, and still have full control over it and himself. Irving said circumstances sometimes influenced an actor. An event which had disturbed him during the day might give extra colour to his acting at night. In fact an actor is influenced by all sorts of causes,—as all other people are in their daily work,—by health or weather. Sometimes the presence of a friend in front, or some current occurrence of the moment, or piece of bad or good news, might influence him; but, as a rule, after an actor had played a particular part for a long time, he generally played it very much in the same way every night. "There is a story," he said, "of Kean and Cooper which is to the purpose. A friend met Kean, and told him that on a particular night he was at the theatre, and thought that Kean played Othello better than ever he had seen him play it. 'Gad, sir,' he said, 'I thought you would have strangled Iago outright!' Now we come to the solution of this extra energy which had impressed Kean's friend. 'Oh, yes,' said Kean; 'it was a Tuesday night, I remember; Cooper tried to get me out of the focus!' In those days the theatre was lighted with oil lamps, and only at one particular place on the stage could the actors be seen. To be in the light was to be in the focus; and that accounts for the old habit they had of getting into a line along the footlights."

go ahead at it as fast as she has done in the production of book-engravings ? "

" I do."

" And they tell me—actors tell me—that they have never had Shakespeare as completely and as worthily represented as at the Star this week. Mr. Gilbert says it will work a revolution in dramatic art in this country."

" The papers are beginning to say so all round."

" I confess I am as surprised as I am delighted. I thought more had been done in the way of harmonious representation, grouping, colour, painting, lighting, than is evidently the case. By the way, I heard a good deal about this on the night of the Century Club reception. They were very like Garrick men, many of them. An excellent idea having an exhibition of pictures at a club ! I suppose it would hardly do in London to allow members such a margin in regard to the friends they introduce as in New York. I wish it could be done, and, especially, that granting of the entire privileges of the club to the stranger whom you invite to dinner. In case of transient membership, the compliment we pay to a stranger at the Garrick does include all the privileges of the club. The Manhattan is a cosy club. We got our first canvas-back in New York there. It was a little too early in the season; but in the way of a terrapin and canvas-back dinner the feast Buck gave us at Sieghortner's was a triumph.

---

[2] This was a very notable gathering on November 18. In nearly every case the guests came from long distances. They were all men of distinction in their several walks of life. Among them were, James H. Rutter, President New York Central and Hudson River Railway ; Hon. Noah Davis, Chief Justice Supreme Court, State of New York; Geo. R. Blanchard, Vice-President New York, Lake Erie, and Western Railway ; Gen. Horace Porter, President New York, West Shore, and Buffalo Railway ; John B. Carson, Vice-President and General Manager Hannibal and St. Joseph Railway, Hannibal, Mo.; Col. P. S. Michie, U.S. Army, West Point ; Hon. A. J. Vanderpoel, New York ; Hon. Wm. Dorsheimer, Member of Congress and ex-

It scored by its simplicity. Let me see, I have the *menu* here. Now to look at it, in comparison with what

Lieut.·Governor New York; Col. L. M. Dayton, Gen. Sherman's Chief of Staff during the war, Cincinnati, O.; Jas. N. Matthews, Proprietor Buffalo *Express*, Buffalo, N.Y.; Hon. Henry Watterson, ex-M.C. and editor *Courier Journal*, Louisville, Ky.; Col. Wm. V. Hutchings, Governor's Staff, Boston, Mass.; Col. H. G. Parker, Proprietor *Saturday Evening Gazette*, Boston, Mass.; Col. Wm. Edwards, Cleveland, O.; Hon. L. I. Powers, Springfield, Mass.; Hon. M. P. Bush, Buffalo, N.Y.; John B. Lyon, Chicago, Ill.; Hon. A. Oakey Hall, ex-Mayor of New York City; Lord Bury, W. J. Florence, William Winter, Stephen Fiske, J. H. French, and Chas. Wyndham. The dinner was not reported in the press; nor were several other entertainments which are briefly sketched in the pages of these " Impressions."

The Chief Justice spoke in eloquent terms of Lord Coléridge, whom the American bar and bench had been proud to honour, and who, in his private and public life, realized the highest ideal of the American people. "It is our desire," he said, "the sincerest wish of America, to like the English people. We are always afraid that our visitors from the old country will not let us like them. When they do, and we can honestly respond, we are glad." Presently, alluding to Irving, he said, "We have watched your career over a long period of time, through the New York papers. We were prepared to be interested in you, and to bid you welcome. No people are more moved than ours to exercise their free and unbiased judgment. We have done so in your case, and are proud to acknowledge the greatness of the work you have done; to welcome you, and to take your hand, not only for what you have achieved in England, but for what you have done for us in America."

Ex-Mayor Oakey Hall, in the course of some remarks supplementary of the speech of the Lord Chief Justice, said, "A morning cable despatch informs me that the Millais portrait of our guest was yesterday added to the walls of the Garrick Club, in completion of its gallery of David Garrick's legitimate successors. But on the walls of our memories to-night has been hung the original, impressive features, poetic eyes and hair, and a face so bright that it this moment reflects our looks of personal affection. I have had the personal felicity, thrice within the past fortnight, of seeing our guest in the serenity of private life. Friends knowing this have said to me, 'How did you like Henry Irving on the stage?' And I have answered, 'I have not yet seen Mr. Irving act.' True, I had seen, on the stage of the Star Theatre, Mathias, and Charles the First, and

is called a swell dinner, some people would think its
dishes wanting in variety and number. Somebody, I
Louis the Eleventh, and Shylock, and Duboscq and Lesergne,
and against these characters I had seen printed on the bills of
the play the name of Henry Irving; but never had it otherwise
occurred to me, as an auditor, that the guest now before us,—
original of the Millais picture,—and whom I saw at the banquets
of the Lotos and Manhattan clubs, was representing these
characters. On the contrary, I cannot connect Henry Irving,
the gentleman of private life, with the actor. If you say he is
the same, I must believe you. Indeed, I am now conscious of
having lived in the seventeenth century, and of having beheld
the veritable Charles as a man caressing his children and his
Henrietta Maria,—a wife rather than a queen,—on the banks of
the Thames, at Hampton Court, or as Majesty rebuking Oliver
Cromwell. Nay, I have stood with Charles himself in the
Whitehall Chamber of Death, and with my own streaming eyes
I have witnessed his touching farewell of home and earth. I
have forgotten the merchants of New York in the boxes, and I
have really seen Shakespeare's Merchant of Venice. I have
seen the dreaming victim of remorse. I have lived in the war-
rent realms of France, while Louis the Eleventh infected his
court with his own moral leprosy. I have known in 'The Lyons
Mail' the self-respecting and shrinking merchant, and I have
known his double, the besotted brute of a murderer. They are
all realities to me at this moment. If you again tell me one man
personated all these, and that this one man was the original
yonder of the Millais portrait, I must believe you, for your
honour's sake. During an active career of a quarter century I
never had seen an approach to such a surrender of personal
identity in an actor, nor such a surrender of the peculiarities of
one representation when the actor grasped another. How all
this contradicts a lively writer in the current (November)
number of Clement Scott's *Theatre*, who declares that every
great success of the stage is due to a correspondence of the
natural peculiarities of an actor with the fictional peculiarities
of the character portrayed. Is yonder gentleman a victim to
remorse? Is he a Shylock? Is he a Duboscq? Has he the
soul of a Charles? Least of all, has he one peculiarity of
Louis? No. Then these great successes are won—if yonder
guest be the actor—by a destruction of personal peculiarities
and by portraying his own precise opposites, in his human
nature. You have all seen these recently enacted characters.
You now—some of you for the first time—behold the man
Henry Irving, and hear him converse. To you as a jury,
then, I appeal. Am I not right? Is not my experience
yours? " (Ay!—Yes!—Yes!—and great applause.)

remember, said at the time, ' This is a man's dinner !
Let us dissect it ! ' "

He had fetched the *menu* from his table, had returned
to his seat by the fire, and was holding the *carte* before
his face, partly to read it, and partly to ward off the
glow of the hot coal.

" Now, *first,* oysters on the half shell, and I noticed
they were on the half shell. That is the proper way
to serve an oyster, and they should be in their own
liquor.³ They were lying on a bed of crushed ice,—
did you notice ? The dainty half of a lemon was
placed in the centre of them. Shall you include this
conversation in the book ? "

This last question he asked suddenly.

" Oh, yes ; I think it will be very interesting."

" Then they will say I am a gourmand." ⁴

" Who ? "

₃ " Bathed in their own liquor."—*Sir Henry Thompson.*

₄ In case this charge against Irving should be exploited by the
" little English correspondent " who undertakes to describe his
" Palace on the Thames," let me say that, for one who talks so
well about eating, Irving—next to a great authority on gourman-
dise—recently dead, alas !—is the most moderate diner I know.
He discourses of dishes with the eloquence of Brillat Savarin,
and eats as frugally as the " Original Walker " did, and is as
easily contented as was my late friend Blanchard Jerrold
(" Fin-Bec "), who wrote so much, and always so well, about the
art of dining, that those who did not know him might naturally
have regarded him as a gourmand. He knew the literature of
" the table " thoroughly, but lived as simply as Irving does. It
will be noted that it is the simplicity of the dinner under notice
that awakens Irving's enthusiasm. New York, by the way,
has many restaurants, in addition to its most famous one (Delmonico's) and the best house in Lafayette Place. The Hoffman
House and the Brunswick are well known for their excellent
cuisine. Among the hotels that are equally famous for their
chefs are the Everett House, the Windsor, the St. James', the
Victoria, and the Clarendon. The latter is to New York what
such establishments as Morley's and the oldest West End hotels
are to London. It is one of the pleasantest, and certainly the
quietest, of New York houses. There are very bad hotels in the
United States, and very good ones ; dear hotels, and hotels where
the charges are fair ; but the general idea of uniform excellence

K

" Some of our friends in London."
He emphasized the word " friends."
" They do now; you are reported as giving suppers
and banquets in London on a grander scale than ever
Lucullus dreamed of ! "
" Am I ? Well, I like to have my friends around
me; but I think they appreciate a mutton-chop, a glass
of fine wine, and a good cigar as much as we do, and,
after all, Dr. Johnson says, ' The man who can't take
care of his stomach can't take care of anything else.'
If to be a gourmand, or, rather, let us say *gourmet*,[5] is to
enjoy a well-cooked and elegantly served little dinner
or supper, then I plead guilty to the soft impeach-
ment; so let us go on eating the Sieghortner banquet
over again, just as we shall, I hope, in future years sit
down and re-fight our American victories by an English
fireside. To return to the bill of fare. *Second*, soup.
A vegetable soup, that reminded me a little of the
cock-a-lnkie which is so well constructed at the Garrick
in London, only that the vegetable basis of it is in
an esculent we have not,—the gumbo, or okra, which is
so delicious here. Sauterne with the oysters, and a
remarkably fine sherry with the soup. *Third*, terrapin.
I am told this came from Baltimore ready for the
cook."
" They are celebrated at Baltimore for the three
great American dishes,—oysters, terrapin, and canvas-

and uniform dearness which obtains in England is incorrect.
One class of houses which the English traveller misses is the
comfortable family inn or tavern (where the landlord and landlady are always at hand), common in England, France, and
Germany; and the other absent luxuries, for the lack of which
oysters and canvas-back ducks do not altogether compensate
him, are the mutton-chop, the beefsteak, the ham and bacon,
the sole, salmon, and bloaters of his own country.

[5] " The difference between a *gourmet* and gourmand we take
to be this : a *gourmet* is he who selects, for his nice and learned
delectation, the most choice delicacies, prepared in the most
scientific manner ; whereas the gourmand bears a closer analogy
to that class of great eaters, ill-naturedly (we dare say) denomi-
nated or classed with aldermen."—*Haywood's Art of Dining.*

back ducks. Terrapin is prepared there and shipped to all parts of the United States, and even to Europe. I am told that a Baltimore firm sends in the season supplies of terrapin and canvas-backs to England for the table of the Prince of Wales."

"Indeed," he answers, "his Royal Highness knows what is good! I wish he could have tasted the Baltimore terrapin at Sieghortner's. Buck is a friend of the Duke of Beaufort, and the Duke, they say, is up to all the luxurious tricks of American cooking.

"Now we are at the terrapin. It was handed round very hot, and, as your plate was removed, a fresh supply, better still, it seemed to me, was placed before you. It is polite to ask for terrapin twice ; but, that no one might be embarrassed, it was served twice. Champagne and Burgundy with the terrapin. I prefer champagne. 'Next to going to heaven,' said a friend near me, 'is to go down to —— , Baltimore, and eat terrapin.' *Fourth,* canvas-back duck. An entire breast of the bird on each plate. A chip-potato and a little celery ; you should eat nothing else with a canvas-back duck, though some persons, I observe, take currant or cranberry jelly with it. As in the case of the terrapin, there were two courses of duck,—the first, roast ; the second, grilled and devilled. An excellent notion this. A *soufflé* followed ; then cheese ; then coffee. That was the dinner ; and it was one of the greatest successes I remember, in the way of dining ; though I do not forget how perfectly we had terrapin and canvas-back cooked in our own humble little kitchen at the Lyceum Theatre."

"In responding to the toast of your health, you were very much moved?"

"I was. Chief Justice Davis supplemented the host's words so eloquently, and with so much heart and earnestness, that he touched me deeply. Then his references to England—to Lord Coleridge representing the high estate of the Bench, and to myself as being considered worthy in every way to represent my art, as he in his way is to represent his high calling—and his tender tributes to the old country, and to the deep, sincere friendship that lies at the root of the relations between England and America,—this was all so sympathetic. And when I knew that many of the men around the board who cheered him so warmly had come as far as a thousand miles to meet me, I could not have attempted to say more than to try and thank them. There are occasions when silence is the best, when ' Gentlemen, I thank you ; my heart is too full to say more,' is about the most eloquent speech you can make. Mr. John B. Lyon came all the way from Chicago in response to Buck's invitation ; Mr. John B. Carson came from Quincy,—a day's journey farther than Chicago ; he had been fifty-two hours on the train ; Mr. Watterson,—what a bright, witty fellow he is !—came almost as far, from Louisville in the South."

II.

" THE supper given to me by Mr. Florence, at the St. James' Hotel, was also an entertainment to remember. Quite a little family party, was it not ? Mr. Jerome — Larry, as his friends call him—was splendid ; and how many years of local dramatic history he had at his fingers' ends ! We were quite a little family party ; Gilbert, Edwards, Jefferson,—God bless him !—they were among the guests. Florence, if you remember, had after supper a great brass urn placed upon the table, sat before it, and made whisky toddy. How well actors understand the art of sociability ! ' Now, friends, let us gather round the tea-table,' said Florence, ' and try the brew ! ' We pronounced it ' nectar for the gods,' and so it was. Do you remember the interesting episode of his boyish days that Florence told us ? I repeated it to some people who supped here the other night. It is worth printing, with his permission."

" And that of Mrs. Florence ? " I suggest.

" Oh, yes, of course. I think I remember it. Florence was a very young man, a boy, in fact, and was

filling one of his first engagements on any stage at the
Bowery Theatre. A girl about his own age (who is
now a wife, and a woman of position, in New York) in
the company, was his first love. His adoration was
mingled with the most gallant respect. Their salaries
were about ten to twelve dollars each a week. For a
time they only played in the first piece; for in those
days two plays a night were more popular on the
American stage than they are now. One evening, at
about nine o'clock, after pulling himself together for
so daring an effort in his course of courtship, he asked
her if she would go to an adjacent restaurant and take
something to eat. The house was kept by a person of
the name of Shields, or Shiells. The supper-room
was arranged something after the manner of the old
London coffee-houses. It had compartments divided
off from each other. Into one of these Florence
escorted his sweetheart. He asked her what she would
take. After some hesitation, and a good deal of
blushing (more probably on his part than on hers), she
said oyster-stew and lemonade. He concluded to have
the same,—an incongruous mixture, perhaps; but
they were boy and girl. Florence was more than once
on the eve of declaring his undying passion and asking
her to name the day. Presently, supper being ended,
they rose to go, and Florence discovered that he had
come away without his purse, or, rather, his pocket-
book, as they call it here. He explained to the Irish
waiter (and Florence, I suspect, is himself of Irish descent), who cut him short by saying, 'No money? Oh,
that won't do; you're not going to damage the moral
character of the house, bringing of your girls here,
and then say you can't pay the bill.'—'How dare
you, sir!' exclaimed Florence, the girl shrinking back.
'Dare! Oh, bedad, if you put it that way, I'll just
give you a piece of my mind;' and he did. It was a dirty
piece, which hurt the poor young fellow. 'Take me to
your master,' he said. The girl was crying; Florence
was heartbroken. The master was not less rude than

the man. 'Very well,' said the boy; 'here's my watch
and ring. I will call and redeem them in the morning
with the money. I am a member of the Bowery Company, and I will ask the manager to call and see you
also. Your conduct is shameful!'—'By heaven, it is!'
exclaimed a stranger, who, with some others, was
smoking near the desk of the clerk, or landlord. 'It
is infamous! Cannot you understand that this young
gentleman is a good, honest young fellow? Damme!
you ought to apologize to him, and kick that waiter-
fellow out. Don't frown at me, sir. Give the young
gentleman his watch and ring. Here is a fifty-dollar
bill; take what he owes, and give me the change.'
The stranger was a well-dressed gentleman, with white
hair; not old, but of a venerable appearance. They
all went out together, Florence, the young lady, and
their benefactor. As they stepped into the street,
Florence said, 'I cannot sufficiently thank you, sir.
Where shall I call and leave the money for you?'—
'Oh, don't trouble yourself about it,' said the benevolent gentleman; 'your surly friend won't make much
out of the transaction,—it was a counterfeit bill that
he changed for me.'"

III.

IRVING did not expect to be called upon for a set
speech at the Lambs Club. The President, Mr.
Florence, did, and was prepared. He made no secret
of his nervousness, nor of his arrangements against
failure. The manuscript of his address was lying
before him during the dinner. He consulted it occasionally, to the amusement of his neighbours. When
the time came he rose, his speech in his hand, his heart
in his mouth. The most eminent of actors have felt
similar sensations under the influence of an exaggerated
sense of the responsibility of making a public speech.
This banquet of the Lambs was not reported in the
newspapers. As in other instances where I have ventured to annex speeches and incidents for these pages,

I have done so with the full consent of all the parties concerned.

"Gentlemen," said President Florence, "we have met to-night to do honour to a brother actor, for in that character do we welcome the distinguished guest of the evening,—an artist who has done more to elevate and dignify our calling than any actor that ever trod the stage."

A ringing cheer greeted these few sentences. The applause evidently disturbed the speaker's memory. He consulted his MS. and could make nothing of it. Throwing it upon the table, he continued his address. The few unstudied sentences that followed came from the heart, and were sufficiently effective. They commended Irving as an example to all of them,—an example of work, of unostentation, of success worthily won and worn, and expressed the gratification it afforded the Lambs—a club largely composed of actors—to welcome him at their board.

"I'll never make another speech as long as I live!" exclaimed the President, as he resumed his seat.

"Give me the manuscript," said Irving. "Do you mind my using it?"

"Not at all, my dear friend; do what you like with it."

Irving, rising to reply, stood up with the President's unspoken speech in his hand. Referring to the difficulties actors often experience in regard to public speaking, he said, "At Edinburgh, recently, looking over the old *Courant,* I came across an incident apropos of the present occasion. It was concerning a dinner given to John Kemble in that city. 'The chair was taken at six o'clock by Francis Jeffrey, Esq., who was most ably assisted by the croupiers, John Wilson and Walter Scott,'—the creator in fiction of poor, old, wretched King Louis XI.—Walter Scott, the mighty master of romance, who also proposed this night 'The memory of Burns.' (Applause.) In reply to the toast of his health, John Kemble said, 'I am not successful in extemporaneous delivery ; actors are so much more in the habit of giving utterance to the thoughts of others than in embodying their own, that we are much in the same position with those animals who, subsisting by the aid of others, are completely lost when abandoned to their own resources.' Gentle-men, brother actors, I feel that I am in a similar condition to-night. (Cries of ' No ! no ! ' and laughter.) But my friend, the President, has given me leave to avail myself of the eloquent speech which he had written, but has not read to you." (Laughter.)

Irving looked down at the President for his final consent.

" Certainly, go ahead," was the response.

" The President," said Irving, reading the MS. amidst shouts of laughter and applause, " was anxious to tell you that ' the efforts of the guest of the evening have always been to make his dramatic work in every way worthy the respect and admiration of those who honour our art ; and at the same time he has been none the less indefatigable in promoting the social and intel-lectual standing of the profession ; this has been to him a labour of love.' "

Irving read these lines with mock-oratorical show ; but when the laughter of his hearers changed to loud applause, he laid aside the written speech of his friend, and in a few simple words expressed himself proud of the honour the club had done him, and grateful for the cordiality of its welcome.

" There is one point, however, in that speech which I would like you to hear," said the President, rising again, and it is this : " We are not here to pass an opinion on Mr. Irving's qualities as an actor,—the critics have done that already ; and, if you had at first any doubts as to the high position he should occupy in our profession, the American critics and your own judgment have removed them. Possibly it was just as well that David Garrick did not live in the White Star epoch, for, had he ever crossed the Atlantic

Ocean, his bones might not now be reposing so peacefully under the ancient towers of Westminster Abbey."

During the evening Mr. Henry Edwards,[6] of Wallack's, recited with stirring effect the following :—

WELCOME TO HENRY IRVING.

Round about the board of banquet
    Blazed the bright wits of the town,
" A royal toast," and well they drank it—
    " 'Tis for a king to wear the crown ;
Thrones may totter in the tempest,
    Empires, too, may rise and fall,
But a king, by grace of Genius,
    Sits secure above them all."

Thus a grave and graceful poet,
    And his glowing glass uplifts,
With a warm eye-flash of welcome
    To the Man of Many Gifts ;
Then a clamour and kindly clinking
    Like sudden song breaks round the board,
And the soul of the wine they're drinking
    Seems into their own souls pour'd.

And " Huzza for our guest, King Irving,"
    From a hundred hearty throats,
And the lovingly lengthen'd greeting,
    Like a chorus'd chime, up floats—
When more swift than an earthly echo
    Bursts a sound over guest and hosts,
Strangely shrill, yet faint and far off—
    " Way there for the coming ghosts ! "

Into statued silence stricken,
    Stand and gaze the speechless throng,
While the walls slide wide from side to side,
    As if moved in grooves along,
And a shadowy stage, whose footlights
    Loom white through a weirdly mist,
Is peopled with phantoms of players
    Trooping in as if keeping a tryst.

---

[6] These lines were written by Mrs. Marion Fortescue, a lady well known in New York society.

Then with buskin'd steps and soundless,
  Streaming forward as a tide,
Surge the serried shades of actors
  Whose greatness time has testified;
And their brows are bound with bay-leaves,
  And their garments' phantom'd fold
Shape out the bygone costumes
  Of the parts they play'd of old.

All the fine and famous faces
  In the records of the stage,
Canonized in highest places
  On the drama's brightest page!
Their "brief hour" made eternal,
  Where the deathless laurel nods,
And where Shakespeare reigns supernal
  In the green-room of the gods!

There, each grandly vision'd visage,
  Looking through a mellow haze
On the spell-bound reverent watchers
  With a long, fraternal gaze,
Whose mute and mighty meaning
  Seems like a benediction cast
O'er the promise of the present
  By the high priests of the past!

Then, at an unseen, silent signal,
  Given by some mystic chief,
Each of the ghosts of great ones
  From his own wreath plucks a leaf,
And fleeter than arrow'd lightning
  Through space a chaplet's sped!
And the brow of the actor living
  Is laurelled by actors dead!

And a sigh sweeps over the silence,
  And the walls are walls again,
While the lights flash up to brightness
  And sparkles the gold champagne;
And the joyous voice of the Poet
  Rings out the blended toasts,
" Huzza for our good guest, Irving!"
  And " Huzza for our grand old ghosts!"

IV.

For the last night of the New York engagement the
programme was a novelty, in every respect, to a New

York audience. Custom confines the night's entertainment in American theatres to one piece. On this occasion the play-bill contained the first act of "Richard III.;" the Lyceum version of "The Belle's Stratagem;" the, in England, well-known recitation of "Eugene Aram;" and Irving was also expected to make a speech. The programme was played to an enthusiastic audience; and, at the close of "The Belle's Stratagem," Mr. Irving addressed them as follows :—

"Ladies and Gentlemen,—A month ago, standing before you for the first time, and stimulated by your most kind welcome, I expressed the hope that our loves might increase as our days did grow. You, on your part, have fulfilled my dearest wishes, and I can but hope that we have not disappointed you. On that same first night I bespoke your good-will for my sister artist, Ellen Terry. I felt sure that she would win all hearts, and I believe she has. For her, for all my comrades, and for myself, I thank you for your enthusiastic and generous endorsement of our work. I am sorry that the time has come when I must leave you. I am glad that I have not yet to say 'Good-bye,' but only '*Au revoir.*' In April next we shall have the honour—if all be well—of appearing before you again, and I would propose to present to you 'Much Ado About Nothing' and 'Hamlet.' In my old home, on the other side of the Atlantic, these plays are often performed by us; and I hope they will be welcome in—if I may say so—my new home on this side of the sea. And now, ladies and gentlemen, with a grateful remembrance of your kindness, I must say '*Au revoir.*' I find no words to adequately express my gratitude to you; indeed, I would feel but little if I could say how much."

Retiring for a few minutes, Irving, in evening dress, returned to the stage. A chair was placed in the centre of it. Now standing, now sitting, he recited Hood's dramatic poem. The audience sat spell-bound. Even as Mathias, with the accessories of the mysterious court-scene, Mr. Irving had not held New York play-goers with a firmer grip. They followed the grim story almost in silence. The ancient mariner's narrative did not more impress the wedding-guest. I have seen all kinds of audiences in both hemispheres, and under all sorts of circumstances, and never saw a theatre full of people more under the control of a story. At the end the applause was loud and continued for some minutes, the reciter having to bow his acknowledgments again and again. The next day a discriminating critic pointed out to one of Irving's few opponents, that "the *pseudo* critic who pronounced Irving's 'Bells' a mere success of lime-lights, properties, scenery, and stage-management," had been quite extinguished "by the recitation of Hood's 'Dream of Eugene Aram,' delivered in evening dress, without any lime-lights, properties, scenery, or stage-management."

"And," added a journalistic writer in the *Herald*, "aside from the artistic success Mr. Irving has made here, the financial result should be considered very satisfactory. The total amount received from subscriptions and box-office sales for the four weeks' engagement is $75,687. The receipts for the first week were $15,772; for the second week, $18,714; for the third week, $18,880; and for the week closing last evening, $22,321." It has been estimated that the public paid altogether, to speculators and to the box-office, upwards of $200,000. Judged, therefore, by the financial standard of the box-office, as well as by that of the highest criticism, New York's answer to the London *Standard* was a full and complete endorsement of the English popularity of Henry Irving and Ellen Terry."

But it remained for Boston, Philadelphia, and Chicago to pronounce upon them. The campaign was only in its infancy, though the first stronghold had been won. An advance was made upon Philadelphia on the day following the recitation of " Eugene Aram." The reader who follows the fortunes of the campaigners in these pages will find the record justified by independent pens, and supported by the current chronicles of the entire Union.

IX.

AT PHILADELPHIA AND "IN CLOVER."

Rivalries of American Cities—Boston and Philadelphia—The
real and the picturesque—Miss Terry's Portia—"Three
kinds of Criticism"—First appearance as Hamlet—Miss
Terry's Ophelia—Journalism and the Stage—Critics, past
and present—Philadelphia and English Cities—A new style
of Newspaper—Bogus Reports and Interviews : an example
of them—The Clover Club—A Letter from an eminent
American Tragedian—Presented with Forrest's Watch—
The Macready trouble—Hamlet, and an invitation from
Guest to Hosts.

I.

" THE rivalries between American cities," said Irving,
" seem to take a far more aggressive form than the
rivalry between England and America, or even between France and England ; I mean in regard to their
criticisms of each other, and their hostile chaff or
badinage in regard to each other's peculiarities."
" Is it not very much the same in England ? "
" Perhaps."
" Sheffield scoffs at Birmingham, Liverpool sneers
at Bristol, Manchester is supercilious concerning
London," I said.
" And London mildly patronizes the whole of them.
I think you are right; but one does not notice the
competition at home so much, perhaps, as in America.
Boston and Philadelphia seem to indulge in a good
deal of badinage at each other's expense."
" And they are both sarcastic about the morality of
Chicago."

" A Boston friend of ours," said Irving, " was telling me yesterday of a little war of words he had with a Philadelphian. Said Boston to the Quaker, 'Well, there is one thing in which you have the best of us.'— ' Glad you admit one point in our favour anyhow; what is it ? '—' You are nearer to New York than we are.' Our Boston friend is fond of New York, takes his holidays there; says he likes it nearly as well as London. A less subtle, but more direct, hit at Philadelphia was that of the Bostonian, who, in reply to the question of a Philadelphian, 'Why don't you lay out your streets properly ? ' said, ' If they were as dead as yours, we would lay them out.' "

" Looked at from a balloon," I said, " Philadelphia would have the appearance of a checker-board. Boston, on the other hand, would present many of the irregular features of an English city. Both cities are eminently representative of American characteristics, and both are possibly more English in their habits, manners, and customs than any other cities of the Union."

"There is nothing dead about the Philadelphia streets so far as I have noticed them," Irving replied. " This morning I walked along Chestnut Street, and thought it particularly lively and pleasant. The absence of the elevated railroad struck me as an advantage. I felt that when walking down Broadway, in New York. Then the cars in the street itself did not rush along at the New York pace. These seem to me to be advantages in their way on the side of life in Philadelphia. Perhaps one feels the rest, too, of a calmer city, a quieter atmosphere."

We are sitting near a front window at the Bellevue, looking out upon Broad Street. Presently we are joined by the interviewer, and Irving is not long before he is engaged in a conversation about the actor's art and his own methods.

" Every character," he says, " has its proper place on the stage, and each should be developed to its greatest excellence, without unduly intruding upon another, or impairing the general harmony of the picture. Nothing, perhaps, is more difficult in a play than to determine the exact relation of the real, and what I may call the picturesque. For instance, it is the custom in Alsatia for men to wear their hats in a public room; but in a play located in that country it would not do to have a room scene in which a number of men should sit around on the stage with their hats on. There are reasons why they should not do that. In the first place, their hats would hide their faces from the audience. It is also an incongruity to see men sitting in the presence of an audience with their heads covered. Then, again, the attention of the audience would be distracted from the play by a feeling of curiosity as to the reason why the hats were not removed. These are little things that should be avoided; but in general they are not likely to intrude themselves where proper regard is paid to the general appearance of a scene. The make-up of the stage is exactly like the drawing of a picture, in which lights and colours are studied, with a view to their effect upon the whole. There is another feature. I would not have the costume and general appearance of a company of soldiers returning from a war exactly the same as they appeared when the men were starting for the battle-field. I would have them dishevel their hair and assume a careworn aspect, but yet appear in clean clothes. Everything on the stage should always be clean and pleasant."

The subject of realism being mentioned, he said his death in "The Bells" had been called very realistic, whereas the entire story was unrealistic, in the strict sense, particularly the trial and death. "Dramatically poetic, if you like," he said, "but not realistic. There are so-called realisms on the stage that are no doubt offensive,—overstrained illustrations of the pangs of death, physical deformities, and such like. As for the interest of an audience in the person who is acting, the knowledge that what they see is an impersonation has its intellectual attractions for them. For instance, it would not be satisfactory to see an old man of eighty play 'King Lear;' but it would be highly satisfactory to an audience to know that the character was being portrayed by a man in the vigour of life. As you look upon a picture you do not see something that is real, but something that draws upon the imagination.

" Perhaps there is no character about which such a variety of opinions has been expressed as that of Hamlet, and there is no book that will give any one as much opportunity of understanding it as the 'Variorum Shakespeare' of Mr. Horace Howard Furness. He is still a young man,—he is not an old man,—and I trust that he will be able to complete the whole of the work that he has begun, and I hope that some one will follow in his footsteps. It was a labour of love, of most intense love to him, and he has earned the gratitude of all readers of Shakespeare. I hope I shall meet him."

II.

Irving's Louis made just as profound an impression here as in New York. "No finer performance has been seen on the Philadelphian stage for many years," said the *Ledger.* "From his first appearance on the stage to the moment when he falls dead upon the floor, he rose from climax to climax, and held, not the hearts, but the minds, of his audience captive," said the *Inquirer;* and these notices give the cue to the general criticisms. The other plays were equally well received. Shylock excited the usual controversy as to Shakespeare's intentions, but none as to Irving's interpretation of his own views. The critics, on the whole, were the honest mouthpieces of the audiences in regard to their enjoyment of the entire play. A writer, who confessed to disappointment in Miss Terry's Portia, and who counted Shylock's business as above his elocution, had " no words to express" his " admiration of the entire setting of the

L

piece," which he described as "a discovery and a conquest." It is no reflection upon the literary skill and critical power of the Philadelphia press, when it has to be admitted that here and there the notices bore evidence of an influence preceding Mr. Irving's appearance, notably in the criticisms of Hamlet.

"There are three kinds of criticisms," said Irving, when discussing this point one evening after a quiet supper : "the criticism that is written before the play ; the criticism that is more or less under the influence of the preconceived ideas that are associated with previous representations by other actors ; and the criticism that is *bonâ fide* a result of the night's performance, and also, in a measure, an interpretation of the opinions of the audience. What I mean by a criticism written before the play, is the notice that has been partially prepared beforehand, in connection with the literature of the subject, and the controversies as to the proper or improper views taken of the character under discussion. These start in on one side or the other, just as the writer feels about it, irrespective of the art that is exercised by the actor. This is more particularly the case in regard to Shylock and Hamlet. As to the latter character there is the natural loyalty some writers feel towards what is called the established or accepted Hamlet of the country. It is not given to all men to feel that art is universal and of no country. Don't think I am complaining ; I am not. I am trying to justify some of the Philadelphian notices of Hamlet, which were in opposition to the verdict of the audience before whom I played it in America for the first time."

"You were warned that Philadelphia claims to occupy the highest critical chair in America; and that, of all other cities, it would be the least likely to accept a new Hamlet, especially a natural and human Hamlet as against the artificial school—an impersonation as opposed to mere declamation."

"I think that decided me to play Hamlet for the

first time in Philadelphia; and I never played it to an audience that entered more fully into the spirit of my work."

"I have never," said a Philadelphian, "seen an audience in this city rise and cheer an actor as they cheered you when you took your call after the play scene in Hamlet. Such enthusiasm is unknown here. Miss Terry and yourself both might have had scene calls of the most cordial character. You refused them; it is a rule, I understand, with you to do so. The excitement of some audiences would have been dampened by these checks. Not so yours,—the calls at the close of the play were quite phenomenal for Philadelphia."

A numerous company of critics and reporters came from New York, Boston, and other cities, to be present at Irving's first appearance in Hamlet. Nowhere at any time during the tour were the influences of London so apparent as in the criticisms of Hamlet at Philadelphia. Some of them were entirely out of harmony with the warmly expressed satisfaction of one of the most intellectual audiences ever gathered together in the Chestnut Street Opera House.[1] For instance, the *Evening Bulletin* found in the duelling scene reminiscences of "æsthetic sketches from *Punch*," and the *Press* said, "It is unfortunate that Du Maurier has taken Miss Terry as the model of the æsthetic set. The curly blonde hair, delicate face, and soft, clinging

---

[1] "Mr. Irving presented a Hamlet last evening that was entirely consistent with itself and with the play, and the most virile, picturesque, and lovable Hamlet that has been seen on the stage. There was great variety in his moods and manners. He realized Goethe's idea of a born prince,—gentle, thoughtful, and of most moral nature, without the strength of nerve to make a hero, and overcome by the responsibility put upon him by a vision whose message he alternately accepts and doubts. There was, indeed, the fullest variety given to the part; it was dramatically interesting, and a clearly marked, intelligent study that more than realized the expectations that had been formed of the personation."—*Philadelphia Ledger.*

robes reminded one so often of *Punch's* caricature, that it was difficult to take it seriously." There is, in certain critical circles of Philadelphia, the same kind of affectation of a knowledge of English thought, and a following of London taste, as there is in London in regard to French art and French criticism. The audience at the Chestnut Street Theatre had no difficulty in taking Miss Terry's Ophelia seriously: There was hardly a dry eye in the house during her mad scene. The *Bulletin* critic aired his knowledge of English affectation by associating her with "Burns-Jonesism;" but the *Times* found "Miss Terry's Ophelia tender and beautiful, and pathetic beyond any Ophelia we have lately seen." The *Record* described it as "sweet and unartificial as the innocent and demented maiden Shakespeare painted for us." Said the *Inquirer*, in a criticism of singular literary force:—

In the play scene, in which he seemed to fill the whole stage, in which a real frenzy appeared to fall upon his mind, he justified by the greatness of his acting almost all that has been or could be said in praise of it. So grandly and impressively did he bring the scene to a close as to call down thunders of applause from an audience that he had thrilled and swayed by a power undeniably great. If that scene was ever before so nobly played, we were not there to see it done. Mr. Irving rose to greater heights of excellence as the play proceeded. From the moment Miss Terry put her foot upon the scene she held and controlled her audience as she would. Never before upon our stage has there appeared an actress who played Ophelia with such lovely grace and piteous pathos. To all who saw this most perfect performance it was a revelation of a higher, purer, and nobler dramatic art than they had ever seen or dreamed. What she did just here or there, or how she did it, cannot be told. Over it all was cast the glamour of the genius in which this fine woman is so greatly blessed. She does not seem to act, but to do that which nature taught her.

III.

TALKING of criticism and the press, the press and the stage, one evening, Irving expressed some views in regard to the influence and relations of the newspaper and the theatre which are full of suggestiveness and point.

" Journalism and the stage," he said, " have always been more or less in sympathy with each other. As they have progressed this sympathy may be said to have grown into an alliance in the best interests of civilization. As exponents of the highest thought of the greatest writers, as educationists of the most comprehensive character, the press and the stage are, I think, two of the most powerful institutions for good in our times, and represent the greatest possibilities in the future.

" It is interesting to contemplate how closely they are associated, these two institutions, artistically and commercially. The advertisements of the theatres represent a large revenue to the newspapers; the employment of writers and reporters in chronicling and commenting upon the work of the theatres represents, on the other hand, an important outlay for the newspapers. The press is telling the story of the theatre from day to day; and, while it extends an earnest and honest sympathy to dramatic art in its highest aspirations, I hope the time will come when the criticism of the work of the stage will be considered one of the most serious features that belong to the general and varied compositions of a newspaper.

" In the past we, in England, at all events, look upon but two men as critics in the most complete sense,—men who, by thought and study, feeling and knowledge, had the power to sympathize with the intention of the artist, to enter into the motives of the actor himself, criticizing his conceptions according to his interpretation of that which he desires to express. These two writers were Lamb and Hazlitt. But nowadays we have thousands of critics. Every newspaper in Great Britain has its critic. Even the trade journals, and some of the professedly religious journals, have their critics, and some of them speak with an emphasis and an authority on the most abstruse principles of art which neither Lamb nor Hazlitt would have dreamed of assuming. I don't know how this contrasts with America; but I am sure that when the conductors of the great journals of the two worlds are fully convinced of the deep interest and the friendly interest the people are taking in the stage, they will give increasing importance to the dramatic departments of their papers."

" You are going to a journalistic breakfast or supper one day this week," I said. " Is this your idea of the sort of speech you will make to them ? " I asked, for he expressed his opinions with more than ordinary firmness, seeing that the topic was comparatively new.

" Well, I thought of saying something," he replied, walking all the time about his room. " Do you think the relations of the stage and the press a good subject ? "

" Excellent," I said ; " a text worthy of an essay in the *Fortnightly* or the *Edinburgh Review.*"

IV.

TAKING a quiet stroll along Broad Street, and occasionally up and down the thoroughfares right and left, on the first Sunday afternoon of our arrival in Philadelphia, we paused to note the people coming out of church and chapel.

" You know that part of Manchester called Hulme," said Irving. " Is not this quarter like that ? Could you not fancy we were in almost any suburban part of Manchester ? And the people, do you see anything in their appearance to denote that they are any other than English ? "

" No ; they might be a Birmingham, or a Manchester, or a Liverpool crowd."

" Better dressed, perhaps, so far as the women go. This absence of strong contrasts between American and English is often noticeable. Nothing in that way struck me more forcibly than the Lotos Club dinner at New York. They might have been a gathering of

London clubmen, only that they all made such singularly humorous speeches. The English after-dinner oratory is more solemn. And the audience here last night,—I could not see their faces, of course; but I felt their influence, and their response to various points was very English. I am told that it is thoroughly American to hurry away the moment the curtain falls on the last act."

" It certainly is the general practice of American audiences. An English friend of ours, and a popular comedian here, was only telling me yesterday how the habit afflicts him and his company. ' At first,' he said, ' it was terrible. We thought we had utterly failed, and we shall never get used to it.' He asked me how it affected you. I would not hurt his feelings, of course, by telling him that your audiences, so far, had waited every night to applaud, and to call you and Miss Terry, and frequently other members of your company. I said you seemed to drop into the habits of the country easily."

" It is very generous, is it not? And I know they are making an exception with us, because my attention has been called to it so often. I drove down Chestnut Street yesterday. Have you noticed what a picturesque effect, both in form and colour, the sign-boards give to Chestnut Street? And there is something very clean and homelike about the private houses,—red brick mostly, with white marble steps and green blinds. The atmosphere of the place is calmer than New York. I have been reading a new daily paper here, the *Evening Call,*—very odd, clever kind of paper."

" Yes," I said; "it is a type of quite a new departure in daily journalism. The *Morning Journal,* in New York, and the *Evening News,* in Chicago, are examples in point. Akin to the first idea of the *Figaro,* in London, they are a little in the style of the *Cuckoo,* which croaked in the London streets for a short time. They may be considered as outside the competition of the regular high-class daily journals.

They occupy ground of their own.   Their leading idea
is to amuse, rather than to instruct. They employ
humorous versifiers, story-tellers, jesters.   They are
the cap and bells in print, the jester, or court-fool, in
newspapers; and sometimes are as personal as that
very strange jester in the American play of 'Francesca
da Rimini.'   How this new form of daily journalism
represents American civilization, or what side of it, is
a point which Mr. Arnold or Spencer may be left to
discuss.   I am glad you have noticed it, because I
have collected a few Philadelphian examples of its
style,—bright, easy, clever, frivolous, perhaps, and
sometimes a trifle broad, but full of go."

We sat down at the hotel to look over my notes, and
here are a few items from them :—

Theatre-goer.—"I notice that a favourite device with Irving,
in a moment of deep feeling, is for him to clutch and perhaps
tear open the collar or loose scarf that is around his neck."

Scarf Manufacturer.—"Well, I declare! That is the best
news that I have heard for a long time. Three cheers for
Irving!"

Theatre-goer.—"Why, man, are you demented?"

Scarf Manufacturer.—"Not at all. Can't you see? The
five hundred thousand amateur actors in this country will all
be imitating Irving, and the result will be the biggest kind of
a boom in scarves."

In the same column it is announced that "James
Malley wants to go on the stage," and the editor adds,
"We hope he will wait until eggs are cheaper." "You
cannot convert 15,000 tons into 20,000 tons," is
quoted as a remark of the late Lord Beaconsfield to
accentuate the general grievance about short weight
in coals. "Dizzy's remark clearly shows that he
knew nothing about the coal business." Plumbers in
America are subjects of much newspaper sarcasm.
"Three weeks ago," says the *Lock Haven Express*,
"the writer sent for a plumber, who never appeared,
but yesterday he sent in his bill." The *Call* prints
this to add, "He must have been a poor sort of plumber
to wait three weeks before sending in a bill." Chicago

looks down upon some of the Eastern cities, and there
is a rivalry between the journals of Chicago and the
cities that are scorned, which is often amusing. " The
only cure for love is marriage," says the *Call;* " the
only cure for marriage, divorce. Beware of imitations;
none genuine without the word ' Chicago ' blown on
the bottle."

An imaginary description of Irving's visit to the Rev.
Henry Ward Beecher, with an account of the family
dinner and conversation, was started by one of these
new daily papers, and it was repeated even by several
of the more serious journals in other cities as a genuine
thing. It is difficult sometimes to know when the news
of some of these papers is true. Ingenious readers
will probably ask in what respect they thus differ from
other papers. But our satirical friends must always
have their little joke. It strikes me as a weakness,
in the programme of some of the new sheets, that you
should for a moment be left in doubt as to when they
are in earnest and when in fun ; when they are recording
real events, or when they are chaffing history. Here
is an extract from the " bogus " report of Irving's visit
to Beecher :—

The party rested in the parlour until the dinner was ready.
The conversation was of an every-day nature, and did not enter
deeply either into theatricals or religion.

The party filed into the dining-room, Mr. Beecher behind,
turning his cuffs end for end as he walked. In this room was
a palatable show,—a big, fat goose, intrenched in gravy, and
flanked by all kinds of vegetables, slept the final sleep in the
centre of the table. Everything necessary accompanied the
star of the feast.

"Dark meat, Miss Terry?" asked the reverend gentleman as
he grasped the carver.

"If you please, with plenty of stuffing," returned the little
lady.

All were helped from the generous goose, and Mr. Beecher
sat down to enjoy his reward. He is very fond of onion
stuffing, and had taken care that it was not all gone before his
turn came.

"This goose," began Mr. Beecher, the bird's biographer, "has
a history. She is the seventh goose of a seventh—"

Just what the reverend gentleman was going to attribute to
the goose will not be known, as just then he tasted the stuffing.
There was no onion in it. A stern look came over his face, and
he was on the point of saying something when he caught the
warning glance from his wife's eyes and kept quiet. Nothing
was heard for ten minutes besides the tuneful play of knives,
forks, and dishes. The dinner was topped off with mince and
pumpkin pies, in whose favour the guests could not say too
much. After dinner a quiet, enjoyable talk was indulged in.
Mr. Beecher neglected his Sunday school to entertain the
artists. He highly complimented Irving by telling him that
he was a born preacher.

"If I were not pastor of Plymouth Church, I would be Henry
Irving," said Mr. Beecher.

"You are a born actor," said Mr. Irving. "As for myself,
there is no one I feel more inclined to envy than the pastor of
Plymouth Church."

Miss Terry was not slighted much in Mr. Beecher's meed of
praise. The topics of discussion momentarily changed from
America to England and back again, both of the leading gentlemen having well-stored minds that relieved them from "talking
shop."

At four o'clock the visitors departed, carrying and leaving
delightful impressions.

"Newspapers are not allowed to be noisily hawked
in the streets here, I find," said Irving; "and ticket
speculators on the sidewalks are also tabooed. A
little newsboy offered me a paper yesterday quite con-
fidentially. By the way, you saw the military band
belonging to the *Evening Call.* It is composed of
the *employés* of the newspaper. It looked like a band
of French guides. It serenaded Miss Terry at her
hotel yesterday, and afterwards serenaded me at mine.
I was just getting up. It quite affected me to hear
"God save the Queen" played as finely almost as if
the band of her Majesty's Guards were under my
window.[2]

[2] "DISTINGUISHED VISITORS.—The *Evening Call* band of fifty-
one pieces and the *Evening Call* flute and drum corps, numbering thirty-five pieces, making a total of eighty-six performers,
formed before the Union League building this morning, and
proceeded down Broad Street a few yards, to the Hotel Bellevue,
and tendered a complimentary serenade to the distinguished .

V.

"IRVING in Clover," was the journalistic title of a report of "a notable breakfast given to the English tragedian," which appeared in the *Philadelphia Press.* "A gathering of distinguished men listen to entertaining words by the famous actor; he is presented with the watch of Edwin Forrest." The "Clover Club" is one of the pleasantest of Philadelphian institutions. Its reception to Mr. Irving, and the Forrest incident, which makes the day historical in the annals of the stage, call for a special record. As I was travelling at this time to another city, I propose to repeat the chronicle of the local journalist, and Mr. Irving's own personal report of the interesting proceedings. Let me say, then, in the language of the *Press,* that on the morning of December 7th Mr. Irving broke his fast with the club

English actor, Henry Irving. Several delightful airs, including 'God save the Queen,' were rendered with fine effect. Mr. J. H. Coplestone, Mr. Abbey's manager for Mr. Irving, acknowledged the compliment on behalf of the eminent tragedian. The band then proceeded to the Aldine Hotel, where Miss Ellen Terry, Mr. Irving's leading lady, was serenaded, following which the musicians gave a short street parade. At the conclusion of the serenade Mr. Irving sent the following pleasant little note to the office of the *Evening Call:—*

" ' HOTEL BELLEVUE,

" 'PHILADELPHIA, 29th November ("Thanksgiving Day"), 1883.

" ' *To the Editor of the " Evening Call ":—*

" 'MY DEAR SIR,—Upon this day of universal thankfulness allow me to add a personal item. My thanks to you and your magnificent band for the honour done to me this morning by their serenade. I enjoyed the music much, and beg to add my tribute of praise to the worth of your band which, to my mind, is amongst the best I have heard. To hear the strains of the national anthem of my own dear land here, and on such a day, touched me much, and assures me again in a forcible manner of the strength of the affection between the two countries, America and England.

" ' Believe me to be, dear sir, yours very faithfully,

" ' HENRY IRVING.' "

Evening Call.

that has a four-leaved Shamrock on which to spread
its bounty, *À votre santé* for its toast cry, and for its
motto the quatrain,—

> While we live,
>   We live in clover;
> When we die,
>   We die all over.

The banqueting-room of the Hotel Bellevue, the
scene of so many memorable gatherings, and the
shrine at which the quadrifoil devotees ever worship,
had been turned into a fairy bower. The regular
clover table had an addition in the shape of a crescent;
spreading on either side from the stem of the club's
emblem, and from its centre, and concealing a pillar
supporting the floor above, arose what the florist's
art made to appear a gigantic plant. Its branches,
bearing numerous camellias, reached to the ceiling.
At its base, in a bed of emerald moss, grew ferns and
lilies. Smilax (a beautiful American creeper), in
graceful windings, covered the entire board, furnishing
a radiant green setting for dazzling glass and shining
silver, and handsome plaques of flowers and fruits.
Directly in front of the president of the club, and the
guest of the occasion, was a handsome floral structure,
from which the modest clover grew around the name
"Henry Irving," composed of radiant blossoms. On
the emblematic gridiron was placed the massive
"loving-cup." The walls of the room were covered
with precious works of art, and over all was shed the
mellow light of many wax candles, with their rays
subdued by crimson shades. The sunlight, so suggestive of business activity and all that rebukes feasting
and frivolity, was rigorously excluded from the scene
of pleasure. An English and American flag entwined
draped one end of the room.
Breakfast was served shortly at noon, fifty-three
gentlemen sitting around the clover-leaf.

After the " Baby "³ member, Colonel John A. McCaull, had descended from the high chair and been divested of his rattle, and the loving-cup had been passed around, and the game on the bill of fare had been reached, President M. P. Handy arose, and in a few fitting remarks introduced Mr. Irving, reminding him, in conclusion, that " this unconventionality is our conventionality," and, further, that he was expected " to stir up the animals."

After the warm applause that greeted him had sub-sided, Mr. Irving, in a conversational, unrestrained manner, spoke as follows :—

" Gentlemen,—I can never forget, so long as I live, the hearty welcome you have given me, coupled with such unusual and hearty hospitality. When it was first known that I was coming to Philadelphia, your club extended to me a most kind invitation,—the first invi-tation I received after my arrival in America, and one that will ever be memorable to me. Your great hospi-tality, and the gridiron there before me, has reminded me of an old organization of which I am a member— the Beefsteak Club. I hope I shall have the pleasure of welcoming some of the members of this club when-ever they cross the water. Should any of them come to London, I will endeavour to make some return for this unexpected welcome. I hope by that time we will have some of your unconventional conventionalities of which you have, in such an excellent manner, given me a specimen. I am told that speech-making is not part of the programme. Therefore I can do no better than follow the suggestion of my friend Dougherty, and give you an experience of my early life. I don't wish to do aught against the rules,—for I am a great stickler for rules,—which I see you carry out ; but I will tell you a little story concerning my early life, or it may possibly be the story of the early life of several of us."

And then Mr. Irving branched off into a recitation

³ The youngest member, who is provided with a tall chair, a rattle, and other things indicative of his " clover" childhood.

descriptive of how "some vast amount of years ago,"
a precocious youth—one Tom by name, and but eleven
years of age—had a prematurely amorous longing for
a spinster of thirty-two, who finally married an elder,
but hated, rival. At the conclusion of the recitation,
which was received with great laughter, he continued
his remarks, as follows :—

"I feel most fondly unto you, O Clovers! Many of
you, I believe, are associated with the press. Between
journalism and the stage there has always been a great
sympathy, and I fancy it will continue so until all
things cease to exist. I have often thought that the
stage is a sort of father of journalism,—it is a sort of
Utopian idea,—but from the days of the Greek drama
to the time of Shakespeare there was much news
discussed at the theatres, such as we now find in the
newspapers. Our interests are mixed. We represent
much of the newspaper treasury I know, in England,
and I fancy it is the same in this country. We are
therefore interested, to a very large amount, in the
newspapers, and I have found my friend, Charles
Wyndham, whom I am glad to meet at this board,
interested to the extent of anxiety concerning some of
his large advertisements.

"But this is not solely a gathering of journalists. I
have to-day the honour of meeting many gentlemen who
represent every class in Philadelphia,—every class of
professional calling. I will say from my very heart that
I thank you. I will remember, as long as I live, the
courtesy that has supplemented this sumptuous banquet,
and your kindness in calling me to meet such representative men. I am living next door to this room, and
had I only heard that I was to meet such a distinguished
gathering I am afraid I would have been deterred
from facing you. Mr. Handy, your president, has told
me that your conventionality consists in being unconventional, and I have tried to be as unconventional as
I possibly can. I thank you with all my heart."

At the conclusion of Irving's remarks, Secretary

Deacon read the following letter from the eminent
American tragedian, James E. Murdoch :—

Previous engagements of a domestic kind induce me to
send " Regrets," in reply to your invitation to breakfast with
the members of the Clover Club and their distinguished guest,
Mr. Henry Irving. In regard to certain " effects, defective "
consequent upon the " feast of reason and the flow of soul," I
am constrained to say, in the language of Cassio [somewhat
altered], " I have but a poor and unhappy stomach for feasting."
I am unfortunate in the infirmity, and dare not task my
weakness with the tempting dishes of mind and matter so
bountifully served up at complimentary festivals. I hope it
will not be considered out of place for me to state that I have
had the pleasure of meeting Mr. Irving socially, and of witnessing
some of his performances. I esteem him as a man of gentle
manners, and regard him as a dramatic genius. He appears
to me to possess, in an eminent degree, all those qualities of
thought and action which marked so strikingly the historical
career of Macready and Charles Kean, and which established
the reputation of those gentlemen for consummate skill in stage
direction, and for exquisite portraiture of dramatic characters.
Desiring to be excused for the obtrusion of my opinion, allow
me to add : although I shall not have the pleasure of sitting
down to your banquet, I take pleasure in saying :—
" Now, good digestion wait on appetite and health on both—"
. . . " Come, love and health, to all " . . .

I drink to the general joy of the whole table, and especially
to the health and happiness of your accomplished and worthy
guest.
Yours, always, in the bonds of good-fellowship,
JAMES E. MURDOCH.

The next episode of the memorable occasion was one
that almost moved Mr. Irving to tears. It was as
great a surprise to many members of the club as it was
to the guest of the day. Thomas Donaldson, a well-
known Clover, after some remarks concerning the
drama, in which he spoke of the United States having
1800 theatres, 20,000 actors and actresses, and
spending $40,000,000 for theatrical entertainment,
said : " Mr. Irving, I desire to present you with the
watch of the greatest genius America ever produced
on the mimic stage,—Edwin Forrest." Mr. Irving

clasped the relic extended to him and reverently kissed
it. He remained on his feet, having impulsively arisen,
and in a voice deep with feeling spoke again :—
" You have bereft me of all words. My blood alone .
can speak for me in my face, and if my heart could tell
it would describe to you my gratitude. This recalls so
many memories that you will pardon me if I am not
able to express my deep gratitude for this mark of
affection. I say affection, for to receive here such a
memento of your great country is more than I could
have dreamt of. To think that to-day, before so many
distinguished Americans, a watch could be given to
me that belonged to Edwin Forrest ! It recalls a most
unfortunate affair; I refer to the *contretemps* between
Forrest and my countryman, Macready. That such a
tribute should have been offered me shows how changed
is your feeling towards art; shows how cosmopolitan
art is in all its phases. I shall wear this watch, Mr.
Donaldson, close to my heart. It will remind me of
you all, and of your city and of your country,—not
that I need anything to remind me,—but close to my
heart it will remind me of your friendship ; and with
all my heart I thank you."
    As Irving sat down he kissed the watch again,
and then placed it in the upper left-hand pocket of
his vest. Accompanying the timepiece, which had
been Mr. Donaldson's private possession, were papers
proving the authenticity of its original ownership.⁴

⁴ The documentary evidence handed to Irving as establishing
the identity of the watch are : (1) a copy of the catalogue of the
sale by auction of " the estate of Edwin Forrest, deceased," at
Davis and Harvey's Art Galleries, No. 1212, Chestnut Street,
Philadelphia, on Feb. 4, 1883 ; (2) a copy of the supplementary
catalogue of " the personal effects of Edwin Forrest," which sets
forth twenty-eight articles, including a silver watch ; (3) the
auctioneer's receipt for " One silver watch, the property of
Edwin Forrest ;" and (4) a voucher from Mr. Donaldson, in which
he states that, until he presented it to Mr. Irving, the watch had
never been out of his possession from the time that he bought
it. Mr. Donaldson is a collector of *bric-à-brac*, and possesses

Ex-Attorney-General MacVeagh was the next speaker, and he paid a very graceful tribute to foreign theatrical and operatic artists, and the welcome they receive in these days on the shores of America.

Mr. Henry Howe (a leading member of Mr. Irving's company), who, for forty consecutive years, was a member of the Haymarket Theatre company, made a warm defence of Macready anent the Forrest trouble. "I have heard him say," said Mr. Howe, "time and time again, ' Never in my life did I do anything that would prevent me from shaking Forrest by the hand. I appreciate his genius, and that I could ever have been thought mean enough to do anything against him is the greatest misfortune of my life.' And henceforth, gentlemen, I believe you will all be ready to defend this man who has been unjustly assailed."

After many other speeches, songs, and recitations, Irving rose to leave. He said :—

" The welcome you have given me has surpassed my most ideal dream. I cannot describe my feelings. Such generosity, such welcome, such friendship, as I have met with here, no act of mine can repay. I hope to be back here in the early part of the coming year, and I ask if you will not all at that time be my guests. If you will come you will only add to the greatness of my obligation."

As Irving left the room he passed around the table and shook hands warmly with each gentleman

many interesting relics of the stage. On Irving's second visit to Philadelphia we called upon him and inspected some of his miscellaneous treasures. They covered a wide range of interest,— antiquarian, geological, historical, artistic, and literary. A white-haired, picturesque-looking old gentleman was there to meet us. " How like Tennyson!" exclaimed Irving. The interesting visitor was Walt Whitman. He expressed great satisfaction on being told that he was well known in England, and, in an amused way, he stood up, that Irving might judge if he was as tall as Tennyson. It is a milder face, and less rugged in its lines, than the face of the great English poet; but, in other respects, suggests the author of " In Memoriam."

M

present. The breakfast party did not arise until five
o'clock. Among those, other than the gentlemen mentioned, who contributed to the pleasure of the occasion,
by speech, song, or recitation, were Dr. Edward
Bedloe, Rufus E. Shapley, John B. Schoeffel, A.
Loudon Snowden, Hon. Robert P. Porter, A. G.
Hetherington, British Consul Clipperton, and Nat.
Childs. At the latter part of the festivities Attorney-
General Brewster entered the room and expressed his
regrets that he had been unable to be present in time
to shake hands with the Clover guest, and add his own
to the club's welcome of England's leading actor.

X.

BOSTON AND SHYLOCK.

Rural Scenes on both Sides of the Atlantic—First Impressions of Railway Travel—The Cars—One of the largest Theatres in America—The Drama in Boston—Early Struggles to represent Plays in Public—" Moral Lectures "—Boston Criticisms—Shylock, Portia, Hamlet, and Ophelia—Different Readings of Shylock—Dressing-room Criticism—Shylock considered—A Reminiscence of Tunis—Shakespeare interpreted on the Stage—Two Methods illustrated—Shylock before the Court of Venice—The Judgment of Actors.

I.

NOTHING in America is so unlike England as the desolate appearance of the meadows in the autumn and early winter months. From New York to Boston, a journey of six hours, in the second week of December, not a blade of green grass was to be seen. The train ran through a wilderness of brown, burnt-up meadows. With a tinge of yellow in the colour of them, they would have resembled the corn-stubbles of an English landscape. But all were a dead, sombre brown, except once in a way, where a clump of oaks still waved their russet leaves. Another noticeable contrast to England is the wooden houses, that look so temporary as compared with the brick and stone of the old country. The absence of the trim gardens of English rural districts also strikes a stranger, as do the curious and ragged fences that take the place of the English hedge-rows. The New England homesteads are, however, more like those of old England than are the farms of other States in the Union.

M 2

The habit of letting out walls and buildings, roofs of barns, and sides of houses, for the black and white advertisements of quack-medicine vendors and others, is a disfigurement of the land which every English visitor notices with regret; and lovers of the picturesque, Americans and English, grow positively angry over the disfigurement of the Hudson by these money-making Goths and Vandals.

A change of scene was promised for the Irving travellers on their return to New York, over the same line. A cold wave from the West was predicted. "We shall have snow before long," said an American friend, "and not unlikely a hard winter. I judge so from the fact that all the great weather prophets say it will be a mild one. Your Canadian seer, for instance, is dead on an exceptionally calm and warm winter. So let us look out."

Boston delighted the members of Irving's company; all of them except Loveday, who contracted, on the way thither, an attack of malarial fever. With true British pluck he fought his assailant until his first spell of important work was over, and then he retreated. Medical assistance, rest, and plenty of quinine pulled him through. But the company were destined later to sustain other climatic shocks; and they all, more or less, had a dread of the threatened winter. Until Loveday broke down everybody had stood the change of climate well. Reports came from England that Miss Ellen Terry was ill in New York. On the contrary, she had never been better than during these first weeks of the tour. She suffered, as all English women do, from heated rooms. "That is my only fear," she said to me. "The climate!—I don't object to it. If they would only be content with it, I would. Some of the days are gorgeous. The snap of cold, as they call it, was delightful to me. But when I would be driving out in open carriages, New York ladies would be muffled up in close broughams. And, oh, the getting home again!—to the hotel, I mean. An

English hothouse, where they grow pine-apples—that is the only comparison I can think of. And their private houses! How the dear people can stand the overwhelming heat of them, I don't know!"

The railway journey from Philadelphia to Boston was Irving's first experience of American travel. "It is splendid," he said, when I met him at his hotel, on the night of his arrival. "Am I not tired? Not a bit. It has been a delightful rest. I slept nearly the whole way, except once when going to the platform and looking out. At a station a man asked me which was Irving, and I pointed to Mead, who had been walking along the track, and was just then getting into his car. No; I enjoyed the ride all the way; never slept better; feel quite refreshed."

Said Miss Terry the next morning, when I saw her at the Tremont House, " Oh, yes, I like the travelling! It did not tire me. Then we had such lovely cars! But how different the stations are compared with ours! No platforms!—you get down really upon the line. And how unfinished it all looks,—except the cars, and they are perfect. Oh, yes, the parlour car beats our first-class carriage. I shall like Boston very much—though I never expect to like any place as well as New York."

II.

THE Boston Theatre is the largest of the houses in which Irving has played on this side of the Atlantic. It is claimed that it is the largest in the Union, though many persons say that the Opera House at the Rocky Mountain city of Denver is the handsomest of all the American theatres. The main entrance to the Boston house is in Washington Street. It has not an imposing exterior. The front entrance is all that is visible, the rest being filled up with stores; but the hall is very spacious, and the vestibule, *foyer*, lobbies, and grand staircase beyond, are worthy of the broad and well-appointed auditorium. The promenade saloon is paved

with marble, and is forty-six feet by twenty-six feet,
and proportionately high. Upon the walls, and here
and there on easels, are portraits of Irving, Booth,
McCullough, Salvini, and other notable persons. The
promenade and entrance hall cover one hundred feet
from the doors to the auditorium, which, in its turn, is
ninety feet from the back row to the footlights. The
stage is one hundred feet wide and ninety feet deep;
and the interior of the house from front to back covers
three hundred feet, the average width being about one
hundred feet. In addition to the parquette, which
occupies the entire floor (as the stalls do at the English
Opera Comique, and, by a recent change, also at the
Haymarket), there are three balconies, severally known
as the dress circle, the family circle, and the gallery.
The house will seat three thousand people. It is built
on a series of arches, or supporting columns, leaving
the basement quite open, giving, so far as the stage is
concerned, great facilities for the manipulation of
scenery and for storage, and allowing space for offices,
drill-rooms for supers, and other purposes.

"It is a magnificent theatre," said Irving; "the
auditorium superb, the stage fine; the pitch of the
auditorium in harmony with the stage—by which I
mean there is an artistic view of the stage from every
seat; the gas managements are perfect, and the system of general ventilation unique; but the dressing-
rooms are small and inconvenient. For anything like
quiet acting, for work in which detail of facial expression, significant gesture, or delicate asides, are important, the theatre is too large."

"Are you acquainted with the history of the stage
in Boston?" I asked him, "or of this theatre in
particular?"

"Only from what I have read or heard in a cursory
way," he said; "but one can readily understand that
our Puritan ancestors would bring with them to these
shores their hatred of plays and players. The actors
persevered in their terrible occupation in New

England, notwithstanding a local ordinance to prevent
stage plays and other theatrical entertainments, passed
in 1750. Otway's 'Orphan' was, I am told, the first
piece done in Boston. It was played at the British
Coffee-house, 'by a company of gentlemen,' and this
gave rise to the passing of the Act in question. Some
five or ten years later a number of Tories got up an
association to promote acting and defy this statute.
They revolted in favour of art; and in these days of
political tolerance that is a good thing to remember.
The members of this society were chiefly British
officers, who, with their subalterns and private soldiers
formed the acting company. I believe one of them
wrote the first piece they attempted to give in public.
It was called 'The Blockade of Boston;' but the
entertainment was stopped by a *ruse*—a sudden report that fighting had begun at Charlestown; a call
to arms, in fact. For many years no more efforts
were made to amuse or instruct the people with semi-
theatrical entertainments or stage plays. The next
attempt was a theatre, or, more properly speaking, a
variety show, in disguise. The house was called 'The
New Exhibition Room,' and the entertainment was announced as 'a moral lecture.' One Joseph Harper
was the manager. The programme of the first night
included tight-rope dancing, and various other athletic
feats; 'an introductory address;' singing, by a Mr.
Woods; tumbling, by Mr. Placide; and, in the course
of the evening, 'will be delivered the Gallery of
Portraits; or, the World as it Goes, by Mr. Harper.'
Later, 'Venice Preserved' was announced as a moral
lecture, 'in which the dreadful effects of conspiracy
will be exemplified.' Mr. Clapp's book on Boston
contains several curious instances of this kind. Shakespeare, it seems, filled the stage as 'a moral lecturer;'
and a familiar old English drama was played as 'a
moral lecture, in five parts, wherein the pernicious
tendency of libertinism will be exemplified in the
tragical history of George Barnwell; or, the London

Merchant.' Eventually, in the year 1793, I think, or thereabouts, Harper was arrested on the stage while playing Richard in one of Shakespeare's moral illustrations of the bane of ambition ~nd the triumph of virtue over vice. The audience protested, and destroyed a portrait of the governor of the city, which hung over the stage-box. They also tore down the State arms, and trampled upon them. At the hearing of the charge against Harper a technical flaw in the indictment procured his discharge. After this, however, the ' Exhibition Room ' did not flourish; but a bold and earnest movement, a year or two later, resulted in the building of the Federal Street Theatre, sometimes also called the Boston, and sometimes Old Drury, after the London house. From this time the stage in Boston is a fact; and one feels at home in reading over the names of the actors who have been well ·known here,—Macready, Charles Kemble and Fanny Kemble, Charlotte Cushman, Ellen Tree, John Vandenhoff, Sheridan Knowles, John Gilbert, Fanny Ellsler, the Booths, our friend Warren, and others. The present theatre, the Boston,[1] in which we are acting, has been built about thirty years. The grand ball given to the Prince of Wales when he visited this country took place here, the auditorium being boarded for the occasion.''

III.

'' THE audience '' on the first night of Irving's appearance in Boston, said the *Post* on the following morning,

---

[1] '' The Boston was built in 1854 by a stock company. It was opened on the 11th of September in that year, under the management of the late Thomas Barry, and for some time was in the hands of Junius Brutus Booth. After a time the company gave up the theatre, and it was acquired by Messrs. Thayer and Tompkins. On the death of Mr. Thayer, Mr. Tompkins associated with himself Mr. Hill, who had been a prominent stockholder, and they have since continued as proprietors. Mr. Eugene Tompkins, son of the chief proprietor, is the general manager.''—*King's Boston.*

" was not made up of average theatre-goers; many regular ' first-nighters ' were there, but a very large majority of those present were people of wealth, who go to the theatre comparatively little." The play was " Louis XI." It excited expressions of admiration in the audience, and was as warmly praised in the press as at New York and Philadelphia. A fine theatre, the scenery appeared almost to greater advantage than in the Lyceum itself; and some of the readers of these pages will be surprised to learn that much of the original scenery was dispensed with. Portions of the sets, indeed, for all the pieces during the week, were painted on the spot by Mr. Hall (a clever young artist, who is devoted to the service of Mr. Irving), and Lyceum draperies, groupings, dresses, and stage manipulation, did the rest. The usual orchestra of the theatre was strengthened, as at New York and Philadelphia, and the conductor had the satisfaction of a call for the repetition of some of the *entr'acte* music.

Among the most remarkable tributes to Irving's genius as an actor are the critical notices that appeared in the Boston newspapers the next day; while the people of Boston gave practical evidence of their satisfaction by attending the theatre in increasing numbers every night. The fortnight's work included, besides the opening play, " The Merchant of Venice," " The Lyons Mail," " Charles I.," " The Bells," " The Belle's Strata-gem," and " Hamlet." The old controversies as to the characters of Hamlet and Shylock, and the interpreta-tion of them, cropped up in the press, and, as before, were entirely absent from the audiences. They evidently had no doubts; they showed no desire to discount their pleasure; they found themselves wrapped up in the stage stories, rejoicing, sorrowing, weeping, laughing, with the varying moods of poet and actor. They did not stop to analyze the reasons for their emotion; it was enough for them that they followed the fortunes of the hero and heroine with absorbing interest. They had no preconceived ideas to vindicate; they were happy in the enjoyment of the highest form of dramatic entertainment which even those critics that are chary of their commendation of individual artists say America has ever seen. Said the *Boston Herald*, in its notice of " Hamlet " :—

"At the end of each act he received one or more calls before the curtain, and after the 'play scene' the demonstrations were really enthusiastic; shouts of 'Bravo!' mingling with the plaudits that summoned him to the footlights again and again. Miss Ellen Terry won all hearts by her exquisite embodiment of Ophelia. A better representative of this lovely character has not been, and is not likely to be, seen here by the present generation of play-goers. She received her full share of the honours of the evening, and her appearance before the curtain was often demanded, and hailed with delight, by the large audience present."

The *Advertiser, Traveller, Globe, Post,*—indeed all the daily press,—were unanimous in recognizing the merits of Irving and his work. The *Transcript* was especially eulogistic in its treatment of Hamlet. As a rule the criticisms were written with excellent literary point.

IV.

ON the first night of the " Merchant of Venice " at Boston, Irving played Shylock, I think, with more than ordinary thoughtfulness in regard to his original treatment of the part. His New York method was, to me, a little more vigorous than his London rendering of the part. Considerations of the emphasis which actors have laid upon certain scenes that are considered as especially favourable to the declamatory methods possibly influenced him. His very marked success in Louis no doubt led some of his admirers in America to expect in his Shylock a very hard, grim, and cruel Jew. Many persons hinted as much to him before they saw his impersonation of this much-discussed character. At Boston I thought he was, if possible, over-conscientious in traversing the lines he laid down for himself when he first decided to produce the "Merchant" at the Lyceum. Singularly sensitive about the feelings of his audiences, and accustomed to judge them as keenly as they judge him, he fancied the Boston audience, which had been very enthusiastic in their applause on the previous nights, were not stirred as they had been by his other work in response to his efforts as Shylock. The play, nevertheless, was received with the utmost cordiality, and the general representation of it was admirable. I found a Londoner in front, who was in raptures with it. "I think the carnival, Belmont, and court scenes," he said, "were never better done at the Lyceum."

At the close of the piece, and after a double call for Irving and Miss Terry, I went to his dressing-room. "Yes," he said, "the play has gone well, very well, indeed; but the audience were not altogether with me. I always feel, in regard to this play, that they do not quite understand what I am doing. They only responded at all to-night where Shylock's rage and mortification get the better of his dignity."

"They are accustomed to have the part of Shylock strongly declaimed; indeed, all the English Shylocks, as well as American representatives of the part, are very demonstrative in it. Phelps was, so was Charles Kean; and I think American audiences look for the declamatory passages in Shylock, to compare your rendering of them with the readings they have previously heard. You omit much of what is considered great business in Shylock, and American audiences are probably a little disappointed that your view of the part forbids anything like what may be called the strident characteristics of most other Shylocks. Charles Kean ranted considerably in Shylock, and Phelps was decidedly noisy,—both fine, no doubt, in their way. Nevertheless they made the Jew a cruel butcher of a Jew. They filled the stage with his sordid greed and malignant desire for vengeance on the Christian, from his first entrance to his final exit."

"I never saw Kean's Shylock, nor Phelps's, nor, indeed, any one's. But I am sure Shylock was not a low person; a miser and usurer, certainly, but a very injured man,—at least he thought so. I felt that my audience to-night had quite a different opinion, and I once wished the house had been composed entirely of Jews. I would like to play Shylock to a Jewish audience."

Mr. Warren,[2] the famous Boston comedian, came into the dressing-room while we were talking. He has been a favourite here for thirty-six years.

"Not so long in one place as Mr. Howe," he says, with a smile, "who tells me he was a member of the Haymarket company for forty years."

"You know Mr. Toole well?" said Mr. Irving.

"Yes," he replied; "it was a pleasure to meet him here."

"He often talks of you."

"I am glad to know it," he replied; "I want to tell you how delighted I have been to-night. It is the 'Merchant of Venice' for the first time. I have never seen the casket scene played before, nor the last act for twenty years. A great audience, and how thoroughly they enjoyed the piece I need not tell you."

"I don't think they cared for me," said Irving.

---

[2] As the position which Mr. John Gilbert holds in New York is akin to that which the elder Farren held in London, so the position which Mr. William Warren occupies in Boston is akin to that which Mr. Buckstone ("Bucky," as his particular friends called him) held in the English metropolis. Mr. Warren's Dogberry and Paul Pry are among the pleasantest reminiscences of Boston play-goers. It fell to Irving's lot to meet Mr. Warren frequently, and perhaps no actor ever received greater compliments from two veterans of his craft than Irving received from Gilbert and Warren. While the favourite of New York never missed an Irving performance at the Star Theatre, his famous contemporary of Boston not only attended all the Lyceum performances at Boston, but later, when Irving went to Chicago, Mr. Warren paid his relatives a visit in the western city, and was as constant an attendant at Haverly's during the Irving engagement as he was at the Boston Theatre.

"Yes, yes, I am sure they did," Mr. Warren replied, at which moment an usher brought Miss Terry, to be introduced to him, and the subject dropped, to be revived over a quiet cigar after supper. "I look on Shylock," says Irving, in response to an invitation to talk about his work in that direction, "as the type of a persecuted race; almost the only gentleman in the play, and most ill-used. He is a merchant, who trades in the Rialto, and Bassanio and Antonio are not ashamed to borrow money of him, nor to carry off his daughter. The position of his child is, more or less, a key to his own. She is the friend of Portia. Shylock was well-to-do—a Bible-read man, as his readiness at quotation shows; and there is nothing in his language, at any time, that indicates the snuffling usurer which some persons regard him, and certainly nothing to justify the use the early actors made of the part for the low comedian. He was a religious Jew; learned, for he conducted his case with masterly skilfulness, and his speech is always lofty and full of dignity. Is there a finer language in Shakespeare than Shylock's defence of his race? ' Hath not a Jew eyes; hath not a Jew hands, organs, dimensions, senses, affections, passions; fed with the same food; hurt with the same weapons; subject to the same diseases; healed by the same means; warmed and cooled by the same winter and summer, as a Christian is?' As to the manner of representing Shylock, take the first part of the story; note his moods. He is, to begin with, quiet, dignified, diplomatic; then satirical; and next, somewhat light and airy in his manner, with a touch of hypocrisy in it. Shakespeare does not indicate at what precise moment Shylock conceives the idea of the bond; but he himself tells us of his anxiety to have Antonio on the hip.

"'I will feed fat the ancient grudge I bear him.
He hates our sacred nation, and he rails,
Even there where merchants most do congregate,
On me, my bargains, and my well-won thrift,
Which he calls interest.'

" His first word is more or less fawning; but it breaks
out into reproach and satire when he recalls the insults
that have been heaped upon him. 'Hath a dog
money?' and so on; still he is diplomatic, for he
wants to make reprisals upon Antonio: 'Cursed be
my tribe if I forgive him!' He is plausible, even
jocular. He speaks of his bond of blood as a merry
sport. Do you think if he were strident or spiteful in
his manner here, loud of voice, bitter, they would
consent to sign a bond having in it such fatal possibilities? One of the interesting things for an actor to
do is to try to show when Shylock is inspired with the
idea of this bargain, and to work out by impersonation
the Jew's thought in his actions. My view is, that
from the moment Antonio turns upon him, declaring
he is 'like to spit upon him again,' and invites him
scornfully to lend the money, not as to his friend, but
rather to his enemy, who, if he break, he may with
better force exact the penalty,—from that moment I
imagine Shylock resolving to propose his pound of
flesh, perhaps without any hope of getting it. Then
he puts on that hypocritical show of pleasantry which
so far deceives them as to elicit from Antonio the
remark that 'The Hebrew will turn Christian; he
grows kind.' Well, the bond is to be sealed, and when
next we meet the Jew he is still brooding over his
wrongs, and there is in his words a constant, though
vague, suggestion of a desire for revenge, nothing
definite or planned, but a continual sense of undeserved
humiliation and persecution :—

> " ' I am bid forth to supper, Jessica.
> There are my keys :—but wherefore should I go?
> I am not bid for love; they flatter me:
> But yet I'll go in hate, to feed upon
> The prodigal Christian.'

" But one would have to write a book to go into
these details, and tell an actor's story of Shylock."

" We are not writing a book of Shylock now, but
only chatting about your purpose and intention gene-

rally in presenting to the public what is literally to
them a new Shylock, and answering, perhaps, a few
points of that conservative kind of criticism which
preaches tradition and custom. Come to the next
phase of Shylock's character, or, let us say, his next
dramatic mood."

"Well, we get at it in the street scene: rage,—a
confused passion; a passion of rage and disappointment, never so confused and mixed; a man beside
himself with vexation and chagrin.

"'My daughter! Oh, my ducats! Oh, my daughter!
Fled with a Christian! Oh, my Christian ducats!
Justice! the law! my ducats and my daughter!'

"I saw a Jew once, in Tunis, tear his hair and
raiment, fling himself in the sand, and writhe in a rage,
about a question of money,—beside himself with
passion. I saw him again, self-possessed and fawning;
and again, expressing real gratitude for a trifling
money courtesy. He was never undignified until he
tore at his hair and flung himself down, and then he
was picturesque; he was old, but erect, even stately,
and full of resource. As he walked behind his team
of mules he carried himself with the lofty air of a
king. He was a Spanish Jew,—Shylock probably
was of Frankfort; but Shakespeare's Jew was a type,
not a mere individual: he was a type of the great,
grand race,—not a mere Hounsditch usurer. He was
a man famous on the Rialto; probably a foremost man
in his synagogue—proud of his descent—conscious of
his moral superiority to many of the Christians who
scoffed at him, and fanatic enough, as a religionist, to
believe that his vengeance had in it the element of a
godlike justice. Now, you say that some of my
critics evidently look for more fire in the delivery of
the speeches to Solanio, and I have heard friends say
that John Kemble and the Keans brought down the
house for the way they thundered out the threats
against Antonio, and the defence of the Jewish race.

It is in this scene that we realize, for the first time, that Shylock has resolved to enforce his bond. Three times, during a very short speech, he says, 'Let him look to his bond!' 'A beggar that was used to come so smug upon the mart; *let him look to his bond :* he was wont to call me usurer; *let him look to his bond ;* he was wont to lend money for a Christian courtesy ; *let him look to his bond.'* Now, even an ordinary man, who had made up his mind to 'have the heart of him if he forfeit,' would not shout and rave and storm. My friend at Tunis tore his hair at a trifling disappointment; if he had resolved to stab his rival he would have muttered his intention between his teeth, not have screeched it. How much less likely still would this bitterly persecuted Jew merchant of Venice have given his resolve a loud and noisy utterance! Would not his settled hate have been more likely to show itself in the clinched hand, the firmly planted foot, the flashing eye, and the deep undertones in which he would utter the closing threat: '*Let him look to his bond*'? I think so."

"And so do the most thoughtful among your audiences. Now and then, however, a critic shows himself so deeply concerned for what is called tradition that he feels it incumbent upon him to protest against a Shylock who is not, from first to last, a transparent and noisy ruffian."

"Tradition! One day we will talk of that. In Davenant's time—and some dare to say he got his tradition from Shakespeare himself—they played Shylock as a comic character, in a red wig ; and to make it, as they thought, consistent, they cut out the noblest lines the author had put into his mouth, and added some of their own. We have no tradition in the sense that those who would insist upon our observance of it means; what we have is bad,— Garrick played Othello in a red coat and epaulettes ; and if we are to go back to Shakespeare's days, these sticklers for so-called tradition forget that

the women were played by boys. Shakespeare did
the best he could in his day, and he would do the
best he could if he were living now. Tradition! It
is enough to make one sick to hear the pretentious
nonsense that is talked about the stage in the name of
tradition! It seems to me that there are two ways of
representing Shakespeare. You have seen David's
picture of Napoleon and that by De la Roche. The
first is a heroic figure,—head thrown back, arm
extended, cloak flying,—on a white horse of the most
powerful, but unreal, character, which is rearing up
almost upon its haunches, its forelegs pawing the air.
That is Napoleon crossing the Alps. I think there is
lightning in the clouds. It is a picture calculated to
terrify; a something so unearthly in its suggestion of
physical power as to cut it off from human comprehen-
sion. Now, this represents to me one way of playing
Shakespeare. The other picture is still the same
subject, 'Napoleon crossing the Alps;' but in this one
we see a reflective, deep-browed man, enveloped in his
cloak, and sitting upon a sturdy mule, which, with a
sure and steady foot, is climbing the mountain, led by
a peasant guide. This picture represents to me the
other way of playing Shakespeare. The question is,
which is right? I think the truer picture is *the right*
cue to the poet who himself described the actor's art
as to hold, as it were, the mirror up to nature."

"Which should bring us very naturally back to
Shylock. Let us return to your brief dissertation at
the point where he is meditating vengeance in case of
forfeiture of the bond."

"Well, the latest mood of Shylock dates from this
time,—it is one of implacable *revenge*. Nothing shakes
him. He thanks God for Antonio's ill-luck. There is
in this darkness of his mind a tender recollection of
Leah. And then the calm command to Tubal, 'Be-
speak me an officer.' What is a little odd is his
request that Tubal shall meet him at the synagogue.
It might be that Shakespeare suggested here the idea

N

of a certain sacredness of justice in Shylock's view of vengeance on Antonio. Or it might be to accentuate the religious character of the Jew's habits; for Shylock was assuredly a religious Jew, strict in his worship, and deeply read in his Bible,—no small thing, this latter knowledge, in those days. I think this idea of something divine in his act of vengeance is the key-note to the trial scene, coupled, of course, with the intense provocation he has received.

> " 'Thou calledst me dog before thou hadst a cause;
> But since I am a dog, beware my fangs!
> The duke shall grant me justice.
> . . . . Follow not,
> I'll have no speaking; I will have my bond.'

" These are the words of a man of fixed, implacable purpose, and his skilful defence of it shows him to be wise and capable. He is the most self-possessed man in the court. Even the duke, in the judge's seat, is moved by the situation. What does he say to Antonio ?

> " 'I am sorry for thee; thou art come to answer
> A stony adversary.'

" Everything indicates a stern, firm, persistent, implacable purpose, which in all our experience of men is, as a rule, accompanied by an apparently calm manner. A man's passion which unpacks itself in oaths and threats, which stamps and swears and shouts, may go out in tears, but not in vengeance. On the other hand, there are those who argue that Antonio's reference to his own patience and to Shylock's fury implies a noisy passion on the part of the Jew; but, without taking advantage of any question as to the meaning of ' fury ' in this connection, it seems to me that Shylock's contempt for his enemies, his sneer at Gratiano,—

> " 'Till thou canst rail the seal from off my bond,
> Thou but offend'st thy lungs to speak so loud '—

and his action throughout the court scene quite out-

weigh any argument in favour of a very demonstrative
and furious representation of the part. ' I stand here
for law ! ' Then note when he realizes the force of
the technical flaws in his bond,—and there are lawyers
who contend the law was severely and unconstitutionally
strained in this decision of the court,—he is willing to
take his bond paid thrice ; he cannot get that, he asks
for the principal; when that is refused he loses his
temper, as it occurs to me, for the first time during the
trial, and in a rage exclaims, ' Why, then, the devil
give him good of it ! ' There is a peculiar and special
touch at the end of that scene which, I think, is
intended to mark and accentuate the crushing nature
of the blow which has fallen upon him. When Antonio
stipulates that Shylock shall become a Christian, and
record a deed of gift to Lorenzo, the Jew cannot
speak. ' He shall do this,' says the duke, ' or else I do
recant the pardon.' Portia turns and questions him.
He is hardly able to utter a word. ' I am content,' is
all he says ; and what follows is as plain an instruction
as was ever written in regard to the conduct and
manner of the Jew. ' Clerk, draw a deed of gift,'
says Portia. Note Shylock's reply, his last words, the
answer of the defeated litigant, who is utterly crushed
and borne down :—

> " ' I pray you give me leave to go from hence;
> I am not well ; send the deed after me,
> And I will sign it.'

" Is it possible to imagine anything more helpless
than this final condition of the Jew ? ' I am not well;
give me leave to go from hence ! ' How interesting it
is to think this out : and how much we all learn from
the actors when, to the best of their ability, they give
the characters they assume as if they were really present, working out their studies, in their own way, and
endowing them with the characterization of their own
individuality ! It is cruel to insist that one actor shall
simply follow in the footsteps of another ; and it is

N 2

unfair to judge an actor's interpretation of a character from the standpoint of another actor; his intention should be considered, and he should be judged from the point of how he succeeds or fails in carrying it out."

XI.

A CITY OF SLEIGHS.

Snow and Sleigh-bells—" Brooks of Sheffield "—In the Boston Suburbs—Smokeless Coal—At the Somerset Club—Miss Ellen Terry and the Papyrus—A Ladies' Night—" Greeting to Ellen Terry "—St. Botolph—Oliver Wendell Holmes and Charles the First—" Good-bye and a Merry Christmas."

I.

" A TRANSFORMATION scene, indeed! " said Irving. " Yesterday, autumn winds, bright streets, a rattle of traffic — to-day, snow and sleigh-bells — yesterday, wheels—to-day, runners, as they call the enormous skating-irons upon which they appear to have placed every vehicle in the city. I have just returned from rehearsal, and find everybody sleighing. The omnibuses are sleighs—the grocer's cart is a sleigh—the express waggons are sleighs—it is a city of sleighs! The snow began to fall in earnest yesterday. Last night it must have been a foot deep. It would have ruined the business at a London theatre. Here it made no difference. We had a splendid house."

" As I walked to my hotel at midnight," I replied, " snow-ploughs were in the streets clearing the roads and scouring the car-tracks. Boston tackles the snow in earnest. The trees on the Common were a marvel of beauty. They looked like an orchard of the Hesperides, all in blossom, and the electric lamps added to the fairy-like beauty of the scene."

" A lovely city. Shall we take a sleigh ride ? "

" ' Why, certainly,' as they say in ' The Colonel,' but rarely in America."

Irving rings for his coloured attendant. He has discovered that his surname is Brooks, and takes a curious pleasure in addressing him as Brooks, sometimes as " Brooks, of Sheffield ! "

" Order me a sleigh, Brooks ! "

" Yes, sah," says Brooks, grinning.

" Two horses, Brooks ! "

" Yes, sah," says the attendant, preparing to go, not hurriedly, for who ever saw a coloured gentleman (they are all coloured gentlemen) in a hurry ?

" And take my rugs down ! "

" Yes, sah," he says, marching slowly into the next room for the rugs.

" And, Brooks—"

" Yes, sah."

" Would you like to go to the theatre one night ? "

" Berry much, sah—yes, sah."

" What play would you like to see ? "

" Hamlet, sah ! "

" Hamlet ! Very good. Is there a Mrs. Brooks ? "

" 'Deed there is, sah," answers the darkey, grinning from ear to ear.

" And some little Brookses—of Sheffield ? "

" Yes, sah ; not ob Sheffield, ob Boston."

" That's all right. Mr. Stoker shall give all of you seats. See if he is in the hotel."

" Yes, sah."

As he stalks to the door Stoker comes bounding in (Stoker is always on the run), to the discomfiture of Brooks and his load of rugs.

Brooks picks himself up with dignity. Stoker assures his chief that there is not a seat in the house for anybody.

" Then buy some for Brooks," says Irving.

" Where ? " asks Stoker, in amazement.

" Anywhere," says Irving, adding, with a significant glance at me, " from the speculators."

" Oh, very well, if you wish it," says Stoker.

" And, Brooks—"

" Yes, sah."

" Anybody else in the hotel like to go ? "

"Oh, yes, indeed, sah," says Brooks—"de cook, sah."

" And what play would the cook like to see ? "

" Hamlet, sah."

" You've been paid to say this ! " says Irving, quoting from Louis. " Who bade you do it ? "

But this was only whispered in a humorous " aside " for me, who know how much he likes Hamlet, and how much he likes other people to like Hamlet.

At the door of the Brunswick we find a sleigh, pair of horses, smart-looking driver, a heap of rugs and furs, under which we ensconce ourselves. The weather is bitterly cold, the sky blue; the windows of the houses in the fine streets of the Back Bay district flash icily; the air is sharp, and the sleigh-bells ring out aggressively as the horses go away.

The snow is too deep for rapid sleighing; there has been no time for it to solidify. It is white and pure as it has fallen, and when we get out into the suburbs it is dazzling to the eyes, almost painful. Crossing the Charles river the scene is singularly picturesque ; a cumbersome old barge in the foreground ; on the opposite shore a long stretch of red-brick buildings, vanishing at the point where the heights of Brookline climb away, in white and green and grey undulations, to the bright blue sky. As we enter Cambridge there are fir-trees growing out of the snow, their sombre greens all the darker for the white weight that bows their branches down to the drifts that wrap their trunks high up; for here and there the snow has drifted until there are banks of it five and six feet deep.

" Very pretty, these villas; nearly all wood,—do you notice ?—very comfortable, I am sure; lined with brick, I am told, some of them. Nearly all have balconies or verandahs; and there are trees and gardens everywhere,—must be lovely in summer; good enough now, for that matter. One thing makes them look a trifle lonely,—no smoke coming from the chimneys. They burn anthracite coal,—good for this atmosphere,—excellent and clean; but how a bit of blue smoke curling up among the trees finishes and gives poetry to a landscape,—suggests home and cosey firesides, eh?"

" Yes. New York owes some of its clear atmosphere to its smokeless coal."

"What a pity we don't have it in London! Only fancy a smokeless London,—what a lovely city?"

" It may come about one day, either by the adoption of smokeless coal or the interposition of the electrician. Last summer I spent some time in the Swansea Valley, England, not far from Craig-y-nos, the British home of Patti. One day I noticed that there was no smoke over the villages; none at some local ironworks, except occasional bursts of white steam from the engine-houses; nothing to blemish the lovely sky that touched the mountain-tops with a grey mist. I was near Ynyscedwyn, the famous smokeless-coal district of South Wales. London need not burn another ounce of soft or bituminous coal; there is enough anthracite in Wales to supply all England for a thousand years."

" What a blessing it would be if London were to use nothing else! "

Through Cambridge, so intimately associated with Longfellow, past its famous colleges, we skirted Brookline, and returned to our head-quarters in Clarendon Street, meeting on the way many stylish sleighs and gay driving-parties.

On another day Irving took luncheon with a little party of undergraduates in Common Hall, was received by the president of the college, inspected the gymnasium, saw the theatre, and had long talks with several of the professors.

Perhaps from a literary and artistic standpoint the

most interesting social event among the many enter-
tainments given to Irving was a dinner given by
Mr. Charles Fairchild and Mr. James R. Osgood, at
the Somerset Club. The company included Messrs.
T. B. Aldrich, A. V. S. Anthony, Francis Bartlett,
William Bliss, George Baty Blake, S. L. Clemens
("Mark Twain"), T. L. Higginson, W. D. Howells,
Laurence Hutton, W. M. Laffan, Francis A. Walker,
George E. Waring, and William Warren. After
dinner the conversation was quite as brilliant as the
company. Mark Twain told some of his best stories
in his best manner. Mr. Howells and Mr. Aldrich in
no wise fell short of their reputations as conversa-
tionalists. There were no drinking of toasts, no
formal speeches, which enhanced the general joy of the
whole company.

Driving homewards along the Common, Irving said,
" By gaslight, and in the snow, is not this a little like
the Green Park, with, yonder, the clock-tower of the
Houses of Parliament ? "

" Do you wish it were ? "

" I wouldn't mind it for an hour or two, eh ?
Although one really sometimes hardly feels that one
is out of London."

II.

" LADIES' NIGHT.—The Papyrus Club request the
pleasure of the company of Miss Ellen Terry at the
Revere House, December 15th, at six o'clock. Boston,
1883. Please reply to J. T. Wheelwright, 39, Court
Street." [1]

[1] LADIES' NIGHT AT THE PAPYRUS.—The Ladies' Night entertainment of the Papyrus Club, which has come to be accepted
as one of the annual features of that organization, took place at
the Revere House last night, and the occasion proved to be one
of exceptional interest and brilliancy. The Papyrus includes in
its membership a large number of clever men, and, with their
guests who assembled last evening to partake of the club's hospitality, the company made up a most delightful and distinguished gathering. The after-dinner exercises, which were not
permitted to be reported in full, were of a most entertaining

Thus ran the invitation, which was adorned with a miniature view of the Pyramids in a decorative setting

character; the speeches of the distinguished gentlemen guests and the contributions in prose and verse by some of the members of the club, being very bright and enjoyable. The members and their guests assembled in the hotel parlours at six o'clock, where they were received by the president of the club, Mr. George F. Babbitt, assisted by Miss Fay. Music was furnished by the Germania Orchestra, and, after an hour spent in introductory ceremonies, the members and their guests, numbering altogether 120 ladies and gentlemen, proceeded to the dining-hall and sat down to the dinner-table, which was arranged in horseshoe form. The tables were artistically decorated with flowers, and at each plate was placed a dinner-card, bearing the name of each guest, and a *menu* of an exceedingly artistic design, the front cover bearing a photograph of the club paraphernalia, very cleverly grouped, and bearing the inscription : " Papyrus, Ladies' Night. December 15th, MDCCCLXXXIII." President Babbitt sat in the centre, with Miss Fay at his right and Miss Ellen Terry at his left. On either side of the president were seated Miss Alcott, Mr. Joseph Hatton, Dr. Burnett and Mrs. Frances Hodgson Burnett, General Francis A. Walker and Mrs. Walker, Mr. Henry Cabot Lodge, Captain Story, U.S.A.; Mr. Guy Carleton, of New York, editor of *Life*, and Mr. J. A. Mitchell, assistant editor; Rev. and Mrs. Brooke Hereford, Dr. John D. Blake and Mrs. Blake, Mr. W. H. Rideing and Mrs. John Lillie, the author of " Prudence," and Rev. and Mrs. H. B. Carpenter. Among the other members and guests present were Miss Nora Perry and Miss Noble, the author of " A Reverend Idol ;" Mr. and Mrs. Robert Grant, Mr. F. J. Stimson, the author of " Guerndale," and Mrs. Stimson; Dr. Harold Williams, the author of " Mr. and Mrs. Morton;" Mr. Arthur Rotch and Mrs. Van Rensselaer, Mr. and Mrs. W. F. Apthorp, Mr. A. H. Dodd, Mrs. Dodd, and Miss Dodd ; Mr. Henry M. Rodgers and Mr. George Abbot James ; Miss Gage, Mr. and Mrs. Howard M. Ticknor, and Mrs. S. A. Bigelow ; Mrs. C. H. Washburne, Mr. George Snell, Mrs. Bacon, and Mrs. Charles Whitmore ; Mr. Alexander Young, Mr. George Roberts, Mr. John T. Wheelwright, Mr. L. S. Ipsen, Mr. Alexander Browne and Miss Edmundson, Mr. Frank Hill Smith, and Mrs. Henry Fay ; Mr. Arlo Bates, Dr. and Mrs. James Chadwick, Colonel Theodore A. Dodge, and Mrs. Crowninshield ; Mr. and Mrs. F. P. Vinton, Mr. Francis Peabody, jun.; Mr. Russell Sullivan, Mr. and Mrs. Charles Albert Prince, Miss Minot, Mr. and Mrs. Gordon Prince, Mr. and Mrs. F. V. Parker, Mr. and Mrs. E. L. Osgood, Mr. and Mrs. George M. Towle, Mr. H. G. Pickering, Mr. and Mrs. W.

of the reed that is familiar to travellers in the Nile valley.

H. Sayward, and Mrs. R. G. Shaw; Mr. T. O. Langerfelt, Mr. and Mrs. Arthur Foote, Mr. Sigourney Butler, Miss Butler, and Miss Shimmin; Mr. and Mrs. R. G. Fitch, Mr. and Mrs. George B. Goodwin, Mr. W. B. Clarke, Mr. and Mrs. C. A. Campbell, Mr. G. W. Chadwick, Mr. Preston, Mr. and Mrs. F. E. Wright, Mrs. G. A. Gibson, Mr. and Mrs. L. L. Scaife, and Mr. and Mrs. J. E. Woods. At the conclusion of the dinner the president proposed the health of the assembled company in the loving-cup, in accordance with a time-honoured custom of the Papyrus, the cup passing from guest to guest until it had made the rounds of the tables. Many of the gentlemen were merrily cheered as they rose to drink from the cup, as were many of the distinguished ladies, who, without rising, simply touched the cup to their lips. After this interesting ceremony had been gone through with, the president welcomed the company in a brief speech, concluding with a toast to the lady guests, which was drunk standing by the gentlemen present. The Rev. H. Bernard Carpenter was called upon to respond to the toast, which he did in a neat speech, in which pleasant allusions were made to the distinguished ladies of the company, and their work. He was followed by Mr. John T. Wheelwright, the secretary of the club, who gave a very bright burlesque report of the proceedings of the monthly Papyrus meetings. It was made up of clever imitations of the poetic and prose contributions of the more active members of the Papyrus, and its numerous hits were received with shouts of laughter. Mr. T. R. Sullivan then read a charming bit of prose; and then came a bright and humorous contribution from Mr. Robert Grant, who described, in a very funny way, his experiences as a member of the committee on ladies' night some years ago. It abounded in witty allusions to the antics of some of the members of the club, and, although the names of the characters who figured in the sketch were assumed for the occasion, the references to the members of the club were readily recognized. Mr. Howard M. Ticknor was then introduced, and read a poem addressed to Miss Terry, concluding with a toast in honour of the distinguished lady, the mention of whose name elicited enthusiastic applause. Mr. Joseph Hatton responded handsomely for Miss Terry, thanking the company for their very cordial welcome and the Papyrus for their elegant hospitality. Mr. Arlo Bates read some very pretty songs, and Mr. Guy Carleton responded to a toast in honour of *Life*, the clever New York paper. Mr. W. H. Sayward gave one of his excellent imitations, and the entertainment concluded with the performance of "a burlesque operatic monodrama," entitled "Titi." The sole *dramatis persona*, Titi,

Miss Terry concluded to accept, and I had the honour of being her escort. The handsome rooms of the Revere House that were devoted to the service of the club on this occasion were crowded with ladies and gentlemen when we arrived. Among the guests in whom Miss Terry was especially interested were Mrs. Burnett, the author of "Joan" and other remarkable novels; Miss Noble, the author of "A Reverend Idol;" Miss Fay, Mrs. John Lillie, Mrs. Washbourne, and other ladies known to the world of letters. She was surrounded for a long time by changing groups of ladies and gentlemen, who were presented in a pleasant, informal way by Mr. Babbitt, the president of the club, and other of its officers.

The dinner was a dainty repast (one of the special dishes was a "baked English turbot with brown sauce"). The details of it were printed upon a photographic card, which represented the loving-cup, punch-bowl, Papyrus' manuscripts, gavel, pen and ink, and treasure-box of the institution.

During dinner Miss Terry was called upon to sign scores of the *menu* cards with her autograph. Upon many of them she scribbled poetic couplets, Shakespearian and otherwise, and on others quaint, appropriate lines of her own. She captivated the women, all of them. It is easier for a clever woman to excite the admiration of her sex in America than in England. A woman who adorns and lifts the feminine intellect into notice in America excites the admiration rather

was assumed by Mr. Wm. F. Apthorp, who sang and recited the monodrama in costume, being accompanied on the piano by Mr. Arthur Foote. The performance of this bright musical composition occupied nearly half an hour, and it was acted and sung by Mr. Apthorp with exquisite *chic* and drollery, serving as a fitting finale to the very pleasant after-dinner entertainment. The company arose from the tables at about half-past ten o'clock, and soon after separated, many of the gentlemen going to the St. Botolph Club reception to Mr. Irving, which was appointed for eleven o'clock.—*Boston Saturday Evening Gazette.*

than the jealousy of her sisters. American women seem to make a higher claim upon the respect and attention of men than belongs to the ambitious English women, and when one of them rises to distinction they all go up with her. They share in her fame; they do not try to dispossess her of the lofty place upon which she stands. There is a sort of trades-unionism among the women of America in this respect. They hold together in a ring against the so-called lords of creation, and the men are content to accept what appears to be a happy form of petticoat government. So the women of Boston took Ellen Terry to their arms and made much of her.

After dinner the President expressed in quaint terms the club's welcome of its guests, and the Secretary having read a quaintly expressed official report of the previous meeting, Mr. Howard M. Ticknor recited, with excellent elocutionary point, the following " Greeting to Ellen Terry " :—

"Honour," said Cassius, " is my story's theme."
Honour shall best my verse to-night beseem.

    ———

For some, how safe, how permanent, how sure !
Written in characters that will endure,
Until this world begins to melt away
And crumble to its ultimate decay.
The picture fades ; but colour still is there,
Even in ruin is the statue fair ;
The province won, the city burnt or built,
The inwrought consequence of good or guilt,
Shape after epochs to time's latest span,
And link enduringly a man to man.

But he who is himself artist and art,
Whose greatest works are of himself a part ;
Who, sculptor, moulds his hand, his form, his face ;
Who, painter, on the air his lines must trace.
Musician, make an instrument his voice,
And tell, not write, the melody of his choice ;
Whose eloquence of gesture, pose, and eye
Flashes aglow, in instant dark to die ;—

Where are for him the honour and the fame
A face on canvas, and perhaps a name
Extolled a while, and then an empty word
At sound of which no real thrill is stirred.

What, then, shall recompense his loss ?   What make
Atonement for the ignorant future's sake ?
What but the tribute of his honour now,
The native wreath to deck his living brow ?
Then, as he passes beyond the mortal ken,
His glory shall go with him even then,
Not as a hope, a doubt, and a desire,
But as a spark of his own living fire,
Of his eternal self a priceless part,
Eternal witness to his mind and heart.

And so, to-night, when she who comes from far
To show in one what many women are,
Sits at our board, and makes our evening shine,
Breaks bread with us, and pledges in our wine,
Let us be quick to honour in our guest
So many a phase of life by her expressed.
Portia's most gracious, yet submissive word—
"You are my king, my governor, my lord ;"
Her courage, dignity, and force,
Warning the Jew that justice shall have course ;
The trenchant wit of Beatrice, and her pride,
Her loyalty as friend, her faith as bride ;
Letitia's stratagems ; the tragic fate
Of sweet Ophelia, crushed by madness' weight.

How many chords of happiness or woe,
Her lips that quiver and her cheeks that glow ;
Her speech now clear, now clouded, and her eyes
Filling by turns with anguish, mirth, surprise—
Can wake to throb, again to rest can still—
Potent her power as Prospero's magic will !

Present alone is hers—alone is ours,
Now, while she plants, must we, too, cull the flowers ?
For future wreaths she has no time to wait ;
Unready now, they are for aye too late.
Now is the moment our regard to show,
Let every face with light of welcome glow ;
Let smiles shine forth, glad words be spoken,
Formality for once be broken.
Let hand strike hand, let kerchiefs wave,
Keep not her laurels for her grave ;

Twine our proud chaplet for her fair, smooth brow,
And bid her take our share of tribute now ;
Then shall it be a recollection dear,
That we to-night greet Ellen Terry here !

III.

IRVING, who could not be present at the Papyrus Club
(it was one of Miss Terry's " off nights," when either
" The Bells " or " Louis XI." was performed), was
received at the St. Botolph's Club soon after the
Papyrus festivities closed.   In the absence of the
President, ex-Mayor Green, the Vice-President, and
Mr. Secretary Sullivan did the honours of the evening.
An interesting meeting on this occasion was the intro-
duction of Irving to Oliver Wendell Holmes, who later,
at the *matinée* performance of " Charles the First,"
was quite overcome with the pathos of the play. Apart
from the number and enthusiasm of his audiences, Mr.
Irving's personal reception by the leading men of
Boston—*littérateurs*, professors, and scholars—might
well have given point to the few eloquent words which
he addressed to the house on the closing performance of
" The Bells " and " The Belle's Stratagem." He said,—
" Ladies and Gentlemen,—I have the privilege of
thanking you, for myself, and in behalf of my comrades, and especially in behalf of my gifted sister, Miss
Ellen Terry, for the way in which you have received
our tragedy, comedy, and melodrama.   In coming to
this country I have often said that I felt I was coming
among friends; and I have had abundant and most
touching proof that I was right.   This I have never
felt more truly than in your historic city of New England, which seems a veritable bit of Old England.   In
this theatre we have been on classic ground, and if we
have, while upon these boards, accomplished anything
tending, in your opinion, to the advancement of a
great art, in which we are all deeply interested, we are
more than repaid, and more than content.   It affords
me great pleasure to tell you that, if all be well, we

shall return to Boston in March, when I hope to present, for the first time on our tour, 'Much Ado About Nothing.'   And now, ladies and gentlemen, in the names of one and all, I gratefully thank you, and respectfully wish you 'Good-bye and a Merry Christmas.' "

XII.

LOOKING FORWARD TO CHRISTMAS.

Interviewing in England and America—Rehearsing Richard
and Lady Ann—Reminiscences of a Christmas Dinner—A
Homely Feast—Joe Robins and Guy Fawkes—He would be
an Actor—The Luxury of Warmth—" One Touch of Nature."

I.

THERE is interviewing and interviewing. How it
comes out depends upon the interviewer and the interviewed. Every phase of the difficult art is shown in
American journalism. Mr. Yates, in the *World*, has
given us the best modern form of interviewing in
" Celebrities at Home." Mr. Blowitz, of the *Times*, and
other foreign correspondents have frequently shown
England how admirably the American system fits a
certain class of news. *The Pall Mall Gazette* has
lately adopted the method of our cousins more in
detail than has been hitherto popular with the London
press. I have always held that interviewing, conducted with discretion and a sense of journalistic
responsibility would be a valuable and entertaining
feature of English newspaper work.

I am prompted to these remarks by the contents of
this chapter. Said Mr. Stephen Fiske, the dramatic
editor of *The Spirit of the Times*, and the author of
a clever book on England, " I am anxious to have Mr.
Irving write a short story for our Christmas number.
Wilkie Collins, as you know, is a constant contributor,
and we have the assistance of some of the best pens,

O

English and American. Irving has written for several
English publications."

" He has a wonderful amount of energy, and can
do more mental work in a given time than any man
I know; but when he is going to get an opportunity
to sit down and write a Christmas story is more than I
can tell."

" I only want a personal reminiscence, an anecdote
or two," said Fiske; " but I must have him in the
Christmas number."

" Why don't you interview him, with Christmas as
the pivot of your interrogations ?" I asked.

" He has been interviewed almost to death, I should
think." [1]

" Oh, no; I believe he likes it. I am sure he does
when a really bright, clever fellow comes along and
engages his attention. Though he does not say so,
and, perhaps, has not thought about it, he is doing
good every time he talks to an American reporter
about the stage and its mission. No actor ever set
people thinking so much in England, and he is proving
himself quite an art missionary on this side of the
Atlantic."

" That's true," said the dramatic editor; " but for
my purpose I only want him to be simply entertaining,
—a bit of personal history, *apropos* of Christmas."

" Play the *rôle* of an interviewer, and write the
stories yourself," I suggested.

" I will," said Fiske. " Your plan has this advantage,—I shall get the copy in proper time for the
printer."

II.

And this Christmas chat is the result of the dramatic
editor's decision.

The trouble touching some of the " Interviews" that appeared
in the journals was that they were not all genuine. Fiske
suggested this fact as discounting a " Christmas chat;" but I
undertook to endorse his work by annexing his "interview " to
these pages; and I have to thank him for his bright contribution.

"It was a gloomy, rainy, miserable day. The theatre, always a dreary place in the morning, seemed even more depressing than usual. Mr. Irving was rehearsing the first act of 'Richard III.,' possibly with a view to Baltimore or Chicago.

"With that infinite patience which some philosophers define as genius, Mr. Irving went over and over the lines of Richard and Lady Ann, and acted all the business of the scene. His street costume and tall silk hat appeared ridiculously incongruous with his sword and his words. He knelt upon the stage and showed Lady Ann how to take hold of the weapon and threaten to kill him. He rose and repeated her speeches with appropriate gestures. He knelt again, gave her the cues, and watched her from under his heavy eyebrows, while she again rehearsed the scene.

"Repeated a dozen times, this performance became as monotonous as the dripping of the rain without, or the slow motions of the cleaners in the front of the theatre. At last, with a few final kindly words, the Lady Ann was dismissed, and Mr. Irving sat down wearily at the prompter's table.

"'Where shall you eat your Christmas dinner?' I inquired.

"'At Baltimore,' replied Mr. Irving. 'Several of my company have brought their home-made Christmas puddings over with them, and are to carry them about, with the rest of the luggage, until the day arrives. I have determined to try the American Christmas puddings, which, I am told, are very good indeed,—like most things American.'

"'Oh, our people manufacture them by thousands. After all, a Christmas pudding is only a mince-pie boiled.'

"'Just so,' said Mr. Irving, laughing in his silent, interior, Leatherstocking manner. 'I am thinking,' he exclaimed, 'of the Christmas dinner I gave last year in the room of the old Beefsteak Club, which, you know, is now part of the Lyceum Theatre. We

o 2

had talked the matter over,—a few friends and myself,
—and decided that we were tired of professional
cooks and conventional bills of fare, and that the best
stimulus for our jaded palates was a return to plain,
homely dishes.

" ' You can fancy Stoker saying that. He said it over
and over for at least a month, and kept humming,
" There's no place—or no dinner—like home," in the
most disquieting way, whenever the matter was mentioned. He also undertook to arrange the whole
affair.

" ' Well, it was arranged. There were to be no professional caterers, no professional waiters, no luxuries
of any kind,—except the wines, which I took under
my own care, being cast for the part of the butler.
Stoker was to buy the material. The property-man's
wife was to roast the beef and the turkey. The mistress of the wardrobe undertook to boil the pudding.
An usher, born with a genius for cookery, who was
discovered by Stoker, had charge of the soup, fish,
and vegetables. We were to wait upon ourselves,—a
genuine family party. A suggestion to order ices
from Gunter's, in case the pudding was a failure, was
voted down indignantly.

" ' As Christmas approached I became quite interested in this home dinner—hungry for it days in
advance, as one may say. I began by inviting one
friend who had a reputation as an epicure; then
another asked to be allowed to share our homely feast.
Presently our family party grew to thirty. I began to
have forebodings. You see, a small family can wait
upon themselves, but not a family of thirty.

" ' However, Stoker appeared cheerily satisfied and
mysteriously complacent, and seemed to think that our
motto should be " The more the merrier ! " I imagined
that he had secretly tested some of the home cooking
beforehand, and rather envied him his position as
taster.

" ' The guests were met; the table set. I had made

sure that the wines were all right. As I looked along at the happy, friendly faces I felt that a home dinner was the most pleasant, after all. The soup-tureen was before me, and I lifted the cover with the anxious pride of a Wellington firing the first gun at Waterloo. "'The chance simile of a battle holds good; for the soup was awfully smoky. Somebody said that it tasted like a chimney on fire. The fish was worse. The roast beef was uneatable. Persistent as I naturally am, I gave up the attempt to carve the turkey. The pudding was as hard as a stone. What little appetite remained to us was lost while carving the meats and passing the plates around. I had felt like Wellington before Waterloo; but when the dinner was over I could appreciate the despair of the defeated Napoleon.

"'Had we been only a family party the *fiasco* would not have been so fatal; but, as I told you, I had invited epicures; I had dragged my friends from their comfortable homes on Christmas Day to partake of this terrible repast. Some of them have never quite forgiven me. Some have forgiven me, because I had a chance to take them aside and put all the blame upon Stoker. But nobody who was present can ever have forgotten it.

"'Like Napoleon, I retreated to Fontainebleau; I fell back upon the wines. One of the guests won my heart by loudly eulogizing the cheese and the crackers. They were not home-made. They had not been cooked in the theatre!

"'Here comes Stoker,' continued Mr. Irving, relapsing into his curious solemnity of manner; 'let us ask him about it.

"'I say, Stoker, do you remember the home dinner you gave us at the Lyceum last Christmas?'

"Mr. Stoker stopped on his way across the stage, and stood like a statue of amazement, of indignation, of outraged virtue. 'The dinner *I* gave you?' he at last exclaimed. Then his loyalty to his chief triumphed, and he added, 'Well, you may call it my dinner, if you like; but I have the original copy of the bill of fare in your own handwriting.'

"'Ah!' resumed Mr. Irving, quite placidly, as his acting manager dashed away, 'I thought Stoker would remember that dinner!'

"'This Christmas you will dine upon roast canvasbacks, instead of roast beef, and stewed terrapin, instead of smoked soup,' I observed.

"'Yes,' replied the English actor; 'I am told that Baltimore is the best place for those delicacies. But they will not seem strange to me; I have eaten canvasbacks at Christmas before.'

"'In England?'

"'Certainly. My first American manager—Papa Bateman you used to call him—had many good friends in this country, who kept him liberally supplied with almost all your American luxuries. Under his tuition I learned to like the oysters, the terrapin, and canvasbacks, upon which my generous hosts are feasting me now, long before I ever thought of coming to America.

"'But perhaps the most remarkable Christmas dinner at which I have ever been present,' continued Mr. Irving, after reflecting for a few moments, 'was the one at which we dined upon underclothing.'

"'Do you mean upon your underclothing or in your underclothing?' queried the astonished interrogator conjuring up visions of Christmas dinners on uninhabited islands, at which shipwrecked mariners had been known to devour their apparel, and of the tropical Christmas dinners in India and Australia, at which scanty costumes are appropriate to the climate.

"'Both!' replied Mr. Irving. 'It is not a story of wonderful adventure; but I'll tell it to you, if you have five minutes more to spare. Do you remember Joe Robins—a nice, genial fellow who played small parts in provinces? Ah, no; that was before your time.

"'Joe Robins was once in the gentleman's furnishing business in London city. I think that he had a wholesale trade, and was doing well. However, he belonged to one of the semi-Bohemian clubs, associated a great deal with actors and journalists, and when an amateur performance was organized for some charitable object, Joe was cast for the clown in a burlesque called "Guy Fawkes."

"'Perhaps he played the part capitally; perhaps his friends were making game of him when they loaded him with praises; perhaps the papers for which his Bohemian associates wrote went rather too far when they asserted that he was the artistic descendant and successor of Grimaldi. At any rate, Joe believed all that was said to him and written about him, and when some wit discovered that Grimaldi's name was also Joe, the fate of Joe Robins was sealed. He determined to go upon the stage professionally and become a great actor.

"'Fortunately Joe was able to dispose of his stock and good-will for a few hundred pounds, which he invested so as to give him an income sufficient to prevent the wolf from getting inside his door, in case he did not eclipse Garrick, Kean, and Kemble. He also packed up for himself a liberal supply of his wares, and started in the profession with enough shirts, collars, handkerchiefs, stockings, and underclothing to equip him for several years.

"'The amateur success of poor Joe was never repeated on the regular stage. He did not make an absolute failure; no manager would entrust him with parts big enough for him to fail in. But he drifted down to general utility, and then out of London, and when I met him he was engaged in a very small way, on a very small salary, at a Manchester theatre.

"'His income eked out his salary; but Joe was a generous, great-hearted fellow, who liked everybody, and whom everybody liked, and when he had money he was always glad to spend it upon a friend or give it away to somebody more needy. So, piece by piece, as necessity demanded, his princely supply of haberdashery had diminished, and now only a few shirts and underclothes remained to him.

"'Christmas came in very bitter weather. Joe had a part in the Christmas pantomime. He dressed with other poor actors, and he saw how thinly some of them were clad when they stripped before him to put on their stage costumes. For one poor fellow in especial his heart ached. In the depth of a very cold winter he was shivering in a suit of very light summer underclothing, and whenever Joe looked at him the warm flannel undergarments snugly packed away in an extra trunk weighed heavily upon his mind.

"'Joe thought the matter over, and determined to give the actors who dressed with him a Christmas dinner. It was literally a dinner upon underclothing ; for the most of the shirts and drawers which Joe had cherished so long went to the pawnbroker's, or the slop-shop, to provide the money for the meal.

"'The guests assembled promptly, for nobody else is ever so hungry as a hungry actor. The dinner was to be served at Joe's lodgings, and before it was placed on the table, Joe beckoned his friend with the gauze underclothes into a bedroom, and, pointing to a chair, silently withdrew.

"'On that chair hung a suit of underwear which had been Joe's pride. It was of a comfortable scarlet colour; it was thick, warm, and heavy; it fitted the poor actor as if it had been manufactured especially to his measure. He put it on, and, as the flaming flannels encased his limbs, he felt his heart glowing within him with gratitude to dear Joe Robins.

"'That actor never knew—or, if he knew, he never could remember—what he had for dinner on that Christmas afternoon. He revelled in the luxury of warm garments. The roast beef was nothing to him in comparison with the comfort of his undervest; he appreciated the drawers more than the plum-pudding. Proud, happy, warm, and comfortable, he felt little inclination to eat, but sat quietly, and thanked Providence and Joe Robins with all his heart.'

" ' You seem to enter into that poor actor's feelings very sympathetically,' I observed, as Mr. Irving paused.

" ' I have good reason to do so,' replied Mr. Irving, with his gentle, sunshiny smile; 'for I was that poor actor ! ' "

XIII.

A WILD RAILWAY JOURNEY.

A Great American Railway Station—Platforms and Waiting-Rooms—A queer Night—" Snow is as Bad as Fog "—A Farmer who suggests Mathias in " The Bells "—A Romance of the Hudson—Looking for the *Maryland* and Finding " The Danites "—Fighting a Snow-Storm—" A Ministering Angel "—The Publicity of Private Cars—Mysterious Proceedings—Strange Lights—Snowed up—Digging out the Railway Points—A Good Samaritan Locomotive—Trains Ahead of Us, Trains Behind Us—Railway Lights and Bells —" What's going on ? "

I.

" THE Irving train is expected to arrive at Jersey City from Boston at about seven o'clock," said a telegraphic despatch which I received in New York on Sunday. I had left the great New England city two days before Irving's special train, with the understanding that I should join him at Jersey City, *en route* for Baltimore.

At half-past six I was on the great steam ferry-boat that plies from the bottom of Desbrosses Street, New York, to the other side of the river. A wintry wind was blowing up from the sea. I preferred the open air to the artificial heat of the cabin. In ten minutes I was landed at the station of the Pennsylvania Railroad.

" Inquire for the steamer *Maryland*," continued that despatch which I have just quoted. " She conveys the train down the Harlem river to connect on the Pennsylvania Road."

The general waiting-room of the station, or depôt, as our American cousins call it, is a characteristic one. Seeing that I was allowed plenty of time to observe it, I propose to describe it. A large square hall, with a high-pitched roof, it has more of a Continental than an English or American appearance. As you enter you find a number of people waiting for the trains. They include a few coloured people and Chinamen. The centre of the room is filled with benches, like the stalls of a London theatre. You wonder why two marble tombs have been erected here. They turn out to be heat-distributors. The hot air pours out from their grated sides. In case you should be in danger of suffocation a drinking fountain is in handy proximity to the blasts of heated air. The right-hand side of the hall is filled with booking-offices, and a clock bell tolls, indicating the times at which the various trains start. On the left is a *café*, and an entrance from Jersey City. Opposite to you as you enter from the ferry are two pairs of doors leading to the trains, and the space between the portals is filled in with a handsome book-stall. The doorways here are jealously guarded by officials who announce the departure of trains and examine your tickets. One of these guards sits near a desk where a little library of city and State directories is placed for the use of passengers. Each volume is chained to the wall. Near the *café* is a post-office box, and hanging hard by are the weather bulletins of the day. A ladies' waiting-room occupies a portion of the hall on the booking-office side. The place is lighted with electric lamps, which occasionally fizz and splutter, and once in a while go out altogether. Nobody pays any attention to this. Everybody is used to the eccentricities of the new and beautiful light.

Obtaining permission to pass the ticket portals, I reach the platform, where I am to find the station-master. The outlook here reminds me of the high-level station of the Crystal Palace. A dim gas-light

exhibits the outlines of a series of long cars, fenced in
with gates, that are every now and then thrown open
to receive batches of passengers from the waiting-
room.

The Irving train has been delayed. She is reported
"to arrive at the Harlem river at half-past eight."
In that case she may be here at a quarter to ten.

I return to the spluttering electric lamps and to the
continually coming and going multitudes of passengers. "No smoking" is one of the notices on the
walls. Two men have lighted their cigars right under
it. They remind one of the duellists in "Marion de
Lorme," who fight beneath the cardinal's proclamation. The *café* is bright and inviting, and its
chocolate is as comforting as the literature of the
book-stall. The novels of Howells and James and
Braddon and Black are here, and the Christmas
numbers of the *Illustrated London News* and the
Graphic; so likewise are the Christmas and New
Year's cards of Marcus Ward, De la Rue, and Lowell.
I purchase the latest novelty in books, "John Bull and
his Island," and try to read. I look up now and then
to see the crowd file off through the ticket doors
to go to Bethlehem, Catasauqua, Lansdown, New
Market, Bloomsbury, Waverly, Linden, Philadelphia,
West Point, Catskill, Albans, New Scotland, Port
Jackson, Schenectady, and other towns and cities,
the names of which stir my thoughts into a strange
jumble of reflections, Biblical, topographical, and
otherwise. Bethlehem and Bloomsbury! ·Were ever
cues for fancy wider apart ? "Over here," I read in
"John Bull and his Island," the writer referring to
London, "you are not locked up in a waiting-room
until your train comes in. You roam where you like
about the station, and your friends may see you off
and give you a handshake as the train leaves the
platform. The functionary is scarcely known. There
are more of them at the station of *Fouilly les Epinards*
than in the most important station in London. You

see placards everywhere: ' Beware of pickpockets ';
' Ascertain that your change is right before leaving
the booking-desk.' The Englishman does not like
being taken in hand like a baby." Curiously the
American is treated on the railroads very much as
in France. As to placard-notices, you see cautions
against pickpockets, and the London warning as to
change. Some of the other notifications in American
stations are curious : "No loafing allowed in this
depôt;" "Don't spit on the floor." Douglas Jerrold's
joke about the two angry foreigners who exclaimed,
"I spit upon you," has more point here than in
England; for no apartment is sacred enough is this
free country to keep out the spittoon, which, in some
places, is designed in such a way as to indicate a
strong intention to make it ornamental as well as
useful.

I seek the station-master again.

"Not sooner than a quarter to eleven," he says.

"Does the weather obstruct the train ? "

"Yes, it's a queer night; snow falling very thickly;
makes the river journey slower than usual; snow is
as bad as fog."

The entire train of eight enormous cars, containing
the Lyceum company and their baggage, is trans-
ported by boat right down the Harlem river, a distance of several miles, the raft and train being
attached to a tug-boat. The train is run upon the
floating track at Harlem, and connected again with
the main line at Jersey City.

"I was to ask for the steamer *Maryland.*"

"Yes, her quay is outside the depôt. I will let you
know when she is reported. You will hear her
whistle."

Trying to return to the waiting-room, I find I am
locked in. Presently a good-natured official lets me
out. In the meantime the *café* has closed, the book-
stall has fastened its windows and put out its lights.
The waiters on trains have thinned in numbers. Two

poor Chinamen who have been here are talking Pigeon English to a porter.

"You missed it at seven," he says ; "no more train till twelve."

"Twelfy!" says John, calmly counting his fingers; "no morey go till twelfy."

"That's so," says the porter.

The two celestials sit down quietly to wait ; the ferry-boats give out their hoarse signals, and presently a number of other people come in, covered with snow, a bitter wind accompanying them, as the doors open and shut. They stamp their feet and shake the snow from off their garments, and you hear the jingle of sleigh-bells without. A farmer whose dress suggests Mathias in "The Bells" comes in. He carries a bundle. There is a slip of green laurel in his buttonhole. I avail myself of the supposed privilege of the country, and talk to him.

"Yes," he says. "Christmas presents; I guess that's what I've been to New York for. I live at Catskill. No, not much in the way of farming. My father had land in Yorkshire. Guess I am an Englishman, as one may say, though born on the Hudson. Did I ever hear of Rip Van Winkle at Catskill? I guess so. Live there now? No, sir; guess it's a story, ain't it? But there was a sort of a hermit feller lived on the Hudson till a year or two ago. He was English. A scholar, they said, and learned. His grandchild, a girl, lived with him. Did nothing but read. Built the hut hisself. Never seen except when he and the girl went to buy stores. It was in the papers when he died, a year or two back. Broke his heart, 'cause his girl skipped."

"'Skipped!' I repeated.

"You are fresh, sir; green—as you say in England, run away—that's skipping. I bought one of his books when his things were sold, because I have a grandchild, and know what it is. Good-night! A merry Christmas to you!"

No other hint of Christmas in the depôt, among the people, or on the walls, except the cards and illustrated English papers inside the book-stall windows. I turn to "John Bull and His Island," and wonder if any English writer will respond with "Jean Crapeaud and His City." No country is more open to satire than France; no people accept it with so little patience. There are some wholesome truths in Max O'Rell's brochure. It is good to see ourselves as others see us.

A quarter to eleven. It is surely time to go forth in search of the *Maryland*.

"Better have a guide," says a courteous official; "you can't find it without; and, by thunder, how it snows! See 'em?"

He points to several new-comers.

"Only a few feet from the ferry—and they're like walking snow-drifts. See 'em!"

The guide, as sturdy as a Derbyshire ploughboy, comes along with his lantern.

"There are three ladies," I tell him, "in the private waiting-room, who are to come with us."

II.

I AM taking my wife and two girls to Baltimore for the Christmas week. Last year we had our Christmas dinner with Irving. This year he has said, "Let us all sup together. The theatres are open on Christmas day; we must, therefore, have our pudding for supper after we have seen the last of poor old Louis."

"Awkward night for ladies getting to the *Maryland*," says the guide.

They are well provided with cloaks and furs and snow-boots, or rubbers (an absolute necessity and a great comfort in America), and we all push along after the guide, across the departure platform, into the snowy night,—the flakes fall in blinding clouds; over railway tracks which men are clearing,—the white carpet soft and yielding; between freight cars, through open sheds—the girls enjoying it all, as only young people can enjoy a snow-storm.

The flickering light of our guide's lantern is at length eclipsed by the radiance of a well-illuminated cabin.

"This is the office; you can wait here; they'll tell you when the *Maryland's* reported."

A snug room, with a great stove in the centre. The men who are sitting around it move to make way for us. They do not disguise their surprise at their arrivals: an English family (one of them very young, with her hair blowing about her face), with snow enough falling from their cloaks to supply material for a snow-balling match. We are evidently regarded as novel visitors. Track labourers and others follow us in. They carry lamps, and their general appearance recalls the mining scene in "The Danites," at the London Olympic. Our entrance seems as much of a surprise to the others as the arrival of "the school-marm" was to the men in the Californian bar-room.

Presently a smart official (not unlike a guard of the Midland Railway in England as to his uniform) enters. There is a swing in his gait and a lamp in his hand, as a smart writer might put it.

"That gentleman will tell you all about the train," says one of the Danites, speaking in the shadow of the stove.

"The *Maryland*," I say, addressing the officer; "I want to get on board her special train from Boston."

"Guess I can't help that! I want to get some cars off her, that's all I know," is the response, the speaker eyeing me loftily, and then pushing his way towards a look-out window on the other side of the cabin.

"Oh, thank you very much," I say. "You are really too good. Is there any other gentleman here who is anxious to tell me where I shall find the *Maryland's* quay, and explain how I am to get on board the

special express, which takes a day to do a five-hours'
journey ? "

" I'll show you," says my surly friend, turning round
upon me and looking me all over. " I am the guard."

" Thank you."

" Here she comes ! " he exclaims.

I forgive him, at once, his brusqueness. He too
has, of course, been waiting six hours for her.

A hoarse whistle is heard on the river. The guard
opens the cabin-door. In rushes the snow and the
wind. The guard's lantern casts a gleam of light on
the white way.

" Be careful here," he says, assisting my girls over
a rough plank road.

It is an open quay over which we are pushing along.
The guard, now full of kind attention, holds up his
lamp for us, and indicates the best paths, the snow
filling our eyes and wetting our faces. Now we
mount a gangway. Then we struggle down a plank.
There are bustle and noise ahead of us, and the plash
" of many waters."

" Hatton ! " shouts the familiar voice of Bram
Stoker, through the darkness.

" Here we are ! " is the prompt reply.

A stalwart figure pushes through the snow, and the
next moment my wife is under the protection of a new
guide. We feel our way along mazy passages—now
upwards, now downwards—that might be mysterious
corridors leading to "dungeons beneath the castle
moat," the darkness made visible by primitive lamps.
Presently we are on the floating raft, and thence we
mount the steps of a railway car.

What a change of scene it is !—from Arctic cold
to summer heat ; from snow and rough ways to a
dainty parlour, with velvet-pile carpets, easy-chairs,
and duplex lamps ; and from the Danites to Irving,
Abbey, Loveday, and Miss Terry. They welcome us
cheerily and with Christmas greetings.

" Oh, don't mind the snow ; shake it off,—it will

P

not hurt us. Come, let me help you. Of course, you
all wear snow-boots,—Arctic rubbers, eh ? That's
right ; off with them first ! " And before we have
done shaking hands she is disrobing the girls, and
helping them off with their wraps and shoes,—this
heroine of the romantic and classic drama, this
favourite of English play-goers, who is now conquer-
ing the New World as surely as she has conquered
the Old.

Every one in the theatrical profession knows how
kindly and natural and human, as a rule, are, and
have ever been, the great women of the English stage.
But the outside public has sometimes strange opinions
concerning the people of this other side of the curtain,
this world of art. Some of them would be surprised
if they could see Ellen Terry attending upon my three
fellow-travellers ; giving them refreshment, and, later
on, helping to put them to bed. They would be interested, also, to have seen her dispensing tea to the
members of the company, or sitting chatting in their
midst about the journey and its incidents. Just as
womanly and tender as is her Desdemona, her Portia,
her Ophelia, so is she off the stage,—full of sympathy,
touched to the quick by a tale of sorrow, excited to
the utmost by a heroic story. Hers is the true artistic
temperament. She treads the path of the highest
comedy as easily and with the same natural grace, as
she manifests in helping these girls of mine, from New
York, to remove their snowy clothes, and as naturally
as she sails through these very practical American
cars to make tea for her brother and sister players,
who love her, and are proud of her art.

III.

HAVING spent an hour in vainly trying to couple
Irving's private car with another in the centre of the
train the guard decides to attach it to the last one.
In this position, which eventually proved an interesting

one, we trundle along through Jersey City, past rows
of shops and stores on a level with the side-walks, the
snow falling all the time. Here and there electric
arcs are shedding weird illuminations upon the un-
familiar scenes. By the lights in many of the houses
we can see that the window-panes are coated with a
thick frost. Now and then we stop without any
apparent warning, certainly without any explanation.
During one of these intervals we take supper, those
of us who have not retired to seek such repose as may
be found in a railroad sleeping-car,—an institution
which some American travellers prefer to a regular
bedroom. Irving, Abbey, Stoker, Loveday, and myself, we sit down to a very excellent supper,—oyster-
pie, cold beef, jelly, eggs, coffee, cigars.

"It is too late to tell you of our adventures prior to
your coming upon the train," says Irving. "We will
have a long chat to-morrow. Good-night; I am going
to try and get a little rest."

He lies down upon a couch adjacent to the apartment in which we have supped. I draw a curtain over
him, that shuts off his bunk from the room and the
general corridor of the car. You hear a good deal
of talk in America about "private cars." Without
disparaging the ingenuity and comfort of the private-
car system of American railroad-travelling, let me
say, once for all, that the term private applied to it
in any sense is a misnomer. There is no privacy about
it,—nothing like as much as you may have in an
English carriage, to the sole occupancy of which you
have bought the right for a railway journey. On an
American train there is a conductor to each car. Then
there are one or more guards to the train. Add to
these officials, baggage-men, who are entitled to come
on at various stations, and news-boys, who also appear
to have special claims on the railway company; and
you count up quite a number of extra passengers who
may appear in your private room at any moment.

It is true that the guard of your car may exclude

some of these persons; but, as a rule, he does not. If
he should be so inhospitable to his fellow-man, there are
still left the conductors and guards, who have business
all over the train at all hours. There is a passage-
way, as you know, right through the train. On a
special car there is a room at each end; one is a
smoking-room. This apartment, with or without your
permission, is occupied by the officials of the train;
and on a cold night not even the most exacting traveller would think of objecting to the arrangement.
But it is easy to see that this does away with all ideas
of privacy.

At 1.30 the train comes to a long standstill. I am
reading. The coloured waiter, a negro with a face
given over to the permanent expression of wonder,
has taken a seat near me, in the opposite corner of the
car. The end of the car opens right upon the line;
the door is half glass, so that we can see out into the
night and away down the track. To keep the outlook
clear I occasionally rub the frosty rime from the glass,
and now and then open the door and clear it from
snow. The negro contemplates me through his wide,
staring eyes. He takes a similar interest in the guards
and other officers of the train, who come through the
cars at intervals, swinging, as they walk, lamps of
singularly artistic patterns when compared with the
English railway lanterns. These guardians of the
train pass out of the door of the room upon the line,
and rarely reappear except when they come back again
right through the train, passing most of the would-
be sleepers. Irving does not, however, appear to be
disturbed.

It is 2.35 when the train once more begins to move.
For nearly an hour both the coloured servant and I
have, off and on, been watching a number of curious
demonstrations of lights away down the line behind
us. First a white light would appear, then a red one,
then a green light would be flashed wildly up and
down.

The negro guesses we must be snowed up. But he doesn't know much of this line, he says, in a deprecatory tone; only been on it once before; doesn't take much stock in it. Then he shakes his woolly head mysteriously; and what an air of mystery and amazement is possible on some dark faces of this African race! We move ahead for five minutes, and then we stop again. There is a clock on the inlaid panel of the car over the negro's head. The time is steadily recorded on the dial. It is 2.45 when we advance once more. A hoarse whistle, like a fog-horn at sea, breaks upon the solemnity of the night; then we pass a signal-box, and a patch of light falls upon our window. This is evidently the signal for another pause. "2.50," says the clock. The line behind us is now alive with lanterns. White lights are moving about with singular eccentricity. With my face close against the glass door-way I count six different lights. I also see dark forms moving about. All the lights are suddenly stationary. One comes on towards the train. Our guard frantically waves his light. Presently we stop with a jerk. The lights we have left in the distance now gyrate with the same inconsequential motion as the witchfires of a fairy tale, or the fiends' lights in the opera of "Robert le Diable." Then they remain still again. I open the door. There is a foot of snow on the platform, and the feathery flakes are steadily falling. A solitary light comes towards us. The bearer of it gets upon the platform,—a solitary sentinel. The negro looks up at me, and asks me in a gentle kind of way, if I ever use sticking-plaster. "Yes," I say, "sometimes." A strange question. My reply appears to be a relief to him. Do I ever use sticking-plaster! There is a long pause outside and inside the car, as if some mysterious conference was going on. "Was you ever on the cars when they was robbed?" the negro asks. "No," I say; "I was not."—"Been on when there was shooting?" he asks. "No."—"Has you ever heard of Jesse James and the

book that was written about him?"—"Yes," I
answer, " but never saw the book."—"Dark night,
eh?"—"Yes, pretty dark."—"They would stop de
train, and get a-shooting right away, would dem James
boys, I tell you! Perfeck terror dey was. No car
was safe. Ise believe dey was not killed at all, and
is only waiting for nex' chance."—"You are not
frightened?" I say.   "Well, not zactly; but don't
know who dis man is standing dere on de platform,
and neber was on any train of cars dat stopped so
much and in such lonely places; and don't like to be
snowed up eider. I spoke to de brakesman about an
hour ago; but he don't say much." Thereupon he
flattens his broad nose against the window, and I take
up " John Bull and his Island " at the description of
the Christmas pudding, which sets me thinking of all
the gloomy things that may and do happen between
one Christmas Day and another; and how once in most
lifetimes some overwhelming calamity occurs that
makes you feel Fate has done its worst, and cannot
hurt you more. This thought is not *apropos* of the
present situation; for, of course, there is nothing to
fear in the direction suggested by the negro, who has
worked himself up into a condition of real alarm. At
the same time the dangers of snow-drifts are not
always confined to mere delays. The newspapers, on
the day following our protracted journey, for example,
chronicled the blowing up of a locomotive, and the
death of driver and stoker, through running into a
snow-drift. The accident occurred not far from the
scene of one of our longest stoppages.

2.55.   The man on the platform cries " Go ahead!"
and as the car moves he steps inside, literally covered
with snow. He makes no apology, but shivers and
shakes his coat.

" What is wrong?" I ask.

" Train stuck in the snow ahead of us. It is an
awful night."

"What were those lights in our rear?—one in particular."

"That was me. I have been out there an hour and a half."

"You are very cold?"

"Frightful."

"Have a little brandy?"

"Think I'll break up if I don't."

I gave him some brandy. From the other end of the car comes the guard.

"Think we'll get round her all right now?" he asks.

"Oh, yes," says the conductor, shaking his snowy clothes.

The guard goes out. He, too, carries a weight of snow on his coat.

Says the officer (whom I have just saved from "breaking up "), "I am the conductor; but if anything is wrong they'd blame me, not him; am sent on to this train,—a special job."

"What were you doing out there so long?"

"Digging the points out of the snow, to push these cars on to another track, and get round ahead of the train that's broke down."

"And have you done it?"

"Guess so."

It is three o'clock as he steps once more upon the platform. At 3.5 the train stops suddenly. I look out into the black and white night. It still snows heavily. At 3.10 the conductor returns.

"When do you think we will get to Baltimore?"

"At about ten."

"What is the difficulty?"

"Trains in front of us, trains behind us, too. You would be surprised at the depth of the snow. A gang of men clearing the track ahead."

At 3.10 he goes out again into the wild night; this time the snow on the platform glows red under the

light of his lamp, which exhibits the danger signal. A
distant whistle is heard. The conductor is pushing the
snow off the platform with his feet. He opens the
door to tell me it is drifting in places to "any height."
At 3.15 he says we have taken *three* hours to go
twenty miles. Looking back on the track the rails
show a black, deep line in the snow. Not a house
or a sign of life anywhere around us. "We are a
heavy train, eight cars," says the conductor. The
negro stares at us through his wide, great eyes.
"At Rahway we hope to get another engine," says the
guard. At 3.25 we are really moving along steadily.
"About twelve miles an hour," says the conductor. The
negro smiles contentedly. "We have not met a single
train since we left Jersey City," says the conductor;
"must be trains behind us,—not far away either." A
signal station with green and red lights slips by us.
The swinging bell of an approaching train is heard.
The conductor stands on the platform and waves his
lamp. Our train stops. There looms suddenly out of
the darkness behind us a vast globe, white and glowing
like a sun. It comes on, growing larger, and accompanying it is the bang, bang, bang, of the engine's
bell, a familiar, but uncanny, sound in America. A
number of minor lights dance about on either side of
the approaching monster. It does not stop until its
great single blazing Cyclopean eye looks straight into
our car. Then a voice says, "Don't you want some
assistance?" The monster is a good Samaritan. "A
freight train," says the conductor, leaping down upon
the line. "Yes, push us along." I follow him into
the snow, up to my knees, and the flakes are falling in
blinding clouds. A man is altering our signal light.
"Are you going to give us another engine?" I ask.
"More than I can say," he replies. "This buffer's no
good; can't push against that," says the guard of the
other train. Then our conductor goes off with him
into the rear. It is 3.40. I turn once more to "John
Bull and His Island." The negro is asleep. We

move on again, and gradually leave the locomotive Cyclops behind, its great, sun-like eye getting smaller. A few minutes more, and it follows us. We pull up at a switch-station. There is some difficulty with the posts. I go out and lend a hand at getting them clear of snow. Return very cold and wet. Happily the car is kept at a standing heat of 80° to 90°. "This freight train started an hour and a half behind us," says the conductor. "What about the train ahead?" —"Just got clear of it at last, switched us on to another line. Hope we'll get on now." At 3.50 we are really going ahead, quite at a brisk pace. Suddenly another light behind us; suddenly that ominous bell. It reminds me of the storm-bell off Whitby, that Irving and I sat listening to, one autumn night, a year or two ago. The conductor had passed through the cars. Is this new train going to run us down? It comes along swinging its bell. Just as the possibility of a collision seems ominous the new-comer veers to the left and passes us. We are evidently on a single line of rails, with switch-stations at intervals for trains to pass and repass. Our unhappy train stops once more. Another comes pounding along, with its one blazing light and its tolling bell. It passes us defiantly, as the other has done. The new-comer is, however, only an engine this time. "Assistance, no doubt," I say to myself. I open the door. The snow beats in with a rush of wind. The glass is covered with ice. All else is quiet,—everybody asleep in the train. The negro is dreaming; he pulls ugly faces. I rub the ice off the window. The conductor is out in the snow with several lamps, searching for points. He is kicking at the rails with his boots. A man joins him with a shovel. They work away. At four o'clock our train groans and screams; it moves very quietly. The conductor plods back through the snow. We stop. At 4.5 the conductor and several others are digging on the line. Clearing points, no doubt. There are switch-lights right and left of them.

Now the conductor climbs once more upon the platform, leaving a red lamp away on the track behind him. Another train is heard bellowing; another bell following; another great lamp gleams along the track, smaller red lights showing upon its white beam, over which the snow falls. This other locomotive comes right into us, its great blinding eye blazing like a furnace. The negro wakes up with a cry. "Ah, you fool!" exclaims the conductor, "what's the matter?"—"Got help now," he says to me, "at last; this will push, and there is another one in front." The rear engine pants and pushes, her cow-catcher literally covered with a snow-bank. There is a great fuss about coupling our car upon this panting assistant. "Is it only an engine, or has it cars to draw?"—"It had a train of cars; we have left them on a siding. We shall be all right now."

"What's going on?" is suddenly asked in words and tones not unlike a voice in "The Bells,"— "what's going on?"—"We are, I hope, soon," I reply to my friend, who has pushed aside his Astrachan cloak and the car-curtains, and is looking curiously at us. The negro attendant wakes up and goes towards him. "What is it?"—"Oh, nothing, sah," says the coloured gentleman. "Only getting another engine," says the conductor. "What for?" asks Irving (he has really been to sleep). "To check our speed," I say; "we have been going too fast."—"Oh, you astonish me!" says Irving. "Good-night, then!" The clock marks 4.30. "Good-night, indeed!" I reply. "So say we all of us," murmurs Loveday, as I pass his bunk in search of my own; "what a time we are having!"

XIV.

CHRISTMAS, AND AN INCIDENT BY THE WAY.

At Baltimore — Street Scenes — Christmas Wares — Pretty Women in "Rubber Cloaks"—Contrasts—Street Hawkers— Southern Blondes—Furs and Diamonds—Rehearsing under Difficulties — Blacks and Whites — Negro Philosophy — Honest Work—"The Best Company on its Legs I have ever seen"—Our Christmas Supper—"Absent Friends"— Pictures in the Fire and afterwards—An intercepted Contribution to Magazine Literature—Correcting a Falsehood —Honesty and Fair Play.

I.

BALTIMORE Street is the Broadway of the Monumental City. It also suggests Chestnut Street in Philadelphia, more particularly in the matter of sign-boards. A city of stores and offices, it proclaims its various businesses in signs of every conceivable shape. They swing from ornamental brackets over doorways, and hang right across the pavements. They are of many shapes, but as to colour are invariably black and gold. The inscriptions upon them are characteristic; some of them are strange to the non-travelled Englishmen. I note a few of them: "Gent's Neck Wear," "Fine Jewellery," "Men's Furnishing,"—this latter is the general sign of American hosiers and shirt-makers,— "Diamonds," "Fine Shoes," "Dry Goods," "Imported Goods," "Books," "Cheap Railroad Tickets," "Cheap Tickets for Chicago," "Saddlery," "Adams'

Express." To these are added the names of the
dealers. The " Cheap Railroad Tickets " is a branch
of the speculative operations in theatrical admissions.
" Adams' Express " is a familiar sign everywhere. It
represents the great and universal system of baggage
distribution. Adams and other firms will take charge
of a traveller's luggage, or any other kind of goods,
and "check" it through to any part of the United
States, possibly to any corner of the world. To-day,
in honour of Christmas, the ordinary signs have been
supplemented by such attractive proclamations as
" Holiday Presents," " Toys for the Season," " For
Christmas and New Year's," " Home-made Christmas
Puddings." At the doors of tobacco stores the figure of
a North American Indian, in complete war-paint, offers
you a bundle of the finest cigars, and his tomahawk is
poised for action in case you decline his invitation to
" Try them." In New York this coloured commercial
statuary is varied with an occasional " Punch," and by
many buxom ballet-girls in short dresses and chignons.
But the taste of Baltimore, Philadelphia, Boston, and
Chicago runs in the direction of the Indian. Nowhere
do you see the blackamoor, once popular at the door of
English tobacconists; nor, except at Brooklyn, have I
seen on the American side of the Atlantic the kilted
Highlander, with his "mull" as a sign for the information or temptation of snuff-takers. At Chicago
there is a Scotch sculptor who has ornamented the exterior of more than one store with life-size realizations
of the heroes of some of Burns's most popular poems.
Several of these are represented as snuff-takers; but
the collection includes a few really admirable studies.
The city architect, by the way, at Chicago, is a Scotchman, and he is responsible for the fine designs of the
chief public buildings. Baltimore is not singular in
its habit of pictorial signs, the origin of which may
possibly be traced to old English custom. The saddler
exhibits the gilded head of a horse; the watchmaker
hangs out a clock; the glover a hand; the dry-goods

stores display bright rugs and carpets. Now and then the cabinet-makers show their goods on the pavements. Many stores erect handsome outside glass-case stands for exhibiting knick-knacks at their doorways. The fruit shops open their windows on the street. Itinerant dealers in oranges, bananas, and grapes rig up tent-like houses of business under the windows of established traders (for which heavy rents are paid, notably "down-town" in New York), and all this gives a pleasant variety of life and colour to the street. One is every-where reminded of the excellence of English manufac-tures, "English Tanned Gloves," "English Storm-coats," "English Cloth;" and many other commercial compliments are paid to "Imported Goods."

It is three o'clock in the day, and while Irving, his lieutenant, Loveday, and his able subalterns, Arnot and Allen, are getting the stage of the Academy of Music into some kind of shape for the Christmas-Eve performance, I plod through the rain and slush to make my first acquaintance with this chief street of Baltimore. It is curiously picturesque, in spite of the weather and the dirty snow, which is melting and freezing almost simultaneously. Here and there the pavements are slabs of ice ; here and there they are sloppy snow-drifts. But a surging crowd covers every foot of them. The roadway presents a continual block of tram-cars, buggies, waggons, carts, and carriages. Women leaving and getting upon the cars plunge in and out of snow-heaps and watery gutters. It is a very democratic institution, the American car. The people crowd it as they please. There is no limit to its capacity. It may carry as many persons as can get into it or stand upon its platforms. This afternoon the cars are human hives on wheels. One notices that the crowd chiefly consists of women. They fill the street. All of them are shopping. They are all talking, and all at the same time. This is a peculiarity of our charming cousins. Their costume on this wet afternoon is a very sensible one. It might almost be

called a uniform. A black water-proof cloak and hood
is all the costume you can see. Often it is a pretty,
bright face that the hood encases. Now and then
some woman, a trifle more vain or reckless than her
sisters, wears a hat and feathers with her water-proof
cloak. This incongruous arrangement, however, helps
to give colour to the crowd,—a desirable point on so
dull, grey, and cloudy a day as this. The men who
move about here are mostly smoking. They do not
appear to have any hand in the shopping. The
ladies are doing all that, and are very much in
earnest. Not one of them but deigns to carry a
parcel. The children are evidently coming in for
precious gifts. In one shop window "Father Christmas " himself is busy showing his toys to a numerous
audience. He is made up with white flowing locks
and beard, and ruddy, though aged, features. His
dress is an ermine tippet, scarlet frock trimmed with
gold, and top-boots of patent leather,—quite the
nursery ideal of his genial majesty. Another store
has filled its window with a skating scene. A company
of gay dolls are sliding for their very lives. They go
through their lively work without any change of
expression, and their gyrations never alter; but the
spectators change, and the store within is full of
bustle. I look around for the poor people we would see
in a London group of this character. I seek in vain
for the Smikes and Twists who would be feasting their
sunken eyes on such a free show in London. I try to
find the slipshod women, with infants huddled to their
cold bosoms. They are not here. A boy of twelve,
with a cigarette in his hand, asks me for a light.
Another " guesses " his " papa " will buy " the whole
concern " for him if he wants it. No poor people.
The Irish are a small community here. How one's
mind goes wandering to the West End of London and
to the Strand and Fleet Street, to the Seven Dials and
to Ratcliffe Highway, where (it is five hours later
there than here) Christmas Eve is being celebrated

with such contrasts of fortune and variations of wealth and poverty, of joy and sorrow, as make the heart ache to think upon. Not a single poor-looking person do I note in this long, busy street of Baltimore. Nobody begs from me; and the hawkers on the pavement offer me their wares with an air of almost aggressive independence. " Japanese silk, ten cents," one cries, with a bundle of small handkerchiefs in his hand. " The magic mouse," says another, vending a mechanical toy. " Now, then, one dime a packet," is the proposal of a third, offering material for decorating Christmas trees. "Try 'em!" almost commands a fourth, as I pause opposite his stand of peanuts. If you buy, nobody thanks you, and if you thank the vendor, he is surprised and will probably stammer out, " You're welcome." Yet "this is the Cavalier city," a friend reminds me, " and aristocratic to the core."

The fruit stores are bright with tropical fruits ; but not with the roses, carnations, pinks, and smilax creeper, so plentiful in New York, Boston, and Philadelphia. I pause to scan the faces of the crowd. It is a popular fiction in England that the women of the South are brunettes. The truth is, the further south you go, the fairer the women, and the more delicate their complexions. In Baltimore Street I observe quite a number of ladies with red hair. Many of them are blondes, who might have been natives of Lincolnshire. They are all pretty ; some are beautiful ; and their charms certainly obtained no fictitious aid from their dress or surroundings. Water-proof cloaks and a muddy street could not help them. Baltimoreans may say I should look for beauty in North Charles Street, or Mount Vernon Place, if I expect to see it *en promenade.* But I am not looking for it. I find it in the great, busy, Christmas crowd, tramping through the snow, and buying toys and candies for the children. The " carriage ladies" wear furs, and those everlasting diamond ear-rings, without which expensive ornament few American women appear to consider themselves "real ladies." New York and Boston modify the fashion in this respect, though you may still see women sitting down to breakfast at hotel restaurants in silks, satins, and diamonds.

II.

WHILE I have been studying Baltimore Street darkness has fallen upon it. The gas-lamps and the electric arcs are beginning their nightly competition as I retrace my steps to the Academy of Music. Irving, who arrived in Baltimore at two, after a journey of forty-two hours, has just left the stage, I am told,—" gone to get a little rest."

" Have you had a rehearsal ? "

" Oh, yes," says Loveday, who is directing the last finishing touches to the throne-room set for "Louis XI." " Tight work, eh ? Got into the town at two—scenery to unpack—some of it is still on the train. But we get through it. The chief has his rehearsal somehow —finished half an hour ago—in two hours the curtain goes up. Had to do it all ourselves. Shall have to turn Arnot's men into Burgundians. No help to be had of any kind,—it is Christmas, you know, and Christmas comes but once a year, thank goodness ! The chief carpenter, who is also the gasman, has not turned up. Some of the other fellows are ' Merrie-Christmasing,' also. Tried to get some additional assistance in the way of labour. Found a few chaps loafing ; asked them if they wanted work. Said they did not mind. Offered them good wages. ' Oh, no,' they said ; ' get niggers to do that.' They were above it. I acted on their advice. The moment it was dark the ' coloured boys,' as they call themselves, knocked off. Said they never worked after dark. ' Night is the time to rest and sleep,' they said. ' For black men, perhaps,' I replied ; ' but not for white.' Seemed to me as if they said, ' You had us for slaves a good many years ; it is our turn now.' Funny, eh ?

They wouldn't go on working. However, we shall be all right. It's a good thing I'm not the only Mark Tapley in the company, don't you know; and the governor, by Jove! he stands it like—well, like only Henry Irving can!"

Two hours later Irving is received with rapturous applause by a comparatively small audience. "More power to them!" he says; "for they have left cosey hearths to drive or tramp through the slush of the first snow of the Baltimore winter." And the company, all round, never played with more spirit. "It is the only return we can make to those who have come to see us on such a night," said Irving to several of them before the curtain went up, "to do our very best." And they did. Terriss was never more successful as Nemours. The audience was cold at first, but as the dramatic story unrolled itself under the grip of the master, they caught the infection of its grim interest, and their applause rang out heartily and long. Irving developed the leading character with more than ordinary care, and was called and recalled after every act,—a triple call at the close including Terriss, whose manliness of gait and manner are peculiarly acceptable to every audience.

"There is one thing I observe about this company," said the Boston manager: "it walks well; it is the best company on its legs I have ever seen. Our young men, as a rule, particularly in costume, turn out their toes too much, or are knock-kneed; all your people stand well on their feet,—it is a treat to see them."

"Yes," says Irving, smiling, when this is reported to him. "I engaged them to show me off. But did not Emerson say that the Englishman is, of all other people, the man who stands firmest in his shoes? There is one thing to be said about our cousins on this side, —they do not stand still; they are like young Rapid in 'A Cure for the Heart-Ache,'—always on the move. And when they are behind a trotting-horse how they go! I am a little disappointed, so far, with the sleighing as a matter of speed; but the snow was too soft when we took our first drive at Boston."

III.

IT is the custom in America to open the theatres on Christmas Day. The doors of the Baltimore house could not have been opened in more wretched weather. The streets were impassable, except for carriages, or for pedestrians in "Arctic rubbers," or on stilts. The snow was melting everywhere. Nothing had been done to clear the pavements. They were full of treacherous puddles, or equally treacherous snowdrifts. The Turks blow horns at certain periods of the year, to frighten away evil spirits. I know of no explanation for the blowing of horns at Baltimore; but the boys indulge themselves in this exercise to a bewildering extent at Christmas. Carol-singing is evidently not a custom there, nor "waits." I heard a boy shouting at the top of his voice the refrain of a popular ditty :—

> "In the morning, in the morning,
> When Gabriel blows his trumpet,
> In the morning."

But I conclude that he had only adapted these modern words to what was evidently an old custom at Baltimore; for he blew his horn vigorously at the end of the refrain, as if competing for supremacy with Gabriel himself.

"You are right; it does not seem like Christmas," said Irving, as we sat down to supper—close upon midnight,—a section of that same party which, a year previously, had gathered about the round table in the host's Beefsteak Club room at the Lyceum Theatre.

"It seems so strange," said Ellen Terry, "to play on Christmas Day; that, to me, makes the time wholly unlike Christmas. On the other hand, there is the snow, and we shall have an English Christmas pudding, —I brought it from home, and my mother made it."

" Well done ; bless her heart ! " said Irving ;. " but I have played before on Christmas Day. They open the theatres in Scotland on Christmas Day. They don't pay much attention, I am told, to church festivals in Boston and New England; but one would have expected it in the South, where they are observing the social character of Christmas, I learn, more and more every year; and not alone to the snow, but to that fact, I am told, we are to attribute the small houses we had last night and to-night." [1]

" Small for America and for us," chimed in Loveday ; " but what we should, after our experience, call bad business here would be very good in England."

" Yes, that's true," said Irving ; " but here's holly and mistletoe,—where did they come from ?·"

He was looking at a very English decoration that swung from the chandelier.

" From London, with the pudding," said Miss Terry.

The coloured attendants took great interest in our celebration of the festival. If they could have put their thoughts into words they would probably have expressed surprise that artists of whom they had heard so much could entertain each other in so simple a fashion.

When the pudding came on the table it was not lighted.

" Who has had charge of this affair ? " Irving asked, looking slyly at everybody but his acting manager.

" I have, of course," replied Stoker.

" That accounts for it," said Irving. " Who ever heard of a Christmas pudding without a blaze, except, perhaps, in Ireland ? "

" Oh, we'll soon light it up," said Stoker. " Waiter, bring some brandy ! "

Presently the pudding flamed up, to the delight of the African gentlemen who served it.

[1] The theatre was crowded during the remainder of the week.

" I fear there is no sauce," said one of the ladies.
" No sauce! Christmas pudding and no sauce ! " I
exclaimed.   " Here's stage management ! "
" Sauce ! " said Stoker,—" to plum pudding ? "
" Yes, always in England," said Loveday.

This kind of mild banter was checked by Irving
filling his glass with champagne, and observing,
" After the experience of last year, of course we ought
not to have entrusted Stoker with the pudding.   However, let us make the best of it.   It seems a very
good pudding, after all.   I want you all to fill your
glasses.   Let us wish each other in the old way, ' A
merry Christmas and a happy New Year,' and ' God
bless our absent friends ! "

Some of us gulped the wine a little spasmodically,
and some of us found it hard to keep back our tears.
Who can pledge that familiar toast, and not think of
the empty chairs that seem so very, very empty at
Christmas !

When the women and my girls had been escorted to
their carriages, and sent home to their hotel, with
flowers and bon-bons on their laps, we three men of
the little party sat round the fire and talked of old
times.   Irving had ordered the biggest logs the hotel's
wood-yard afforded to be heaped into the grate.   The
fire cracked and spluttered and blazed, and had in the
lower bars of the grate a solid, steady glow of white
ash that was truly English ; and I think we each
looked into it for a time, busy with our own individual
thoughts and reflections.   Presently, under the more
cheerful influences of the season, we talked of many
things, and finally drifted into " shop."   The chief
subject was started by Irving himself, and it dealt
with the novel treatment of the next Shakespeare play
which he intends to produce at the Lyceum.   He
looked into the fire and saw it there, scene by scene,
act by act.   As he saw it, he described it.

It was in the glamour of Irving's rosiest pictures
that I said good-night, to have the witchery of the fire-

light dispelled by the outer bitterness of the weather, and the lonely, desolate appearance of the city. The streets were now as hard as they had been soft; the pools were ice, the snow adamant; icicles hung down from the eaves of every house. The roadways glistened in the lamplight. Not a soul was abroad. It might have been a city of the dead. A strain of Christmas music would have redeemed the situation. Even a London " waits " at its worst, such as one awakens to with a growl on cold nights at home, would have been a God-send. Not a sound; not a footstep; no distant jangle of car-bells; not even a policeman; only the winter night itself, with a few chilly-looking stars above, and the hard, icy streets below.

IV.

IT is a long way from Baltimore to Brooklyn,— five or six hundred miles,—Brooklyn to Chicago is over a thousand; yet these were the journeys that followed each other. The company, as you already know, travelled from Boston to Baltimore; from Baltimore it went to Brooklyn; and from the city of churches its next trip was to the great city on Lake Michigan. But, not to get ahead of events, we will pause at Brooklyn : first, to say that the theatre was crowded there all the week; secondly, for Irving to relate an incident by the way; and, thirdly, to introduce the succeeding chapter, which will describe our departure therefrom.

Irving was a little ruffled during his journey from Baltimore by the sting of one of those vagrant gad-flies of the press that are not confined to the American continent, but, as a matter of course, exist in that broader field in large numbers, and are of greater variety than in the narrower limits of Great Britain.

" I promised to write a little gossip of my experiences in America for the —— magazine, and I think the Baltimore incident is a very good subject, told as an episode of the trip, with just a few lines about my reception. What do you think ? "

" Very good, indeed," I said.

" Ah, I'm glad you like the notion, because I have written it. Here it is ; I'll read it to you."

" The Baltimore man will feel flattered when he learns how much you have taken his *Tribune* despatch to heart," I said.

" I don't care for that at all ; nor would I, as you know, have thought of answering him, only that he put his falsehood into so ingeniously damaging a shape. But no matter, this is what I have written :—

"AN INCIDENT OF MY AMERICAN TOUR.

" The Sunday newspapers of America are the largest and certainly the most amusing of the week. They were especially welcome to me during the railway journey between Baltimore and Brooklyn. The landscape was striking now and then; but we were travelling literally through a snow world, and the monotony of it was a trifle tedious.

" I turned to the New York papers, a bundle of which had been brought ' on board ' (this term is applied to railway trains as to ships in America), and was not long in coming upon a surprise. It was in the shape of a special telegraphic despatch from Baltimore to the *Tribune*, of December 30th. I read that ' Henry Irving closed a very successful week at the Academy of Music ;'. that his ' audiences were large ;' that ' his success was due to curiosity ;' that ' " Hamlet " raised a storm of criticism about his newfangled ideas, and when the ghost appeared on the stage in a green gown the audience roared at the strange sight, to the evident embarrassment of the ghost ;' that ' individually, however, Henry Irving's stay in Baltimore was of the pleasantest nature ;' and that ' Dr. W. Crim,' the well-known surgeon, gave him

---

² A reception was given to Mr. Henry Irving, the distinguished English actor, by Dr. Wm. H. Crim, at his residence, 185, W. Fayette Street, last evening. At the close of the performance

a reception, where he proved himself an entertaining conversationalist. He was favourably impressed with Americans, but said they were not yet fully educated to appreciate true artistic ability; they were progressing.'

"As I had never remembered the closet scene in ' Hamlet' to have been more impressive, and particularly as regarded the appearance of the ghost; as the question of curiosity, *per se,* had never been raised by the local press; as on our first two nights we had bad

at the Academy, Mr. Irving, accompanied by his stage manager, H. J. Loveday; acting manager, Bram Stoker; J. H. Copleston, and James H. Plaser, representing Manager Abbey, of New York, and Mr. Joseph Hatton, the English author, drove to Dr. Crim's residence, where they were received by the host, and presented to a number of journalists, representing the city press, and other gentlemen. Among those present were Messrs. John W. McCoy, Wm. T. Croasdale, John V. Hood, Innes Randolph, Harry J. Ford, Henry D. Beall, C. M. Fairbanks, E. N. Vallandigham, Frederick L. Holmes, Prof. Charles G. Edwards, Samuel W. Fort, Manager of the Academy; Harry P. Wilson, Harry F. Powell, Harry J. Conway, Charles F. Meany, John W. Albaugh, of Holliday-street Theatre; Chas. Reynolds, and W. I. Cook. The affair was wholly informal, but was apparently all the more agreeable on that account. Mr. Irving, upon being presented, expressed his gratification at meeting the representatives of the Baltimore press, and during the evening manifested the utmost cordiality of manner. He is a delightful conversationalist, and for a couple of hours entertained groups of attentive listeners. His impressions of Baltimore, as far as he had seen, were very favourable, and he was much pleased with the audiences that had greeted him during the week at the Academy. Speaking of the Academy, he remarked that its acoustic properties—a rare quality in a theatre of that size—were among the very best he had ever known. About midnight the visitors repaired to the dining-room, where a tempting repast, with choice wines, was enjoyed. Adjourning thence to the library, the guests indulged in a fragrant Havana, and another hour slipped by almost unconsciously in pleasant social intercourse. During the evening Mr. Irving appeared much interested in the rare collection of antiques, art-works, *bric-à-brac,* and articles of *virtu* that adorn the parlour and library of the genial host, and in the collection of which he has spent much time and labour.—*The Day (Baltimore), Dec.* 28, 1883.

houses, and on our last two the theatre was crowded ; as the remark attributed to me at Dr. Crim's was a false report, calculated to injure me in the eyes of the American people,—this newspaper despatch, I confess, annoyed me.

" I consulted my friends on the train as to the advisability of contradicting the latter part of it.

" The general verdict was against me. Said an American journalistic friend, ' If you get into a controversy of that kind, it will be never-ending.'

" ' But it is not a question for controversy ; it is a question of fact. If this man's statement is allowed to go forth, I simply stand before the American people as a downright prig.'

" ' If you take the trouble to contradict every misrepresentation of what you say and do, you will have no other occupation.'

" ' So far this is the only thing I have cared to contradict ; for I think the press, as a rule, has been generous to me, and to all of us. As for the point about the " ghost," that does not matter ; it is a lie, and, even if it be malicious, it will be corrected wherever we play " Hamlet." It is true, our friend of the *Standard* may publish it ; but truth will prevail even against his curiously persistent misrepresentations.'

" ' Oh, but,' said my adviser, and he was backed by others, the London *Standard* will not repeat such obvious nonsense, and the American people will not believe a mere Baltimore correspondent. Take no notice of it.'

"Thus the matter rested until the close of the journey. I hope I endure criticism with becoming fortitude, but a wilful and malicious falsehood reflecting upon my personal conduct frets me. I therefore resolved to send the following letter to the editor of the *Tribune* (who had devoted much valuable space to my work, and whose personal courtesy I shall always remember) :—

" ' SIR,—I value so highly the good opinion of the American people that it is painful to me to see any estimate of their education and culture misrepresented. In your journal of to-day a Baltimore despatch states that I have said: " The Americans are not yet fully educated to appreciate true artistic ability; they are progressing." This statement is utterly untrue; and, while I take this opportunity to contradict it, I feel sure that America by this time knows me sufficiently well to believe that I am incapable of uttering such conceited nonsense, or of the bad taste and ingratitude which the correspondent desires to fix upon me.

" ' Faithfully yours,
" ' HENRY IRVING.'

" Sometimes instinct is one's best guide in dealing with mere personal matters. The invidious character of the newspaper report in this case is apparent, and my letter was, in many directions, referred to as a well-advised and necessary rejoinder to a calumny. The *Tribune* mentioned it in the following terms, a day or two afterwards :—

" ' Mr. Irving's recent card in the *Tribune*, concerning the absurd charge that he had disparaged American audiences, was graceful and manly. An imputation of invidious remarks to those persons who are prosperous in the public esteem is one of the commonest methods of malicious detraction. It has been used, of course, against Mr. Irving, who is altogether too fortunate a man for envy and malice to endure. An old remark, made by the poet Samuel Rogers, applies to this case: " To succeed is no little crime in the eyes of those who fail; and those who cannot climb will endeavour to pull you down by the skirts." '

" The ' absurd charge ' was not too absurd, I learned later, for it appeared in the cable correspondence of the *Standard*. You ask me for a few notes on my work in this great country. I hope you may consider this personal matter of sufficient interest. From the first I have been received with unbounded kindness; from the first I have played to large and enthusiastic audiences. My most sanguine hopes never reached so high as the success I have realized. Here and there, prompted, possibly, by the preliminary appeal of the *Standard* to the American people ' not to nail my ears to the pump ' (as the *Herald* put it in commenting

upon the article), and, encouraged by a parchment
pamphlet circulated here, some few press-men, of the
Baltimore stamp, have had their malicious fling at me;
but I have reason to be deeply grateful to the American
critics and to the American people for judging me and
my work in a spirit of honesty and fair play. The
study of a life-time, and the conscientious working out
of my own convictions in regard to the representation
of stage stories in a natural manner, have been stamped
with the approval of the American people; and I shall
return to my native land very proud of their artistic
endorsement and their personal friendship.

"HENRY IRVING.

"There!   What do you think of it?"

"It is excellent," I said, "and most interesting; but
I would rather see it in 'Henry Irving's Impressions of
America' than in the ——"

And here it is accordingly, an intercepted contribution to an English magazine.

"I thought," he said, "the editor would publish it
as a 'P.S.,' after the manner of other contributions
about the stage."

"No doubt," I replied; "but I think we will sand-
wich it between our chapters on Baltimore and the trip
to Chicago."

XV.

FROM BROOKLYN TO CHICAGO.

" Fussy "—The Brooklyn Ferry— Crossing the North River—
A Picturesque Crowd—Brooklyn Bridge at Night—Warned
against Chicago—Conservatism of American Critics—Dangers
of the Road—Railway-train Bandits—An early Interviewer
—A Reporter's Story—Life on a Private Car—Miss Terry
and her " Luck "—American Women.

I.

THE clocks are hammering out the midnight hour
on Saturday, January 5th, as several carriages dash
over the snowy streets of Brooklyn, one of them made
more conspicuous than the rest by the antics of an
attendant dog. It is a black and white fox terrier,
with a suggestion of the lurcher in its pedigree. Busy
with many tram-cars and a variety of other traffic, the
streets are bright with gas and electric lamps. " Fussy "
is quite a foreigner in Brooklyn ; carriage, horses,
and driver are strange to him. One looks out to see
the sagacious animal leaping along through the crowd,
never heeding the calls of boys and men, now making
short cuts to head the vehicle, and now dropping
behind.

" You will lose him one day," I say to Fussy's owner,
by way of warning.

" Oh, no," says Miss Terry. " He follows my carriage
everywhere, day or night, going to the theatre or leaving
it, strange town or otherwise. I have a small piece
of carpet for him to lie upon in my dressing-room.

Sometimes, just as we are leaving for the theatre, my maid pretends to forget it. But Fussy will dart back to my room and bring it, dragging it downstairs into the street, and only dropping it by the carriage-door. One day, at New York, he leaped into the hotel elevator with it, and out again on the ground floor, as if he had been accustomed to elevators all his life."

We are three,—Miss Terry, Irving, and myself. We are making our way to the Brooklyn ferry. The boat belonging to the Pennsylvania Railroad is waiting to convey us across the North River to the Desbrosses-street Depôt of that well-known corporation. "Fussy" is there as soon as we are, and poor "Charlie," who is getting blind, has to be carried aboard. Nearly all the members of the company are here already. They are a picturesque group in the somewhat uncertain light of distant lamps, and a world of stars sparkling in a frosty sky that seems further away from the earth than our English firmament. Mr. Terriss looks like a dashing Capt. Hawksley on his travels,—fur coat, cap, self-possessed air, and all. Mr. Tyars wears a "Tam O'Shanter" and ulster. He might be the laird of a Scotch county, just come down from the hills. The grey-haired, pale-faced gentleman, muffled to the eyes in fur cap and comforter, is Mr. Mead, whose imperial stride as "the buried majesty of Denmark" is repeated here in response to the call of a friend in the cabin. Mr. Howe carries his years and experience with an elastic gait, and a fresh, pleasant face. He is a notable figure in the group, dressed in every respect like an English gentleman,—overcoat, hat, gloves. He has a breezy, country manner, and, if one did not know him, one might say, "this is a Yorkshire man, who farms his own land, going to the West to have a look at Kansas, and perhaps at Manitoba." Mr. Ball, the musical conductor, wears his fur collar and spectacles with quite a professional air. Norman Forbes brings with him ideas of Bond Street, and Robertson, who sings "Hey, Nonnie," to the swells in Leonato's gar-

den, is wrapped up as a tenor should be, though he
has the carriage of an athlete. The American winter
lends itself to artistic considerations in the matter of
cloaks, coats, leggings, scarfs, and " head-gear." The
ladies of the company have sought the hot shelter of
the spacious saloon. Miss Terry pushes the swinging-
door.

" I shall be stifled in there," she says, retreating
before a blast of hot air.

" And starved to death out here," says Irving.

" Well, I prefer the latter," she replies, taking her
place among the crowd on the outer platform.

" Our English friends would complain of heat at the
North Pole," says an American gentleman to another
as they push their way into the saloon.

It is an impressive sight, this great, rolling flood of
the North River at midnight. The reflection of the
boat's lights upon the tide gives it an oily appearance.

" Looks harmless enough, eh?" remarks an American
friend, answering his own question; "but it ain't.
The strongest swimmer might fail in breasting the
current at this state of the tide."

Bright electric lamps mark out the graceful lines of
the Brooklyn bridge. The twinkling signals of river
craft are seen afar off beneath the span of the suspended
roadway, along which gay-looking cars are flashing
their white and red and green lights. We pass and
meet gigantic ferry-boats, as large as the Terrace at
Henley-on-Thames would be if converted into a house-
boat, but a thousand times brighter, with tier upon
tier of illuminated windows. Irving, in his great
Astrachan overcoat, contemplates the scene with deep
interest.

" It is, indeed, very wonderful," he says. " We
could give an idea of the bridge at night on the
Lyceum stage; but these ferry-boats would bother
us, eh, Loveday?"

" Not more than they do now with their heat and

cold. Don't you think Miss Terry ought to go inside ? It is very bitter here."

" No, I'll die first ! " said the lady, amidst a general laugh.

II.

PRESENTLY we run into dock, and are as firmly part of it as if the two structures were one, and so we land and struggle along in groups to the platform, where our special train is to start for Chicago, a run of 1000 miles. Mr. Carpenter, the traffic-manager of this road, is here to receive us. He and Mr. Abbey exchange some not unpleasant badinage about the tribulations of our previous journey from Boston to Baltimore, and we get aboard. Mr. Blanchard, the President of the Erie Railroad, has lent Mr. Irving his own parlour-car for the journey, although it is necessary that the company shall travel over the Pennsylvania road. He has provisioned it also. It contains a private room for Miss Terry, a special room for Irving, and sections for myself and other friends. There is also a smoking-room and little parlour, besides, of course, a well-appointed kitchen. Mr. Blanchard's own *chef* is in the car, with a couple of servants ; they are coloured gentlemen, and very attentive to our wants. Miss Terry and her maid go straight to bed ; so likewise do the other occupants of the car, except Irving and my-self. We think there may be much rest for mind and body in a quiet chat before turning in for the night.

" Besides," says Irving, lighting a cigar, " we may not be in the humour for such recreation after Monday night. I am to get it hot in Chicago, they tell me.'

" I believe you will find the gate of the West wide open to receive you, and the people of Chicago quick to recognize all that is good in your work, and not a whit behind the other cities in its appreciation of it."

" They can have no prejudices, at all events," he re-plied ; "there has been no time for tradition to take root there. They will not be afraid to say what they think, one way or the other. I would not feel anxious at all if we had to stay there a month instead of a fortnight."

" I should not wonder if reporters meet the train and ask for interviews long before we arrive at Chicago."

" Is it possible ? Well, let them come. I am told that if we should be snowed up, there are much worse persons to fear than our friends the reporters. Mr. Abbey carries pistols, and the conductors and guards are armed. During the Bernhardt tour more than one plot to stop Abbey's special trains was discovered. A band of masked men were disappointed at one place, and a company of desperadoes from a western camp at another. One of Abbey's agents was attacked in his sleeping-car and badly wounded by men who sneaked on board during a stoppage near a signal station ; but he made a good fight, and the guard coming quickly to his aid, the fellows got off. Travelling as we did, even from Boston to Baltimore, pulling up at lonely and unpeopled points, one can understand how easily a gang of reckless robbers might capture a train, the facilities for getting aboard and walking right through the cars being largely in favour of success. It was known, Mr. Abbey tells me, that Madame Bernhardt carried her diamonds about with her ; and, acting on reliable information, he found it desirable to have a smart chief of police on the train, who had each end of her car protected at night by an armed guard. No such honour is, I suppose, provided for us ; and then we do not go so far West, nor so near the frontiers, as she and her company went. I suppose Abbey is not chaffing us, as Raymond and those other fellows tried to do in London ? "[1]

---

[1] The coloured gentleman who asked me, during the " wild railway journey " of a previous chapter, if I used " sticking plaster," referred to the exploits of the James boys. Their murderous adventures, I find, cover a period of over twenty years, beginning, some people allege, with a sort of guerilla warfare

"Oh, no; Abbey's is a true bill. In the West a detective well known to the thieves sat by Madame Bernhardt's coachman whenever she went out, to or from the theatre, or anywhere else; and, apart from the weapons he carried, his courage and skill made him a terror to evil-doers. The Western bandit is singularly discreet when he knows the reputation of the police is pledged against him in a public enterprise.

during the war. A reward was offered a few years ago for the capture of the leader, Jesse James, dead or alive, and he was treacherously murdered by one of his confederates, who, being tried and sentenced to death, was reprieved and rewarded in accordance with the State proclamation. He and several other members of the gang are still occasionally before the courts, I believe, on various charges; some appealing to the superior power of the law, others working out their various sentences, and some of them free. One of their most daring adventures is a tragedy that is not likely to be forgotten in the criminal history of America. The story is to railway travel, so far as the mere robbery itself is concerned, what the robbery of "The Lyons Mail" is to the history of posting in France and England a century ago. It is a truly dramatic story, in two acts. The first scene discovers the postmaster and two or three friends of the village of Glendale, at a flag station on the Kansas City branch of the Chicago and Alton Railway. It is a pleasant October evening. Suddenly they are made prisoners by a band of twelve masked and heavily-armed men. They are marched to the little railway station, where the telegraph-operator, an old woman, and the railway auditor, are added to the number. They comprise the entire population of the very picturesque and romantic station. The telegraphic instrument is destroyed, and the station-master compelled to lower his signal lights and stop the mail then due. This ends the first act. The second is the arrival of the train, the sudden and expert seizure of engine-driver and guard (the latter battered almost to death with the butt-end of a pistol), the overawing of the passengers with revolvers, and the plunder of the mails. Horses are then brought up to the track, the men mount with their booty, and order the train to proceed. As the cars move away, the robbers write a despatch that the telegraph operator is directed to send off as soon as his instrument is in order:— " We are the boys who are hard to handle, and we will make it hot for the boys who try to take us. Signed, Jesse and Frank James, Jack Bishop, Irwin Cohens, Cool Carter," &c. The plunder was 30,000 dollars in gold.

III.

THE Chicago press justified my forecast of its enterprise.. The story of one of its representatives (he was a baron, by the way, in his German Fatherland, though content to be a reporter in Chicago) is best told in his own way. He begins it with rather a series of "catching" titles, thus:—

A CHAT WITH MR. IRVING.

A DAILY NEWS *Reporter climbs into the English Tragedian's Special Train, and Interviews Him.*

MISS ELLEN TERRY thinks her AMERICAN SISTERS 'Very nice,' but she has not yet seen DAISY MILLER.

Then he goes on to narrate his own adventures, and the results, and without much exaggeration, almost as follows:—

" Mr. Henry Irving, the notable English actor, is in Chicago now, and so is the *Daily News* man, who accompanied him part of the way. The manner in which these two—the great representative of the British stage and its latest and finest fruition, and the modest representative of the *Daily News*—met was quite peculiar; and it may be amusing to a discerning public to, for once, learn that the interviewer's path is not always strewn with roses when he sets out upon his way past the thorny hedges that beset his road. Who doesn't pity him in his various plights, and concede that naught but the reputation of Chicago for having the pluckiest and most irrepressible reporters did not make him wilt long before accomplishing his task, must bear a stone in his bosom, instead of the usual muscular fibre called a human heart.

" It is well known to the newspaper fraternity that Mr. Irving holds the interviewer in dread, and that nearly all the so-called interviews with him published in the American papers have been spurious. Duly appreciating this fact, the *Daily News* man had not

R

only been munificently fitted out with the requisite
lucre by the business department, but had furthermore been furnished with a letter of introduction,—
one of the combination sort,—addressed to both Mr.
Copleston, Manager Abbey's representative, and to
Mr. Palser,[2] couched in terms to make the flintiest
heart melt. Thus attired, then, the emissary boarded
at Fort Wayne the train which had carried safely thus
far Cæsar and his luck from Jersey City. Entry to
the cars was effected with difficulty, the rules pro-
scribing any but the theatrical company for whom the
train was chartered from riding in it. Perseverance
and gall in equal doses prevailed, however, as they
usually do, and the drowsy Senegambian, who was
doing the Cerberus act, at the entrance of the car,
yielded to an amount of eloquence perhaps never before brought to bear upon his pachydermatous ana-
tomy. As soon as the train had started, a still-hunt
was begun for the two prospective victims, Miss Terry
and Mr. Irving. Alas! they had both obeyed nature's
call, and were at that moment sweetly slumbering,
oblivious even of the Chicago interviewer. Everybody
else was likewise sleeping, even unto the dusky porters.
Passing up and down the train from end to end,
nothing but the cheerful and melodious British snore
greeted the attentive ear. Here, to the right, it was
the wheezing note of a snore combined with a cold ;
there, it was the thundering roll of a *snoro basso pro-
fundo ;* across the aisle the gentler breathing of some
youthful British blonde struck the expectant senses,
and again a confused jumble of snores, of all sexes and
ages, would fall 'with a dull thud' upon the tympanum
of the investigator. It forced itself upon the latter's
conviction that it would be a difficult matter to attain
the object for which he had been deputed. It was
then after three o'clock. The train was due in Chicago
at eight, and it looked very unlikely that Mr. Irving
would overcome his aversion to interviewing and grant

[2] Mr. Abbey's excellent business manager and treasurer.

audience to a stranger at such a time. This was a hiatus which had not been thought of, and the *Daily News* man sat down in an abandoned chair (on which were peacefully reclining some articles of feminine attire), and reflected. Reflecting, he caught himself in a nap, and woke out of it with a slight shudder. He gave himself a poke in the rib and muttered, in grave-like accents, *Nil desperandum.*

"The next move in the direction of the desired interview was a vigorous rap administered to the saddle-coloured individual who in that car discharged the duties of collecting '50 cents all 'round.' When the kicked one had gathered up his portly limbs, he was sent on a search for Mr. Palser first, and that proving unavailing, on a hunt for Mr. Copleston. The latter, after considerable energy had been expended by the coloured brother, awoke and gave vent to his indignation at having been thus rudely snatched from Morpheus's arms. He did so in rather vigorous style and language, which, under the circumstances, was hardly to be wondered at. He declined to come forth from under his blankets, and not even the cutting repartee of the reporter could rouse him. He said he had been but an hour and a half asleep, he and some friends in another car having played poker till very late, and he, the speaker, having lost quite heavily. He wouldn't, couldn't, shouldn't get up and wake Mr. Irving, and an interview, he concluded, on the train was an impossibility.

"'Here is a fix,' was the mental commentary. Poking his hand in here and there into berths, and being startled now by the apparition of a female face, then by a powerful snort of defiance from some male actor, the investigator finally groped his way back into the rear car, one of the palace pattern, placed at Mr. Irving's disposal by Mr. Blanchard of the Erie Road. And there he found, at last, Mr. Irving, who being duly apprised of the mission of his unwelcome visitor, and having a bit of pasteboard with the latter's address thrust into his unwilling palm, murmured plaintively, but politely, that he would see him before reaching Chicago. Later on Mr. Abbey's services were enlisted in the same cause, and his promise to the same effect obtained. Wearily the time dragged on, till but another twenty-five miles lay between the train and its destination. Just at this opportune moment the great actor's friend, Mr. Joseph Hatton, stepped up and invited the hungry, wild, and desperate minion of the press to partake of a cup of coffee. Gladly this was accepted, and being made aware of what was wanted, he, with the sympathizing spirit of a brother journalist, said he would try and have Mr. Irving appear. Mr. Hatton, by the way, is accompanying Mr. Irving for the purpose of gathering material for a book, in which jointly the impressions of American travel of himself and the eminent actor will be deposited. While he went off to wake Mr. Irving, another trip was taken to Mr. Abbey's room, in doing which, both coming and returning, the reporter's modesty underwent the severe ordeal of passing in review a large array of British beauties, all in different stages of evolution—as to dress—and all talking sauce in choice Cockney English at him for his "shocking impropriety." When the somewhat cowed Daily Newsian returned to his cup of coffee he found not only Mr. Copleston, the surly bear of a few hours ago, transformed into a most amiable gentleman, but also among the other gentlemen, Mr. Irving himself.

"After the tedious business of introduction had been gone through with all around; after it had been remarked that the trip had been a trying one to them all, as not being used to these long journeys in their tight little island, where a twelve-hours ride was considered the utmost,—after saying this, all felt broke up, and, expressing anxiety as to the Siberian climate of Chicago, Mr. Irving took out his cigar-case, invited his *vis-à-vis* to light one of his choice weeds, and then prepared himself for the torture to be inflicted.

" 'How are you pleased with your reception in America?'

" ' Beyond all expectation and desert. I have been treated with a kindness, courteousness, and hospitality that have been really touching to me. And this, you know, has been done despite the fact that my trip to America had not been endorsed by all. While on my way across the Atlantic, for instance, a London daily paper published a leading article on me, suggesting to the Americans not to receive me cordially, and, not satisfied with this, the article was cabled over before our arrival. I thought this unfair and ungenerous. I like America, of course, though " like " is hardly the proper term. I feel deeply grateful to the American people for the very kind manner in which they have treated me. But you must come to the theatre to-night. I am sorry that Miss Terry will not play to-night.'

" 'Now, Mr. Irving, shirking your modesty for a moment, and assuming as a settled fact that you are one of the most eminent actors living, what made you such? What cause or causes do you attribute your good acting to?'

" ' To acting.'

" ' What do you mean by that? This answer is not quite clear to me.'

" ' I merely want to say that by incessant acting, and love and study of my art, I have attained whatever position I hold in my profession. This is a leading cause, as it is, I believe, in every other art.'

" 'What made you choose "Louis XI." in pre-ference to " The Bells " as your first piece here, Mr. Irving?'

" 'Because it takes the least amount of stage pre-paration, that's all. That reminds me to say that the reports you have heard about my gorgeous scenery, &c., you will find, I think, exaggerated. Our stage decorations are quite simple, and their beauty consists merely in their nice adjustment, and the scrupulous calculation of the effect produced by them on the audience.'

" Meanwhile Miss Terry's maid had been very busy preparing tea and buttered toast for her mistress, taking dainty little things for wear out of a big lock-basket. Being repeatedly asked if Miss Terry could not be seen a moment, the train meanwhile arrived in Chicago, and most of the other actors and actresses having got off, she made evasive answers. Suddenly, however, the door opened, and a very pretty lady looked briskly around. This, then, was Miss Ellen Terry! A beautiful woman, indeed! Lustrous eyes of rare azure; a profuseness of wavy blonde hair, long and of a luminous shade and silky texture; the form lithe, yet full, every motion of a natural supple grace. She was shaking hands with the *Daily News* man, even while Mr. Copleston introduced him, and then scurried back into the dark depths of her room, where she continued wailing, ' I've lost my luck! I've lost my luck,—my beautiful horse-shoe brooch, which I wouldn't have missed for the world!' And maid and mistress went down on their knees, peering into every nook and cranny. While still thus employed: ' You see, Miss Terry, the Chicago reporter is the first introduced to give you a hearty greeting to this city, and to hope you'll like your stay here as well as I am sure Chicago will like to hold you within her walls.'

" ' Thanks! thanks!' said Miss Terry, and then continued her search for that obstreperous brooch.

" ' And what do you think of America?'

" Miss Terry held up a round, well-shaped arm appealingly, and merely said, ' No, no. You mustn't try to interview me. I won't stumble into that pit-fall.'

" ' How do you like the American women, then?'

" ' Very nice and pretty they are,—those I've seen, at least. I think we must say, in this regard, what Lord Coleridge did: "They can't be all so nice and

pretty; I suppose I've only seen the nicest ones."
And one thing I'll tell you which I have not seen;
I've never set eyes on any Daisy Millers.'

" ' Of course not,' rejoined the reporter. ' Who
ever heard of or saw a Daisy Miller outside of a book?
That's a character you'll only find in James's novel,—
not in America, Miss Terry.'

" And thus, still hunting for that unfortunate
brooch, which she plaintively called her ' lost luck,'
and so apparently a kind of voodoo or talisman, the
reporter left her, momentarily feeling a ray out of the
sun of her glorious eyes lighting up his departure.
It was a little after eight o'clock then, and, while she
soon after went by carriage to the Leland Hotel, Mr.
Irving put up at the Grand Pacific, and was, two
hours later, busily arranging things at Haverly's
Theatre."

XVI.

THE PRAIRIE CITY.

First Impressions of Chicago—A Bitter Winter—Great Storms
—Thirty Degrees below Zero—On the Shores of Lake
Michigan—Street Architecture—Pullman City—Western
Journalism—Chicago Criticism—Notable Entertainments
—At the Press Club—The Club Life of America—What
America has done—Unfair Comparisons between the
Great New World and the Older Civilizations of Europe
—Mistaking Notoriety for Fame—A Speech of Thanks—
Facts, Figures, and Tests of Popularity, past and to come.

I.

THROUGH piles of lumber, into back streets filled with
liquor bars, " side shows," and decorated with flaming
posters, into fine, stately thoroughfares, crowded with
people, past imposing buildings marked with architectural dignity, to the Grand Pacific Hotel.

" It is as if Manchester had given Greenwich Fair a
blow in the face," said Irving,—" that is my first
impression of Chicago. 'The Living Skeleton,' 'The
Tattooed Man,' 'The Heaviest Woman in the World,'
' The Museum of Wonders,' with the painted show-
pictures of our youth; public-houses, old-clothes shops,
picturesque squalor. And then great warehouses,
handsome shops, and magnificent civic buildings,—
what a change! There is something of the 'go' of
Liverpool and Manchester about it. If I was ever
afraid of Chicago, I am afraid no longer. A people
that have rebuilt this city within a comparatively few
years must be great, broad-minded, and ready in

appreciating what is good. We have something to
show them in the way of dramatic art,—they will
' catch on,' as they say on this side of the Atlantic, I
am sure of it."

The city was more or less snow-bound. Little or
no effort had been made to remove the white downfall,
either from road or pavement. The sun was shining.
The air was, nevertheless, very cold. Within a few
days of our arrival the thermometer had fallen to twenty
and thirty degrees below zero. We had selected for
our visit to America what was destined to be the
bitterest winter that had been known in the United
States for over twenty years. There were storms on
sea and land; storms of rain, and snow, and wind,
followed by frosts that closed the great rivers, and
made even Lake Michigan solid for ice-boats a dozen
or twenty miles out. The South Jersey coast was
strewn with wreckage. Railway tracks were swept
away. At Cape May the principal pier was destroyed.
The sea demolished the piles of Coney Island's iron
piers. At Long Branch cottages were undermined by
the water, and their contents carried out to sea. The
well-known dancing platform and piazza of the Grand
Union Hotel, on Rockaway Beach, were washed away.
Terrific winds blew over Boston and New England. A
little fleet of schooners were driven ashore at Portland.
Vessels broke from their moorings in the adjacent
harbours. Atlantic City had boarding-houses, stores,
and dwellings carried away by high tides.

The mails were delayed for hours, and in some
cases for days, on the principal railroads. Where the
obstacles were not rain and flood, they were wind and
snow. Lockport, New York, reported that the snow
on that day was four feet on the level, and still falling.
Bradford, telegraphing for Pennsylvania generally,
announced that fourteen inches of snow had fallen
within a few hours, the weight of it crushing in many
roofs and awnings. "The narrow-gauge railways,"
ran the despatch, "five in number, have been closed

all day; the trains are stalled a few miles from the city." Even at Louisville, in Kentucky, navigation was suspended, and floating ice-blocks were battering in the sides of steamers lying at the wharves of Baltimore. On the Rappahannock river, in Virginia, a ship laden with corn was cut down and sunk by floating ice. These and kindred incidents occurred on or about the day of our arrival in Chicago. The record of the few previous days, judged from the official reports of Washington, and the ordinary chronicles of the times, was a very remarkable one, even for the coldest States of America. In some places the weather had been the coldest known for more than fifty years. Canada had had the most extreme experiences in this respect. At Winnipeg, Manitoba, the thermometer had fallen as low as forty-five degrees below zero.

On the day we were travelling to the prairie city, while the thermometer was rising in that section of the country, it was falling in the eastern and southern States, registering thirty degrees below zero at Whitehall, New York. The Straits of Mackinaw, connecting Lake Michigan and Lake Huron, were navigable only on foot or runners. We arrived in Chicago on Monday, Jan. 7. On the 6th the thermometer registered twenty-two degrees below zero. Monday's newspapers congratulated their readers that "the wave had passed over." Incidents of its severity were curious and numerous. Hundreds of hogs had been frozen to death on freight trains. The Terre Haute express from Chicago was snowed up for thirty-one hours. At fires which had broken out, water from the engines froze as it fell, and covered the buildings with strange, fantastic shapes.

I had arranged to visit Gunnison (Colorado), and other mining cities, within a reasonable distance from Chicago and St. Louis, but was persuaded to postpone my trip by private and public reports of the storm in those regions. One day's newspaper (the *Daily-News-*

Democrat, of Gunnison) contained startling evidence
of the difficulties I should have had to encounter.
Within a few days twenty-seven men had been killed
by snow-slides in the mountains between Ouray and
Telluride. A local mail-carrier was among the victims.
All the available snow-ploughs and engines of the
various districts were at work on the tracks. Engines
were helplessly stuck in the snow on the Rio Grande.
" The miner," remarked the *Daily News* editor, " who
goes into the mountains at this season takes his life in
his hands." I remained in Chicago with Irving, and
am spared to chronicle these things. The weather was
sufficiently cold for both of us in Chicago. It varied,
too, with a persistency of variation that is trying to the
strongest constitution. One hour the thermometer
would be fairly above zero, the next it would be far
below it. Men went about the frozen streets in fur·
coats and caps, carefully protecting their ears and
hands. Along the shores of Lake Michigan were
barricades of ice ; they looked like solid palisades of
marble. Here and there, where tiny icebergs had
been formed, the polar bear would not have looked out
of place. It was strange to see the ice-boats, with
their bending sails, literally flying along, while away
out lay ships at anchor. Mr. Lyon took Miss Terry,
Irving, and myself sleighing along the lake shore and
upon the prairie beyond. My friends were delighted
with the novel excursion, astonished at the fine boulevards through which we passed, amazed at the possibilities of Chicago, as they realized what had been done
and what space had been laid out for the future. A
forty-mile drive through great, wide boulevards designed to encompass the city, is the biggest of the
city's schemes, and it is in vigorous course of for-
mation.

" One is forced to admire the pluck of Chicago,"
said Irving, after our first drive. " Twice burnt down,
twice built up, and laid out anew, on a plan that is
magnificent. Some of the houses along Prairie and

Michigan Avenues are palaces.[1]   The art revival in
street architecture and house decoration is as actively
rife here as in London.   And what a superb stone they
have for building purposes in their yellow cream-
coloured marble !   It is marvellous to see how they
have taken hold of the new ideas.   The Calumet and
the Chicago club-houses, nothing could be more chaste
than their decorations."

One day we went to Pullman City, an industrial
town, akin to Saltaire, near Bradford, in its scope and
enterprise.   We were invited and accompanied by Mr.
and Mrs. Pullman, Miss Terry, Mr. and Mrs. Dexter,
Mr. and Mrs. James Runnion, and several other ladies
and gentlemen.   Going out in Mr. Pullman's private
car, we lunched with him at the pretty hotel of the
novel city, and afterwards inspected the workshops
and principal buildings.

"The story of the conception and creation of this
Pullman City," said Irving, "interested me very much,
though I confess the method of it all strikes me as
somewhat like living by machinery : the private houses
being massed, as it were, *en bloc ;* the shops collected
together like arcades ; the whole place laid out with
geometrical system ; and yet one feels that there
are fine principles underlying it ; that the scheme is
founded upon wise plans ; and that, from a moral and
sanitary stand-point, the city is an ideal combination of
work and rest, of capital and labour.   Pullman's idea
was a lofty one, and the result is very remarkable : a
centre of industry that should give to labour its best
chance, with capital taking its place on a platform

---

[1] " Miss Ellen Terry is said to have a broad knowledge and
high appreciation of decorative art.   During the past two or
three days she has been doing Michigan and Prairie Avenues in
this city with a critical eye. ' I noticed a good many houses,'
she says, ' that I did not like at all, but many others that are
truly beautiful.   The red brick ones and the yellow marble
fronts are mostly exquisite in design and colour.   Here and there
Michigan Avenue reminds me of Brighton in England.' "—*Daily
News.*

as human as labour. That is the notion, as Pullman explained it to me. What a square, level head
it is! Just the determined kind of man to be the
author of a new city on new lines. He told me that
Charles Reade's novel, ' Put Yourself in his Place,' had
influenced him greatly in his ambition to found this
place ; that it has affected all his relations towards his
people. Reade would be glad to know that, I am sure.
Politically, Pullman City is a paradox. A despotism, it
is nevertheless very democratic. It owes its successful
administration to a benevolent autocracy. The theatre,
I am told, is more prosperous than the church proper,
though religion is represented by several earnest com-
munities. The idea of giving the people a chance to
buy land and build cottage homes for themselves, at a
reasonable distance beyond Pullman, appears to be a
good one. Pullman may well be proud of his work.
It is worthy of Chicago and the West."

II.

In spite of " wind and weather " the people of Chicago
crowded Haverly's Theatre, where Irving and Miss
Terry appeared, night after night, for two weeks ; and
the critics of the great papers of the West, the *Times,
Tribune, Inter-Ocean,* and *Daily News,* were equal to
the occasion. They showed a knowledge of their work,
and an appreciation of dramatic art, as illustrated by
Irving, quite in keeping with the spirit and ambition of
their new and wonderful city. A news-collector having
in view the prejudices of New York and London, as to
the literary and journalistic cultivation of Chicago,
selected an enthusiastic line or two from the Chicago
notices of Irving and Miss Terry, with a view to cast
ridicule upon western criticism. This kind of thing
is common to news-collectors on both sides of the
Atlantic. A reporter desires to please his editor, and
to cater for his public. In London, believing that
New York will be stirred with the report of a hostile

demonstration against an American artist, he makes the most of the working of a rival American clique there against Lotta. New York looks down loftily upon the art culture of Chicago, and London chiefly knows Chicago through its great fire, borne with so much fortitude, and for its "corners in pork." The local caterer for the news columns of New York and London panders to these ideas. The best-educated writer, the neatest essayist, might be made to appear foolish if we were to cut unconnected sentences out of his work, and print them alone.

In the journalistic literature of modern criticism there is nothing better than some of the essays on Irving and his art that appeared in the papers of Chicago and the West. In this connection it is worth while pointing out that the absence of an international copyright between England and America forces native writers, who otherwise would be writing books, into the newspaper press. So long as publishers can steal or buy "for a mere song" the works of popular English authors, they will not give a remunerative wage to the comparatively unknown writers of their own country. Therefore, busy thinkers, men and women with literary inspirations, devote themselves to journalism. It would be surprising if, under these circumstances, the Western press should not here and there entertain and instruct its readers with literary and critical work as much entitled to respect, and as worthy to live, as the more pretentious and more happily and fortunately placed literature of London, Boston, and New York. The American authors best known to-day, and most praised in both hemispheres, have written for the newspapers, and some of them had their training on the press: Bret Harte, Mark Twain, Howells, Aldrich, John Hay, James, Haberton, Winter, Bryant, Artemus Ward (I leave the reader to complete the list, for I mention these names *en passant* and at random); and how many others are coming on through the columns of the newspapers to take up the running, who shall say?

The Chicago press often sacrifices dignity and good taste in the headings with which it seeks to surprise and excite its readers. But this is a feature of Western journalism that will go out with the disappearance of the lower civilization to which, in covering the entire ground of its circulation, it unhesitatingly appeals. The London press is not free from the charge of pandering to depraved tastes in its reports of sensational murders and divorce cases, though the great body of its writers and contributors no doubt sit down to their work with a higher sense of their responsibility to the public than is felt by their American contemporaries.

"Do you think that is so?" Irving asked, when I was propounding this view to an American colleague.

" Yes," said the journalist addressed; "but I think our newspapers are far more interesting than yours. At the same time you beat us in essay writing, for that is what your editorials are,—they are essays."

"That is true," said Irving, "and very fine some of them are."

· But to return to Chicago criticism,—I repeat that among the best and most appreciative and most scholarly of the criticisms upon Irving and his art, in England and America, are the writings of the Chicago journalists,—McPhelin, of the *Tribune*, Barron, of the *Inter-Ocean*, McConnell, of the *Times*, and Pierce, of the *Daily News*. The two first-mentioned are quite young men, not either of them more than twenty-five. I am tempted to quote, in justification of this opinion, and as an example of Chicago work, the following extracts from one of several equally well-written criticisms in the *Tribune* :—

There is nothing phenomenal or meteoric about this new actor. Henry Irving is not what Diderot would have us believe a great actor should be, namely, a man without sensibility. Diderot said that sensibility was organic weakness; that it crippled the intelligence, rendering acting alternately warm and cold; and that the great actor should have penetration, without any sensibility whatever. But Talma called sensibility the faculty of exaltation which shakes an actor' very soul, and which enables him to enter into the most tragic situations and the most terrible of passions as if they were his own. In the discussion of these conflicting theories Henry Irving has always taken Talma's view. He comes nearer realizing Diderot's ideal of greatness than any other actor of whom we have record.

His imagination is picturesque almost to the verge of sublimity. His fancy is lively and apparently inexhaustible. When he unrolls before us the varied-coloured robe of life, we look in vain to find one colour missing. It is a fancy that is not only vivid, but that is most poetic. How touching is that return of Shylock to his lonely home, walking wearily over the deserted bridge,—the bridge that echoed only a moment before to the shouts and laughter of the merry maskers! The old man walks to the house from which his daughter has fled, knocks twice at the door, and looks up patiently and expectantly towards the casement. Then the curtain falls. The people who do not applaud such a tender touch as this should stop going to the theatre.

In saying that Irving is realistic, that word is not used in its grosser sense. Realism should be the union of the ideal and the true. There may be truth in Zola's realism, but there is no ideality; for ideality rejects the trivial, the vulgar, the earthly, and grasps the essence. There may be ideality in Mrs. Burnett's novels, but sentiment is substituted for truth. The realism of Howells, for instance, is a union of the ideal and the true. Irving's ideals are in harmony with the realistic tendency of literary thought, because they are drawn from humanity, and not from Olympus. His are human, not heroic, ideals. His Louis XI. is as true to nature as any impersonation can be; and yet it is ideal, inasmuch as the essence of the character is incorporated in action, and the baseness, the cruelty, the bigotry of the king are not repugnant. Here is the union of the ideal and the true. If a man like Zola were playing Louis XI. he would shock and disgust us by a portrayal not essential, but of superficial grossness.

In attempting to estimate Irving's genius one cannot catalogue qualities, but must indicate in a general way the nature of that genius as it is judged from its manifestations. Irving cannot be classified, for he is the leader of a new school of acting, as Tennyson is the leader of a new school of poetry. They who in the future will write of the great Victorian Era will find, perhaps, a resemblance between the actor and the poet, not only because both have opened up new fields of art, but because the chief characteristic of each is originality in form. If Tennyson is the poet who should be read by poets, Irving is the actor who should be studied by actors. The idea intended to be conveyed is, that both Tennyson and Irving excel in perfection of detail; in other words, of technique, or form. The great poet who wishes to be heard in the future must give us the polish and the intensity of Tennyson; the actor who would be great must give us the polish and the intensity of Irving.

Any line in Irving's acting will illustrate his intensity, by which is meant the grasping of a fuller meaning than appears on the surface. When Shylock is flattering Portia in the trial scene, exclaiming, "A Daniel come to judgment," &c., it is startling the manner in which he leans forward suddenly and whispers with venomous unction and cunning the insidious compliment, "How much more elder art thou than thy looks!" The words are very simple, but their effects depend on the intensity of meaning with which they are uttered.

Praise has already been accorded Irving's Shylock, because it is a type of the medieval Jew, interpreted, not according to the traditions of a bigoted age, but in the light of the liberality of the nineteenth century. This creation is, perhaps, the best proof of the assertion that Henry Irving has embodied in his art the spirit of his age, and therein lies his greatness.

Several lessons American managers will draw from the success of the Irving engagement. One is that Shakespearian plays must not be mutilated to give prominence to one actor. Artistic harmony must not be sacrificed to personal ambition. Another lesson is that an actor must not undertake all alone to act a play; he must have a company of actors, not a company of incompetent amateurs. A third is that Shakespearian plays are the jewels of dramatic literature, and their setting should surely be as rich as that given to the extravagant productions that are doing so much to vitiate popular taste.

In conclusion, it may be remarked that it is gratifying that Henry Irving in his American tour has been regarded, not from a fashionable or a national, but from a purely artistic stand-point. In art the Spartan and the Athenian are brothers; the same love of beauty lives in Rome and in Geneva, in London and in New York. In the sunshine of art the national merges into the universal, and the mists of prejudice die away upon the horizon of the world.

III.

ALL the forecasts that warned Irving to expect in Chicago a coarse fibre of civilization and an absence of artistic appreciation were reversed in the Prairie

city. Night after night, great, generous, enthusiastic
audiences crowded Haverly's Theatre. Quick of perception, frank in their recognition of the best features
of Irving's work, they were cordial in their applause,
and hearty in their greetings of the novelty of it. The
critics interpreted the sentiments of the audiences, and
put their feelings into eloquent sentences. They
showed knowledge and sincerity of intention and purpose, and some of them criticized severely the carping
spirit in which one or two Eastern contemporaries
had dealt with the London actors. The hospitality of
Chicago is proverbial. It was made manifest in many
ways,—in offers of carriages for sleigh-riding, of ice-
boats, of railway cars. Irving and Miss Terry had to
decline more invitations than they accepted. Members
of the company were also entertained at breakfasts
and suppers. After the first night, with its ac-
ceptation of Irving as a reformer of the stage, and
as the author of what to Chicago was a new pleasure,
the city literally opened all its doors to him. Among
the receptions was a breakfast given by Mr. John
B. Carson,[2] at which the Mayor spoke of the

---

[1] The company included his Worship the Mayor of Chicago
(the Hon. Carter Harrison), G. M. Pullman (of Pullman City),
J. Medill (editor of the *Tribune*), Murray Nelson, Mr. Gage
(banker), Major-General Schofield, Marshal Field, Mr. Dexter,
George Dunlap, C. R. Cummings, General A. Stager, and J.
B. Lyon. The *menu* was remarkable for its luxurious elegance,
and the speaking, though informal, and in no sense pre-arranged,
was notable for being chiefly confined to the arts and their
influences on civilization. Mr. John B. Carson proposed
" Health and continued success to Henry Irving," and welcomed him to the West in terms of hearty friendship. " And
I only hope," he said, "you will one day come to Quincy,
which is my head-quarters ; we are not a very great population,
but we have a fine theatre, and we enjoy a good play." Quincy
has a population of 25,000, is beautifully situated on a limestone
bluff, 125 feet above the Mississippi River. Mr. Carson and
his friends at Quincy sent Mr. Abbey a guarantee of $4000, for
one night's visit of the Irving Company. It will be interesting
to add, in this place, that many " theatre parties " came to

pleasure Chicago experienced in Irving's visit, and upon which occasion Mr. Joseph Medill, the editor of the *Tribune*, who had seen Irving in London, as well as in Chicago, proclaimed him the one Shakespearian actor who interprets and exhibits the conceptions of the poet with a proper naturalness, and in such a manner as to make people regret that Shakespeare could not revisit the world to see what had at last been done for his plays. The health of Miss Terry was proposed and drunk with all the honours; as it was, also, at a very dainty reception given one night after the play to Miss Terry herself, at the Calumet Club, by Mr. and Mrs. John B. Jeffery,[3] and, on a later occasion, at the Leland Hotel, at a supper given by Mr. Emery A. Storrs[4] to Mr. Irving. Pro-

Chicago, from distant cities, to see Irving. Some of them travelled all day, and several of their newspapers contained reports and criticisms of the performances.

[3] The *menu* cards on this occasion were gems in the way of printing and binding. They were exquisitely encased in alligator-leather and silver. With each of them was a guest-card, on which was written a poetic welcome, couched in bright, humorous, and complimentary terms,—the work of the hostess. Many ladies and gentlemen of position were present, and the affair was one of the pleasantest in the history of the Calumet Club.

[4] At eleven o'clock last evening Mr. Emery A. Storrs gave a supper in honour of Mr. Henry Irving, at the Leland Hotel, and pleasantly entertained thirty-five well-known gentlemen. The guests assembled about ten o'clock, in room No. 20, and shortly afterwards adjourned to Mr. Storrs' suite of parlours on the Michigan Avenue front of the hotel. Mr. Irving and Mr. Hatton arrived soon after eleven o'clock, and, after a few minutes' social chat, the party proceeded to the small dining-hall. The arrangements were elaborate and perfect, and the decorations were very handsome. Lines of flags of all nations extended from the four corners of the room, crossing one another just under the dome in the centre. Hanging by an invisible wire from the electric light in the dome was a double-faced floral circle, edged with smilax, through the centre of which was a floral bar. On one side of this was the name "Irving," and on the other side "Terry," in red carnations upon a white ground. The walls were hung with the English and American colours, and directly behind the guest's seat was a bust of Shakespeare,

fessor Swing was among the speakers on this occasion, and during the evening pleasant allusion was made to

over which was looped the English flag, caught up by a shield, bearing the arms of Great Britain and Ireland. Above this was a banner bearing the following inscription: "'One touch of nature makes the whole world kin'—Irving and Booth." At the opposite end of the room, just above the door, was a similar banner, inscribed as follows: "'To hold, as 'twere, the mirror up to nature.'—Ellen Terry and Mary Anderson." Immediately opposite the entrance to the room was the inscription, "Greeting and Welcome," and over the entrance was inscribed, "Not that we think us worthy such a guest, but that your worth will dignify our feast." To the left of this was a banner, bearing the following: "Suit the action to the word, the word to the action, with the special observation that you overstep not the modesty of Nature." And to the right was a banner, inscribed as follows: "All the world's a stage, and all the men and women merely players; they have their exits and their entrances." The table was arranged in the shape of a "T," with the host, the guest of the evening, and a few of the more favoured sitting at the cross of the "T." Immediately in front of the seats of Mr. Irving and Mr. Storrs was an immense basket of flowers,—which was sent later in the evening to Miss Terry, with Mr. Storrs' compliments,—and to the right and left of this was a floral bell, suggesting the actor's favourite play, "The Bells." In the body of the "T" was a huge *épergne* of fruit and flowers, and trails of smilax were laid the length of the cloth. In front of each one of the thirty-five plates was a fragrant *boutonnière*, and a satin-covered card bearing the name of the guest diagonally across a marine scene. Delicate-tinted glasses to the right of each plate suggested liquid enjoyment to follow. The following is a list of the guests as they sat at table:—Emery A. Storrs, Henry Irving, Joseph Hatton, General Schofield, Professor Swing, Perry H. Smith, Professor Fraser, William Balcom, F. B. Wilkie, F. H. Winston, J. D. Harvey, M. E. Stone, Alfred Cowles, D. B. Shipman, W. C. D. Grannis, W. P. Nixon, W. S. Walker, Dr. Jackson, Mr. Phinney, Leonard Hodges, Canon Knowles, A. F. Seeberger, Louis Wahl, S. D. Kimbark, C. P. Kimball, J. L. High, Mr. Clement, Washington Hesing, J. M. Dandy, Mr. Lewis, Mr. Griswola, Mr. Harper, Mr. Dewey, Mr. Thayer, Mr. Hord, and Mr. Bacon. After supper Mr. Storrs, in a witty prelude, explaining that there were to be no speeches, proposed the health of Mr. Irving. The famous actor having responded, Joseph Hatton, who, by his works and in his own person, is well known in Chicago, was the visit of Lord Chief Justice Coleridge, and to English writers who had not confined their attention solely to the shortcomings of Chicago. Irving, in responding to the toast of his health, described his sensations on entering Chicago; "I came warned against you; but knowing your history. When I saw your great city, and felt how much you had done, and how much that was broad and generous and courageous belonged to such enterprise and ambition, my instinct told me that you would be with me in my work; that you would, at least, respect it; and that if you liked it, no jealousies, no prejudices, would stand in the way of your saying so."

The Press Club [5] "received" Irving and Miss Terry and several members of the Lyceum company. "Nothing could have been conceived or carried out in a more frank and friendly spirit than the Press Club reception," said Irving, on returning to his hotel; "no pretence, no affectation, a hearty crowd. They treated us as if we had known each other all our lives, and I begin to feel as if they were old friends. It is the absence of caste in America, I conclude, that gives a meeting of this kind its real cordiality. Nobody is afraid of anybody else; there is an absence of self-restraint, and, at the same time, of self-consciousness. I liked them, too, for not apologizing for their very unpretentious rooms; and I think they are right in

---

toasted. Miss Terry was not forgotten during the unstudied and informal eloquence of the evening. A magnificent basket of flowers was sent to her, with the respectful compliments of the host and his friends.—*Tribune and other newspaper reports.*

[5] The reception to Henry Irving and Miss Ellen Terry by the Chicago Press Club last evening was a brilliant social and professional event. It was a graceful recognition of Great Britain's greatest histrionic stars. Many professional people, including Mdlle. Rhea, Mrs. Jessie Bartlett-Davis, and others of note on the dramatic and operatic stage, were present, and were presented to the distinguished guests of the evening, together with a large number of *littérateurs,* journalists, and members of the bar.—*Morning News.*

adhering to the principles on which the club is founded, that it shall be purely a press club. Do you remember the evening at the journalists' club in Philadelphia? But that was a man's night only. Very delightful too, eh? I thought so. Indeed, the club life of America, from the humblest to the highest, is characterized by a cordiality and freedom that is glorious; I think so. No nonsense, no unnecessary formality; they give you the best, and make you at home at once. So nice to be introduced straightway, and be on terms with all the fellows! I find, by one of the newspapers, that I am keeping a scrap-book; they have seen Houson's handiwork, I imagine. I was just thinking that if one indulged in that sort of thing, what a collection of club cards and *menus* one would have! There is not a city we have visited where we have not been made free of all the clubs, from Boston to Chicago. The Boston clubs are very fine, English-like in many respects. But there is nothing, I suppose, more gorgeous than the Union League at New York. I'll tell you what strikes me most about America—the immensity of the work it has done in regard to the material welfare of its people; in building up a new civilization; providing for the comforts of the thousands who crowd into its ports from the Old World; taking care of them and governing them, giving them a share of their wealth, and welding the incongruous mass into one great people. I don't wonder that young men who have only their honest hands and hopes as legacies from parents come here to make homes and names, to found families, and lay up for their old age. It is a wonderful country; the thought of it almost inspires me with eloquence, and I think on many a night it has given me a new energy and a new love for my own work. I notice, by the papers, that some English visitor has been writing in one of the English periodicals what is called 'a slashing criticism' upon American habits and customs, and making unfair comparisons between the life-objects of the men and women of this great New World and the older civilizations of Europe. This sort of criticism can only be mere surface-work; it does not consider and weigh results; it does not count how great a thing has been done in a short time; it does not see how marvellously successful this people has been in making a law unto itself, a civilization unto itself, and how it has not yet had time to rest and tack on to its great, sweeping garments the fringes and ribbons and jewels that belong to an age of rest, and luxury, and art. They are but small critics, and they are not respectfully conscious of the possibilities of the close union of England and America, who discuss America in a petty way, and do not give her the credit she deserves for all she has done in the cause of freedom and of humanity."

He paced the room as he talked, and I applauded his peroration.

"And you say you cannot 'orate,' to use a local phrase, except about acting."

"It is an easy thing to make a speech in one's own room, but a different thing standing up before an audience, eh?"

"Anyhow," I said, "we will make a point about that hap-hazard criticism of irresponsible persons, who do not consider either the truth, or the feelings of a nation, so long as they can put together a few smart things for their own glorification. Nobody ever heard of the writer you mention until he abused America; and there are men who mistake notoriety for fame."

IV.

THE pieces produced during the two weeks of Irving's stay in Chicago were "Louis XI.," "The Merchant of Venice," "The Bells," "The Belle's Stratagem," and "The Lyons Mail." On the last night, being called before the curtain by one of the most crowded houses of the season, he addressed the audience as follows:—

"Ladies and Gentlemen,—It is my privilege to thank you for the hearty and enthusiastic welcome which you have given us during our too short stay amongst you. Many years ago, when a boy in England, I remember a song,—

> " 'To the West! to the West!
> To the land of the free!'

I little dreamed in those days I should ever see your fair city—the Queen of the West. For the welcome you have given my colleagues and myself I thank you— especially I thank you on behalf of Miss Ellen Terry, whose indebtedness to you is equal to my own. I was good-humouredly told the other day that I was too pleased with America, especially with Chicago; and if I were to find some faults it might be a relief, and would vary the monotony a little. (Laughter.)

"Well, I hope I am not naturally a fault-finder; but if I were, you have afforded me no opening ; for you have loaded us with gratitude, and extended to us a welcome as broad as the prairie upon which you stand. I cannot leave you without thanking the press of Chicago for its sympathy, its eloquent and its un-grudging recognition of at least a sincere, although incomplete, effort to bring the dramatic art abreast of the other arts, and not leave the art of the stage behind and out in the cold in the general march of progress.

"I am very glad to tell you that we shall soon meet again ; for we shall have the honour of appearing before you on the 11th of next month, when we shall have the gratification of spending another week amongst you. And now I beg to thank you again and again, and I can but hope that we may live in your memories as you will live in ours." (Applause.)

The receipts for the first week in Chicago were $17,048, and for the second, $19,117; making a total of $36,166. From a mere box-office point of view the success of Irving's visit is unprecedented ; the increase of the receipts at the close of the engagement dissipating the last "weak invention of the enemy," that he only excites curiosity. If this shallow nonsense merited the smallest attention, the figures already quoted would be a sufficient answer. A truer test of the genuineness of Irving's popularity, and the hold his work has obtained upon the intelligent and intellectual public of America, will be the character of his reception when, in the course of the present tour, he begins to pay return visits to Chicago, Boston, Philadelphia, and New York; for he goes back to these cities when their enthusiasm may be said to have cooled, and in the Lenten season, which is largely observed in the chief cities of the United States.

XVII.

ST. LOUIS, CINCINNATI, INDIANAPOLIS, COLUMBUS.

Sunshine and Snow—Wintry Landscapes—Fire and Frost—
Picturesque St. Louis—"The Elks"—A Notable Reception—
"Dime Shows"—Under-studies—Germany in America—
"On the Ohio"—Printing under Difficulties—"Baggage-
smashing"—Handsome Negroes and Sunday Papers—The
Wonders of Chicago.

I.

THERE was a little crowd of friends at the railway
station, to see us take our leave of Chicago, at noon on
Sunday, January 20, 1884. The weather was cold,
but there was a bright, sunny sky. Everybody was
in good spirits. The "Edwin Forrest" car, in which
we travelled, had now quite a familiar appearance.
George, a coloured attendant who had charge of it, was
there, with a merry grin upon his broad, intelligent
features. "A right good fellow, George," said Irving.
"Yes, that's so," was George's response, as he relieved
him of his coat and stick, and led the way to the pretty
little suite of rooms on wheels allotted to Irving and
his friends. The other cars were also admirably appointed.

"This is something like a day for travelling!"
said one member of the company to another. The sun
blazed down upon them as they walked about, awaiting
the signal for departure, but there appeared to be very
little warmth in it. The sunbeams were bright, but

they seemed to have contracted a chill as they fell. Every now and then a gust of icy wind would come along, as if to put truth into this conclusion. Terriss and Tyars, braving the weather without overcoats, as Englishmen delight to do, soon discovered that, after all, the winter was still with us. As the cry "All aboard," followed by the clanging of the engine-bell, set the train in motion, we entered once more upon severely wintry scenes of ice and snow.

Within a very short time we found ourselves in the midst of snow-drifts, out of which preceding trains had had to cut their way. Gangs of men were clearing the track, flinging up the snow on both sides of the road in solid shovelfuls. The white *debris* was piled up six and eight feet high, where the snow had settled down in great drifts upon the line. "One train was stuck here five hours yesterday," said the guard. "It is the heaviest snow in my experience."

Moving onwards once more, we travelled through a world of snow : through prairie-lands, where the wind came tearing after us, waited upon by scudding clouds of snow, that rose like spray, to fall in its wake as if the prairie were a snow-sea ; past forests of oak, with the brown leaves clinging to the tough branches, that moved with a sturdy kind of protest against the boisterous wind ; across great rivers, that were closed to navigation. Now and then skating-parties flitted by us in sheltered bends of the great silent water-ways, and at intervals the sun would burst out upon the white world and fill it with icy diamonds.

We met a train with five engines. It came plunging along—a veritable procession of locomotives. The foremost of them were mighty ploughs, to charge the growing snow-drifts we had left behind us. By-and-by the sun went down, and when our lamps were lighted, and it was night, as we thought, we looked out to see one of the magnificent sunsets which had been puzzling for many weeks the wise men of both worlds,—a wide red glare in the sky, stretching away as far as the eye could see, with a white foreground, the line of the horizon dotted with the dark configuration of farm buildings and forest trees.

At three o'clock in the morning we arrived at St. Louis, and on the next day I walked across the ice-locked Mississippi. In a street adjacent to the quay with its frozen-up steamers and boats of all kinds, were the remains of an old hotel, that had been burnt out a short time previously. The thermometer stood at twenty degrees below zero. A first glance at the place, from a short distance, showed a house with packs of wool thrust out at the windows, and great bundles and entanglements of wool hanging down to the ground from eaves and window-sills. On examination, these strange appearances turned out to be excrescences of ice,—part of the water that had been poured upon the flames by the fire-brigades, whose engines had literally frozen up in the street. Inside the devastated buildings the ruins were hung with icicles many feet in length, with others rising to meet them, mimicking the stalactites and stalagmites of the Cheddar caverns, in England, not to mention the more famous caves of Kentucky.

A picturesque city, St. Louis, smoky and not over-clean, but seated grandly upon the broad river which local enterprise has spanned with a roadway that is worthy of the engineering skill of the people whose locomotives climb the Rocky mountains, and whose bridges are the admiration of the world. One of the picturesque memories of the tour, that will reappear at odd times in " the magic lantern of the mental vision," will be the procession of carts and waggons, drawn by teams of mules driven by coloured drivers, that is continually passing over the bridge across the Mississippi at St. Louis. The English Government have obtained a great many mules from this part of the United States. There could be no finer breed of this useful animal than the examples one saw at St. Louis. The drivers, almost to a man, appeared to be wearing old army cloaks.

The greyish-blue of the cloth and the red linings, toned
down to rare "symphonies" of worn colour, were in
perfect harmony with the atmospheric and material
surroundings. Smoke hanging like a pall over the
city; a wintry mist creeping along the icy river; the
approaches to the bridge lost in the local haze of smoke
and snowy clouds; the great mercantile procession of
mules, and carelessly laden waggons, bursting with
cotton, corn, and hides, made a fine busy foreground
to a very novel scene.

St. Louis accepted the plays, the acting, the scenery,
and the stage management of the Lyceum with much
of the earnest admiration that had characterized the
Chicago audiences. The *Republican*, the *Globe-Democrat*,
the *Post-Dispatch*, and the *Chronicle* had lengthy and
appreciative notices of "The Lyons Mail," "The Bells,"
and "The Merchant of Venice." The spirit of the
criticism is crystallized in the following remarks, which
appeared as an editorial in the *Post-Dispatch* of
January 22 :—

"To the delighted audience which hung with rapt attention
last night on each word and look, each tone and motion, of
Henry Irving, there was only one element of disappointment.
This was that they had not been prepared at all for any such
magnificent revelation of dramatic genius. . . . As far as
the people of St. Louis are concerned, we have only to say
that those who miss seeing him will sustain a loss that can
never be made good."

II.

AMONG the social events of the visit to St. Louis
was a reception given in the lodge and club rooms of
the "Elks." [1] The event was regarded as of so much

---

[1] The institution of "The Elks" is one of influence and
importance. Its objects are to promote and advance the
material and social interests of the theatrical profession, and to
give mutual aid and assistance to the members in case of pecuniary need. Candidates for admission to the order must be
"proposed and vouched for" by existing members; and before
election they must pass through the ordeal of the ballot "after

interest and importance, and the Elks is so excellent
an institution, and the affair so different to anything
associated with the theatre in England, that it merits
special attention.   The local reporter will not, I am
sure, feel annoyed if I call in his aid to make the
record complete.

The lodge and club rooms, the hall-ways, and the
corridors, were decorated for the occasion.   The
room where the formal introductions took place was
festooned with flags and evergreens.   The yellow
light of the chandeliers was in striking contrast with
the white rays of two Edison lamps, that were artistically hung at each end of the hall.   Two handsome
crayon portraits of Irving and Miss Terry were displayed above the platform at the east end of the
room.   Directly above them was the coat-of-arms of
England, draped with the English flag and the Union
Jack, while below and immediately over the lounge
was a bank of white immortelles, framed in flowers
and evergreens, and bearing in the centre the words
"Our Guests," worked in purple flowers.   The platforms at either end of the hall were decorated with

an investigation as to character by a committee of the lodge."
Membership is a title to relief in distress wherever there is a
lodge ; but a "black book" is kept and circulated containing
the names of members who have proved unworthy of their
privileges.   Members need not necessarily be actors.   Many
lawyers and journalists are Elks.   The charity of the order is
secretly dispensed by an executive committee, sworn not to
divulge the channels into which it flows, or the names of those
who request assistance.   Annual performances in aid of the
"charity fund" are given at the theatres.   One of these
"benefits" occurred during Mr. Irving's first visit to New
York.   Irving finding it impossible to accept an invitation to
be present, either as a performer or a spectator, sent a dona-
tion; and this was acknowledged by a formal resolution of
thanks, which, beautifully illuminated and framed, was presented to Irving at the Brevoort House by a deputation of the
members, headed by A. C. Morland, Exalted Ruler and Secretary of the lodge; A. L. Heckler, J. Steinfeld, George Clarke,
J. W. Hamilton, and James W. Collier, Chairman of the Committee of Arrangements.

rare plants and exotics, interspersed with evergreens. In one corner of the main room supper was spread upon a table, the decorations of which were very dainty flowers interspersed with culinary trophies. About half-past nine o'clock the guests began to arrive and disperse themselves here and there about the rooms. An orchestra, under the direction of Professor Maddern, furnished the music for promenading; and an agreeable little concert of instrumental and vocal music led up to the entrance of the guests of the evening. " About eleven," says the local chronicler, "they arrived, and were escorted to the lodge-room, where all the other guests had assembled to receive them. Mr. Irving entered, escorting Mrs. John W. Norton, while Miss Terry was escorted by Mr. John A. Dillon. As they strolled here and there about the hall, they were introduced to those present. Mr. Irving's countenance, when in repose, was rather inclined to be sombre and solemn, but immediately assumed a pleasant expression when he was introduced to the ladies and gentlemen who had assembled to do him honour." Mr. and Mrs. Howe, Mr. Wenman, and several other members of Irving's company, were present, and as one strolled through the rooms there was something very homelike in these familiar faces intermingled with the crowd. Says the local chronicler :—

" Miss Terry was the soul of life and animation. When she was not chatting gaily with some lady or gentleman, who had just been presented, she walked about with her escort, and commented in a bright and interesting way on the decorations, pictures, &c., that adorned the walls. She was becomingly dressed in white silk, trimmed with Spanish lace, flowing brocade train of white and crushed strawberry. Her only jewellery were gold bracelets and a pearl necklace. On her bosom she wore a bunch of natural flowers.

" After half an hour or so spent in conversation and promenading the guests repaired to the club-room and partook of supper. Here the greatest sociability prevailed. Mr. Irving walked here and there, and conversed pleasantly and informally with all the people he met; while Miss Terry, seated in a large

chair, was surrounded by a gay throng of young folk, and
appeared the youngest and gayest of them all. A number of
beautiful roses were taken from the table and presented to her
by ardent admirers, for all of whom she had a pleasant word,
and some little coquettish reply for their gallantry. About
twelve o'clock they left the rooms, and the guests slowly dispersed. Upwards of five hundred hosts and guests were
present.[2]

A newspaper correspondent telegraphed to a Chicago
journal the startling information that Irving was
dissatisfied with this entertainment, and left early.
This was probably the reporter's sly way of com-
plimenting Chicago. The rivalry between these two
cities is often humorously illustrated in the press. St.
Louis is the elder and most historical city of the two;
but Chicago is the most prosperous, and has, no
doubt, the greatest future. St. Louis, nevertheless,
claims to have a population of nearly 500,000; it
boasts double the park area of New York, and stands
"second only to Philadelphia in point of territory
devoted to public recreation."

II.

Two weeks were spent between St. Louis, Cincinnati,
Indianapolis, and Columbus. The New York *répertoire*
was played with excellent results in every way.

"Indianapolis and Columbus," said Irving, "are
evidently behind St. Louis and Cincinnati in their
appreciation of the arts; though I have no reason to
complain, nor has Miss Terry. They came to the
theatre in large numbers, were most excellent

[2] The Irving-Terry reception, by the Elks, Wednesday evening, was a notable social event. The Elks were there, of
course; but it is worthy of notice that, at this testimonial
offered to two eminent members of the dramatic profession,
the attendance of ladies represented the most exclusive and
aristocratic circles of St. Louis society; and quite a number of
the most liberal and eminent of the clergymen were there also.
"Society" in St. Louis has more good common-sense than in
any other city in the Union.—*Post-Dispatch, Jan.* 26.

audiences, cordial in their reception of us, and flattering in their applause; but in walking through their
streets one could not help seeing that there was a good
deal too much of the 'Dime Museum' business in
these places for art in its best forms to flourish liberally
at present. 'The Fat Lady,' 'The Two-headed Pig,'
'The Tattooed Man,' and 'The Wild Men of the
Woods,' appear to have a great hold on Indianapolis
and Columbus. Indeed, they make a fight for it
against the theatres, even in St. Louis and Cincinnati.
You remember the great wide street, in Birmingham,
called the Bull Ring? Well, the show-streets of these
cities remind me of a concentrated Bull Ring in Birmingham, where 'Living Wonders,' 'The Wizard of the
North,' and 'The Fortune-Telling Pony,' are always,
more or less, challenging public attention. I believe
Ball, the leader of our orchestra, had some special
trouble at Indianapolis. The violoncello, for example,
had only two strings. Ball, on the second night,
chaffingly said, 'I suppose you will consider two
strings sufficient for to-night?'—'No,' was the reply;
'I stick to three, on principle.'"

"Did you hear about the manager who gave the
extra musicians in his orchestra something less than
usual," I asked, "because, as he said, they would see
you for nothing, and that should be considered when
every seat was taken? At night they complained;
they said, 'You have swindled us; we have not seen
Irving act at all; we have only seen him at rehearsal.
We have been playing under the stage, at the back of
it, behind flats, or smothered up at the wings, where
we could see nothing, and you have got to give us our
full pay.'"

It is quite new in American theatres for the orchestra
to be put into such frequent requisition behind the
scenes, as is the case in Irving's representations. The
special engagement of a tenor (Mr. J. Robertson)
to sing the ballad in "Much Ado" is an unheard-of
extravagance. Mr. Robertson also gave very valuable

T

assistance in the quartettes and choruses introduced with fine effect in "The Merchant," "The Bells," and other plays; which reminds me that among the saddening incidents of the tour were the sudden recall to England of Mr. Johnson, the low comedian, to the sick-bed of his wife; and the withdrawal of Mr. Norman Forbes from the cast of "The Merchant," through illness. We left Forbes at one of the cities, with a serious attack of rheumatic fever. The "understudies" had to be employed, necessitating many new rehearsals. Mr. Howe, at a moment's notice, undertook the part of Dogberry, and played it admirably; while Mr. Carter took the part of Richard in "Louis XI.," and Mr. Harbury gave extra and efficient service in the graveyard scene in "Hamlet." Mr. Andrews was cast for the part of Lancelot in "The Merchant," replacing Mr. Johnson, and Mr. Lyndal played Claudio in "Much Ado" in such a way as to entitle him to the compliments of Irving, which were generously and ungrudgingly given.

"Cincinnati," said Irving, "has great aims in the direction of art. It has a grand public hall, endowed by a local philanthropist, in which it gives musical, operatic, and dramatic festivals. This year the opera occupies its enormous stage. The Festival Committee gave me a dinner at the Queen City Club. It was a most interesting reunion.[3] The city is very picturesque,

---

[3] The Dramatic Festival Association tendered a dinner to Mr. Henry Irving, at the Queen City Club rooms, last evening, after the great actor's final performance at the Grand Opera House. There were present, besides the distinguished guest, Governor Noyes, ex-president of the association; Manager Henry E. Abbey; Colonel Miles, city dramatic director; Secretary Hall, Mr. Halstead, Judge Force, Colonel Dayton, Mr. Alter, Mr. Huntington, Mr. J. W. Miller, Mr. Nat. H. Davis, Mr. Devereux, Mr. Chatfield, Mr. Bram Stoker, manager for Mr. Irving; Mr. Wetherby, Mr. Stevens, Copleston, agent of Mr. Abbey; Mr. Charles Taft, Mr. Leonard, Colonel Markbreit, Mr. Will. Carlisle, Mr. Frank Alter, and others, to the number of thirty or more.—*Cincinnati News Journal*, Feb. 3, 1884.

I should say, if one could only have seen it; but it was choked with snow, and in a continual mist or fog. The ice in the river broke up before we left,—a wonderful sight it was; a great rising flood, filled with ice and snow,—along the wharves silent ships and steamers, —surprising to look down upon from the hills. As the city has grown the people have had to build on the heights, and the street-cars are hauled up on elevators —you drive your carriage upon these platforms and are raised to the roads above,—it is something like going up in a balloon. A mist hung over the river, the water was rising rapidly, and people were expressing fears that the place would be flooded, as it had been a year or two previously.[4] There is a German quarter.

[4] Irving saw the beginning of one of the periodical disasters to which Cincinnati is subjected,—the overflowing of the Ohio. Within a few days after his visit the city was inundated, thousands of people were homeless, entire families flying from their homes, their houses wrecked, their property floating down the river. Many lives were lost up and down stream. Great floods occurred in other districts, the busy manufacturing city of Pittsburg being among the most serious sufferers. Cincinnati had hardly recovered from the floods, and thought out new devices for dealing with any future trouble of the kind, when she was visited with another disaster,—a great and fatal riot. All countries have their public abuses, their governmental shortcomings. England has plenty of them; the administration of the law in America is far from perfect. As long as judges are elected by popular vote, so long will there be serious miscarriages of justice; so long as juries can be packed, intimidated, and bribed, so long will the jury system be found defective. Such glaring instances of malfeasance and failure in the administration of justice had, from time to time, occurred at Cincinnati that (upon the principle that it is the last straw that breaks the camel's back), when "another notorious murderer was let off," the populace arose, attacked the jail where a company of other ruffians were imprisoned, with a view to taking the law into their own hands. The militia, being called out, fired into the rioters. Many persons were killed and wounded before order could be restored. The press of the country, while regretting the breach of the peace and the loss of life, generally insist upon the moral that governments must not look for people to respect the law in face of corruption in high places and notorious compromises with thieves and murderers. "The objec-

It is called 'Germany,' and has all the characteristics of the Fatherland in its beer-gardens, concert-rooms, theatres, and general mode of life.   Next to the native Americans the Germans are the most influential people. They have several newspapers printed in their own language, and in the regular German type.[5]   The

---

tive point of the mob," wrote the special correspondent of the *New York Sun*, " was the jail, and the murderers it contained, whom they meant to hang. Twenty-three murderers are in that . jail, none of whom have had a trial, except William Hugh, who is to be hanged; and Emil Trompeter, who has had two trials, and is to have a third.   In the list are William Hartnett, who murdered his wife with an axe ; Joe Palmer, the negro confederate of William Berner in murdering William Kirk, and Allen Ingalls and Ben Johnson, the Avondale negro burkers.   In addition to these there are several murderers out on bail and walking the streets. They have not been tried, though the murders for which they were indicted were committed months ago."   The *New York Herald*, editorially discussing "the results of the riot," says that, in the first place, "no jury in that city for some time to come will outrage justice and public decency by making a mockery of murder-trials," and that, "in the next place, the people of Cincinnati have become deeply impressed with the importance of divorcing partisan politics from the administration of justice and municipal affairs generally. Before the echoes of the riot have died away they have started a citizens' movement, with the determination to put in the field and elect at the coming municipal election candidates not identified with either party machine, but representative of the highest order of citizenship.   When this is done there will be a more effective administration of law and justice, and a reform of abuses which contributed, directly or indirectly, in no small degree, to the disastrous events of the past few days."

[5] " Louis XI.," " Charles the First," " The Merchant of Venice," " The Bells," and " The Lyons Mail," drew great and fashionable houses at Cincinnati, and the criticisms in the native press and in the German newspapers were written in a spirit of cordiality, much of it descriptive, and all of it recognizing the possibilities of a speedy reformation in the existing method of representing the classic drama in the West.   The following translation of some of the most prominent passages in a lengthy criticism of " The Merchant of Venice " is from *Tagliches Cincinnati Volksblatt*, one of the principal German newspapers of the district :—

" The court-scene is a masterpiece, and is filled with so many

sudden rises of the Ohio appear to be the chief draw-
back. They are very philosophical about it, and try
to console themselves on the ground that, if they
suffer from water, they have not been burned out, as
some other cities have. Cincinnati has a noble
ambition : it aims at becoming a great centre of culture,
more particularly in art and science. It is making a
magnificent start in its schools of design, its art leagues,
its university, and the museum which is being built
in Eden Park. I was struck with an incident related
to me by a friend of yours. One of the newspaper

details that the spectator follows the action with lively interest,
and imagines himself in a real court of law. The decoration of
the last act, a wonderful park scene, with moonlight, was
ravishing, and the madrigals behind the scene were charmingly
melodious, and were also excellently sung ; in a word, one saw a
great performance of 'The Merchant of Venice,' and not only
Mr. Irving, as Shylock, or Miss Terry, as Portia. By that we
do not mean to say that Henry Irving's performance was less
great; on the contrary, he confirmed and fortified, through his
Shylock, the judgment we pronounced upon his Louis XI. His
reading is entirely the same as Döring's, who ranked as the best
Shylock in Germany, and who has not yet found a successor.
It is the covetous, vindictive Jew; but he is rather an object of
pity than of scorn. It was the Jew whose passionate temperament and inexorable vengeance naturally seized upon the first
opportunity of gratifying his hatred towards the Christians, who
heaped mockeries, insults, and injustice upon him, particularly
Antonio, who treated him with the utmost scorn. This was the
Jew Shakespeare drew, played by Mr. Irving with the refinement of an artist and the sharp observance of a philologist.
. . . His facial expression is mobile and most expressive . . .
and his speech has only just the accent by which the Jews
of that class are known. His acting in the first scene, in the
scene with Tubal, and, above all, in the court scene (particularly the passing from cruel, passionate joy to the consciousness
of his own torpid despair), was the true work of a great actor.
. . . Miss Ellen Terry, who plays Portia, was reported from
other towns where she had appeared to be a great actress :
the audience was, therefore, highly expectant. . . . She took
the public from first to last by storm. . . . She is one of those
endowed actresses, who shine so completely in the character
they represent that the spectator forgets the actress, and only
sees the person represented in the piece."

offices was burned down. The fire took place while
the paper was at press. Seeing that it was impossible
to save the machinery, they put on the highest speed
and worked off the sheets until the place was too hot
to hold them; and the men stepped out with the printed
sheets, almost as the ceiling fell in upon the machinery.
By the aid of a neighbour, and the presses of a rival
who had failed, they came out the next day with a full
report of the calamity, in which, I believe, some lives
were lost. An example of American enterprise that,
eh ? "

" At Columbus I went to the State house while
the General Assembly and Senate were sitting. If
one were a politician, I can imagine nothing more interesting than to study the details of the American
system of government, the question of State rights,
and other features of the general administration. Each
State seems very distinct and independent of the
other. For instance, some States and cities have
special laws of their own, and many complications
which seem inexplicable would be more easily explained if this were more understood. It is not the
government of the United States which can control all
matters; it is the State which sometimes plays the
principal part. I did not quite understand that until
recently. For instance, in New York City or State,
there is a law giving certain privileges to ticket speculators; while at Philadelphia, and at Boston, I believe,
there is a law against speculators selling tickets on the
pavements. Talking upon this subject to a lawyer in
Baltimore, he told me that baggage-smashing on the
railroads had reached such a pitch that a State law had
been passed in Maryland making it a misdemeanour.
English and indeed European travellers generally, who
have had no experience of America, can have no conception of the way in which baggage is treated; it
seems to me as if the intention often is really to stave
in trunks and boxes. The credulous Britisher, who
should put on his trunk, ' This side up, with care,'

would have a fit if he saw the porter throw it down with
a crash on the other side, and then pile a ton or two
of the heaviest kind of merchandise upon it. When
you think of the respect with which a traveller's
trunks are treated on European railways, it is startling
to encounter a general sort of conspiracy to break
them up, and in a country which has invented the
best system of 'expressing' and delivering baggage
known to modern travel,—to me this is incompre-
hensible."

" From Columbus we went back to Chicago, the first
of our return visits. I felt quite at home again at the
Grand Pacific Hotel,—one of the finest and most comfortable houses of the entire tour. The coloured
attendant, Walter, who is told off for my service, is the
most intelligent and courteous fellow I have ever met
in the position he holds. Singularly handsome, too,
is he not? Indeed one is struck with the physical
beauty of some of these half-breeds, mulattoes, creoles
—wonderful fellows! I remember that Sala describes
the Grand Pacific as ' Wonder number One ' among the
marvels of Chicago, and the newspaper press as
' Wonder number Two.' I should put the press first,—
did you ever see such papers as the Sunday journals?
Sixteen to twenty and twenty-four pages,—why, it's
marvellous how they get the matter for them together !
One of the St. Louis papers I noticed was also a very
large one. What a deftness of allusion and adaptation
of events to personal criticism there is in these western
journals ! The Standard oil affair,—I don't know the
merits of it; but charges of unfairness in connection
with the enterprise are before the public. Somebody
has sent me this paragraph about it, from the *Columbus Times* :—

" The members of the General Assembly who looked upon
the Standard oil, when it flowed with unction in the recent
senatorial struggle, might get a few points on the effects of the
remorse of conscience by seeing Henry Irving in ' The Bells.' "

" Flattering, eh ? "

XVIII.

CHIEFLY CONCERNING A HOLIDAY AT NIAGARA.

The Return Visit to Chicago—Welcomed back again—Farewell Speech—Niagara in the Winter—A Sensation at the Hotel—Requisitioning adjacent Towns for Chickens and Turkeys—Ira Aldridge and a Coloured Dramatic Club—A Blizzard from the North-West—The Scene of Webb's Death—"A great Stage-manager, Nature"—Life and Death of "The Hermit of Niagara"—A fatal Picnic—The Lyceum Company at Dinner—Mr. Howe proposes a Toast —Terriss meets with an Accident that recalls a Romantic Tragedy.

I.

"The fact of Mr. Irving and Miss Terry and their company attracting an audience to fill Haverly's Theatre on so speedy a return after leaving us, and that, too, following a rugged strain of grand opera," said the *Chicago Inter-Ocean* of February 12, "may be accepted as conclusive evidence of genuine appreciation and admiration of their worth. This testimony is much strengthened by the fact that the plays presented were those most frequently seen during the original engagements,—' The Bells,' and ' The Belle's Stratagem,'—for, though it is thought Mr. Irving is seen to exceptional advantage as Mathias, mere curiosity would have held off to see him in a new character. It was a generous and highly gratifying welcome back; and it is certainly a great pleasure, as well as an artistic privilege worthy to be acknowledged, that we have Mr. Irving and his superb surroundings again before us. We are in no danger of seeing too much of this sort of work." "Hamlet" and "Much Ado" were produced for the first time at Chicago during this second season. Both excited genuine interest, and were received with as much favour by audiences and critics as his previous work. Only two weeks had intervened between his first and second visit. More money was paid at the doors of Haverly's during the week than had gone into the treasury for a week of grand opera. The programme for the last night was "Much Ado," and the recitation of Hood's "Eugene Aram." After enthusiastic calls for Irving and Miss Terry, at the close of the comedy, there were cries of "Speech! Speech!" Irving, in evening dress for the recitation, presently responded to the wishes of his audience. He said he would be made of sterner stuff—and he was glad that such was not the case—if he failed to feel profoundly the welcome that had been accorded him in Chicago. Not one shadow had fallen across the brightness of that welcome; there was not a jarring note in the generous applause that had greeted the company's efforts. The encouragement had been most grateful, and it had urged himself and his associates to do their best work. He thanked the press of the city for overlooking shortcomings, and for recognizing so generously what they found to be good. The notices had been most eloquent and sympathetic. He wished to thank the audience on behalf of his associates, and particularly on behalf of Miss Ellen Terry, whose great gifts had been so quickly recognized. If he might be permitted to say so in public, he himself heartily joined in their appreciation of Miss Terry's work.

Parting was a "sweet sorrow," and the sweet part of his leave-taking was in expressing his deep sense of Chicago's great welcome. Again he would say good-bye to every one; but he hoped circumstances would make it possible to meet a Chicago audience in the future, and he trusted that "you will remember us as we will surely remember you."

"The speaker," says the *Tribune*, "was frequently interrupted by applause, his reference to Miss Terry especially awakening enthusiasm. He then recited 'Eugene Aram's Dream' with fine effect, and after inducing him to respond to a fifth and last recall, the audience dispersed."

II.

ON the following Monday and Tuesday the company appeared for two nights at Detroit,[1] the chief city of Michigan, to large and most friendly audiences. I was in New York at this time, and had arranged to meet Irving, Miss Terry, and a few friends, at Niagara, on Wednesday. "If Abbey is agreeable, I shall give the company a holiday, so that they can go to Niagara,[2]

---

[1] Detroit is a handsome and populous city on the banks of a noble river that connects Lake Erie and St. Clair. The company gave two performances at Whitney's Opera House, to large audiences, by whom they were heartily received. The *Post* and *Tribune* contained long and complimentary notices of the plays and the actors, with lists of the principal people in the audiences. "The coming of Mr. Irving and Miss Terry," it says, "was a great event in dramatic circles here, and has long been looked forward to with expectancy. The audience that greeted them completely filled the house, every seat being occupied, while many were content to stand during the entire performance. It was also a fashionable audience, in the fullest sense of the word, all of Detroit's most pronounced society people being there."

[2] The *Niagara Falls Courier* has an interesting article on the many orthographical changes of the name of Niagara. In 1687 it was written Oniogoragn. In 1686 Gov. Dongan appeared uncertain about it, and spelled it Onniagero, Onyagara, and Onyagro. The French, in 1638 to 1709, wrote it Niaguro, Onyagare, Onyagra and Oneygra. Philip Livingstone wrote in 1720 to 1730 Octjagara, Jagera, and Yagerah; and Schuyler and Livingston, Commissioners of Indian Affairs, wrote it in 1720 Onjagerae, Ocniagara, &c. In 1721 it was written Onja-

spend the day, and sleep in Toronto at night. It will do us all good." Abbey was agreeable, and Wednesday, February 20th, was one of the most memorable days of the tour.

I travelled from New York by the West Shore Road, an admirably equipped railway (and having at Syracuse the most picturesque and one of the finest stations in America), to meet my friends at the Falls. At two o'clock, on Tuesday, I arrived on the Canadian side of the river. The country was covered with snow, but a thaw had set in during the morning. Driving from the railway station the scene was wild, weird, and impressive. The steep banks of the Niagara River were seamed and furrowed with ice and snow. The American side of the ravine was ploughed by the weather into ridges. One might say the river-banks were corrugated, cracked, grooved into strange lines, every channel ribbed with ice. Here and there tiny falls, that had mimicked the colossal ones beyond, were frozen into columns. Others had been converted into pillars that seemed to be supporting white, ghost-like figures. Further on there was a cluster of fountains gushing out of the rocks beneath a number of mills, the wheels of which they had turned on their way to the river. These waters leaped down some fifty or sixty feet into great ice-bowls. You would think they had found an outlet other than the river but for its discoloration at the base of the natural urns, or bowls, into which they fell. There were ponderous heaps of ice at the bed of the American falls. A section of them was literally frozen into a

gora, Oniagara, and accidentally, probably, Niagara, as at present. Lieut. Lindsay wrote it Niagara in 1751. So did Capt. De Lancey (son of Gov. De Lancey), who was an officer in the English army that captured Fort Niagara from the French in 1759. "These pioneers," says the local journalist, "may, however, be excused in view of the fact—as will be attested by postmasters—that some letter-writers of to-day seem quite as undecided about the orthography of this world-wide familiar name."

curious mass of icicles. The ice was not bright, but had a dull, woolly appearance. Coming upon a slight bend of the river, you see the two great falls almost at the same moment. On this day they were almost enveloped in spray. Our horses splashed through thawing snow, and picked their way over a road broken up with scoriated ice and flooded with water. A strong, but not a cold, wind blew in our faces, and covered us with spray. The water was pouring down the abyss in greater masses it seemed to me than usual ; and this was my third visit to Niagara. I had seen the falls in summer and in autumn. Their winter aspect has not the fascinating charm of the softer periods of the year, when the banks are green, and the leaves are rustling on the trees of the islands. The Clifton House was closed, and its balconies, upon which merry parties sit and chat on summer evenings, were empty. Even the Prospect House looked chilly. The flood fell into its awful gulf with a dull, thudding boom, and the rapids above were white and angry.

I wondered what Irving would think of the scene. Some persons profess that they are disappointed with the first sight of Niagara. There are also people who look upon the ocean without surprise ; and some who see the curtain go up on a grand opera, for the first time in their lives, without experiencing one throb of the sensation which Bulwer describes with pathetic eloquence. The Rev. Dr. Thomas, a popular preacher in the Prairie city, went to his first play while Irving was at Chicago, and was greatly impressed ; although he half confessed that, on the whole, he liked a good lecture quite as well. A coloured man and his wife, at Philadelphia, told me they had always considered the play wicked, and would never have thought to go to a theatre, had not one of their clergymen done so. "But," said the husband, "I see noffin' wicked nor wrong, and it did my heart good to see all dem white folk bowing to de coloured gentleman and making much of him." It was the casket scene in "The Merchant" that had most delighted these people.

Almost the first thing I did on arriving at Niagara was to send Irving a telegram, asking if he had settled where to stay, and advising him that for a brief visit the Prospect House was most conveniently placed for seeing the falls. The response was a request for rooms. This was followed by an inquiry if the house could provide a dinner for seventy ; and from that moment I found myself actively engaged, not in reviving my former recollections of Niagara, but in preparing to receive the Irving company. The proprietor of the Prospect House is a land-owner in Manitoba. He was looking after his interests in those distant regions. The landlady, a bright, clever woman of business, however, undertook to "run the dinner."

"The house is partially closed, as you know," she said, "and it is small. We have only a few servants during the winter, and it is difficult to get provisions at short notice. But we have the Western Union telegraph in the house, and a telephone. We will do our best."

The intelligent coloured waiter found it "impossible to seat seventy persons in the dining-room."

"They must dine at twice," he said ; "that's the only chance ; no help for it."

It was night before the order for dinner was really closed and settled, many telegrams passing between Detroit and Niagara ; and, as I found to my consternation, between Niagara and several adjacent towns.

"Not a turkey nor a chicken to be got for love or money," said the landlady. "I have telegraphed and telephoned the whole neighbourhood,—just going to try Buffalo, as a last resort. You see the hotels here are closed, and it is very quiet in the winter."

"As good a dinner as can be provided," was one of Stoker's latest telegrams, "and it must be ready at half-past three to the minute."

The excitement at the Prospect House was tremendous. The falls were quite discounted. They were of no moment for the time being, compared with the question of turkeys and the seating of the coming guests.

" You have beef, mutton, ham, you say ? "

" Yes, and we can make excellent soup,—a nice lot of fish has come in from Toronto, lake fish,— but turkeys, no ; chickens, no ; though I have telegraphed everywhere and offered any price for them. Ah, if we had only known two days ago ! " said the landlady.

" Never mind, let it be a plain English dinner, horseradish sauce with the beef,—can you manage that ? "

" Yes. Oh, yes ! ".

" And boiled legs of mutton, eh ? "

" Yes, with caper sauce."

" Capital. And what do you say to plum-pudding ?"

" I fear there will not be time to stone the raisins ; but I'll telephone into the town at once and see."

While she was gone I surveyed the dining-room once more. "If you moved the stove, and placed forms against the walls, instead of chairs, how would that be ? " I asked.

It was a great problem, this. My coloured ally and his two assistants set to measuring with a foot-rule. They had their woolly heads together when I looked in upon them an hour later.

"Yes, I believe it can be done," said the chief waiter ; and before midnight the tables were arranged, the stove cleared out, and the room almost ready for the feasters. As he was leaving for the night he said, " The people of my race honour Mr. Irving. He knew our great actor, Ira Aldridge. There was a letter from Mr. Irving about him, and a dramatic club started by our folk in the New York papers. Rely on me, sir, to have this dinner a success." [3]

[3] The following is the correspondence alluded to :—

" MR. IRVING :—   *New York*, Jan. 20, 1884.

    " DEAR SIR,—The creation and development of a taste for true dramatic art among the coloured citizens of culture in New

III.

WEDNESDAY morning was ushered in with a blizzard from the north-west. The roads that had been slushy the day before were hard as adamant. There was ice

York city, having been long regarded as a necessity to their intellectual growth, a number of ladies and gentlemen, selected for their evidences of dramatic ability, which they have shown from time to time, met on the evening of January 7, and perfected the organization of the 'Irving Dramatic Club.' In apprising you of this fact, we beg leave to assure you, sir, that, in selecting your name for the title of our club, we did not choose it because we felt we were conferring an honour,—far from it,—for we well know that the mere naming of an amateur club could add nothing to the lustre of the laurels so deservedly won by one who so fittingly represents as yourself all that is noble and grand in dramatic art. But, having in our mind the record of past events, we could not fail to recognize that the English stage and its representatives were but the synonyms of equity and justice.

" Thus, in searching for a patron, we naturally reverted to that source from which our efforts were mostly to be regarded with favour; and, acting upon this impulse, we could think of no name that would be a greater incentive to conscientious and praiseworthy effort than that of Irving.

" Hoping that this action will meet with your approval, we remain, with best wishes for your health and prosperity, respectfully yours,

"IRVING DRAMATIC CLUB.

"CHARLES G. BOWSER, *Pres.*

"W. H. A. MOORE, *Sec.*"

" ST. LOUIS, Jan. 26, 1884.

" DEAR SIR,—I have received your letter of the 20th, and it gives me great pleasure to have my name associated with so gratifying an intellectual movement among the coloured citizens of New York as the establishment of a Dramatic Club. Art is of no country, and has no nationality. Europe is deeply indebted to the artistic culture of the great coloured people of the Eastern World, and there is promise of a future for your race, in the fact that you have ceased to feel the disabilities of colour in your association with your white fellow-citizens. I once had the pleasure of knowing a very famous actor of your race,—Ira Aldridge. I wish for your club a prosperous career, and beg to subscribe myself,

" Yours truly,   HENRY IRVING."

in the wind.   The air was keen as a knife.   A traveller
who had come in from Manitoba said that during the
night it was "as much as your life was worth to pass
from one car to another."   Towards noon the weather
moderated.   The sun came out, the wind changed, the
spray from the falls fell into the river.   A rainbow
stretched its luminous arch over the American falls.

"I have often thought," I said to Irving, "during
this tour, how surprised any English traveller who knew
London well would be, if he encountered the Lyceum
Company by accident at some wayside American railway station, not knowing of this visit to the States."

"Yes," he said, "do you remember the people at
Amsterdam, in Holland, who followed us to the hotel
there, one of them, a German, making a bet about us,
the others ridiculing the idea that I could be out of
London, when he had seen me acting there a few days
before ?"

We were on our way to the falls, driving in a close
carriage, Irving, Miss Terry, and myself, and I think
we talked on general topics a little, while they were
trying to take in the approaches to the great scene
of all.

"Toole and his dear boy, Frank, lost their way, one
night, about here," said Irving.   "I remember his
telling me of it—couldn't get a carriage—were belated,
I remember.   There was no fence to the river then, I
expect,—a dangerous place to lose your way in.   How
weird it looks!"

"Oh, there are the falls!" Miss Terry exclaimed,
looking through the glass window in front of us.
"Surely!   Yes, indeed!   There they are!   How
wonderful!"

I had told the driver to pull up at the bend of the
river, where we should get the first view of them.
Irving turned to look.

"Drive on," I said, and in a few minutes we pulled
up in full view of both falls.

"Very marvellous!" said Irving.   "Do you see

those gulls sailing through the spray? How regularly the water comes over! It hardly looks like water,—there seems to be no variety in its grand, liquid roll; and, do you notice, in parts it curls like long, broken ringlets, curls and ripples, but is always the same. What a power it suggests! Of course, the colour will vary in the light. It is blue and green in the summer, I suppose; now it is yellowish here and there, and gray. There have been great floods above, —yonder are the rapids above the falls, I suppose? How wonderfully the waters come leaping along,—like an angry sea! "

He watched the scene, and noted everything that struck him. Miss Terry joined some members of the company, and went driving. Later a party of us went to the rapids and the whirlpool, where Webb was drowned. Irving discussed the fatal feat with one of the men who saw the swimmer take his courageous header and go bounding through the rapids.

" It was there where he disappeared," said the man, pointing to a spot where the waters appeared to leap as if clearing an obstruction; " he dived, intending to go through that wave, and never was seen again alive. It is believed his head struck a sunken rock there, which stunned him."

Irving stood for a long time looking at this part of the river, discussing the various theories as to its depth. " A bold fellow!" he exclaimed, as he left the place; " he deserved to get through it. Imagine the coolness, the daring of it! he takes a quiet dinner, it seems, at his hotel, rests a little, then hires a boat, rows to the place where the rapids fairly begin, strips and dives into this awful torrent,—a great soul, sir, any man who has the nerve for such an enterprise!"

We walked back to the falls, and on our return observed a great change in the colour of the scene.

" Quite a transformation in its way, is it not?" said

U

Irving; "let us take in the picture, as a painter might. The horizon, you see, is a bluish-purple; the Canadian falls have a grayish-blue tint, except where the positive golden yellow of the water comes in; then, as it plunges below, the foam is of a creamy whiteness; the mist and spray rise up a warmish-gray in the half-shaded sunlight; the snowy rocks are white against it. The sun is about to set, I suppose, and these are some of its premonitory colours. The river, you see, is now a deep blue,—it was muddy-looking this morning,—and the trees on the banks are a warm grayish-brown. Beyond the American falls, above there, where it is like a lake, the white houses are whiter still, the red ones redder, and the country looks as if it had quite changed its atmosphere. A great stage-manager, Nature! What wonders can be done with effective lighting!"

Then, turning away to go into the house, he said, " Do you remember the lighting of the garden scene in 'Romeo and Juliet,'—the change from sunset to night, from sunset to moonlight, from moonlight to morning, and the motion of the sunlit trees, as if a zephyr had touched them?"

" I do, indeed!"

"Well, let us talk of something else. Niagara must offer to artist or poet a continual study. Did you notice how the fir-trees on the little island close to the Canadian falls are twisted and warped, as if they had tried to turn away from the tempest, and had been beaten down with the wind and snow? You were telling me one day about a scholarly hermit who had spent his life at a lonely place on the Hudson. That is also a curious story,—the life and death of Francis Abbott, 'the hermit of Niagara,' as they call him in one of the old guide-books. He first appeared here, it seems, on a summer day in 1839,—a young man, tall, well-built, but pale and haggard. He carried a bundle of blankets, a portfolio, a book, and a flute; went to a little out-of-the-way inn and took a room; visited the local library; played his flute, and rambled about the country; got permission to live in a deserted log-house near the head of Goat Island; lived there in a strange seclusion during two winters, then built himself a cabin at Point View, near the American falls, and did not appear to shun his fellow-man so much as formerly. A local judge became quite friendly with him; they would meet and have long talks. Sometimes, too, he would enter into conversation with the villagers, and others whom he encountered on his rambles. He talked well, they say; spoke of Asia and Greece with familiarity, and liked to discuss theological questions. His religious views were akin to Quakerism. He was a fine figure, had a sorrowful face, and was attended by a dog, which trotted at his heels always. During the summer he lived in his cabin at Point View; he went down the ferry-steps and bathed in the river, and, on June 10, 1841, he lost his life there,—after two years of this strange solitude. The body had been in the water ten days before it was found at the outlet of the river. The villagers brought it back and buried it. They went to his cabin. His dog guarded the door, a cat lay asleep on his rough sofa, books and music scattered about. There was no writing to be found, though the local judge said he wrote a great deal, chiefly in Latin, and, as a rule, burned his work, whatever it was. In later days friends and relatives of the poor young fellow came to Niagara, and identified him as the son of a Quaker gentleman of Plymouth. Rather a sad story, eh?"

"Yes, very, and there are others, less romantic, but more tragic, in connection with the falls."

"None more sad, after all, than the death of poor Webb. It is true, he deliberately risked his life. I have seen it stated that the rapids where he dived are by some persons estimated as only twenty or thirty feet deep. Of course nothing can be more absurd. The channel is only three hundred feet wide, and through this gorge rush the waters of five great lakes.

Calculating the volume of water, and the velocity of it, the scientists who estimate the depth at two hundred and fifty feet .are nearer the mark. The most surprising thing to me about Niagara is the fact—it must be a fact—that this mighty torrent, after falling into the river, ploughs its way along the bottom,—the surface being comparatively calm,—drives along for two miles, and then leaps up from its imprisonment, as it were, into the general view, a wild, fierce torrent, with, further down, that awful whirlpool. Webb knew the force of it all; he had surveyed it,—the cruellest stretch of waters in the world, I suppose,—and yet he took that header, and went along with it hand-over-hand, as the man told us, and with an easy confidence that was heroic,—one would have thought the water would have beaten the life out of him before he had time to rise and fight it ! "

" Not long since," I said, " there was a picnic party on Goat Island. A young fellow, I think the father of the child itself, picked up a little girl, and in fun held it over the rapids above the falls. The child struggled and fell; he leaped in after it, caught it, struggled gallantly in presence of the child's mother and the distracted friends, but went over the falls. I read the incident in a newspaper, and have it put away at home with many other notes about the falls, which I hoped to use in this book. Our critics will, of course, recognize the difficulties attending the preparation of these Impressions. We have worked at them in odd places, and at curious times. One wonders how they will come out."

" Oh, all right, I am sure ! " Irving replied ; " they are quite unpretentious, and it is delightful to note how they grow up and assume shape and form."

IV.

But nobody will ever know, except those who took part in the work, how much ingenuity, patience, and enterprise were expended on that dinner. It was ready to the minute. The guests all sat down together. There were turkeys and there were chickens, too. Horsemen had ridden hard half the night to bring them in. There were plum-puddings, also. Lovely maidens at Buffalo and Niagara had been pressed into the service of stoning them. When Stoker, at midnight, in order to smooth the way, had telegraphed that "rare flowers and hot-house fruits can be dispensed with " (he was thinking of New York, Boston, Chicago, and Philadelphia), the landlady had looked at me in dismay. "There isn't a flower in the whole neighbourhood! I'm afraid they are expecting too much," she said. "Not at all; it is only Mr. Stoker's little joke," I replied, fearing that at the last moment the entire business might fall through. As the reader already understands, it did not fall through ; but, on the contrary, was a great and surprising success; for, when Mr. Howe got up to propose the health of the founder of the feast, he said, "This has been the first English dinner we have had since we left home, and, what is more, we have eaten it off English plates,—not those little dishes and saucers they give us everywhere in America. Not, ladies and gentlemen, that I have a word to say against the American food—not I,—because it is good and abundant; but I do like large plates, and I love to see the joints on the table and carved before our eyes." Everybody laughed at this and applauded; but the cheering increased, and was followed by "three times three " and the chorus, " He's a jolly good fellow ! " when Howe thanked their "host and chief, Mr. Irving, for his hospitality and kindness that day, and for his energy and courage in bringing them all from the old country on a tour in the New World."

It was nearly six when we left Niagara for the railway station, in every kind of vehicle, omnibus, buggy, brougham, and carriage. Mr. McHenry and a party of ladies and gentlemen came to see us off. The members of the company were loud in their expressions of wonder at the falls. " So strange," said one, " to be sitting down to dinner in view of them." " What a day to remember!" exclaimed another. Tyars, Andrews, Terriss, Arnot, and some others, had donned the water-proof dress, known to every visitor, and explored the regions below the falls. Terriss had a narrow escape. There were special dangers to be encountered, owing to the accumulatious of ice ; and, at the hands of a party of Englishmen, the dangers were of course duly attacked. Terriss slipped upon an icy descent, and saved himself from going headlong into the torrent by clutching a jagged rock which severely lacerated his right hand. He played with his arm in a sling for several nights afterwards.

One of the saddest stories of the falls is the history of a calamity that occurred almost at this very spot, in the autumn of 1875. Miss Philpott, her two brothers, a sister-in-law, and Miss Philpott's lover, Ethelbert Parsons, went through the Cave of the Winds, and climbed over the rocks towards the American falls. They were residents of Niagara, and knew the ground. The sheltered eddies in the lighter currents under the falls are pleasant bathing-places. The Philpott party took advantage of them. Miss Philpott was venturesome. She bathed near one of the strongest currents. Mr. Parsons, seeing her in danger, went to her rescue. Seeking for a firm foothold for both of them, the girl slipped and fell. Parsons sprang for her, and both were carried into the current. He caught her around the waist. The young lady could swim, and Parsons was an expert; they struck out for the rocks on the other side of the current. The torrent carried them out. By-and-by Parsons swam on his back, the girl cleverly supporting herself with her hand upon his shoulder. Then she suddenly pushed him away from her,—the inference being that she discovered the impossibility of both being saved,—flung up her arms and sank. Parsons turned and dived after her. They were seen no more until some days afterwards, when the bodies were recovered at the whirlpool.

Terriss and his friends had more reason than they quite realized to congratulate themselves upon the fact that they were enabled to comply with the kindly and considerate programme of the holiday, which arranged that they should sleep that night in Toronto.

XIX.

FROM TORONTO TO BOSTON.

Lake Ontario—Canadian Pastimes—Tobogganing—On an Ice
Slide—" Shooting Niagara and After "—Toronto Students
—Dressing for the Theatre—" God save the Queen "—Inci-
dents of Travel—Locomotive Vagaries—Stopping the Train
—"Fined one hundred Dollars "—The Hotels and the Poor—
Tenement Houses—The Stage and the Pulpit—Actors, past
and present—The Stage and the Bar-room—The second
Visit to Boston—Enormous Receipts—A Glance at the
Financial Results of the Tour.

I.

THE blizzard was in full possession of Toronto, but
the air was dry, the sky blue and sunny. There was
a brief interval for a snow-storm. But it came in a
bright, frosty fashion. The footpaths were hard.
Sleighs dashed along the leading thoroughfares. Lake
Ontario was a vast plain, upon which disported skaters,
walkers, riders, drivers, and that most fairy-like of
" white-wings," the ice-boat. Did you ever fly across
the silvery ice on runners, with sails bending before
the wind ? It is an experience. You may spin along
at sixty miles an hour, or more. If you are not
wrapped to the eyes in fur, you may also freeze to
death. The sensation of wild, unchecked motion is in-
tensely exhilarating ; but, if you are a novice, want of
care or lack of grip may send you flying into space, or
scudding over the ice on your own account. A secure
seat is only obtained by accommodating yourself all

the time to the motion of your most frail, but elegant,
arrangement of timbers and skating-irons.

The leading characteristic winter sport of Canada is
Tobogganing. The word "toboggan" is Indian for
"sled." The French call it *Traîne sauvage*. Two or
three light boards deftly fastened together, a mattress
laid upon them, a sort of hollow prow in front, into
which a lady thrusts her feet,—that is a "toboggan."
It is like a toy canoe, or boat, with a flat bottom and no
sides. The lady passenger sits in front; the gentleman
behind. He trails his legs upon the ice-slide, and thus
guides the machine. It is not necessary, of course,
that there should be two passengers; nor, being two,
that one of them should be a lady. The contrivance
was invented by the North American Indians. They
used it for the transportation of burdens. The squaws
sometimes made it available for hauling along their
children. The pioneer troops of Courcelles, Tracy,
and Montcalm made a kit carriage of it.

There is a famous Tobogganing Club at Toronto.
It has a slide of half a mile in length, down the side
of a hill in a picturesque suburban valley. The slide
starts at an angle of about forty-five degrees; then it
runs along a short flat; then it drops, as if going
over a frozen Niagara, to shoot out along a great
incline, that might be the frozen rapids. To stand at
the summit and watch the gay toboggans slip away,
and then disappear down the Niagara-like precipice,
to shoot out as a bolt from a gun along the remainder
of the pass, is to realize the possible terrors of a first
trip.

Miss Terry watched the wild-looking business with
amazement, and built up her courage on the experiences
of the ladies who took the flying leap with delight.
They were dressed in pretty flannel costumes, and their
faces glowed with healthful excitement. But they
were practised tobogganers. Some of them could not
remember when they took their first slide. A sturdy
officer of the club explained the simplicity of the sport

to the famous actress, and offered to let her try half
the slide, beginning at the section below Niagara.
"I ought to have made my will first; but you can
give my diamond ring to your wife," she exclaimed,
waving her hand to me, as she drew her cloak about
her shoulders and stepped into the frail-looking sled.

As she and her stalwart cavalier, in his Canadian
flannels, flew safely along the slide, her young English
friend and admirer followed. They had not been upon
the wintry scene ten minutes, in fact, before both of
them were to be seen skimming the mountain-slide at
the speed of the Flying Dutchman of the Midland
Railway, and at one point, much faster, I expect.

"Oh, it was awful—wonderful—magnificent!"
Miss Terry exclaimed, when she had mounted the hill
again, ready for a second flight. "I have never experienced anything so surprising,—it is like flying;
for a moment you cannot breathe!"

And away she went again, followed at respectful
distances, to avoid collision, by other excursionists, the
slide fairly flashing with the bright flannels and gay
head-dresses of the merry tobogganers.

"Yes," she said, on her return, "it is a splendid
pastime. The Canadians are quite right,—it beats
skating, ice-boating, trotting, everything in the way
of locomotion; what matters the cold, with such
exercise as tobogganing?"[1]

[1] TOBOGGANING.—Saturday, February 24th, was a gala day in
the annals of the Toronto Toboggan Club. The slide was in
perfect condition,—glare ice from top to bottom. About eighty
members were out with their toboggans, enjoying the slide, the
only fault of which is that it is too fast for the length of run at
the bottom. The committee are, however, making arrangements
to overcome this defect. During the latter part of the afternoon
several members of Mr. Irving's company and friends were
present by invitation, escorted by Mr. Bram Stoker. Miss
Terry drove a young friend, Miss Helen H. Hatton (who is
visiting Toronto with her father), out to the grounds, and they
were both initiated into the Canadian winter sport. Miss
Terry was completely captivated by this entirely new sensation,
and only regretted that she was unable to enjoy it longer.

The *Montreal Daily Star*, during this Toronto week,
had a brief description of tobogganing, *apropos* of the
winter carnival that was being held in the neighbouring
city, during our too brief visit to Canada. A proper
slide is constructed on "scientific principles, and blends
a maximum of enjoyment with a minimum of danger."
The *Star* has a picture of the enjoyment and the
danger. It depicts an enormous mountain slide by
torchlight. Many sleds are coming down in fine, picturesque style. There are wayside incidents of spills,
however, which suggest a good deal of possible dis-
comfort. "Try your luck on one of these sleds," says
the descriptive text. "Take two or three girls with
you. That is indispensable; and there is a shrewd
suspicion that much of the popularity of tobogganing
comes from its almost essential admission of ladies.
Let them be well wrapped up. Take a firm seat on
the cushions, never stir an inch, and all will be right.
They may shut their eyes and utter their little shrieks;
but, at their peril, they must not move. You occupy
your station at the rear. The position is optional.
The general mode is to lie on the left side, propped on
one arm, with right leg extended; but some sit, others
kneel, and on short, easy inclines some venture to
stand. One invariable rule is to hold on to your girl;
an occasional squeeze may be allowed; indeed, there
are critical moments when it cannot be helped. All is
ready; the signal is given, and the descent begins.
At first it is gradual, and one might fancy that he
could regulate it; but, like a flash, the grand propul-
sion is given; like an arrow's, the speed is instanta-
neous and resistless. A film passes before your eyes;
your breath is caught. One moment you feel yourself
thrown into space; the next you hear the welcome
crunch of the firm snow, and then comes the final
tumble, topsy-turvy, higgledy-piggledy, in the fleecy

She entered into it with the greatest zest. The ladies and
gentlemen of the club gave her a very hearty welcome.—*Newspaper Reports.*

bank at the foot.   There is the crisis of the fun, and
you must take particular care of the girls just then.
The weary ascent next begins, to be followed by
another vertiginous descent, and still another, till the
whole afternoon, or the whole of the starry evening,
is spent in this exquisite amusement."

II.

THE short season at Toronto was very successful in
every way.   A great body of students filled the
gallery of the Opera House every night.   Stalls, boxes,
and dress circle were crowded, the audience being in
full evening dress.   The house looked like a London
theatre on a first night.   Boston and Philadelphia
were the only cities that had shown anything like an
approach to uniformity in dressing for the theatre in
America, though New York made a good deal of display in regard to bonnets, costumes, and diamonds.
New York copies the French more than the English
in the matter of dressing for the theatre, consulting
convenience rather than style—a very sensible plan.

On the Saturday night, after repeated calls and loud
requests for a speech, Irving, in his Louis XI. robes,
stepped down to the footlights, amidst thunders of
applause.

"Ladies and gentlemen," he said, " I regret that I
have to appear before you as somebody else, though I
feel quite incompetent in my own person to respond to
your kindness at all as I could wish, or in such a way
as to make you understand how keenly I feel the compliment of your enthusiastic welcome.   I thank you
with all my heart for myself and comrades, and more
especially for my co-worker, Miss Terry, for the right-
royal Canadian, I will say British, welcome you have
given us.   I can only regret that the arrangements of
this present tour do not enable me to extend my
personal knowledge of Canada beyond Toronto."

"Come again !" shouted a voice from the gallery,

quite after the manner of the London gods ; "come again, sir ! "

"Thank you very much," Irving replied, amidst shouts of laughter and applause. "I will accept your invitation."

"Hurrah ! " shouted the gallery ; and the house generally applauded Mr. Irving's prompt and gratifying repartee.

"I would have liked," said Irving, pulling his Louis XI. robes around him, "to have travelled right through the Dominion, and have shaken hands with your neighbours of Montreal, Quebec, and Ottawa. That, however, is only a pleasure deferred. In the Indian language, I am told, Toronto means 'The place of meeting.' To you and me, ladies and gentlemen, brother and sister subjects of the English throne—"

A burst of applause compelled the speaker to pause for some seconds.

"To us, ladies and gentlemen, to you before the curtain, to us behind it, I hope Toronto may mean 'The place of meeting again and again.'"

His last words of thanks were drowned in applause. The students tried to recall him again, even after he had spoken. The band struck up "God save the Queen," and a few minutes later the audience was on its way home, and Irving was conducting a rehearsal of scenes in "Much Ado," and "The Merchant of Venice," rendered necessary by the illnesses which are referred to in another chapter.

III.

Two hours after midnight we were once more on the cars, bound for Boston.[2]

[2] Mr. Henry Irving, Miss Ellen Terry, and their company left for Boston early in the morning, by special train, over the 'West Shore route.' The train consisted of Mr. Irving's private car, two Pullmans, and three baggage-cars. The Pullmans, two of those in ordinary use on the West Shore road,

"These long journeys," said Irving, "are most distressing. I wonder what sort of a trip this will be. We ought to arrive at Boston on Sunday, at about six, they say."

"The agent of the road," replied Mr. Palser, "tells me he hopes to make good time. But I told him that the only occasion when we have done a long journey on time has been when we had no railroad agent to take care of us. They are very good fellows, and anxious to help us, but they have been unfortunate. Our flat baggage-car is a trouble. You will remember that the Erie could not take it, and some of the other companies consider it an extra risk. It affords an excuse for not exceeding a certain speed. Besides this, we have not had so much snow in America for over twenty years as this winter. Our trains have been snowed up, and this has occasioned all sorts of delays, as you know. But I hope we will get through to Boston in good time."

We did not, "by a large majority," as Bardwell Slote says. It was a tedious and unsatisfactory journey. So soon as we left the West Shore line we began to have trouble. It was on a short section of an unimportant road that we encountered most delay, the character of which will be best illustrated by a brief conversation between Irving and several other persons :—

"Well, what is the matter now, George?" Irving asked the coloured conductor of the private car.

are simply magnificent in their internal arrangements, possessing the latest improvements, and affording to the traveller the greatest possible comfort. Among the innovations not found in the ordinary 'sleepers' are the racks on which clothes may be deposited; electric call-bells attached to each berth, communicating with the porter's berth; a small kitchen, where light refreshments may be prepared, and the whole structure running on paper wheels, so that the rattle and jar of the ordinary car is entirely abolished. The train was in charge of Mr. G. J. Weeks, of Buffalo, northern passenger agent of the company, who accompanied the party to Boston."—*Toronto Mail.*

"Oh, this is the third time he's stopped in the woods to tinker up his darned old engine," said George; "seems it needs it!"

Everybody laughed at this rough criticism of the engineer and his locomotive.

"Stops in the woods, eh?" says Irving,—"that nobody may see him? But suppose another train comes along?"

"If the brakeman should neglect to go back and flag it, there might be no performance at the Boston Theatre on Monday," said Palser; "that is how Wagner, the car-builder, lost his life. He was killed in one of his own cars, on the New York Central. The train stopped suddenly,—it is said somebody on board pulled the check-string in joke,[3]—and an oncoming

[3] During the journey from Boston to Baltimore an inquiring member of Mr. Irving's company pulled the check-string, "just to see what the thing was." There was great consternation on board, neither guard nor driver knowing what had happened. The inquiring gentleman offered a frank explanation, and the train went on again; but the monotony of the remainder of the journey was relieved by a little practical joke at our friend's expense. An official was introduced into the conspiracy, and the delinquent was formally fined a hundred dollars. The rules of the company and the law of the land were quoted against him. Irving explained to him the enormity of his offence, and, after a little outburst against the tyranny of American laws as compared with those of England, the defendant paid twenty dollars on account, and a subscription was started to raise the remainder. "I am glad the affair occurred," said the offender, an hour or two later, "if only for the pleasure it has given me to find how well I stand with my colleagues; it is quite touching the way they have stood by me in purse and in friendly words." Alas for the sentiment of the thing!—most of the subscribers were in the secret. At Baltimore imaginary despatches passed between Mr. Abbey and the railway authorities, and the fine was withdrawn, the President, at New York, being satisfied that there was no malice in Mr. ——'s strange interference with the working of the train. The victim thereupon wrote a letter of thanks to Mr. Abbey, had quite a pathetic interview with Irving on the happy termination of the *contretemps*, and insisted upon treating the chief subscribers to champagne, over which he made so cordial and excellent a

train, not being warned, ran into them, and Mr. Wagner was killed."

"Ah," Irving replied, "there must have been a good deal of flag-signalling done on this journey of ours, seeing how often we have stopped."

"Yes, that's so; yah, yah!" remarks the privileged coloured servant.

"I don't think any of the tracks we have crossed are as good as the Pennsylvania," said Irving; "they are certainly not as good as the Midland or Great Western in England. The West Shore road is evidently a fine one; but I have more than once during our travels been reminded of a story I came across recently, relating to a passenger's question : 'We've struck a smoother strip of road, have we not?' The Arkansas railway conductor replied, 'No, we've only run off the track.'"

"Yah! yah!" shouted George, as he disappeared to tell the story to Peter in the kitchen.

"The newspaper that told the story added, as American journals are apt to do, a line or two of its own, to the effect that the Arkansas conductor's reply was almost as uncomplimentary as that of an Eastern conductor, who, upon being discharged, said, 'Well, I was intending to quit anyway, for there is nothing left of your old road but two streaks of iron rust and a right of way.'"

IV.

DURING one of the very long delays in question Irving and I talked of many things.

"You were speaking of the waste of food at hotels and restaurants one day," Irving remarked. "I am told that at some of the best houses in Chicago the clean scraps that are left on dishes after each meal are

speech that everybody shook hands with him, and said he was "a real good fellow,"—which is perfectly true, and a good actor to boot. I would not have mentioned this incident but that the opportunity of an appropriate foot-note overbears my self-denial; and, after all, it was a very harmless piece of fun.

collected and given to poor families every day. Children with large baskets call for them. Another class of scraps go to charitable institutions, more particularly Roman Catholic establishments. These are the leavings of the carvers' tables in the kitchens. One is glad to know this, for I, too, have often been struck with the abundance that is taken away un-touched from tables where I have dined; though I have seen nothing of the public breakfast and dining rooms. It is quite a system in England, I believe, the collection of food for the humbler 'homes' and charities; but one does not see in America any poor of the abject, poverty-stricken class that is familiar at home. Life to many must, nevertheless, be a bitter struggle."

"There are many who are well off; thousands who would be happier even in the most wretched districts of Ireland. An Irish friend of mine, in New York, said to me only the other day, 'The worst hut in Con-nemara is a palace to some of the tenement-house dens where my countrymen herd together in New York.'"

"They don't go West, I am told, as the Germans and Swedes and Norwegians do. It is a little odd that they do not take full advantage of the unrestricted freedom of the West, and the gift of land which can be obtained from the American government. Sixty acres, is it not?"

"Yes, that is the endowment America offers to settlers in some of her finest territory; and it is true that, as a rule, the Irish do not become farmers on this side of the Atlantic. They prefer city life, even with its disabilities. When I was in America one hot summer, two years ago, children of the poor, who live in the common tenement-houses down-town in New York, were dying of the heat at the rate of hundreds a day. In her most crowded alleys London has no-thing to compare with the lodging-houses in the poorer districts of New York for squalor and misery. But human nature is alike all the world over ; more than one rich man collects heavy rents from these death-traps."

"Just as a few of our fellow-countrymen in London supplement their rents by the contributions of infamous tenants. I dare say some of these hypocrites make speeches against the stage, and go ostentatiously to church; otherwise they would be found out by their associates. Religion is, indeed, a useful cloak for these gentry. It is gratifying to find that in some American cities, that are noted for their church discipline, the preachers are not afraid to tell their flocks that, properly used, the stage, as a moral teacher, is not unworthy of alliance with the pulpit."

"Did Mr. Beecher talk about the morality of the stage, or its relations to the public ?"

"No, but one of the writers for a Brooklyn journal asked me some questions on the subject. I told him that the world has found out that they live just like other people, and that, as a rule, they are observant of all that makes for the sweet sanctities of life, and they are as readily recognized and welcomed in the social circle as the members of any other profession. The stage has literally lived down the rebuke and reproach under which it formerly cowered, and actors and actresses receive in society, as do the members of other professions, exactly the treatment which is earned by their personal conduct. He asked me about the morality of attending the theatre, and I said I should think the worst performances seen on any of our stages cannot be so bad as drinking for a corresponding time in what you call here a bar-room, and what we term a gin-palace. The drinking is usually done in bad company, and is often accompanied by obscenity. Where drink and low people come together these things must be. The worst that can come of stage pandering to the corrupt tastes of its basest patrons cannot be anything like this, and, as a rule, the stage holds out long against the invitation to pander; and such invitations, from the publicity and decorum that attend the whole matter, are neither frequent nor eager. He informed me that the clergy, as a rule,—he used the term dissenting clergy, I suppose, as an explanation to me to denote the class who are not Episcopalians, that I might the better compare them with the ministers at home,—he told me that they are opposed to theatres. He asked me what I felt about this. I told him I thought that both here and in England the clerical profession are becoming more liberal in their views. Some people think they can live and bring up their children in such a way as to avoid all temptation of body and mind, and be saved nine-tenths of the responsibility of self-control. But that seems to me to be a foolish notion. You must be in the world, though you need not be of it. The best way for the clergy to make the theatre better is not to stay away from it, and shun the people who play in it, but to bring public opinion to bear upon it,—to denounce what is bad and to encourage what is good. When I was a boy I never went to the theatre except to see a Shakespearian play, and I endeavoured to make my theatrical experiences not only a source of amusement, but of instruction."

V.

" IT was a glorious audience," said the *Boston Daily Globe*, of February 26, "that welcomed Irving and Terry back to Boston last evening. No better evidence of the great popularity of the English artists could have been given than that which was implied in the presence of such an assemblage. The Boston was thronged, and the gathering represented the best class of our play-goers,—a company that accorded the stars a cordial greeting both, and that was appreciative of all the excellencies that marked the entertainment."

The theatre was crowded in all parts. "Louis XI." and "The Belle's Stratagem" were played. "Much Ado" closed the engagement. It was received by the audience as if it were a revelation of stage work, and criticized in the press in a similar spirit. At the end of the play the audience summoned the leading actors before the curtain over and over again. It was a scene of the most unaffected excitement. At last there arose cries of " A speech ! " " A speech ! " to which Irving responded, visibly moved by the enthusiasm of his Boston admirers and friends. He said,—

" Gentlemen and Ladies,—I have no words in which to express my thanks for your kindness; 'only my blood speaks to you in my veins.' A few weeks since we came here, and you received us with unbounded hospitality, and gave us a welcome that touched us deeply,—a true Boston welcome. (Applause.) We come back, and you treat us not as strangers, but as old friends. (Applause.) Again, I say, I can find no words adequately to convey our thanks. I need not tell you that this is to us a matter of the deepest gratitude and pleasure, for it is a proof that we have perhaps realized some of your expectations, and have not absolutely disappointed you. (Applause.) I say ' we,' because I speak in behalf of all,—not for myself alone, but for my comrades, and especially for one who has, I am sure, won golden opinions; you know to whom I allude (applause, and cries of " Yes ! " " Yes ! ")—my friend, and fellow-artist, Miss Ellen Terry. (Applause and cheers.) When we have recrossed the Atlantic, and are in our homes, we shall ever bear you in our kindliest memories. I hope to be here again. (Applause, cheers, and shouts, " Come again ! " " That's right ! ") Even before the present year closes I hope to be with you. (Cheers.) Once more I thank you with all my heart, and bid you good-night, only hoping that your memories of us may be as agreeable as those we shall cherish of you." (Applause and cheers.)

This second visit, it is agreed on all hands, brought more money into the treasury of the Boston than had ever before been taken during one week at that or any other theatre in the city, namely, $24,087,—and this was the largest sum that had been received during any previous week of the Irving engagement.

It will be interesting, at this period of the tour, to glance at its financial results. The following figures are taken from the cash book of Mr. J. H. Palser, the business manager and treasurer, who supplied them to the *Boston Herald,* and "vouched for their absolute accuracy":—

	$
New York—first week	15,772 00
New York—second week	18,714 00
New York—third week	18,880 00
New York—fourth week	22,321 50
Philadelphia—first week	16,128 50
Philadelphia—second week	16,780 50
Boston—first week	18,845 50
Boston—second week	16,885 00
Baltimore—one week	9,952 00
Brooklyn—one week	12,468 00
Chicago—first week	17,048 75
Chicago—second week	19,117 50
St. Louis—one week	13,719 00
Cincinnati—one week	11,412 00
Indianapolis (4 nights) and Columbus (2 nights).	8,700 50
Chicago (return)—one week	18,308 75
Detroit (2 nights) and Toronto (3 nights)[4] . .	13,430 50
Boston (return)—one week	24,087 00

The total receipts in cities where Mr. Irving has played more than one week were as follows :—

	$
New York—four weeks	75,687 50
Boston—three weeks	59,817 50
Chicago—three weeks	54,475 00
Philadelphia—two weeks	32,909 00

The total receipts of the tour, thus far, have been $292,571.

[4] One day's rest was taken at Niagara Falls.

XX.

WASHINGTON, NEW ENGLAND, AND SOME "RETURN VISITS."

From Rail to River—Once more on board the *Maryland*—Re-
collections of President Arthur—At the White House—
Washington Society—An apt Shakespearian Quotation—
Distinguished People—" Hamlet "—A Council of War—
Making out the Route of a new Tour—A Week in New
England Cities—Brooklyn and Philadelphia Re-visited.

I.

WE left Boston at about two o'clock in the morning
of the 3rd of March, and after breakfast, at half-past
ten, some of us turn out to stretch our legs on the
railroad track by the side of the Harlem River. Once
more we are shunted on board the *Maryland*, that is
to convey us " down stream, to connect with the Pennsylvania Road."

At about eleven o'clock we are afloat. Presently
we pass Blackwell's Island. The pretty villas on the
opposite bank are in notable contrast with the hard,
prosaic buildings of the island. The morning is
grey and cold. The snow is falling lightly and is full
of crystals. Most of the company are on deck, which
stretches right over the snow-covered cars. Some are
promenading and enjoying the change from railway to
river travel. Others are breakfasting in the steamer's
spacious saloon. Howe and his wife; Terriss (his hand
in a sling); Tyars (in his long Scotch ulster, which
was evidently new to the gamins of Philadelphia, where

they said, as he passed, " Here's a dude ! ") ; Mrs.
Pauncefort, and others, are defying the sharp weather
at the bows of the vessel, which, with its freight, is a
continual surprise to them; Miss Millward, the picturesque Jessica of "'The Merchant," is romping merrily
with the children of the company, who are quite a
feature in the garden and church scenes of " Much
Ado."

We steal quietly along the river without noise,
but with a steady progression. Blackwell's Island
prisons are enlivened in colour by a little company of
women, who are being marched into the penitentiary.
They turn to look at the *Maryland* as they enter
the stony portals. As we creep along, villas on
our left give place to lumber-yards, with coasting-
vessels lying alongside. Leaving Blackwell's on the
right, the shore breaks up into picturesque wharfage,
backed, in the distance, by the first of the steeples of
Fifth Avenue. The eye follows them along ; wharves
and river-craft in front; the spires against the grey sky,
until they are repeated, as it were, by forests of masts,
—first a few, and then a cluster. We meet another
train coming up the river, then another; and now we
get glimpses, through the haze, of distant ferry-boats
ahead. There is a dull mist on the river, and here and
there it hangs about in clouds. We pass Long Island
railroad pier. It is very cold ; but the children of the
company still trot about ruddy and merry.

"You don't say so ! " exclaims somebody. "Is it
true, the train we saw at Harlem, which we thought full
of poor emigrants, was the Opera Company on their
way to Boston,—the chorus ? "

" Quite true."

" Then I can now understand," is the rejoinder,
" that the passengers on board the *Rome*, when we came
out, thought us a most respectable crowd ? "

" That has been remarked before," says the buxom
Martha of "Louis XI.," " and in far more complimentary terms."

Presently, through the mist on the larboard side, we catch a glimpse of the Brooklyn Bridge. A few gulls are sweeping down the river before us. On both banks there are wharves and ships. One of the vessels flies the British flag, which is greeted with a cheer from some of our people. On the left bank of the river is a great sugar factory, with a picturesque red-brick tower. We have now left the Harlem river, and for some little time have been steaming down the East towards the North River, with Bedloe's Island—a dot in the distant Sound—and Sandy Hook somewhere in the mist beyond. We now pass Hunter's Point, and slue gradually round towards the North River. We glide along beneath the wonderful bridge, and look up among its network of roads and rails; past piers 50 and 51 on our right, with freight-cars and steamers ready for the river; past the New York, New Haven, and Hartford Railway quays, hugging the South Street Docks and ship-repairing yards, Governor's Island at our bow. Ships and steamers stretch along to Battery Point, which we round into the North River, and pass Castle Garden. It is here that we catch sight of Bedloe's and other distant islands, and look far in the direction of Sandy Hook, whence fierce tug-boats are steaming along, with great barges in tow. Now we cross the river to Jersey City. It is two o'clock. Our cars are once more on the rails, and, at about nine o'clock that night, we ran into Washington.

II.

"You know the President," said Irving, while we were travelling from Boston to Washington.

"Yes; I met him once or twice during the contest when he was ultimately returned as Vice-President with General Garfield. His likeness had become very familiar to me before I saw him. Candidates for the high offices of state are not only photographed, but their pictures are painted in heroic proportions. You see them everywhere,—on flags and banners, in shop-windows, in the newspapers. But you will be in the thick of it next autumn, since you have really decided to return this year."

" Oh, yes; but tell me about your meeting with the President,—what is he like ? "

" Tall and handsome ; frank and genial in manner ; an excellent conversationalist; well read,—a gentle-man. I became acquainted with him on the eve of his election to the Vice-Presidential chair. At his installation hundreds of his personal friends and admirers from eastern and western cities made ' high festival,' in his honour at Washington. Two years later I saw him, with sorrowful face and head bowed down, start for the capital, to stand by the bedside of the dying President, with whom he had been elected. Soon afterwards the friends, who had metaphorically flung up their caps for him on the merry day of his installation with Garfield, went, ' with solemn tread and slow,' to assist at his inauguration into the chair which, for a second time, the hand of the assassin had rendered vacant. My recollection of Mr. Arthur pic-tured a stout, ruddy-complexioned man, with dark hair and whiskers, and a certain elasticity in his gait that betokened strong physical health. I remember that we sat together by the taffrail of a Sound steamer, and talked of the vicissitudes of life and its uncer-tainties, and that I was deeply moved with sympathy for him in regard to the death of his most ac-complished and amiable wife, of whom he spoke (apropos of some remark that led up to his bereavement) with a quivering lip and a moistened eye. The day had been a very pleasant one ; the bay of New York was sleeping in the sun ; the air was balmy; the time gracious in all respects ; but, while doing his best to enliven the passing hour, Arthur's thoughts had wandered to the grave of his wife. She was a very accomplished woman, I am told; musical, a sweet disposition, refined and cultivated in her tastes. Friends of mine who knew her say that she, above all others, would have rejoiced in her husband's victory; and, while inspiring him with fortitude under the calamity that lay beyond, would have lent a grace to his reign at the White House that alone was necessary to complete the simple dignity of his administration, social and otherwise, which will always be remembered at Washington in connection with the Presidentship of Chester A. Arthur."

"I have letters to the President, which I shall certainly take the first opportunity to deliver," said Irving.

When I met Mr. Arthur again in his own room, at the Executive Mansion, I was struck with the change which the anxieties and responsibilites of office, entered upon under circumstances of the most painful character, had wrought upon him. His face was careworn; his hair white; his manner subdued. He stooped in his gait; the old brightness had gone out of his eyes, and there was what seemed to be a permanently saddened expression about the corners of his mouth. He did not look sick; there was nothing in his face or figure denoting ill-health or physical weakness; but in the course of four years he appeared to me to have aged twenty. I had not been in Washington a day before he sent for me and my family, with a pleasant reference to the time when last we met. Looking back over these four years, and considering its record of trouble and anxiety, I could well have forgiven him if he had forgotten my very existence. That he recalled the occasion of our meeting, and was still touched with the spirit of it, I mention to do him honour, not myself; though, had it pleased Providence not to have afflicted me with a never-ending sorrow, I could have felt a high sense of personal pride in the home-like reception which the President of the United States gave to me and my family, in his own room at the Executive Mansion, sitting down with us and chatting in a pleasant, unconstrained, familiar way, that is characteristic of American manners, and eminently becomes the chief of a great republic.

Were this book only intended for English readers, I would hesitate (even with the friendly approval of my collaborator) about publishing these few sentences, so personal to myself, lest it should be thought I might be "airing my connections;" but a President *per se* is not held in such profound estimation or reverence in America as in England, where we rank him with the most powerful of reigning monarchs, and give him a royal personality. Moreover, I should be ungrateful did I not take the best possible opportunity to acknowledge a conspicuous act of kindliness and grace on the part of one who, since I last met him, had stepped from the private station of mere citizenship to the chief office of state over fifty millions of people, wielding an individual power in their government that belongs to no constitutional sovereign, nor to any prince or minister in the most despotic courts or cabinets of Europe.

III.

"AND I can only say," remarked Irving, as we left the White House together, after his first interview with the President, "that, if his re-election depended on my vote, he should have it. I know nothing about the political situation; but the man we have just left has evidently several qualities that I should say fit him for his office,—foremost among them is patience. I would also say that he has the virtue of self-denial, and he is certainly not impulsive. A kind-hearted man, I am sure, capable of the highest sentiment of friendship, of a gentle disposition, and with great repose of character."

"You have made quite a study of him," I said;

"and I am glad you like him, for I am sure he likes you."

They had had a long chat at the White House. Mr. Congressman Phelps accompanied Irving, and introduced him to the Secretary of the Navy, and to other ministers who came and went during the first part of the informal reception. The President talked of plays and general literature; regretted that Washington, which had so many fine buildings, did not yet possess a theatre worthy of the city.

"A beautiful city, Mr. President," said Irving. "I had heard much of Washington, but am agreeably surprised at its fine buildings, its handsome houses, its splendid proportions; and the plan of it seems to be unique."

"The original design was the work of a French engineer," said the President, "who served under Washington. His idea, evidently, was that a republic would have continually to contend with revolutions at the capital. He, therefore, kept in view the military exigencies of the government. The main streets of the city radiate upon a centre that is occupied by the legislative and executive buildings, like the spokes of a wheel, so that they could be dominated by artillery. This was the French idea of the dangers and duties of that republican form of government, which has never been contested here, nor is ever likely to be. While but a village, Washington was laid out for a great city, and, without any seeming prospect of the grand idea being realized, the original lines have, nevertheless, always been adhered to."

"And with glorious results," said Irving. "Washington is one of the most beautiful cities I have ever seen. There is no reason why the highest architectural ambition should not be realized in such broad avenues and boulevards, and with such a site."

IV.

"MANY Americans underrate the beauty of Washington," I said. "Comparatively few of them have seen it, and hundreds who criticize it have not been south for a number of years. The growth of Washington is not only modern, it is of yesterday. The city was really little more than a village up to the date of the late war; and it was only in 1871 that the impetus was given to the public enterprise that has covered it with palaces, private and public. It is the only city of America in which the streets are kept as cleanly and as orderly as London and Paris. The streets are asphalted, and you may drive over them everywhere without inconvenience or obstruction. There is an individuality about the houses that is one of Washington's most notable architectural characteristics."

"Yes," said Irving, "that is a great point. New York is lacking in that respect, the reason being, I suppose, its want of space. Some of the houses in Washington suggest Bedford Park, Fitzjohn's Avenue, and the street of artists' houses at Kensington. The same may be said of portions of Chicago and Boston. The so-called Queen Anne order of architecture is very prevalent in Washington,—take Pennsylvania Avenue, for instance. On a fine summer's day it must be a picture, with its trees in leaf and its gardens in bloom."

Irving went more than once to the White House, and was greatly impressed with the dignified informality of one of its evening receptions.

"No ceremonious pomp, no show, and yet an air of conscious power," he said; "the house might be the modest country-seat of an English noble, or wealthy commoner, the President the host, receiving his intimate friends. No formal announcements; presentations made just as if we were in a quiet country house. Soon after supper, when the ladies took their leave, and most of the gentlemen with them, I and one or two others went into the President's room, and chatted, I fear, until morning. It was to me very enjoyable. President Arthur would shine in any society. He has a large acquaintance with the best literature, dramatic and general, is apt at quotation, an excellent story-teller, a gentleman, and a good fellow. When I had said good-night, and was on my way to the hotel, I could not help my own thoughts wandering back to thoughts of Lincoln and Garfield, whose portraits I had noticed in prominent positions on the walls of the Executive Mansion. I remember Mr. Noah Brooks, of New York, telling us the story of Lincoln's death, and how he was to have been in the box with him at the theatre that same night, and how vividly he recounted the chief incidents of the tragedy. And Garfield,—I can quite understand that terrible business making his successor prematurely old, called as he was into office under such painful circumstances, and with so great a responsibility. A distinguished American was telling me yesterday that only the wisest discretion and personal self-denial in regard to the filling of offices saved America from the possibilities of riot and bloodshed. He said Arthur's singularly quiet administration of affairs—the one necessity of the time—would be taken into account at the polls, if he is nominated for re-election."

v.

WASHINGTON society made itself most agreeable to both Irving and Miss Terry, though "Portia, on a trip from the Venetian seas," to quote the New York reporter, made her visit to the capital an opportunity for rest. Electing this city for a holiday, being relieved of a week's journey through New England, she remained at the capital on a visit to her friend, Miss Olive Seward, the adopted daughter of the famous minister of Lincoln's administration.

Among the social entertainments given in Irving's honour were two notable little suppers,—one at the Metropolitan Club, by Mr. H. J. Nelson, Secretary

to the Speaker, and a journalist of well-won renown.
There were present, the Speaker (the Hon. John G.
Carlisle), Senator Bayard, Representatives Dorsheimer
(ex-Lieut. Governor of the State of New York), T.
B. Reed, Dr. George B. Loring (Commissioner of
Agriculture), and Messrs. John Davis (Assistant Secretary of State), and F. E. Leupp. The other "evening after the play" was spent at Mr. Dorsheimer's
house, in Connecticut Avenue, where the guests included
several distinguished judges, senators, and government
officials. The conversation on both occasions was
chiefly about plays. It was a great relief from law and
politics, one of the learned judges said, to discuss
Shakespeare and the stage. They all talked well upon
the drama ; some of them had known Forrest ; others,
the elder Booth. Irving was more than usually talkative in such congenial company. He related many
reminiscences of the English stage, none of which
interested his Washington friends more than his
anecdotes of Macready. Several instances of apt
Shakespearian quotations were given ; but they were
all capped by a story which Nelson told of Judge
Jeremiah S. Black, Mr. Buchanan's Attorney-General
and Secretary of State. Judge Black was holding
court at Chambersburgh, Pa., when he was on the
circuit in that State, forty years or more ago. His
manners were rough, but more from absent-mindedness
than any other cause, for he was one of the kindest of
men. He would almost invariably find the strong
point in a cause that was on trial before him, and go on
thinking about it without reference to the point which
counsel might be considering ; so that his questions
often seemed impertinent to the bar. One of the
lawyers of Chambersburgh was a man of the name of
Chambers, a soft-spoken, mild-mannered kind of man.
Chambers suffered especially from what he supposed
was Black's intentional rudeness to him, and, one day,
he came to the conclusion that his burdens were
intolerable ; therefore he stopped in the midst ·of his

argument, and expostulated with the judge, telling him that he always tried to treat the court deferentially, but the judge did not reciprocate.   The judge sat smiling through Chambers's long reproof, and briefly answered,—

> " Haply, for I am *black*,
> And have not those soft parts of conversation
> That *chamberers* have."

During the week Irving visited the capitol, and was introduced to the highest officers of state.   He heard debates in both houses, visited the law courts, and received many kindly attentions, public and private. The theatre was crowded every night.   On the first night the President sat in the stalls, and the Russian Ambassador contented himself with quite a back seat. Mr. Bancroft, the white-haired historian, was a constant attendant.   Mr. Charles Nordhoff (whose graphic stories are not sufficiently well known) was in the stalls; so, also, were the authors of " Democracy." (It is rumoured that they are a society syndicate; but there is more authority in the statement that they are two, and I could give their names.   I forbear, for the sake of the American lady who was pointed out to me in London, last year, as the undoubted author of the " scurrilous burlesque ").   Mr. Blaine (one of the most famous and learned of American statesmen) was also present, and he was one of the prominent men who showed Irving much social attention.[1]   A list of the

[1] The President went last evening to witness the final performance of Mr. Henry Irving and his company at the National Theatre, in " Louis XI." and " The Belle's Stratagem."   Mrs. McElroy and Miss Nellie Arthur were with him in the box. Subsequently he entertained at the White House, Mr. Irving, the members of the President's cabinet and the ladies of their families; Mrs. McElroy and Miss McElroy, the sister and niece of the President; Colonel and Mrs. Bonaparte; General and Mrs. P. H. Sheridan, United States Army; General E. F. Beale; Mr. and Mrs. Marcellus Bailey; Mr. Walker Blaine; Mr. and Mrs. N. L. Anderson; Lieut. T. B. M. Mason, United States Navy, and Mrs. Mason; Commissioner of Agriculture

distinguished people present would include a majority
of the great personages at Washington during the
season of 1884. All the plays were enthusiastically
received.[2]

George B. Loring, Mrs. and Miss Loring; Assistant Attorney-
General William A. Maury, Mrs. and Miss Maury; Assistant
Secretary of State John Davis and Mrs. Davis; John P. Jones,
United States Senate, and Mrs. Jones, Nevada; Senator M. C.
Butler, South Carolina; Senator Aldrich, Rhode Island; Mr.
and Mrs. H. S. Sanford; Mr. John Field; Mr. F. J. Phillips,
secretary to the President; Senator and Mrs. John F. Miller,
California; Mr. and Mrs. Theodore Lyman, of Massachusetts
House of Representatives; Mr. and Mrs. William Walter Phelps,
New Jersey House of Representatives; Mr. Clayton McMichael,
United States Marshal, and Mrs. McMichael; Mr. and Mrs.
Charles Nordhoff, *New York Herald ;* Mr. Stillson Hutchings,
Washington Post ; Mr. Albert Pulitzer, *New York Journal;*
Mr. and Mrs. Isaac Bell, of New York; Mr. and Mrs. Joseph
Hatton, of England.—No actor was ever so entertained in
Washington as Mr. Irving has been. He attended a supper at
the Metropolitan Club on Wednesday evening; a breakfast
given by Mr. Bayard on Thursday; gave a supper to Mr. Blaine
and a party of friends on Thursday evening, after the play;
was the guest of Mr. William Walter Phelps on Friday morning;
attended a supper given to him by Mr. Dorsheimer on Friday
evening; and last night was the President's guest, as stated.
Miss Terry has received more social attentions here than in any
other American city.—*The Capital, March* 9.

[2] We thoroughly believe that the time will never come when
any actor can present a Hamlet that will be universally regarded
as a correct interpretation of the master poet's sublime creation.
Mr. Irving's impersonation was brilliantly bold in execution,
replete with new readings and stage business, and magnificent
bursts of feeling, arising from his changeableness of moods.
There does not seem to be a scene in the entire tragedy which
he has not touched with his own subtle and delicate refinement,
and removed far above the conventionalities of other actors
whom we have seen. His first soliloquy, "Oh, that this too, too
solid flesh would melt!" was rendered as though it were the
unconscious utterance of a thought. He displayed but little
interest in the return to earth of his father's spirit until he met
it face to face; and then he surrounded himself with a solemn
supernaturalism, tinged with glow of superb filial affection.
This, in turn, seemed to give way to a sort of nervous terror,
and he became hysterical, which presented to the oath of secrecy
an added reverential awe. The first long interview between

Called on, as usual, to speak when the curtain had gone down for the last time, after three recalls, Irving thanked the audience for the kind reception and liberal patronage which had been accorded himself and his company. They had during the past few months appeared in all the leading cities of the country, and he felt that this cordial welcome in the beautiful capital of the Union might fairly be regarded as the crowning engagement of a most happy and prosperous tour. He returned heartfelt thanks, not alone for himself, but for his company, and especially for his fair comrade and friend, Miss Ellen Terry, of whom he felt he could heartily say : " She came, she saw, she conquered." He said farewell with the greater ease in the expectation of having the privilege of again appearing in Washington early in the coming season. Again returning thanks, and saying good-bye, Mr. Irving bowed himself off the stage amid very demonstrative applause.

VI.

It was quite like a council of war to see Irving, Loveday, Palser, and Stoker, bending over a map of the United States, during the journey from Washington to New York, *en route* for several New England cities. The chart was scanned with careful interest, Irving passing his finger over it here and there, not with the intensity of the overthrown monarch in " Charles the First," but with a close scrutiny of routes. The chief was sketching out his next tour in America.

" No more long journeys," he said.

" They are not necessary," Loveday replied.

Hamlet and Ophelia was played with splendid dramatic force and fire. His simulation of passion, his deep longing for its gratification, and his recklessness consequent upon his recollection of the stern duty to which he had devoted himself,—alternately flying from her, and then returning,—was a part of the performance which created a most profound impression upon our mind.—*The National Republican, March* 6.

"No jumping from Brooklyn to Chicago, and from Chicago to Boston. This sort of thing may have been necessary by our relinquishment of the one-night places set down for us in the original plan of the tour ; but we'll reform that altogether."

Then all the heads went down upon the chart; and pencil-marks begin to appear, dotting out a route which began at Quebec, and traversed, by easy stages, Canada and the United States,—from Quebec to Toronto, from Toronto to New York, and thence to Chicago, and, by easy calls, back again to the Empire city.

An hour or two later and the route was settled, Palser remarking, "It is the most complete and easiest tour that has ever been mapped out."

"And we will begin it in the autumn of this year. We have sowed the seed; we are entitled to reap the harvest. All my American friends say so; and the great American play-going public would like me to do so. I am sure of it. My pulses quickened at the great cheer that went up at Boston when I said I hoped to come back this year. Let us consider it settled. We will come in September."

The map was folded up, and the work of organizing the next tour was at once commenced. Telegraphic "feelers," in regard to "dates," had already been sent to the leading theatres. The best of them were ready to accept for the time proposed; and a week or so later the business was settled.

Meanwhile we arrived at New York (the trees in Washington and Union Squares, and Fifth Avenue were crystal trees ; every house was coated with ice that sparkled under the electric lamps), and the next day "Louis XI." was given at New Haven. The week was spent between this picturesque city and Worcester, Springfield, Hartford, and Providence. Only "Louis XI." and The Bells" were played, Miss Terry taking a week's rest at Washington. The New England audiences were as cordial at these cities as they had been at Boston; the critics interpreted their senti-

ments. At Hartford, Mark Twain (S. L. Clemens)
entertained Irving under his hospitable roof, and at
Springfield there was a memorable gathering at the
Springfield Club,—in fact, Irving was welcomed
everywhere with tokens of respect and esteem. One
regrets that these pages and the time of the patient
reader are not sufficiently elastic to allow of one de-
voting a volume to the New England cities, so interesting as they are, historically and otherwise, from
American as well as English points of view.

VII.

FOLLOWING the New England cities come the last of
the return visits,—Philadelphia, Brooklyn,³ New York.
They reindorsed the previous successes, and fully justified the decision of a second visit next season.

³ Mr. Henry Irving and Miss Terry were tendered a reception
by the Hamilton Club yesterday afternoon. The quaint old
mansion in Clinton Street was filled between the hours of three
and five. The reception, which was informal, was held in the
library on the second floor, an inviting apartment papered in old
gold, with a frieze of olive-green with conventionalized flowers.
The walls are lined with mahogany bookcases filled with well-
bound books, largely historical. An oil painting of Alexander
Hamilton, in an old-fashioned frame, hangs in the west hall,
where it is lighted by the flickering gleams of the wood-fire in a
tiled fireplace opposite. An antique chandelier, with imitation
candles, completes the effect. At half-past three Mr. Irving
and Miss Terry were found in opposite corners of the room,
each surrounded by an animated group. Miss Terry, over
whom some of the younger ladies were mad with curiosity,
was completely hemmed in, and was given no opportunity to
move about, as Irving did. She sat during intervals in an
old arm-chair, covered with red plush. She wore an artistic
gown, with a Watteau plait. Her fair hair curled from beneath a round French hat, covered with brown velvet, and
with a dark feather. At her neck was an eccentric scarf of
orange-coloured satin. Prior to the reception, Mr. Irving and
Miss Terry lunched with Mr. Samuel McLean, president of the
club, at his residence, 47, Pierrepoint Street; among his fourteen
guests being Mrs. Buckstone (his sister), Mr. and Mrs. Henry
Ward Beecher, and Mr. and Mrs. John Foord.—*Brooklyn Times*,
and *Brooklyn Union*, March 30.

One of the most interesting incidents of the second
visit to Philadelphia was Irving's entertainment in
the new rooms of the " Clover Club." [4] Accustomed

[4] When Henry Irving was here, in December last, the
" Clover Club " tendered him a breakfast, and at that time he
stated that when he returned to the city he hoped again to meet
his genial hosts. Last night he kept his promise. Upwards of
sixty gentlemen, members of the club, and friends whom he had
met elsewhere, were invited to take supper with him at the
Bellevue, after the performance at the Chestnut Street Opera
House, and the occasion was a most delightful one. The celebrated table of the club, in the shape of a four-leaved clover, was
spread in the banqueting-hall. On it were two lofty forms of
flowers, in the midst of which rose two fountains, throwing up
crystal streams of water, which fell in spray over the blossoms.
There were also several little plots of growing clover, shaped in
the form of the quadrifoliate. The company did not assemble
until after the performance of " Much Ado About Nothing." It
was 11.30 when they were seated at the table, with Mr. Irving at
the head. Among the many present were Ex-Gov. Hoyt, Dion
Boucicault, Attorney-General Cassidy, Col. A. Loudon Snowden,
A. K. McClure, M. P. Handy, and J. H. Heverin. Mr. Joseph
Hatton and Mr. Montague Marks from New York. The occasion was one long to be remembered. Mr. Irving, in proposing
the toast of the " Clover Club," thanked the members for their
hospitality, and Philadelphia for its welcome of him, and, with
characteristic modesty, spoke of his tour through the country, the
welcome which he had everywhere received, and the love of dramatic art which he found among the people. Mr. Handy replied
for the " Clover Club," with his customary felicitous eloquence,
and concluded by informing Mr. Irving of his election as an
honorary member of the club. While Mr. Irving was bowing his
thanks, Mr. Handy decorated him with the jewelled badge of
membership. Dion Boucicault told how Mr. Irving, to his mind,
had banished the pedestal actor from the stage, and presented
Shakespeare as the dramatist himself would have wished to
see his works given. Mr. A. K. McClure pointed out how the
dramatic art had knit the Anglo-Saxon race in a close bond of
union. Mr. Howe, the "old man" of Mr. Irving's company,
gave some interesting reminiscences of how he, as a Quaker boy,
and dressed in a Quaker garb, applied to Edmund Kean to be
allowed to go on the stage. Mr. Terriss, the leading man, gave
a recitation. Dr. Bedloe offered a new version of Shakespeare's
" Seven Ages," and before the close Miss Terry was toasted in
a bumper of three times three. Seldom has such a merry party
sat down to supper, and the evening, when it is brought to mind,

to play the host, the club found itself in a novel position when it accepted that of guest. The occasion was one not likely to be forgotten in the annals of an institution which interprets the best and highest social instincts of an eminently hospitable city. The club-room was decorated with its characteristic taste.

Mr. Dion Boucicault, in a brief address, spoke of the beneficent change which Irving had wrought in the methods of the English stage; Mr. McClure, the popular and powerful director of the *Times*, thanked him, in the name of all lovers of art, for extending that reformation to the American stage; Col. Snow depicted his high place in the history of the best civilization of America; and Irving, while accepting with pride the honours which had been conferred upon him, defended the great actors of America's past and present from the criticism of several speakers, who complained of their adherence to what Boucicault called "the pedestal style" of acting Shakespeare. Irving described to them how, in years gone by, both England and America had possessed provincial schools of acting, in the stock companies that had flourished in such cities as Boston, New York, Philadelphia, Chicago, and other cities on one side of the Atlantic, and Bristol, Bath, Manchester, Birmingham, on the other; how these had been broken up by "combinations" in travelling companies; and how the leading actors of America had thus been disabled from presenting the dramas of the great masters in a manner they would, no doubt, have desired to present them. He said he had found similar difficulties in his own country; but, actuated by the resolute purpose of a sense of duty to his art, and a devoted love for it, he had overcome them. For some eight or ten years he had worked with a company, trained with the object

will never call up any but the most delightful recollections.— *The Day*, Baltimore, and *The Call*, Philadelphia, March 20, 1884.

of interpreting, to the best of their ability, the work of
the dramatist. They subordinated themselves to the
objects and intentions of the play they had to illustrate,
and only by such self-abnegations to the harmony of
the entire play, he said, could anything like an approach be made to the realization of a dramatic theme.
He disclaimed any such ambition as to be ranked
foremost among the great actors whose names had been
mentioned ; but he confessed to a feeling of intense
satisfaction that America should have accepted with a
generous, and he must say a remarkable, spontaneity,
the methods which he had inaugurated at the Lyceum
Theatre.

Among other " sight-seeing " and calls which we
made together in Philadelphia, was a visit to Mr.
Childs, at the *Ledger* office, and an hour or two spent
at Independence Hall. Irving was much interested
in the new private office of Mr. Childs. Decorated in
the so-called style of Queen Anne, it is a fine example
of the progress in art which America has made within
the past few years. It contains many precious reminiscences of the Centennial Exhibition. A screen in
front of the street windows is not the least artistic
feature of the apartment. It is formed by six square
pillars, with arched openings, which, save the centre,
are closed to the height of three feet from the floor,
the space between the back of these and the windows
forming a kind of recess, where have been gathered
some very valuable specimens of plastic and mechanical art. Over the screen, or arcade, are ten painted
glass panels ; the centre one contains the portraits of
Guttenberg, Faust, and Schœffer, inventors of the art
of printing with type ; the other four contain figures
representing the art of book-making. The left-hand
panel contains a sitting figure, intently engaged on an
article for the press, which, with two figures, a man
and a boy, the latter of singularly fine action, forms
the second panel. Passing over the centre, the story
is continued by the proof-reader, and concluded in the

last panel, which represents a standing figure perusing the finished book in the shape of a Bible, chained to a lectern. The centre panel of five smaller panels, over those just mentioned, exhibits Mr. Childs' motto, " *Nihil sine labore,*" and on the remaining four, in old English, is painted the command, "Let there be light, and there was light."

Mr. Childs is one of the best known and one of the most popular journalists in the United States. His name is familiar to the newspaper men of England, and his offices are models, both as regards the mechanical departments and the rooms set apart for his editorial associates and writers. Mr. Cooke, the able and trusted correspondent of the London *Times,* is the financial editor of the *Ledger.*

The porter at Independence Hall was glad to get the English actor's signature in the visitors' book. From the moment that Irving entered the place he attracted more attention than even the bell of liberty itself. Long before American independence was even dreamed of, this bell (originally cast at Whitechapel, London, and afterwards recast in Philadelphia) bore the inscription, " Proclaim liberty throughout all the land, to all the inhabitants thereof ! " Having taken in the historic room which was formerly the Judicial Hall of the English colony of Pennsylvania, Irving said, " How English it all is ; how typical of the revolt the portraits of these great fellows who headed it ! " Then he traced likeness to living Englishmen in several of the pictures. " One hundred and thirty portraits, nearly all of them by one artist ! " he exclaimed. " He has done wonderfully, I think, to get such variety of style, and yet so much individuality." In modern days this chamber has been the scene of the lying-in-state of several prominent statesmen, on the way to burial. Among them were John Quincy Adams, Henry Clay, and Abraham Lincoln.

American history proudly recalls that " here, on the 3rd of November, 1781, twenty-four British standards and colours, taken from the army under Cornwallis, which had surrendered at Yorktown, were laid at the feet of Congress, amidst the shouts of the people and volleys of musketry, for they had been escorted to the door of the State House by the volunteer cavalry of the city, and greeted by the huzzas of the people." " But let us not forget," said an American speaker, discoursing on this theme at an Irving entertainment, " that we were all British until we had signed that Declaration of Independence ! "

XXI.

"BY THE WAY."

I.

"Yes," said Irving, "I, too, have made a few notes of
'things to be remembered,' as we passed together some
of the last proofs of these chronicles and impressions.
For instance, here is a memorandum, ' Politics ;' and
it refers to General Horace Porter's anecdotical illustration of ward politics, and to Mr. Millett's letter on
art and tariffs."

"Let us take the story first," I suggested.

We both remembered it ; so, likewise, will several
American friends of that excellent *raconteur*, Horace
Porter, one of New York's brightest post-prandial
orators.

Irving had been making inquiries about the city
government of New York, and remarking upon the
curious little wooden houses away up at the further
end of New York city.

" Oh," said Porter, "those places belong to the last of the Manhattan squatters. Most of them are occupied by families, who, as a rule, pay little or no rent at all. They are on the outskirts of progress. As the city extends into their district they disappear, seeking 'fresh woods and pastures new.' Nevertheless some of them become quite firmly established there. They are included, for voting purposes, in the Twenty-fourth ward of the city. The houses, as you have observed, are not architecturally beautiful. All the inhabitants keep fowls and animals in their basements or cellars. As a rule nobody repairs or attends to their abodes. Occasionally in wet weather they could bathe in their cellars. Recently one of the most important men in the district was a Mr. Mulldoon, whose very practical views of city politics will be gathered by the story I am going to tell you, which also illustrates the local troubles from a sanitary point of view. Mulldoon's premises were flooded. He was advised to apply to the Commissioner of Public Works on the subject, and to use his political influence in the matter; and he did. Entering the office of the commissioner, he said,—

" ' My name is Mulldoon. I live in the Twenty-fourth ward ; I conthrol forty votes there ; I kape hens ; the wather has inundated my cellar, and I want it pumped out at the public expinse.'

" ' We have no machinery to do that kind of work ; it does not belong to our department,' said the officer.

" ' And be jabers if I don't get that wather removed it will go hard wid the party. I'll cast thim forty votes for a Dutchman.'

" ' You had better go to the fire department.'

" ' Divil a bit ; it's the wather department I'm afther.'

" ' The fire department have appliances for pumping, we have not ; I recommend you to see the fire department.'

" He does so.

" Arrived at the proper officer's desk, he says, ' My

name is Mulldoon; I live in the Twenty-fourth ward; I conthrol forty votes there; I kape hens; the wather has inundated my cellar, and I want it pumped out at the public expinse.'

"'The work does not belong to this department, Mr. Mulldoon; we put out fires, not water. I—'

"'Indade,' said Mulldoon calmly; 'thin let the party look to it, for I'll rather cast thim forty votes for a nigger than Tammany Hall shall get wan o' them.'

"'I was going to say, when you interrupted me, that you had better see the mayor, and get an appropriation for the sum necessary to be expended, and then you'll have the business done right away.'

"'An appropriation, is it? Thank ye! I've niver gone ag'in' my party; but I object to having my hens drowned under my very roof.'

"Going straight for the mayor, he said, 'Mr. Mayor, sorr, my name is Mulldoon; I live in the Twenty-fourth ward; I conthrol forty votes there; I kape hens; the wather has inundated my cellar, and I want it pumped out at the public expinse.'

"'I am sorry I cannot help you, Mr. Mulldoon; but—'

"'Not help me!' exclaimed the chief of the little caucus in the Twenty-fourth ward; 'then, by my soul, I'll cast them forty votes for a hathen Chinee—'

"'If you had not interrupted me, I was going to say that—'.

"'Oh, then, I beg your honour's pardon; it is only just my bare rights that I am saking.'

"'If you go to the Board of Aldermen and get an appropriation, and bring it to me, I will see that the work you claim shall be done.'

"'Very well, then, and thank your honour,' said Mulldoon, who in due course presented himself before the principal officer of the Board, an Irishman like himself, and having considerable power.

"'My name is Mulldoon; I live in the Twenty-fourth ward; I conthrol forty votes there; I kape

hens; my cellar is inundated, and I want it pumped
out at the public expinse. The mayor's sent me to
you for an appropriation, and, by St. Patrick! if you
refuse it, divil a wan o' them votes will ye ever get.
I'll cast them for a native American first!'

"'I don't see how I can get you an appropriation,
Mr. Mulldoon.'

"'You don't; well, then, the party may go to the
divil, and Tammany Hall wid it! I'm ag'in' the lot o'
ye!'

"'Don't lose your temper, Mr. Mulldoon, I'll see
what can be done for you; but, in the meantime, will
you allow me to suggest that it would be less dangerous for the party, considering the situation of your
residence, if, in the future, *you would arrange to keep
ducks?*'"

II.

"WE have not talked much about politics, eh? And
a good thing, too! One only got really well into the
atmosphere of political life at Washington; and then,
after all, one heard more about literary copyright than
anything else. I find I have made a note of a letter I
read somewhere recently from an American painter, in
support of taxing importations of fine art, more particularly pictures. It seems to me this is a grave mistake. I had no idea that protection, as it is called,
existed so generally in America."

"You have here," I said, "the extreme of protective
duties, as we in England have the other extreme of an
unreciprocal free trade."

"I can understand a reasonable protective tariff for
a commercial industry; but art should surely go free.
For a country that as yet possesses no great school of
painting nor sculpture of her own, to obstruct, nay,
almost prohibit, the entry of foreign work, must be
to handicap her own rising genius. The examples of
the famous masters of Greece and Rome, of France,
and Holland, and England, are necessary for the

American student, and free traffic in the works of great modern artists would have an elevating tendency on public taste."

" As a rule American artists are favourable to the free importation of foreign pictures. They favour it from your own stand-point, the educational point of view," I said.

" Moreover, I can quite imagine American artists who are permitted all the privileges of the art schools and galleries of Europe, and who sell their pictures in the Old World without let or hindrance, being annoyed at the inhospitality of their own country in this respect," he replied; " Boughton, Bierstadt, Whistler, and other well-known American painters, for example."

" And so they are, no doubt."

" As a matter of fact, public opinion in the United States, if it could be tested, would, I imagine, be on the side of admitting pictures, *bric-à-brac,* and books without duty; though the progress of what is called the modern free-trade movement is likely rather to retard than advance the interests of a free importation of fine-art productions."

" In what way? " he asked. " The leading idea of a great reduction of tariffs is in the direction of abolition for protective purposes, a tariff for revenue only. In that case luxuries only would be heavily taxed, and the so-called free-traders, who support this view, would probably count in pictures and *bric-à-brac* with luxuries."

" I should call them necessities," Irving replied; " for the mind and the imagination require feeding just as much as the body. Besides, how are the Americans going to judge of the work of their own painters without comparison, and current daily comparison too, with foreign artists? The stage is as much of a luxury as paintings. Why let the English actor and his artistic baggage and belongings come in? It is a pleasant thing to remember that, under all circumstances, whatever the troubles between the two countries, America has always welcomed English players, and that has given her some of the best theatrical families she has,—the Booths, Jeffersons, Wallacks, and others. If the same enlightened policy in regard to painting, pottery, and *bric-à-brac* had been carried out in the matter of the stage, we should have seen just as fine an art appreciation applied to pictures as to plays and players. I am sure of it. If the musician and his works, if the opera, had been handicapped as art in other directions is, would America hold her high place in respect of choral societies, orchestral bands ? And would she enjoy, as she does, the grand operas that are now produced in all her great cities ? No. While, as you know, I claim no other credit for my method of presenting Shakespeare and the legitimate drama upon the stage than a performance of managerial duty, I am quite sure that had European stage art and artists been hampered for twenty years by restrictive taxes and other fiscal obstructions, the Lyceum Company and work would not have been welcomed as they have been, wherever we have pitched our tent. The same freedom for paintings would have made Watts, Millais, Tadema, Leighton, Pettie, Leader, Cole, Long, not to mention the works of earlier masters, as familiar here as at home, and would have crowded American houses with examples, original and copies, of the best schools of Europe. Would not that have helped American painters ? Of course it would."

III.

"Your work among New England cities," I said, on his return visit to Brooklyn, "should impress upon you the grim quaintness of the story Mr. Emery Storrs told you concerning the annual festival called the 'general muster.'"

" Yes ; a queer story, was it not ? And, no doubt,

characteristic of some of the more remote little towns."

This is the story :—

The militia muster, once a year, is a celebration peculiar more particularly to New England. It is called the "general muster." Each little town comes in with its quota of militia ; the bands as numerous as the troops. They make a holiday of it. One after-noon an old couple on the hillside of the little town go out to catch a glimpse of the festivities. They are old and alone, managing to drag a mere subsistence out of the sour soil. Their children have gone West,—a son here, a daughter there. They are content to spend the winter of their days in the old, hard nest where they have reared their young; old folks, so old!—parchment faces, bony hands. They totter to the town, and rest on the way in the cemetery, or church-yard, and look at the graves as such grizzly veterans will. One of the militia fellows, going home,—he had got fuddled rather earlier than usual,—sees them. "Halloo!" he shouts. "Go right back, right back, my friends; *this is not the general resurrection, it is the general muster!*"

"By the way," said Irving, "did I tell you of the amusing incident that occurred at Philadelphia? It was on the last night of the first visit. We were playing 'The Belle's Stratagem.' You know how difficult it is sometimes to keep the wings clear of people,—goodness knows who they are! Well, my way was continually blocked by a strange-looking crowd. I remonstrated with them once, and they moved ; but they were back again. The cue for my entrance during the mad scene was at hand, as I said to these fellows, 'Who are you? What do you want?' 'Baggage!' exclaimed two of them, both in a breath. I did not know what the deuce baggage meant: whether the reply was a piece of information or a piece of impertinence; so I thought I would astonish them a little. Getting my cue on the instant, I stepped back a yard or two, and dashed in among them, yelling my entrance line, 'Bring me a pickled elephant!' They scattered right and left, and fell over each other; but before they had time to defend themselves from what they evidently thought was a furious attack I was on the stage."

IV.

I HAVE referred to the "theatre parties" of ladies and gentlemen who travelled many miles by railway to be present at the Irving performances. Several invitations to visit distant cities were also given, with guarantees of financial profit. Among these the most interesting and complimentary was a requisition from Kansas City, which is worth printing. I append it, with Irving's reply :—

"Warwick Club, Kansas City, Mo., Jan. 4th, 1884.
"MR. HENRY IRVING.

"DEAR SIR,—We, the citizens of Kansas City, respectfully request that you honour this city and the West with a professional visit before your return to London. We hold in profound admiration your great histrionic ability and success in the legitimate drama, and your reputation as the leading representative of the English stage.

"We will endeavour to make the season both pleasant and profitable to yourself and Miss Terry, the brilliant and accomplished tragedienne. On behalf of one hundred members of the Warwick Club,

"Yours respectfully,
"T. C. TRUEBLOOD, *President.*
"F. E. HOLLAND, *Secretary.*

Alden J. Buthen, *Kansas City Journal;* Morrison Mumford, *Kansas City Times;* George W. Warder, John Taylor, Smith & Rieger, Holman & French, Robert Keith, Cady & Olmstead, D. Austin, George H. Conover, M. H. Shepard, W. B. Wright, John H. Worth, Woolf Bros., C. J. Waples, John Cutt, John Walmsley, John Sorg, J. V. C. Kames, Jos. Cahn, H. N. Eps, Milton Moore, R. O. Boggers, Gardiner Lathrop, B. R. Conklin, W. R. Nelson, Homer Reed, Albert C. Hasty, L. E. Irwin, the Irwin & Eaton Ckg. Co., Meyer Bros. Drug Co., Charles L. Dobson, Fred Howard, James Scammon, A. Holland, H. T.

z

Wright, Jun., N. W. McLain, W. B. Grimes and W. B. Grimes
Dry Goods Co., Charles S. Wheeler & F. H. Underwood,
Merchants' National Bank, A. W. Atmour, W. H. Winants,
Henry J. Lotshaw, Web. Withers, W. A. M. Vaughan, B. O.
Christakker, F. B. Nopinger, John W. Moore, W. H. Miller,
Charles E. Hasbrook, H. H. Craige, Levi Hammersleigh, B. R.
Bacon, Morse Bros. & Co."

" MY DEAR SIR,—Your invitation, on behalf of one hundred
members of the Warwick Club, is one of the most gratifying
incidents of a very pleasant tour. I cannot sufficiently thank
you for the compliment it conveys to myself, to my sister in
art, Miss Terry, and to my entire company. We shall all of
us treasure it as a delightful memory of the West, and, for my
own part, I shall never be content until I can respond to it as
I wish. I hope the day is not far distant when I may be able
to visit you and your interesting city. I regret, however, that,
so far as the present tour is concerned, Mr. Abbey finds it
impossible to change our programme so as to make it fit your
most kind and hospitable invitation.

" With sincere thanks and good wishes, in which Miss Terry
joins,

"I am,

" St. Louis, January 7th.   HENRY IRVING."

V.

" ONE thing I notice about the American cabmen
and drivers generally," said Irving ; " they do not chaff
each other as the London men in the same positions do.
They don't appear to be cheerful ; don't discuss among
themselves the news of the day ; they treat each other
as if they were strangers. English people, as a rule,
complain of the cab fares here ; but they forget, on the
other hand, to say that the cabs, or *coupés*, as they
call them, are beautifully appointed vehicles ; private
broughams, in fact. The only inconvenience is, that
unless you make a bargain with a driver beforehand, he
may charge you, it seems, what he likes. Against
that, again, is this set-off : you can order your cab at
your hotel, or your club, and have it charged in your
bill, and in that case there is no extortion. Each
leading hotel and club has telephonic communication
with livery stables ; and what a comfort that is ! Then

the messenger system,—one almost wonders how we do without it in London. If London can give New York 'points' in some things, New York can certainly return the compliment."

Asked by a Boston journalist "how he considered he had been treated by his American critics," Irving said "I am exceedingly gratified by the intelligent and fair manner in which I have been treated by the press wherever I have gone. The Boston critics have been just and generous to me. Of course I read what the press has to say of my work, and, while I think it is not the proper province of an actor to criticize his critics, I will say generally that I have been pleased to note in how very few instances I have had to encounter on this side of the Atlantic anything in the nature of personal or petty feeling. I have been struck, too, by the power, vigour, and critical acumen which your leading papers, both here and elsewhere, have displayed in passing judgment upon my work and that of my company. I have a feeling that an actor should be content with what he gets, and that it is his duty to accept patiently any reproach, and to profit by it if he can. After all, criticism, if unjust, never harms a man ; because any final appeal is always to the public, and, if any wrong is done, their ultimate judgment invariably corrects it."

VI.

THE Southern Hotel, at St. Louis, displayed prominently engraven upon a tablet, near the principal staircase, the dates when it had been burned down and rebuilt. The Tremont, at Chicago, recorded on its handsome new building the fact that it had been destroyed by fire, Oct. 27, 1839 ; July 9, 1849 ; and Oct. 9, 1871. "Having dwelt upon these dates with a little misgiving," said a member of Mr. Irving's company, "some of us felt almost alarmed when, on closing our bedroom doors, a card headed 'Fire !' printed in red ink, attracted our attention. I have asked permission to carry one of them away with me, thinking you would like to have it."   The notice is as follows :—

"FIRE! FIRE! FIRE!

"There have been placed in the halls of the Tremont House GONGS, which will be rung by electricity, as an

"ALARM IN CASE OF FIRE.

" They are under control of the office, and will be set going INSTANTLY, on the slightest alarm, and continue to ring.

" This ringing, with the system of calling each room by watchmen stationed on the floors, will insure the speediest alarm to guests it is possible to give in case of accident.

" On being awakened, guests and employés will protect themselves, each other, and property, to the greatest possible extent.

" There are four RED LANTERNS in each hall, at the corners, showing the stairways, and at the end of every corridor outside the building there are IRON LADDER FIRE-ESCAPES to the ground.

" Passage along the halls and corridors, if dark and filled with smoke, can be made by crawling close to the floor with the face covered, to prevent the inhalation of smoke and consequent suffocation.

" From the roof and the three stories below it there is access from the service stairs to the tops of the adjoining buildings, making a way of escape over the roofs, from Dearborn to State Street,—a full block.

"JOHN A. RICE & CO."

The fire service at Chicago is, no doubt, the finest and most complete organization in the world.   Situated

as the city is, on a vast plain, with prairie winds and
lake winds that sweep the entire country for hundreds
of miles without obstruction, the fire department has to
consider, not only the question of extinguishing a con-
flagration, but protecting the property adjacent to a fire
from ignition, in regard to which it has a series of wise
precautionary measures. In former days Chicago, like
many other American cities, was largely built of wood,
and there are still outlying districts of timber houses.
There are also enormous lumber-yards in Chicago,
which are a source of danger during fires that rage
when a high wind is blowing. Not long since Capt.
Shaw gave an exhibition to a royal party in London,
demonstrating how quickly the engines and fire-escapes
can be signalled and despatched to a fire. So far as I
remember the time was about fifteen minutes. In
Chicago they take less than as many seconds to com- .
plete a similar operation. The system of fire-alarms in
all American cities is superior to ours, and the arrangements for starting engines to the rescue insure far
more expedition. We have a less number of fires in
England, many conflagrations taking place in America
through carelessness in connection with the furnaces
that are used for heating the houses ; then shingle roofs
are not uncommon in America; and in England the
party-walls that separate houses are, as a rule, thicker
and higher. This was the explanation which the
American consul gave me at Birmingham, England,
recently, for the fact that during a whole year in Birmingham (with a population equal to Chicago) every
fire that had occurred had been extinguished with a
hand-engine and hose; it had not been necessary in a
single case to use the steam-engines. In Chicago and
other cities the electric signal announcing a fire at the
same time releases the horses that are tethered close
to the engines, alarms the reclining (sometimes sleeping) firemen in their bunks above, withdraws the bolts
of trap-doors in the floor ; and by the time the horses
are in the shafts and harnessed the men drop from

their bunks upon the engine. From a calm interior, occupied by an engine with its fire banked up, and one attendant officer, to a scene of bustle and excitement with an engine, fully equipped, dashing out into the street, is a transformation sufficiently theatrical in its effect to make the fortune of an Adelphi drama. I once engaged to time the operation with a stop-watch, and before I was fairly ready to count the seconds the engine was in the street and away. These exhibitions of skill, speed, and mechanical contrivance, can be seen every day at the quarters of the Fire Insurance Patrol. Chief Bulwinkle is one of the most obliging of officers, and many a famous English name has been inscribed in his visitors' book.[1]

[1] " The head-quarters of the Fire Insurance Patrol are eighty-five feet wide and one hundred feet long. The first floor or room is sixteen feet eight inches high, with black walnut and maple wainscoting. In the front of the room there are two pairs of stairs, one each side. Under these are the horses' stalls. Between the stairs and stalls is the patrol-waggon, the pole of which is ten feet from the front doors, which open out in a vestibule by electricity, and are held by weights. On the right of the room, as you enter, are all the telegraphic instruments connected with the patrol, with no wires visible; a raised panelled black-walnut wall, consisting of the Electric Mercurial Fire-Alarm, which is connected with seventy different business buildings, concealing the wires. This is a system which gives the alarm automatically, giving the exact location of the fire in any building. Over this annunciator is a large clock. On panels, on the right and left of the above, are two gongs, one giving the fire-alarms from the city, the other connected with the Mercurial Fire-alarm Annunciator. Under one gong there are three small gongs, one connecting directly with the Western Union Telegraph Office, one with Marshal Field & Co.'s retail store, and the other with the City Fire Department. In another panel are the American District Telegraph connections. In the ceiling over the waggon is a large reflecting gas-light, which shines directly over the horses when hitching. Just in the rear of the reflector are three raps, that work automatically when an alarm is received, opening the floor on the second story, and ceiling of the first, to enable the driver and assistants to have easy access to their seats; two other members, who sleep on the second floor, make use of the same means of ready exit.

VII.

"Do you remember the poetic speech, in verse and prose, that William Winter[²] made at the banquet in Lafayette Place ? " I asked.

" Yes, indeed," Irving replied. " The two stanzas with which he introduced it were singularly musical, I thought."

" Here they are. I wanted him to write out the

The same telegraphic instrument sets in motion appliances which take off the bed-clothing from ten beds on the second floor, and four berths on the first, relieving the men from all incumbrances in an instant. On the second floor is the dormitory for the men, which is carpeted with English body Brussels. There are heavy black-walnut bedsteads, with F.I.P. carved in head-board, inlaid with gold. The front part of this room is partitioned off and used as Captain Bulwinkle's room, which is carpeted with Wilton carpet, bordered with white, papered and frescoed on all sides in handsome style. Conspicuous here are white marble mantels and grates. On a table in the centre of this room is an album, with autographs of noted people from all parts of the world who have been visitors, and left their names as a testimonial of the excellent qualities of this department. The time required by this patrol to get out of bed, dress, hitch the horses, and get out of the building, is four and one-half seconds."—*Stranger's Guide to the Garden City.*

[²] William Winter is probably best known in America and England as the accomplished and scholarly critic of the *New York Tribune*. As an authority on the drama he holds in New York a similar position to that which the late John Oxenford held on the *Times*. While there are other professional critics in the Empire city who write admirably, and with the authority of knowledge and experience about the stage, William Winter is the only one among them who has made for himself a prominent name apart from the paper with which he is associated. There is no other critic sufficiently well known to be entitled to have his name mentioned in news' cables or telegrams aside from the journal which engages his pen. Winter has broken through the anonymous character of his journalistic work as successfully as Oxenford and Sala. He is the author of several volumes of lyrics; he is the biographer of the Jeffersons; and since Washington Irving nothing more charming has been written about "the old country" than his "Trip to England."

heads of his speech for me; but he had only written down his verses, and here they are, as dainty as they are fraternal."

I.

If we could win from Shakespeare's river
 The music of its murmuring flow,
With all the wild-bird notes that quiver
 Where Avon's scarlet meadows glow;
If we could twine with joy at meeting
 Their prayers who lately grieved to part,
Ah, then, indeed, our song of greeting
 Might find an echo in his heart!

II.

But since we cannot in our singing
 That music and those prayers entwine,
At least, we'll set our blue-bells ringing,
 And he shall hear our whispering pine;
And there shall breathe a welcome royal,
 In accents tender, sweet, and kind,
From lips as fond and hearts as loyal
 As any that he left behind.

Among the curious notices, serious and humorous, which were posted in the offices and dressing-rooms of the various theatres, the following satirical regulations are somewhat incongruous when considered with the handsome furniture which generally belongs to managerial rooms in America:—

" OFFICE RULES.

"1. Gentlemen entering this office will please leave the door open.

"2. Those having no business should remain as long as possible, take a chair and lean against the wall,—it will prevent it falling upon us.

"3. Gentlemen are requested to smoke, particularly during office hours. Tobacco and cigars will be furnished.

" 4. Spit on the floor,—the spittoons are merely for ornament.

" 5. Talk loud or whistle, particularly when we are engaged; if this does not have the desired effect, SING.

" 6. Put your feet on the table, or lean against the desk ; it will be a great benefit to those who are using it.

" 7. Persons having no business with this office will please call again when they can't stay so long."

VIII.

" WILL you please tell me about the report cabled from London to the American press, that you propose to stand for Parliament in the Liberal interest, on your return to England?" asked a journalistic interviewer, at Boston.

"I can only say that the report is entirely unfounded. It arose, I imagine, from my election to the Reform Club. You know they do occasionally elect out-of-the-way fellows, such as I am, in the matter of politics. The welcome news reached me last night in my dressing-room at the theatre. To be elected in my absence adds to the pleasure of the thing. I have only that interest in politics which all honest men should have, but it exists only under my own roof. I do not think artists should mix up in politics. Art is my vocation, and I confine myself to it."

" Then I assume you have never cherished political aspirations ? "

" Oh, no, never ! In fact, I should be totally unfit for Parliament. I am not eloquent, and should be unfit in other ways. We do not look upon politics in England as you do here. Here political life is an avenue to office and to emoluments, in a broader and deeper sense than is possible in England, and many choose the law as a profession, with a view to politics. Do they not ? It is not so with us. A seat in the

House of Commons, as a rule, involves great expense, as well as a claim upon a man's time ; and he may sit there all his life, if he is returned often enough, and spend every year a large income, socially, in London, and locally, on charities, hospitals, reading-rooms, churches and chapels, among his constituents. We do not pay our representatives salaries ; and I believe, particularly in the country, the constituencies watch with the greatest jealousy every vote a member records. The House of Commons is not a bed of roses."

I have said, in a previous chapter, that the trouble in respect to the new form of journalism in some of the cities of the United States is, that the reader is left too much in doubt as to the truth of the daily chronicles. The Chicago reporter, who held up the "interviews" of other journals as more or less "bogus," would himself have found it difficult in this respect to winnow the chaff from the wheat. At St. Louis a reporter professed to have taken an engagement as a "super" in the Irving Company. He wrote a description of "behind the scenes" in that capacity, but "gave himself away" by making all the company, from the leading actor down to the call-boy, drop their "h's." The American reporter's leading idea when burlesquing the English is to take every "h" out of a Britisher's conversation, and even to make the Queen herself drop the aspirate or misuse it ; for instance, here is a summary of the royal speech on the opening of Parliament, which appeared in a Philadelphia journal : "We're pretty well, I thank you, and we 'opes to remain so, we does." If in our stage and journalistic satire we make Jonathan "guess," "calkalate," and "lick all creation, you bet," he "gets even" with "yahs, deah boy," and "'ow har' you," and "'pon my honor, don't cher know ?" But, referring back to the many imaginary interviews and fictitious sketches of Irving and his life behind the scenes, here is an extract from an account of "Irving's day," which appeared in one of the light-headed dailies, that is, in some respects, truer than I dare say any of its readers believed it to be. The introduction of "the secretaries" is worthy of *Punch*, and in its earnestness funnier than some of the great humorist's sketches of the Irving tour in America. Here are the leading points of the article :—

THE METHODICAL WAY IN WHICH IRVING PASSES HIS TIME.

Henry Irving is a man of simple, but regular, habits. He has gained the hearts of everybody in the Bellevue, from the proprietor to the bell-boy, by his courteous demeanour and his desire to give as little trouble as possible. He rises at nine o'clock, and drinks a cup of coffee with milk. Breakfast is served in his private sitting-room at ten o'clock, consisting of tea, boiled eggs, and some other simple dish. The eggs he cooks himself in a little spirit-lamp arrangement of his own. He eats the meal alone, and glances at his mail while at table. The budget of correspondence is usually large, and in-cludes letters from all over the world. After breakfast one or two secretaries pay their respects to him, and receive his in-structions in regard to the replies to the missives. The daily papers are then carefully read, and any visitors who call are received.

Between twelve and one he leaves the hotel, generally in a carriage, and always accompanied by a secretary. The theatre is the first destination. In everything concerning the stage arrangements, indeed, even the most minute details, Mr. Irving is consulted. A skye-terrier is also a persistent companion of the English actor, and follows wherever he goes.

Mr. Irving dines at 3.30. A course dinner is served,— oysters, soup, fish, a cutlet, and a bird. Canvas-back duck has a preference among the feathery food. He dines by himself, does his own carving, and dismisses the servants as soon as the dishes are placed in front of him. From the dinner hour until he goes to the theatre he is denied to everybody. No matter whose card arrives for him, there is no passport for the paste-board through the portals of the actor's apartments. The interval after dinner is passed in study and meditation. Mr. Irving is, above all, a student, and every gesture and motion he makes on the stage have been previously considered, and a reason found for the change of position or features.

After the theatre Mr. Irving throws off the restraint of the day, and sups at his ease with some of his friends. A secretary or two are included in the party. Supper lasts sometimes until two or three in the morning. Last Sunday, when Attorney-General Brewster was Mr. Irving's guest, it was 3 a.m. before the party exchanged adieux.

Among the visitors who have called on Mr. Irving, Viscount Bury, James McHenry, and General Collis, were among the favoured ones who were admitted to audience. Scores of invitations for every kind of entertainment have overwhelmed him, keeping three or four of his secretaries busy with writing his expression of regrets.

When Irving was at Philadelphia he had a young English friend visiting him. The waiter (who was evidently in the confidence of the local reporter, or might have been the reporter himself masquerading as a waiter) pressed him in as a secretary. Abbey's manager, Mr. Palser, Mr. Stoker, Mr. Loveday, and another friend, a resident of Philadelphia, were all promoted to the secretarial office. There is a sublime touch of unconscious satire in this staff of secretaries, engaged upon the work of answering Irving's letters, which will be particularly appreciated in London, where that one special sin of his—neglecting to answer letters—is even commented upon in learned reviews. The after-dinner " study and meditations " is " Jeames's " view of the siesta, which is a needful incident of every actor's day. The data of the sketch being fairly correct, the *bonâ fides* of it, from the reporter's point of view, makes it interesting as well as characteristic of the " personal " character of some of the clever news journals of the day.

IX.

ONE day, during " this interval after dinner," which is " passed in study and meditation," Irving said, " Have you followed out all the story of the Bisbee murderers ? "

" Yes," I said. " It is one of those strange cases of lawlessness, that I have taken out of the newspapers for my scrap-book. Charles Reade[3] would have been interested in it. Have you ever seen his scrap-books ? "

" No," said Irving ; " are they very remarkable ? "

" Yes, and in my slovenly attempts to save newspaper cuttings I often think of him. I once spent a whole day with him, looking over his journalistic extracts, and he was lamenting all the time the trouble involved in their arrangement and indexing. He subscribed to many odd, out-of-the-way newspapers for his collections. If he had ever visited America he would have been tempted to make a very formidable addition to his list.

" Do you know the beginning of the Bisbee business ? I have only seen the account of the hunting down of one of the murderers, which has interested me tremendously. Have you seen any accounts of the capture ? "

" No."

" Well, then, curiously enough I have received a San Francisco *Chronicle*, with the entire story of it, and I believe it is worth putting into the book. Can you tell me the nature of this crime ? "

" Yes. One day several strangers arrived suddenly in the little town of Bisbee, on the outskirts of Western civilization. They went into the principal store, shot down tho owner of it, fired at anybody they saw in the street, killed a woman who was passing the store, and, having generally, as it were, bombarded the little town, left as mysteriously as they came. That is briefly the story, as it was repeated to me a week ago by Dr. Gil-

---

[3] Among the cablegrams that cast English shadows upon the tour was the announcement of Charles Reade's death. This had already been preceded by obituary notices of Blanchard Jerrold. It was followed, at a later date, by the chronicle that Henry J. Byron had also "joined the majority." The sudden death of the Duke of Albany was chronicled by the leading American newspapers, with touching sentiments of sympathy for the Queen of England.

man, of Chicago, who has recently returned from the scene of the tragedy, and other mining camps and towns, about which he entertained me with a dozen almost equally startling stories."

"Well," said Irving, "the hunt after these Bisbee ruffians is about as dramatic an episode of police work as I ever came across. A reward being offered for the chief of the gang who raided Bisbee, it was soon discovered that 'Big Dan,' a notorious ruffian, was the criminal. The entire business was after his most approved method, and it was finally proved, beyond doubt, that this was the latest of 'Big Dan Dowd's' crimes. On the 6th of January, Deputy Sheriff Daniels brought him in custody into Tombstone, and this is the story of the capture :—

"'On December 23rd, Daniels learned in Bisbee from some Mexicans just in from Sonora, that two men answering the description of 'Big Dan' and Billy Delaney, were in Bavispe, Sonora. This place will be remembered as the point from which Crook started on his trip into the defiles of the Sierra Madre, and lies on the western slope of that range. Satisfying himself that the information furnished by the Mexicans was correct, Daniels communicated with the sheriff's office, and, after making all necessary arrangements, started, on the morning of December 26, for that place. Accompanying the officer was a Mexican named Lucero, on whom Daniels knew he could rely as a guide and a fighter. On the morning of the 30th, after a ride of about 200 miles, Daniels and his two companions (he having picked up another Mexican at Frontera) reached Bavispe. Here it was learned that Delaney and Dowd had separated five days previously, Dowd remaining in Bavispe, which point he had left that morning, about an hour prior to the arrival of Daniels and his posse. Additional inquiries elicted the information that Dowd had struck across the Sierra Madre for Janos, in the State of Chihuahua, distant about seventy-five miles. After taking a short rest, and perfecting plans for the capture of Delaney, the officer started in pursuit of the other bandit.

" ' The route of travel led through the defiles of the Sièrra Madre, by rocks and precipitous trails, and it was not until the morning of January 1st that Daniels reached Janos, where he learned, as at Bavispe, that the bird had flown, having left Janos a few hours ahead of him for Coralitos, distant about twenty-seven miles. Procuring fresh horses, the posse started at once for Coralitos, which place was reached about eight o'clock that evening. The town is in the centre of a mining country, and is composed principally of Mexicans, there being but half a dozen Americans in the place. The whole neighbourhood, as described by Daniels, seems to belong to the Coralitos Mining Company, of which Ad Menzenberger is superintendent. Daniels went at once to him, and communicating the object of his visit, learned that ' Big Dan ' had arrived a short time previously, and was then in what was known as the house of the Americans. The superintendent, having learned the character of Dowd, was only too willing to assist in his capture, and, under the cover of darkness, he and Daniels proceeded to the house. Prior to reaching it, it was agreed that the superintendent should enter in advance of Daniels, in order to prevent any interference by the Americans who were in his employ, in the capture of Dowd.

" ' As agreed, the superintendent entered the room first, with Daniels at his heels. Dowd was sitting on a table facing the fire, and the rest of the party were scattered about the room. On the table was standing also a bottle of whisky, which had not been uncorked. Everything indicated that Dowd had no idea of the presence of an officer, and was preparing for a jolly night with his companions. He did not even look around when the men entered the room, and his first knowledge that he was in the clutches of the law was when Menzenberger, who had reached his side, caught hold of his arms, and, throwing them above his head, said, 'Throw up your hands.' Daniels, at the same time, with a cocked pistol in each hand, made the demand to surrender. A word from the superintendent to the Americans present showed Dowd, who was unarmed at the time, that he was powerless to escape, and he quietly submitted to being manacled. Daniels remained until the following morning, when he was furnished with an ambulance and escort by the superintendent, and driven to San José station, on the line of the Mexican Central Railroad, 110 miles distant, and about ninety miles south of El Paso del Norte. Here he telegraphed to Sheriff Ward of the capture, and, putting his prisoner on board the train, started for home. Upon nearing Paso del Norte, he feared that Dowd might raise a question of extradition, and put him to much trouble ; so he made arrangements with the railroad officials, and, together with his prisoner, was locked in the express car until reaching the American line.' "

Irving recited most of the *Chronicle's* narrative. The close, terse particulars of its details leave sufficient colour of surroundings to the imagination of the reader.

X.

" TOMBSTONE," he said presently, "is a curious name for a town."

" Some friends of mine," I said, "have business interests there. It got its name in this way : a party of young pioneers decided to go there on a prospecting expedition. They were ridiculed, and told by another party, who had refused to join them, that all they would find would be a tomb. The adventurers, however, discovered mineral treasures of enormous extent, started a town, and, as a derisive answer to their prophetic friend, called it Tombstone. This is the story of only a few years. Tombstone is now a prosperous community, and has a daily paper. What do you think its title is ? "

" I cannot guess."

" Eugene Field, a journalist whose name is well known throughout the West, gave me a copy of it only yesterday."

I went to my room and brought down a well-printed, four-page paper, entitled *The Tombstone Epitaph.*

" And not a funny paper at all," said Irving, examining it; " a regular business-like paper, newsy and prosaic, except for the short literary story and the poem that begin its pages."

" Mr. Field gave me some remarkable newspaper trophies of these mining towns, that may be said to grow up outside the pale of civilization, to be eventually incorporated into the world of law and order. Here for instance, is a placard issued by *The Bazoo*, a newspaper published at the little town of Sedalia :—

BAZOO NEWS TRAIN !

— to —

NEVADA, MO.,

FRIDAY, DECEMBER 28TH, 1883.

BILL FOX'S PUBLIC EXECUTION

For the murder of Tom Howard, at Nevada, Mo., May 20, 1883.

The *Sedalia Bazoo* has chartered a special train, which will run to Nevada from Joplin on that day. Leaving Joplin at 8.10 o'clock a.m., and returning in thirty minutes after the death-scene at the gallows.

TIME-TABLE.			Rates of Fare for Round Trip.
Leave Joplin	.	.	8.10 a.m.	. . . . $2.00
„ Webb City	.	.	8.25 „	. . . . 1.75
„ Edwin	.	.	8.43 „	. . . . 1.50
„ Carthage	.	.	8.53 „	. . . . 1.45
„ Carey	.	.	9.05 „	. . . . 1.25
„ Jasper	.	.	9.15 „	. . . . 1.10
„ Carleton	.	.	9.27 „	95
„ Lamar	.	.	9.40 „	75
„ Irwin	.	.	9.57 „	60
„ Sheldon	.	.	10.07 „	50
„ Milo	.	.	10.35 „	25
Arrive Nevada	.	.	10.20.	

☞ Tickets for Sale at the Depôt. ☜

A a

Returning, the train will leave Nevada thirty minutes after the execution, giving plenty of time for all to get to the train. Tickets sold for this train will not be good on any other but the *Bazoo* News Train, this day only.

THE BAZOO!
Is a Daily and Weekly newspaper published at
SEDALIA, MO.,
For the People now on Earth.

TERMS.

Daily, per Annum $10.00
Sunday, ,, ... 2.50
Weekly, ,, ... 1.00
☞ Subscriptions will be received on the Train by a Solicitor. ☜

The *Sedalia Morning Bazoo* of December 29 will contain a picture of FOX, who is to be executed, with a full history of his crime, his trial, and the last words of the dying man on the gallows.

Secure a copy of the news-agent on the train, or of your news-dealer for FIVE CENTS.

And here is the free pass (printed on a mourning card) which accompanied the announcement that was sent to Mr. Field in his journalistic capacity :—

Good for Special News Train only.

THE BAZOO NEWS TRAIN,
On the occasion of the
PUBLIC EXECUTION OF BILL FOX.
Pass Miss Eugenia Field,
Acc't of Boss Bog,
TO NEVADA AND RETURN,
Dec. 28, 1883.
J. WEST GOODWIN.

" Bill Fox, I understood, was a noted criminal, and

everybody was glad to have him hanged out of the way."

XI.

" IT is a lesson in the evolution of towns, these incidents of the pushing out of the frontiers of a great country," said Irving. " I dare say Denver began its career as a mining-camp."

" It did ; and only a few years ago."

" And now they tell me it is a beautiful and well-ordered city, with the finest opera-house in all America."

" That is so ; and one day you ought to play there."

" I hope I may; I would like it very much. By the way, your bill about *The Bazoo* excursion reminds me of two curious placards which the manager of Haverly's gave me. They tell the story of the fate of a new play that was once produced at his theatre. It was called ' Hix's Fix,' and was a terrible failure. The theatre had been engaged for a short season for ' Hix's Fix,' and the proprietors of it were at their wits' ends to know what to do. They were not prepared to play any other piece; so they hit upon the expedient of ' pushing the failure.' They printed half a million handbills, and circulated them diligently. This is one of them; it reads as follows :—

HAVERLY'S THEATRE.

In obedience to the Unanimous Opinion of the Daily Press
MESTAYER & BARTON
Seriously think of Changing the name of their Play,
HIX'S FIX, TO ROT.
In sober truth, this is about the right thing,
☞ BUT ☜
It is the funniest rot you have ever seen, and stands pre-eminent and alone the
WORST PLAY OF THE AGE.

OPINIONS OF THE PRESS :

Hix's Fix is bad enough, but think of the poor audience.—*News.*

All that is not idiotic is vile.—*Tribune.*

The piece is sheer nonsense, to speak mildly.—*Times.*

The most painful dramatic infliction we have suffered this season.—*Evening News.*

EVERYBODY'S JUDGMENT WANTED.

TURN OUT AND JOIN THE MOURNERS.

Every Night this Week and Wednesday and Saturday Matinées.

"Under the influence of this extraordinary announcement, the business improved, stimulated by which cheering result the managers issued a new proclamation, to this effect :—

HAVERLY'S THEATRE.

Every Night this Week and usual Matinées.
HIX'S FIX
Is unquestionably the worst Play ever produced.

It is so much worse that no one should miss it!

THIS IS CONFIDENTIAL (?)

To illustrate how good people will sometimes go wrong, read the list of talent engaged in playing this vile trash.

WILLIAM A. MESTAYER,
The heaviest of heavy Tragedians.

Rob't E. Graham,
Unequalled in Character Impersonations.
Harry Bloodgood, Fred. Turner, Chas. A. Stedman,
H. A. Cripps.

Miss Kate Foley,
As bright as a sunbeam,
Sophie Hummell, Helen Lowell, Lisle Riddell, with
James Barton as Manager.

Here you have the novelty of a very Good Company in an
unpardonably Bad Play.

AND THEY KNOW IT!

You must admire their Candour, if you will condemn the Play.

" Many curious people were drawn to the theatre in
this way; but the attraction of failure only lasted a
few nights. The invitation to turn out and join the
mourners strikes one as funny. ' It helped them to
pay expenses,' said the manager; ' but it is the most
novel effort to " turn diseases to commodities," as
Falstaff says, that ever came under my notice.' "

XII.

" And now," continued Irving, " to go back to your
opening, where we rather discount Raymond's stories
of the wild life of Texas. Have you seen the *Herald's*
latest sensation ? "
" No."
" Not the Texan tragedy ? "
" No."
" Here it is, then; listen to the heads of it: ' Two
Crime-stained Ruffians die with their Boots on—Pistol
Shots in a Theatre—Killed in Self-defence by Men
whose Lives they sought—The Heroes of many
Murders !' "
He handed me the paper, saying, " Read that ! And
yet we chaffed poor Raymond ! "
I read a " special telegram " to the *Herald* (and

verified the report at a later day by the records of other journals, local, and of the *Empire City*), reporting that on the 11th of March, between ten and twelve at night, San Antonio, Texas, was " thrown into a state of wild excitement, by the report that Ben Thompson and King Fisher had been shot and killed at the Vaudeville Theatre. An immense crowd thronged around the doors of the theatre, but were denied admission by the officers who had taken possession of the building.

" It seems that Ben Thompson, who is noted throughout Texas as one of the most reckless and desperate characters in the State, and King Fisher, who also had the reputation of a desperado, arrived at San Antonio together, from Austin, by the international train. After enjoying the performance at Turner Hall for a time, they left before the curtain fell, and went to the Vaudeville Theatre, in company with another person. As soon as it became known that Thompson was in the city the police were on the alert, expecting trouble. Fisher and Thompson entered the Vaudeville, and, after taking a drink at the bar, went upstairs and took seats. They engaged in a brief conversation with Simms, one of the proprietors, and the whole party took drinks and cigars together. Thompson and Fisher then rose, and, in company with Simms and Coy, a special policeman at the theatre, started downstairs.

" The party was joined by Joe Foster, another of the Vaudeville proprietors, and an excited and heated conversation followed, during which Thompson called Foster a liar, a thief, and other vile names. Firing then commenced, and some ten or twelve shots were heard in rapid succession. Police Captain Shardein and another officer rushed upstairs, to find Ben Thompson and King Fisher weltering in their blood in the corner of a room near the door leading downstairs. Joe Foster was badly wounded in the leg, and Officer Coy slightly grazed on the shin.

" A scene of the wildest confusion ensued as soon as the shooting commenced. All who were in the theatre knew of the presence of Thompson and Fisher, and were well acquainted with their desperate character. When the first shot was fired the whole crowd seemed to be panic-stricken. The dress circle was quickly cleared, the occupants jumping into the parquet below and through the side windows into the street. No one seems to know who fired the first shot, or how many were engaged in the shooting. Before the theatre was fairly cleared of its occupants, 1500 persons on the outside were clamouring at the closed doors for admittance, which was resolutely denied by the police, who had taken possession of the building. Subsequently the dead bodies of Thompson and Fisher were removed to the city jail, where they were washed and laid out.

" Bill Thompson, the brother of Ben, was at the White Elephant at the time of the shooting, waiting for Ben to return from Turner Hall. He rushed out as soon as he saw that there was some trouble ; but, as he was unarmed, he was stopped at the entrance to the Vaudeville by Captain Shardein, and kept outside the building.

" An immense crowd followed the remains of the two desperadoes when they were carried to the jail, and this morning the plaza around the building was thronged.

" From the statements of those connected with the theatre, the killing was unavoidable, as it seemed to be understood when Thompson entered the house that his purpose was to raise a disturbance ; but whether King Fisher shared in this design is not known.

" A coroner's jury was summoned at once. They viewed the bodies, and the inquest was held the next morning. After hearing the testimony of eye-witnesses and others, a verdict was returned to the effect that Ben Thompson and J. King Fisher came to their deaths by means of pistol-bullets fired from weapons in the hands of W. Simms, Joseph C. Foster, and Jacob Coy; and, further, that the killing was justifiable, being done in self-defence. Coy, the special policeman on duty at the theatre, testified that Thompson drew his weapon first; but it was seized by witness, who held it in his grasp during the affray. Thompson, however, fired four shots, one of which took effect in Foster's leg.

"Foster's leg has been amputated, and there are no hopes of his recovery."

The newspaper man gives "Thompson's antecedents" and "Fisher's record" as follows:—

Ben Thompson was born in Knottingley, a town in Yorkshire, England, in 1844. His father was a sea-captain. Ben leaves a wife and two children in Austin—a bright boy of fourteen years and a girl of eleven. He has a brother here, who took charge of his body, and carried it to Austin to-day. Thompson's record is a bloody one. He is said to have slain probably twenty men. His last victim was Jack Harris, proprietor of the Vaudeville, whom he shot in June, 1882, in the same house in which he himself was slain last night. His death is little regretted here.

King Fisher was a young man of some twenty-eight years, and his record was, if possible, more bloody than Thompson's. For years he was feared as a frontier desperado, and killed Mexicans almost for pastime. Of late he had reformed a little, and when killed was deputy-sheriff of Walde county. Both men were strikingly handsome, and noted as quick dead-shots with six-shooters, or Winchesters. Fisher's remains were shipped home to-night.

The reporter adds: "The city is now quiet, though the death of two such notorious desperadoes is still a topic of conversation."

"Thompson was an Englishman, you see," remarked Irving, "which verifies to some extent what I have often been told, that England has to answer for a full share of the ruffianly element of the States. The mining regions of California at one time were crowded with English adventurers. What a vast country it is that encircles in its territories every climate—tropical heat and arctic cold! To-day, while we are ice-bound,

a journey of two or three days would take us to Florida
and orange-groves, and a day's travel from the heart
of a highly civilized city, of refined cultivation and
well-ordered society, would carry us into a region
where men live in primitive state, so far as the law
is concerned, and yet are the pioneers of a great
empire. What a story, the history of America, when
somebody tells it from its picturesque and romantic
side! "

XXII.

"THE LONGEST JOURNEY COMES TO AN END."

" Our closing Month in New York "—Lent—At Rehearsal—
Finishing Touches—Behind the Scenes at the Lyceum and
the Star—The Story of the production of " Much Ado "
in New York—Scenery and Properties on the Tour—
Tone—Surprises for Agents in Advance—Interesting
Technicalities—An Incident of the mounting of " Much
Ado "—The Tomb Scene—A great Achievement—The
End.

I.

" It is almost like getting home again," said Irving,
" to find one's self in New York once more. The first
place one stops at in a new country always impresses
the imagination and lives in the memory. I should
say that is so with pioneers, and more particularly
when your first resting-place has been pleasant. Let
us get Monday night well over, and we may look for
something like a little leisure during our closing month
in New York. We shall produce ' Much Ado ' as
completely as it is possible for us to do it, outside of
our own theatre. If no hitch occurs, I think we will
run it for two, Palser even proposes three, weeks.
If we have been complimented upon our scenic and
stage-managerial work on the other pieces, what may
we expect for ' Much Ado ' ? Lent is severely kept
in New York, I am told ; Holy Week being among the
churches, if not a fast in regard to food, a fast from
amusements. We must therefore be content, I sup-

pose, to let ' Much Ado ' grow in time for the restoration of social pleasures at Easter." [1]

On Monday, at a quarter to eleven, Irving was at his post, on the stage of the Star Theatre, for a complete rehearsal. Scenery, properties, lighting, grouping of supernumeraries, the entire business of the piece, was gone through. Not a detail was overlooked, not a set but was viewed as completely from the stalls as from the stage.

" Pardon me," says Irving to Claudio, " if you get your hand above your head in that position, you will never get it down again. Suppose you adopt this idea, eh? What do you think?"

" Certainly, it is better," says Claudio.

Irving, as he speaks, illustrates his own view of the scene.

" Then we will try it again."

The scene is repeated.

" Yes, very good, that will do."

---

[1] " Much Ado " did " grow," and was played for three weeks a " mixed bill " closing the last six nights. The receipts during Lent were unprecedentedly large in the history of New York theatres. These pages go to press before the financial returns are completely made up; but it is known to-day (April 25) that the receipts for the entire tour will be more than $400,000. The social hospitalities in honour of Irving and Miss Terry, which characterized their first visit to New York, were continued on their return. Among the notable breakfasts of the time was one given to Irving by Edwin Booth, at Delmonico's, on April 14. The *Times*, in chronicling it, says : " Mr. Booth sat at the head of the table, with Mr. Irving on his right, and Chief-Justice Charles P. Daly on his left. John McCullough knocked elbows with Parke Godwin. The other guests included Jervis McEntee, Launt Thompson, Charles E. Carryl, Richard Henry Stoddard, William Bispham, Eastman Johnson, William Winter, Bram Stoker, Lawrence Hutton, Frank P. Millett, Junius Henri Browne, H. J. Loveday, and E. C. Benedict. No speeches were made, but in the course of an informal chat Mr. Irving was asked about ' Hamlet.' He said that he hardly thought it policy to produce the play for three or four nights at the end of a season, and on the eve of his departure, particularly as he contemplated so speedy a return."

The rehearsal goes on.

" No, no," says Irving, " there must be no wait; the second procession must come on promptly at the cue. Try it again. And hold your halberd like this, my boy; not as if you were afraid of it. There, that's it."

The supernumerary accepts his lesson; the music cue is repeated; the halberdiers file in; the military strains cease, the organ peals out, the wedding procession comes on.

" Bow, bow,—don't nod," says Irving, stepping forward to instruct a subordinate in the scene; " that's better—go on."

The solemn voice of Mead opens the scene, and as it proceeds, Irving calls Loveday aside.

" Too much light at the back there, eh ? "

" Do you think so ? " says Loveday. " Lower the light there,—the blue medium."

Steps have been placed as a way from the stage to the stalls. Irving (" Charlie " following at his heels) goes into the third row, Loveday watching and waiting.

" Yes, that will do," says Irving, at the same time turning to me to remark, " Do you see what a difference that makes ? You have no difficulty now in imagining the distance the subdued light suggests,—chapels, vestries, dim cathedral vistas. Do you notice what a last touch of reality to the scene the hurried entrance of the pages give ?—they break up the measured solemnity of the processions with a different step, a lighter manner, the carelessness of youth; they have no censers to carry, no ecclesiastical robes to wear."

As he is speaking he strides up the steps and upon the stage once more.

" Mr. Ball ! Call Mr. Ball, please."

The musical director appears.

" The basses are too loud; they spoil the closing movement, which is too quick altogether. Come into the stalls and hear it."

" Howson ! " says Ball, " please give them the time."

Ball goes into the stalls. The movement is repeated

and repeated again, the last time entirely to Irving's satisfaction.

In these passing notes I merely desire to give the reader a hint at the kind of work which was done at rehearsal on the Monday of the production of " Much Ado." It lasted until a quarter-past five. Irving was there until the end. Out of sight of the audience he had done enough work to entitle him to a night's rest ; but, so far as the critics and the public were concerned, his labours were only just beginning. Shortly after seven he was on the stage again, and when the play began he was never more heartily engaged in his *rôle* as actor.

"Yes, I am rather tired," he said, in his quiet way, when I spoke to him at the wing ; " feel inclined to sit down,—hard work, standing about all day,—but this is the reward."

He pointed to the setting of the garden scene, which was progressing quite smoothly.

" If we pull through with the cathedral set all right, one will not mind being a little tired."

I waited to see the work done, and, though I am familiar with the business behind the scenes, I was glad to escape from the " rush and tumble " of it on this occasion. At the Lyceum every man knows the piece, or flat, for the position of which he is responsible. He goes about his work silently, and in list slippers ; he fetches and carries without hurry ; nothing seems more simple ; you see the scene grow into completeness, silently but surely. At the Star, on this first night, it was, to all appearance, chaos. Wings were slid about ; curtains unrolled ; tapestries hauled up by unseen strings ; great pillars were pushed here and there ; images of saints were launched into space from the flies, to be checked by ropes, just as you might think they were coming to grief ; a massive altar-piece was being railed in, while a painted canopy was hoisted over it ; a company of musicians were led out of the way of falling scenes to join a chorus party of ladies and gentlemen,

who were gradually losing themselves among a
picturesque crowd of halberdiers. Everybody seemed
to be in everybody's way; it looked like a general
scramble. Irving, with " Less noise, my boys—less
noise," continually on his lips, moved about among
the throng; and as Ball, who had made a third and
last effort to find a prominent position from which to
conduct his band, stepped upon a bench which was
instantly drawn from under him by the stage hands
who had it in charge I went to the front of the house.
Ball's musicians struck up their impressive strains of
the " Gloria," and the curtain slowly rose upon the
cathedral at Messina as if it had been there all the
time, only waiting the prompter's signal. Pande-
monium behind the curtain had given place to
Paradise in front. It was a triumph of willing hands
under intelligent and earnest direction.

II.

NEXT day, when the success of the night had been
duly chronicled in the press,[2] I suggested to Irving

[2] " The excitement of that cheerful October evening last year
when Henry Irving made his first appearance in New York,
was repeated last night at the Star Theatre, where ' Much Ado
about Nothing' was presented, and where Mr. Irving and Miss
Terry effected their re-entrance, and were welcomed by a great
and brilliant company with acclamations, with floral tributes
and in a charmingly manifest spirit of the heartiest admiration
and good-will. The scene, indeed, was one of unusual brightness,
kindliness, and enjoyment, both before the curtain and upon
the stage. The applause, upon the entrance of Beatrice, a rare
vision of imperial yet gentle beauty!—broke forth impetuously
and continued long; and, upon the subsequent entrance of
Benedict, it rose into a storm of gladness and welcome."—
Tribune.

" The performance at the Star Theatre last evening was
one of remarkable interest. ' Much Ado about Nothing' was
produced, and Mr. Irving and his company furnished a dramatic
representation more complete and artistic, and in every way
more admirable, than any that has been seen upon our stage.
The audience was large and brilliant, and the reappearance of
Mr. Irving and Miss Ellen Terry was greeted with every demonstration of pleasure."—*Sun.*

that we should place on record some account of the
manner in which the Lyceum scenery, dresses, and
properties had been dealt with on the tour ; to what
extent the equipment with which he had set out had
been used; and, as a concluding chapter, that we
should tell the story of the production of " Much Ado "
in New York. After a consultation with Loveday, and
the verification of some necessary statistics, Irving
exhausted the subject in a very pleasant and instructive chat, the points of which are not too technical to
mislead the general reader, while they are sufficiently
technical to be of special interest to actors and
managers.

" After the Philadelphia engagement," said Irving,
" I discussed the question of scenery with Loveday, and
we found that it was impossible to carry or to use many
of our largest set-pieces. Even if we could have
carried them conveniently, we would not have got them
into many of the theatres. Loveday, therefore, packed
a mass of it up and sent it back to New York. What
we had left was enormous in its bulk, filling two
sixty-two-feet cars, and one huge gondola-car, which
was made to carry all the flat scenery. We took on
with us, however, all the cloths for our entire *répertoire*,
and many of the small practical set-pieces. We carried
every property of the entire *répertoire*,—the bedstead
of ' The Belle's Stratagem,' the altar of ' Much Ado,'
the horse of ' The Bells,' down to Cattermole's picture
of Letitia Hardy, some Chippendale furniture of the
period, and other minor things that are characteristic
or useful decoration in the furnishing of interiors and
exteriors. All our dresses were included,—principals
and " supers." Loveday tells me they filled 120 great
baskets, the properties being packed in thirty baskets,
making a total of 150.

" We took everything to Boston and Philadelphia
It was at the latter city that, as I say, we decided to
modify our arrangements. We sent back to New
York twenty-seven cloths, eighty flats, sixty wings,

ninety set-pieces, and twelve framed cloths; so that
we had to adapt our requirements to the local situation.

"As regards such of our scenery as is painted in
tone, you know that one of the most remarkable we
have is the frescoed interior of the hall of justice in
'The Merchant of Venice,'—a complete reproduction
of the period. I had the portraits of the Doges
painted by White and Cattermole. I think it is one of
the most superb pictures ever seen upon the stage. I
understand that some people thought it worn, mistaking
the tone for dirt. Here and there, I think we found
the tapestries, which we used instead of the frescoes,
more acceptable.

"Some of the scenes in 'Hamlet,' 'The Bells,' and
'Much ado,' we had specially reproduced ahead of us.
Indeed, the companies following us will find portions
of the cathedral of Messina around the walls of many
an American theatre; and in every house where we
have played, travelling stage-managers, asking for a
cottage scene, will find a reminiscence of 'The
Lyons Mail' in the inn at Lieursaint. We have
left one in each town. As they are fac-similes, they
will, I should think, bewilder some of the agents in
advance.

"As to our full Lyceum scenery, and what may be
called the administration of it, we achieved our greatest
triumph this week, presenting 'Much Ado' as nearly
like the Lyceum production as the space at our disposal
would permit. Our stage at home, including the scene
dock, which we always use, is seventy feet long,
measuring from the footlights; the Star stage is fifty
feet. We took possession of the theatre on Sunday
morning, March 30, the stage having been occupied
until Saturday night. A small army of men, besides
our own, aided by the heads of departments in Mr.
Wallack's employment, began work, under Loveday's
direction, at seven o'clock a.m., and by four o'clock on
Monday morning every scene had been set, lighted, and

rehearsed three times over. At four they adjourned, and came on again to meet me at a quarter to eleven, when we had a full rehearsal of scenery, properties, lighting, and of the entire company. I was impressed and delighted with the earnestness of everybody employed in the work, Wallack's people showing as great a desire as our own to do their best to achieve the success we were all striving for. This is very gratifying; and it has been our experience, wherever we have reappeared, that the *employés* have thoroughly entered into our work, and shown something like pride in being associated with us. Our experience was not as pleasant at first. Here and there they thought our labours affected, and considered that we gave them unnecessary trouble. In one or two instances they put great and serious difficulties in our way. When, however, they saw the results of our labours they became more amenable to orders; and when we returned to Chicago, Boston, Philadelphia, and now to New York, there was no trouble too great for them to undertake for us. I thank all these good fellows heartily."

" But to return to ' Much Ado,' " I said; " let us go a little into detail as to the number of scenes, cloths, flats, properties, and changes there are in the work. To have got through the piece, without a hitch, within three hours on the first night, is a very remarkable performance."

" Well, then, there are five acts in the play, thirteen scenes. Every scene is a set, except two, and they are front cloths; there is not a carpenter's scene proper in the entire representation. To begin with, there is the opening scene,—the bay, with Leonatas' palace built out twenty-four feet high,—a solid-looking piece, that has all the appearance of real masonry. I am giving you these details now from a cold, practical stage-manager's point of view,—fact without colour. Well, this scene—the outside of Leonatas' house—has to be closed in two minutes and a half, discovering the inside, the ball-room, which extends right round the walls of the theatre. This finishes the first act.

"Now, the second act was rung up in eight minutes, showing Craven's beautiful garden scene,—terraces, glades, and arbours,—in which set the business of the entire act occurs.

"The next act opens in front of Craven's cloth,—the terrace, which changes to the morning view of the garden, which, in its turn, is covered with the cedar cloth ; thus accounting for three scenes. After the last one, in two minutes the change was made to the effective representation of the town at night ; the riverside street ; the quay with its boats moored ; the houses on the other side of the river illuminated, Leonatas' palace among them. This closes the second act.

"Our great anxiety, as you know, centred in the cathedral set. We calculated that a wait of eighteen to twenty minutes would be required to send the curtain up on that, no doubt, very remarkable scene. It was rung up in fifteen minutes, displaying Telbin's master-piece,—the cathedral at Messina, with its real, built-out, round pillars, thirty feet high; its canopied roof of crimson plush, from which hung the golden lamps universally used in Italian cathedrals; its painted canopy overhanging the altar ; its great iron-work gates (fac-similes of the originals) ; its altar, with vases of flowers and flaming candles, rising to a height of eighteen feet ; its stained-glass windows and statues of saints ; its carved stalls, and all the other details that are now almost as well known in New York as in London. What a fine, impressive effect is the entrance of the vergers ! "

"Yes, you were telling me once, when we were interrupted, how you came to introduce this body of men into the scene ; it might be worth while to mention the incident along with these practical details of the working of the piece."

"It came about in this wise. I went into Quaritch'

bookstore one day, and among other curious books I picked up an old, black-letter volume. It was a work on 'Ceremonies,' with four large illustrations. I went into the shop to spend four or five pounds; I spent eighty-four or five, and carried off the black-letter book on 'Ceremonies,'—all Italian. I was at the time preparing 'Much Ado' for the Lyceum. In the picture of a wedding ceremony I saw what struck me at once as a wonderful effect, and of the period too,—the Shakespeare period. The effect was a mass of vergers, or javelin men,—officers of the church, I should imagine. They were dressed in long robes, and each carried a halberd. I pressed these men at once into the service of Shakespeare and his cathedral scene at Messina, and got that impressive effect of their entrance and the background of sombre colour they formed for the dresses of the bridal party. And it is right too,— that's the best of it. Not long ago I was at Seville, and saw a church ceremony there, where the various parties came on in something like the fashion of our people on the stage; but we never did anything so fine in that way as the entrances of the visitors at the Capulets' in 'Romeo and Juliet.' Do you remember the different companies of maskers, with their separate retainers and torch-bearers? But I see you are about to suggest that we get back to the stage of the Star Theatre; and so we will.

"The last act of 'Much Ado' was rung up in seven minutes, disclosing the scene where Dogberry holds his court; this is withdrawn upon the garden scene. Then we come to the tomb of Hero, never before presented, except by us, since, I believe, Shakespeare's own time. This scene, with its processions of monks, vergers, and mourners, and the few lines that are spoken, gives us four minutes to make a remarkable change, back to the ball-room in Leonatas' house, where the story is concluded.

"As you say, to have moved all this scenery, and represented the piece, with its many characters,

smoothly and without a blemish, in the various pictures,
—and when you think what trifling mistakes will upset
the effect of the finest scenes,—to have done all this
within three hours is a great achievement. The theatre
was handed over to us on Sunday morning; on
Monday night at a quarter-past eight the curtain rose
on 'Much Ado,' mounted and set with our Lyceum
effects,—scenery, properties, company,—and fell at
twelve minutes past eleven."

"And the longest journey comes to an end," said
Irving.

FINIS.

PRINTED BY GILBERT AND RIVINGTON, LIMITED, ST. JOHN'S SQUARE, E.C.

PRICE 6s.

HENRY IRVING'S
IMPRESSIONS OF AMERICA.

*NARRATED IN A SERIES OF SKETCHES, CHRONICLES,
AND CONVERSATIONS.*

By JOSEPH HATTON,

AUTHOR OF "CLYTIE," "CRUEL LONDON," "THREE RECRUITS," "TO-DAY IN
AMERICA," "JOURNALISTIC LONDON," ETC.

OPINIONS OF THE PRESS.

"Mr. Hatton has interspersed his work with some bright writing on general subjects, and with some clever bits of description. He knows America and the Americans exceedingly well. . . . Many of Mr. Irving's remarks upon stage business and on his own rendering of his own favourite parts are of great interest, and Mr. Hatton's labours have so far been crowned with success that he has produced a couple of very presentable volumes, from which we proceed to pick out some of the plums. . . . Mr. Irving's remarks on acting, as we have said, would be well worth reproducing. Perhaps the most striking and suggestive is his conception of Shylock, which we have unfortunately no space to give at length, and which we should only spoil by condensing. And in justice to Mr. Hatton, we must repeat that, more especially in his second volume, there are lively pictures of American scenery, of American life, and of American travel."—*Times.*

"Happily the expedition included a gentleman well qualified for the work of furnishing a permanent chronicle of its 'faictes et gestes.' When the Society of the Comédie Française made their memorable visit to England, that distinguished critic, M. Francisque Sarcey, elected to travel with them in the quality of historiographer. Mr. Hatton, in like manner, shared all the long journeys of the Lyceum Company on the American continent; joined in all their public and private festivities; assisted at their councils of war and anxious scrutinies of maps and routes; and witnessed all their receptions by first-night and other audiences in American cities far and wide. . . . We have not space to quote at length any of the numerous passages containing Mr. Irving's views on the art with which his name is inseparably associated; though probably no portions of Mr. Hatton's volumes will be of more enduring interest to those who concern themselves with dramatic history."—*Daily News.*

"Mr. Hatton has not indulged in any attempt at book-making, resting content to present the 'sketches, chronicles, and conversations' with a lightness and fidelity that will cause them to be treasured as an interesting and faithful record of what Mr. Irving so happily calls a 'delightful progress.'"—*Daily Chronicle.*

"As we always wish to think favourably of that great nation of the English race, of their manners, institutions, public and private life, of their character, sentiments, ideas, and all their concerns present and future, it is satisfactory to find Mr. Henry Irving so well pleased with all that he saw and heard amongst them. Mr. Hatton, his literary ally, whose shrewdness as an observer of men and cities has been proved on former occasions, contributes plenty of lively descriptive and narrative incidents, for the most part friendly and agreeable, which have an interest beyond that of the personal experiences of the Lyceum Company there. But these experiences make very tolerable light reading, being told without reserve in a spirit of frank and jovial goodfellowship, an enjoying, sociable, mutually diverting spirit, with a keen perception of the humorous, quaint, and comical aspects of their situation as favourite guests in a country which is but half-foreign and half-homely to English visitors coming with the best credentials, and fully deserving, in every respect, the hearty reception they everywhere met."—*Illustrated London News.*

"Mr. Irving returns to his numerous friends and admirers, simultaneously with the issue of the record of his wanderings in America, and the impressions of his experience there. These 'Impressions of America,' as narrated by Mr. Joseph Hatton, are remarkably pleasant reading. There are descriptions of the great tragedian in his London rooms and at his suburban domicile, immersed in his art, or quietly discussing it and its professors with his friends; giving his views on the new life unfolding before his eyes in the great American cities, or telling apt stories for the amusement of his companions in the cars. The book is, naturally, a sonata on one string; but the player knows his business, and handles his bow with excellent taste."— *World.*

"Mr. Hatton has performed with phenomenal success and tact a task which few literary men would have undertaken without great misgivings. He had to incorporate in his volumes everything worthy of note in Mr. Irving's travels, and much that was very worthy of note was necessarily of a kind which is generally lost in the ephemeral columns of newspapers. He had to give the necessary degree of dignity to a considerable number of newspaper excerpts, and to preserve, without an appearance of fuss or overdoing it, a number of impromptu speeches. Many business details had to be brought in, or the work would have been very incomplete. But all the time Mr. Hatton had to remember that he was the literary companion and Boswell of a distinguished actor, who had set his mark, and was setting his mark continuously, not only on the stage art, but on the Shakespearian and other poetical interpretations of the age. And along with all this, Mr. Irving's Boswell had to be perpetually lively, on pain of losing that great circulation which, of course, it would be a principal aim of such a work to secure. In all this we say Mr. Hatton has succeeded. His book will have a great sale now, and it will be sought after generations hence as one of the most interesting mementoes of artistic life in our time. On its serious side, perhaps the best example in the book is to be found in Mr. Hatton's recital of Mr. Irving's conception of Shylock as given by himself in one of the most intellectual of conversations."—*Liverpool Daily Post.*

"Mr. Irving understood his position. . . . And it redounds to Mr. Irving's praise that he adopted the proper means for preserving his impressions, by bringing with and carrying with him everywhere a skilled and accomplished writer. . . . All nationalities have their weaknesses, and it is easy enough to make them the subject of ridicule. Mr. Irving was not blind to our foibles and peculiarities; but he found in America and in the American people much to admire, and Mr. Hatton's book cannot fail to strengthen those ties of friendship which exist between the younger and the older country."—*New York Herald.*

"Mr. Joseph Hatton, who is one of Mr. Irving's intimate friends, and who was his companion in this country, has written the greater part of the record, and the object sought and accomplished by him was a history of Mr. Irving's American tour. This the volume presents in copious fulness and minute accuracy. No such work has ever before been done for an actor. The narrative glows with the excitement that attended Mr. Irving's remarkable progress through our country, and fairly teems with the multitudinous incidents that steadily attended his course. There will, at least, be no complaint from the future historian of the stage that this book passed over the actual details, and in the desire to theorize and reflect, omitted the common and essential facts. Viewed as material for history in this especial department, the volume is a trustworthy contribution to literature, for it is comprehensive, it is thorough, it is explicit, and it is true. With a clear and fresh recollection of Mr. Irving's tour, this can be said, very heartily, for Mr. Hatton's account of it. The atmosphere of travel is preserved; there is no constraint or squeamish fastidiousness in the style or the substance; the twenty-two chapters are full of diversity, and they convey a just impression of the most remarkable theatrical journey that has ever been made in America, scarcely excepting those of Jenny Lind and Charles Dickens; and, furthermore, by means of brief biographies in foot-notes, a considerable quantity of useful theatrical information has here been made convenient of access. A sketch of Miss Ellen Terry, for example, finds its place in this way, and is of obvious worth. To Mr. Irving's part in the book it is possible to do justice only by extract; and several parts of his talk are given herewith. But that which is most impressive in the actor's share is the remarkable figure that he himself presents amid all these scenes of novelty, excitement, artistic effort, and exacting circumstance."—*New York Tribune.*

"Mr. Irving's occasional expressions of opinion upon things American are scattered through the book. . . . They are such expressions as might be expected from a cultivated gentleman who is not in the least disposed to take the world in hand for its immediate and compulsory reformation. They are pleasant things to read, and the whole book, indeed, may be characterized as an agreeable one."—*New York Commercial Advertiser.*

"Mr. Hatton is a competent Boswell or Eckermann to Mr. Irving's Johnson or Goethe. . . . A mere short review can do no justice to the minute and most captivating descriptions of breakfasts, luncheons, dinners, suppers, first-nights' speeches, and complimentary addresses, and play-bills, which form the staple of Mr. Hatton's book."—*Harper's Magazine.*

"Covering a volume of 475 pages, it is an uninterrupted tale of interest from beginning to end. Commencing to read it, one dislikes very much to lay it down until he has read every word."—*New York Newsdealer.*

"Written in a chatty, pleasant style, and gives a picturesque account of the great actor's tour throughout the country, and the impressions made on him during the trip."—*Albany Express.*

SAMPSON LOW, MARSTON, SEARLE, & RIVINGTON,

CROWN BUILDINGS, 188, FLEET STREET, LONDON.